Discover Sociology

Discover

Sociology

Ray Power · Don Robinson
with additional material provided by Alex Popowicz

Pitman

PITMAN PUBLISHING LIMITED
128 Long Acre, London WC2E 9AN

A Longman Group Company

© Ray Power, Don Robinson & Alex Popowicz 1986

First published in Great Britain 1986

British Library Cataloguing in Publication Data
Power, Ray
  Discover sociology.
  1. Sociology
  I. Title   II. Robinson, Don, *1940–*
  III. Popowicz, Alex
  301   HM51

  ISBN 0–273–02282–2

Printed in Great Britain at The Bath Press, Avon

Contents

Preface

Discover Sociology has been written for students on social science courses who are studying for CSE, GCE O Level or GCSE examinations. It covers the syllabus requirements of all 6 GCE Examination Boards and deals in full with key sociological terms and concepts. It should also be helpful to students who choose a vocational route on BTEC or RSA courses, in that it covers most of the social and community studies components of these syllabuses. The book may also provide a useful introduction to sociology for students who are attempting A Level sociology directly, without first completing the O Level course.

Although each of the 12 chapters deals with a specific area of the subject, every opportunity has been taken to present sociology as an interesting and coherent whole. This has been made possible largely through the use of real-life exercises and tasks that bring relevance and meaning to the topic under study. Every chapter is divided into convenient parts, with each part carrying at least one exercise that aims to test the student's grasp of the material. Supporting each chapter there are:

- An invitation to the student to survey the range of topics and important concepts to be covered.
- A summing up of the main ideas under the heading **Important points.**
- Three structured questions of the type that are found in GCE O Level examination papers.
- A glossary at the end of the book that provides further information or more precise definitions of words or concepts not fully explained in the text.
- At least 2 substantial tasks or case studies that offer a meeting point, a focus, for students to explore the relationship between sociological theory and its value as an interpreter of the social world. Students are asked to deal with questions demanding short-response, written answers, and there is an opportunity, time allowing, to throw the subject open for group discussion.

A word of caution. Teachers are asked not to insist that students complete every exercise and task in the form that is presented. This would call for a course length of many years. However, by modifying and fitting the exercises and tasks (perhaps by using only parts of them) to the needs of students, and within practical class-time limits, it should be possible to produce a package that meets the demands of the course.

Acknowledgements

The authors and publishers would like to thank the following for permission to reproduce copyright material:

Associated Examining Board
Avantgarde

Birmingham Evening Mail
British Medical Journal

Cambridge University Press
COPEC Housing Trust

Daily Mail
Daily Mirror

Fontana

Guardian

HMSO

Longman

Macmillan
Martin Robertson

New Society

Observer
Oxford University Press

Penguin

Race Relations Publications
Radio Times
Routledge

Schools and Race
Straits Times
Stratford upon Avon Herald
Sun

The Sunday Times

United Nations

The authors would also like to thank Aleck and Jean Green, Carole Smith, Nick Daws, Eileen Gibbs, and many of our teaching colleagues who have helped with contributions and advice.

1 Sociology and your world

When you have worked through this chapter you should have a clearer understanding of

The nature and purpose of sociology · **Culture** · **The social construction of self** · **Methodology** · **Pilot study** · **Qualitative and quantitative data** · **Social surveys** · **Sampling** · **Participant and non-participant observation** · **Argot** · **Observer bias** · **Primary and secondary sources of information** · **Sociological theory** · **Conflict and consensus views of society**

What is sociology?

The world we live in can at times seem strange and confusing. We are often faced with puzzling questions about what is happening in our society and, try as we might, we usually fail to come up with any satisfactory answers. Why do people live in extreme poverty whilst others enjoy great wealth? Why do young people find themselves in conflict with their parents and with others in authority? Why are certain groups, for example blacks, women and Asians, discriminated against? What is clear is that on our own we are not going to get far in our attempts to provide meaningful answers to these and other questions. This is where sociology can help. Although the study of sociology will not provide answers to all our questions it will provide us with the opportunity of taking a more logical and objective view of the world.

There are some people – usually those with little or no understanding of sociology – who argue that sociology has little to offer other than a collection of wishy-washy theories that have nothing to do with the real world. This view is misguided. Any course of study that attempts to provide us with a deeper and clearer understanding of our society has to be of value, and the opportunity to study sociology should be an interesting and rewarding activity. Students who are interested in the way past events have influenced the present, study history in order to make more sense of the world they live in. The study of geography provides information about climate, terrain and raw materials of our own and other countries. As the world we live in becomes more and more complicated we need a science of society to unravel this complexity so we can see more clearly how our society works.

Sociology has been described as the **science of society**, which might strike you as curious. When we think of science our mind conjures up images of people in white coats working in laboratories carrying out experiments. The question that people rightly ask is how can sociologists study people in a laboratory and carry out experiments on them. The answer is that they can't and they don't. This is how sociologists might conduct their research:

- they collect as much information as possible about a particular topic,
- then sift through this information to see if any recurring patterns emerge, and
- on the basis of this they are in a position to offer some form of explanation about the behaviour under study.

To explain this further, let us examine an article which appeared in a newspaper. It describes a trend in some young people's behaviour:

The new menace

What is the popular image of the football hooligan? Close-cropped hair, Doctor Martens (just the thing for kicking innocent passers-by), a scarf tied around the wrist, and obscene chanting? If that's what you think you're a little out of date.

Today's menace is well-groomed, often wears designer knitwear, carries a telescopic umbrella and travels strictly first-class to the away games. However, behind this veneer lies the same old vicious thug who is eager to inflict pain and misery, just like his scruffy predecessor, except that our travelling toff could easily pull out a razor-sharp blade from his brolly!

Where they get their money from is a mystery but one young man told me outside a football ground that street theft from frightened pedestrians was a major source of income. Shoplifting is another way of obtaining the well-cut smarty clothes these louts like to wear. In fact anything illegal is considered. As my young informant told me only 'dip-sticks' go out to work.

So beware. That clean-cut youth sitting opposite you on the train could be a thug intent on relieving you of your hard-earned cash. It's about time society did something about these gentlemen muggers. Let's not be taken in with fancy clothes and hairstyles – and keep an eye on that brolly!

What kind of picture does this article paint of young football supporters? What evidence does the journalist provide to back up the story?

If we look closely at the article we can see that few facts are presented. The journalist acknowledges only one source of information and the style of writing obviously is meant to appeal to our emotions. This is not to say that he is trying to mislead us, but some stories which appear in newspapers can distort and sensationalise people's behaviour and social happenings.

EXERCISE

You want to gather information from young people about their attitudes and experiences of football hooliganism. Working with a colleague, draw up 10 suitable questions that could be answered by an average football supporter.

The first thing we would want to know is how much football hooliganism actually takes place at, or is associated with, football matches. Millions of people attend football matches simply to enjoy the game, yet their behaviour is never featured on the front pages of newspapers. So the sociologist would first attempt to place the behaviour described in the *The new menace* into some form of context. He would probably find that such groups are in the minority and the publicity they generate in the media is out of all proportion to their actual size and significance.

The sociologist would not offer any points for discussion about such behaviour until he was sure that he had made enough observations on which he could reliably base his arguments. This would not mean talking to one football supporter for a couple of minutes outside a football ground. His work may well involve him in hundreds of interviews with all kinds of football supporters – young, old, male and female. Equally we should be aware that this research wouldn't take place on one day, it would spread over weeks and months. Some studies take years to complete. This is because the sociologist has to be certain that the explanation he offers is based on reliable evidence, on as much information as can reasonably be collected. It is this thoroughness in collecting and assessing information that justifies the use of the definition of sociology as the **science of society** (the word science roughly means knowledge) and helps us to answer some of the questions we ask about our society.

Sociology then *is* the science of society and in this the sociologist tries to be as rigorous and as analytical in his work as possible. As the historian tries to understand the past and the economist grapples with solutions to inflation, so the sociologist tries to provide us with a framework by which we can understand the range of complex social behaviour in our society and the societies of others.

EXERCISE

In about 100 words, using the information in this chapter as a guide, complete with as much information as possible the statement: The purpose of sociology is . . .

Sociology and culture

Although sociology is the study of social behaviour, this does not mean that sociologists spend their time studying individuals. They are more concerned with the different social groups to which these individuals belong. For example, you as an individual are unique but as a member of different social groups your experience of the world will be shared by others who find themselves in similar social situations. You may be a member of a family group and your family – if we wanted to study it – would have much in common with other families.

Think about your own family. What does your family have in common with other families in your locality?

You may have thought about factors such as the size of your house, the income earned by your family, the type of holidays you enjoy, or the number of people living in your house. You might even find that you and your neighbours have similar leisure interests, job prospects, tastes in furniture, transport facilities, attitudes towards politics and favourite television programmes. All these form what sociologists refer to as the **culture of a group**.

Using this concept of culture the sociologist is describing a way of life which exists and persists in all the communities which make up our complex industrial world. This is not to say that there is one dominant culture within our society. It would be silly to suggest that. Although we all live in the same country with its particular traditions and institutions – like the right to vote or not to vote and political rule through an elected parliament – ours is a complex society making it fascinating for the sociologist to study.

To give you an example of a particular culture, here is an extract from an interview where a member of the aristocracy is describing aspects of his childhood. This gives us a clue to the culture of his social group:

One grew up in this terribly large house in about 400 acres of ground although one did not think there was anything unusual about the size of it at the time. All one's friends lived in such houses so no one imagined when we were children that any one lived on huge housing estates. I had a nanny – dear Miss Walcott – and she looked after me most of the time. Mother and father travelled a lot and it wasn't until much later that I and my sister went with them ... One had servants of course and sometimes cook would take me downstairs into the kitchen. It was wonderful seeing all the food being prepared, especially when my parents were having people for dinner ... I went away to school and spent most of the holidays in the south of France. When I look back one can only remember coming into contact with people just like oneself. One's cousins, friends, people who were I suppose wealthy. When I was 14 and 15 my father arranged for me to spend all my summer holidays with a family of farm labourers. He never failed to remind one that we were very fortunate and not to look down on anyone ... Yes I knew – I couldn't put a precise date on it – that one day I would go into banking after

Cambridge. It was all mapped out, I suppose ... Yes one could say that I have had a somewhat privileged life but I do work jolly hard. I am a member of the upper class and I am proud of it. I think people who are critical of people like me are simply jealous. I work jolly hard – harder than a factory worker or a miner I would think. I mean to say I have an awful lot of responsibility.

These experiences are interesting in a variety of ways because here we are given an insight into a world which is remote from most of us and our social experiences.

EXERCISE

Draw out from the previous extract the main features that characterise the culture of this individual's social group. Compare them with similar influences from your own culture.

In your answer to the previous exercise you may have included points about servants, wealth, education, and possibly the way he uses language: all of these are part of his particular culture and background. This leads us to another key point about sociology. Although we have suggested that sociologists are not particularly interested in the individual, they do have something important to say about the individual and his or her personal experiences. It is that the people we are – the person you are – is the sum total of all the experiences we have had in our lives. In other words, the experiences you have had within your family, schools, neighbourhood and friendship groups have greatly influenced you as a person.

To fully appreciate this important point read the following extract, again featuring a description of a childhood experience. You will see an interesting contrast with the previous example:

My father was always a trade union

activist. So was my mother. In fact my mother always told me that women had every right to be involved in the trade union movement. In no way was she prepared to be the 'little wife at home' cooking and cleaning and being a general skivvy. My father would take us all to the union meetings and from an early age I developed my interest in politics. I remember going with my brother to watch the men being given work down by the dockside gates. They would stand in line and wait for the foreman to turn up. Then he would say: 'I'll take you-and-you-and-you-and-you' until he had about a dozen men – depending on how much work there was and how much work he could reasonably expect one man to do – and then the remaining men would be turned away. No one was guaranteed work. Well, those who didn't belong to the union had the best chance of being taken on. I remember my father and uncle going down every day for eight months and they were never taken on because they were in the union. When people ask me why I'm now active in the trade union movement and why I'm a socialist, it doesn't take me long to answer them. I just think back to those days down on the quayside and the desperation in the faces of all those men who were turned away not knowing how they were going to feed their families.

This person lived in a community of dockworkers where unemployment was high and where there was an obvious shortage of money. She was also encouraged to involve herself in trade union activities. As she suggests, the person she is today has been strongly influenced by those early and later experiences. This means that she was not born with her particular views and attitudes. The views she holds were socially learned as she grew up within a particular culture and community. This is a vital point for you to consider when studying sociology. For the sociologist it is the experiences we have in the world, in our environment, which are of prime importance in shaping us as people.

Hopefully we have established that the sociologist's task is to study, systematically, the patterns of behaviour amongst the various social groups in our society. We should also understand that the sociologist is interested in how the culture of these social groups influences the development of the individual personality. The way society and our experience of the social world influence us as individuals is a process known as the **social construction of self**, which means that most behaviour is socially learned through the life experiences we all have. Our experiences of the world have an enormous influence on us in terms of our behaviour, attitudes and the development of our personalities.

EXERCISE

This illustrates some of the ways in which society influences us. Write a few notes on each item giving as much

factual information on your own culture as you can. You may be asked to read aloud your notes to compare your cultural influences with others in your group.

The sociologist at work

We have explained that the sociologist carries out his investigations in a scientific way, and whilst he is aware that he cannot conduct his research in a laboratory setting – this would be far too artificial – he nevertheless has a number of techniques on hand to use in his research work. The techniques used by the sociologist form part of his **methodology**. This word simply refers to the range of research methods available for the study of society and social behaviour.

Before we look at specific methods, let us put the scientific approach into some form of perspective. Here is a simple guide showing the steps a sociologist might take during a research investigation:

Research procedure

1 **Identifying the Research Problem**

2 **Selecting the Research Method**

3 **Collecting the Data**

4 **Understanding and Interpreting the Data**

5 **Producing a Report of Findings**

In your study of sociology you should take every opportunity of reading as many research findings as you can. One easily available source of findings is the weekly journal *New Society*.

Findings

Not redundant
Everyone knows that being made redundant is, psychologically, hardly a barrel of laughs. But what if you stay, while your colleagues go? Audrey Mathews of the University of Kent has been interviewing 177 factory workers, who were left behind after a third of the 810-strong workforce had been made redundant. Redundancy, it transpires, has bad effects even on those who escape it.

During the 90-day statutory notification period, when no one knew what was happening and who would have to go, anxiety and

- Neighbourhood
- Family income
- Leisure activities
- Mass media
- Work experience
- Family
- Friends
- Religion
- Schooling

YOU

The sociologist may himself identify an interesting social problem to investigate or be directed to a particular area of research because an organisation is offering money and facilities. For example, the government might be willing to fund research and provide computer support into how UK families are spending their income.

This will be determined by the nature of the information required, the size of the group under study, and the time and finance available. The researcher sometimes conducts a preliminary investigation called a **pilot study** to test out his ideas and iron out any snags.

This is the hard work of sociological research and takes up most of the time and money available.

Data are usually of 2 types: **qualitative** and **quantitative**. Qualitative data require careful interpretation because their purpose is to throw light on what might be very complex social problems (why do addicts take drugs?). Quantitative data is basically information that can be counted, measured and presented in statistical form, often with the aid of computers (how much money is spent on drugs by addicts?).

The final report will first set out the nature of the problem under investigation, then explain the choice of research method, how the data were analysed, explain the results and suggest conclusions that can be drawn from the results.

---

tension became serious problems. One man said, 'It was affecting my home life, I was taking it out on my wife and kids.' A woman confessed, 'I worried a lot, I went quiet and went off my food.' According to Mathews, 'Many described their feelings of frustration and despair, their utter helplessness while it was all going on.'

Even for those who survived, everything was far from rosy. Long-standing and close-knit work groups were torn apart. One worker summed it up: 'You lost contact with some close friends. You spend more time with them than you do your family and then suddenly they're not there any more.' The shift system had completely altered. 'We can't identify with each other as workmates on shifts now,' another respondent said, 'because we're a nine-week cycle and we never work together for more than two days at a time.' All the activities workers on the same shifts used to do together

– 'hire fishing boats, arrange bowls fixtures, and outings to London shows' – had collapsed.

'The active social lives,' Mathews says, 'had tended to compensate for the boredom and poor working conditions most experienced.' Not only had this aspect of their lives disintegrated, but they all had to work even harder. 'Overtime was now being forced on them. Many were being phoned or "sent round for".'

The people who had escaped redundancy were still feeling insecure and vulnerable. But, Mathews concludes, they were thankful to be in work. As one employee put it, 'I knock this place a bit but I'd still rather have my job than be on the dole.' **Maryon Tysoe**
Source: *New Society*, 2 August 1984

Victims ignored
How does the victim of a crime of violence feel in its aftermath? To find out how their plight changed in the

light of official action, Joanna Shapland of Oxford University has interviewed 278 adult victims of violent crimes in the Midlands, contacting them up to four times each over a two year period (*British Journal of Criminology*, vol 24, No. 2, page 131).

Initially, the victims were pleased with their treatment by the police, and with the care and the courtesy shown to them. However, as time passed, the extent to which they still suffered social, psychological and even physical after-effects showed little, if any, diminution. Matters did gradually improve financially, in that they ceased to be afflicted by any loss of earnings or other out-of-pocket expenses. Nevertheless, most of them had not even been told how to claim the criminal injuries compensation which they were legally entitled to have.

During the two years, the victims became steadily more critical of the police and the courts, not because of any feeling that their assailants were being treated too leniently, but simply because they themselves were not kept informed of developments. Additionally, if required in court as witnesses, little or nothing was done to assist them in an unfamiliar situation.

Indeed, by the end of the two years one in seven victims was sufficiently embittered to say that they would not report a similar offence to the police – an outcome which, so Joanna Shapland maintains, could have been avoided if just a little more were done to keep victims in the picture.

Source: *New Society*, 9 August 1984

EXERCISE

Using the 5 headings in the previous guide, work through both of these research findings, making notes to show that you understand the sequence of the research methods.

Social surveys

By far the most important technique used in sociological research is the social survey. The social survey is a systematic way of collecting information about people who live in a particular area or who belong to a defined social or economic group. One of the earliest social surveys was carried out by Charles Booth in 1897. This survey – *Life and Labour of the People of London* – contains information about people's incomes, domestic circumstances and religious beliefs.

Social surveys provide us with a means of comparing how different social groups might behave in similar circumstances. For instance, how would a working class family spend extra income compared with a family from the middle class. Surveys may also demonstrate links between factors and help us to identify the reasons for certain types of behaviour. Criminal behaviour in children, for example, might be found to be more common in criminal families, and to be even more common in criminal families involved in divorce or separation.

The most common type of survey is the **cross-sectional** or **snap-shot survey**. The researcher gets his information from a cross-section of the group under study at one point in time (hence the phrase 'snap-shot'). Thus the findings are gathered fairly quickly and cheaply to provide useful information. An example of this would be the researcher who asks people about their voting intentions at a forthcoming general election. Unfortunately

the findings are usually valid only for a short period of time and take no account of long-term changes in attitude or behaviour.

A less common and more expensive type of social survey is the **longitudinal** or **cohort survey**. In this, a selected group (the **cohort**) is studied over a period of time (**longitudinally**). This enables the researcher to gain not only current information but also insights into the way people are changing their attitudes or behaviour over a much longer time-span. So if you wanted to find out in what way a massive pit closure is affecting a coal-mining community, a longitudinal survey might be the best technique to use.

The social survey is very much a part of our everyday lives. It is frequently used in market research as a means of assessing our attitudes and preferences about consumer products – from margarine to dog food. Probably the most important of all social surveys provides the government with invaluable information about the economic, social and cultural conditions of Britain today. This information is collected by the **Office of Population Census and Surveys** which is responsible for one of the most famous and extensive social surveys called the **Census**. The Census is carried out every 10 years and it provides information about every household in Britain (the next Census will be in 1991).

EXERCISE

Explain what kind of social survey you would consider for the following:
- A headmaster of a large school wishes to know the views of parents and pupils about the wearing of school uniforms.
- A trade union requires information about the effects of poverty on striking workers.
- A government department wants to

know how families are spending their supplementary benefit.

Sampling

What is unusual about the Census is that every householder in Britain is compelled by law to provide personal information on a questionnaire that is delivered to their home. For the bulk of sociological research, however, this method would not only be questionable but far too expensive and time-consuming. Most sociologists resort to what is termed **sampling**.

A sample is a small number of people who fairly represent a cross-section of the group under study. For example, if you wanted to find out how much time is spent by pupils in a school watching sport on TV it would be more sensible to conduct your investigation thoroughly with a representative sample, rather than attempt to interview the whole school population. To ensure that your sample is taken from the greatest number of pupils you would need a complete list of the names, say from all the class registers. This source, from which a sample can be drawn, whether they are class registers, lists of voters, a computer printout of addresses, is known as a **sampling frame**.

When a suitable sampling frame has been chosen, the sociologist is ready to take his sample. The easiest sample to take is a simple **random sampling**. This is sampling on the basis of pure chance. It might mean picking names out of a hat or choosing every third name in the school's registers.

Another form of random sampling is called **stratified sampling**. Here the sociologist ensures that the correct proportion of the elements that make up the group under study (the **strata**) is fairly represented before sampling takes place. Take a college of 2000 students aged between 16 and 20 with 80% males and 20% females. How would the sociologist go about getting the proportions of his sample right? He might draw up a simple table:

Total number of students	2000
Age groups	16 17 18 19 20
Sex breakdown	Males 80% Females 20%
Stratified sample required	10% (based on sex and age)

Age Group	Total Students	Sex breakdown		Required for sample	
		Males	Females	Males	Females
16	700	560	140	56	14
17	600	480	120	48	12
18	400	320	80	32	8
19	200	160	40	16	4
20	100	80	20	8	2
Totals	2000	1600	400	160	40

Lexbridge college

After the sociologist has done his sums he can make his random sample from each stratum. For example, he could choose his 19-year-old female sample by picking 4 names out of a hat containing the names of 40 females.

Two other useful forms of random sampling are:

- **Cluster sampling** This economical method is used by researchers who want to take a small sample from a large population that may be spread over a wide geographical area. In a large town, for example, a researcher might decide to do her sampling from limited 'clusters' of streets or districts in carefully selected areas of the town.
- **Filter sampling** As the name suggests, this is a method of filtering out the people who are not wanted from a main sample group until the researcher is left with a smaller sub-group that is wanted. For instance, from a sample of 1000 women, 400 may be filtered out leaving a group of 600, each aged between 20 and 25 with at least one child under 5 years of age. This sub-group of 600 may itself be further filtered to a group of say 50 pregnant women who smoke over 10 cigarettes per day.

Another type of sampling, which is rather less scientific, is **quota sampling**. In this the sociologist exercises his own judgment in selecting a quota or a number of people with certain characteristics *before* he subjects them to investigation. It is a fast and cheap way of finding things out and it is often used in opinion polls. So if a researcher wants to know what people think of the Prime Minister's performance in the last year he might decide to question a group of 1000 voters according to the following quotas:

Voters		Number or Quota in Sample
Conservatives	Males	200
Conservatives	Females	200
Labour	Males	150
Labour	Females	150
Lib/Alliance	Males	100
Lib/Alliance	Females	100
Don't Knows	Males	50
Don't Knows	Females	50
	Total	1000

The researcher is then free to choose the people who fit into these categories.

EXERCISE

You want to know how the 450 boys and girls in a junior school spend their time between 6pm and 8pm. How would you go about getting a sample of children to investigate? You have a calculator and this information:
Sex breakdown: *Girls 70% Boys 30%*
Numbers of pupils: *1st year 110*
                    2nd year 150
                    3rd year 190
You must state clearly what method of sampling you are using.

The questionnaire

Almost always used as part of a social survey is the **questionnaire**. This is where the sociologist designs a set of questions about a particular subject to be answered by respondents (the people being surveyed). Here is a real-life example of part of a postal questionnaire designed to find out more about how people use buses in a major British city:

Travel survey

1 What address have you come from? (Please give as full an address as possible).

Number and Street ....
(or firm/shop/building)
District/Town ....

---

2 How did you get to the bus stop?

Walk	Bus	Cycle	Taxi	Train	Car Driver	Car Passenger	Motor Cycle	Other
☐	☐	☐	☐	☐	☐	☐	☐	☐
0	1	2	3	4	5	6	7	8

---

3 How long did it take to reach the stop?

Less than 1 minute	1-2 minutes	2-3 minutes	3-4 minutes	4-5 minutes	5-7 minutes	7-10 minutes	10-15 minutes	15-20 minutes	more than 20 minutes
☐	☐	☐	☐	☐	☐	☐	☐	☐	☐
0	1	2	3	4	5	6	7	8	9

---

4 How many buses will you use on this journey?

..............................Bus(es)

---

5 What address will you be going to when you leave the bus? (Please give as full an address as possible).

Number and Street ....
(or firm/shop/building)

District/Town ....

---

6 What is the purpose of your journey? Please tick one FROM box and one TO box.

	Home	Work	School/ College	Firms Business	Shopping	Sport/Social/ Entertainment	Other
FROM	☐	☐	☐	☐	☐	☐	☐
	0	1	2	3	4	5	6
TO	☐	☐	☐	☐	☐	☐	☐
	0	1	2	3	4	5	6

---

7 How will you get to your destination when you leave the (last – if more than one) bus?

Walk	Bus	Cycle	Taxi	Train	Car Driver	Car Passenger	Motor Cycle	Other
☐	☐	☐	☐	☐	☐	☐	☐	☐
0	1	2	3	4	5	6	7	8

---

8 How long will this take?

Less than 1 minute	1-2 minutes	2-3 minutes	3-4 minutes	4-5 minutes	5-7 minutes	7-10 minutes	10-15 minutes	15-20 minutes	more than 20 minutes
☐	☐	☐	☐	☐	☐	☐	☐	☐	☐
0	1	2	3	4	5	6	7	8	9

9 What type of ticket will you use for the bus journey(s)?

Single	Countrywide Travelcard	Area Travelcard	Off Peak Travelcard	OAP Pass	Scholars Pass	Other Please specify
☐	☐	☐	☐	☐	☐	....
0	1	2	3	4	5	

---

10 Are you

Male ☐ 0   Female ☐ 1

---

11 What is your age group?

Under 11	11-15	16-24	25-44	45-59	60-65	65+
☐	☐	☐	☐	☐	☐	☐
0	1	2	3	4	5	6

---

12 Do you hold a full driving licence?

YES ☐ 0   NO ☐ 1

---

13 Was there a car available to you that could have been used for the whole of this journey?

YES ☐ 0   NO ☐ 1

---

14 Are you

In full or part time employment	Unemployed or seeking work	In full time education				Other
☐ 0	☐ 1	☐ 2	Housewife ☐ 3	Retired ☐ 4		....

---

15 Please state your occupation. .... Please give full description

---

16 If you are travelling from home when do you plan to return home?

Before 1500 (3 pm) today	After 1500 (3 pm) today	Not today
☐	☐	☐
0	1	2

---

17 Are you prepared to answer further questions about your journey today? (You have the chance to win a 13 week travelcard if you participate in this further survey).

YES ☐ 0   NO ☐ 1

There are a couple of interesting features about this questionnaire. First note that questions of a personal nature (questions **11**, **14** and **15**) appear quite low down. This is to reduce the risk of embarrassing respondents too soon by giving them time to gain confidence. Question 17 helps the sociologist to improve his chances of getting more information by the offer of a reward.

Questionnaires are very difficult to write but are worth the effort because the sociologist can get a lot of information from respondents to help him with his research. Once the questionnaire has been successfully designed, the way it is used can vary. Sending it through the post to individuals is cheap, in that it saves paying for interviewers and cuts out the high cost of travel. There are nonetheless problems. The biggest problem is that people may not return the questionnaire so the response rate is often very low. Another problem with **postal questionnaires** is that if the respondent has problems filling in the form there is no one there to help. Even when questionnaires are completed and returned satisfactorily, this does not necessarily guarantee a successful survey. Sometimes only those respondents who feel strongly about a topic or who find it particularly interesting may respond, thus distorting results. A personal visit by the researcher can reduce these risks, but only at great expense.

The most reliable and efficient way of using questionnaires is by **direct interviewing**. In this the researchers approach people and ask them if they would like to answer questions on the particular topic. Needless to say the researchers have to be carefully briefed about whom to stop and interview. If the research team is interested in questioning females aged between 25-35 this should, in theory, pose few problems, but there is still an element of hit-and-miss about the operation. Misjudging the ages of people, for example, can be time-consuming and embarrassing and slow the progress of the survey.

We have said that questionnaires are difficult to write although vital in any social investigation. However some questions are easier for the sociologist to handle than others. For example, factual questions about whether someone is married, single, divorced, widowed or living with someone, or the person's occupation and age, are fairly straightforward. However the sociologist may want

to know about people's views and opinions:

- What are your views on Race Relations?
- What do you believe trade unions contribute to society?
- Are there any crimes that you think should be punishable by death?

These are called open-ended questions because there are many ways of answering them. Unfortunately they make life difficult for the sociologist, and during the analysis great care has to be taken when sifting through this kind of response if an accurate picture of people's views is to be established.

EXERCISE

What follows is an example of a postal questionnaire that has been badly written. Examine each question carefully and say why you think it is unsatisfactory. You might wish to refer to the previous survey on bus travel for guidance.

Alcoholic consumption – young people

We are conducting a survey into the excessive drinking habits of young people and we think you could help us with our research. Please answer all the questions as honestly as you can by drawing a circle around the appropriate answers. You will notice that your name and address are not required.

1 How old are you? – 12 12–13 13–14 14–15 15–16 16–17 17–19 19–20 20–21 21+
2 What is your marital status? Married Single
3 What sex are you? Male Female Other
4 How often do you drink alcohol? Occasionally Sometimes Frequently
5 How would you define your

weekly consumption of ethyl alcohol? Less than 1 drink 2–5 drinks 6–10 drinks 11–15 drinks 16–20 drinks 21 drinks or more
6 When you drink alcohol do you smoke? Yes No
7 Do you usually drink alone or in company? Yes No
8 What percentage of your available spending money is spent on alcohol? Not less than 10% Between 10% and 30% Between 30% and 50% Between 50% and 70%. Over 70%
9 Where do you normally buy your alcohol? In a public house In a wine bar In an off-licence
10 Do you believe that drinking encourages promiscuity and deviant behaviour?

When you have completed your criticisms you might like to redesign the whole questionnaire in a more satisfactory way. You may change or add questions in any way you wish. The introduction requires rewording.

Observation

Although social surveys and questionnaires are at their most effective in large scale sociological research, another method, **participant observation**, is more appropriate when studying small group behaviour. For this the sociologist actually joins the group he wishes to study and becomes as much involved as possible in all its activities. This gives him an insider's view of the culture of the group.

If the sociologist reveals both himself and the nature of his research to the group he joins he is conducting what is known as **open participant observation**.

However, if he chooses not to reveal himself or his true purpose, he is practising **concealed participant observation**, which of course involves wholesale deception on the part of the researcher.

In certain circumstances the sociologist may choose not to join the group's activity but simply to observe behaviour as unobtrusively as possible (like the school inspector sitting at the back of the class). This is called **non-participant observation** or **direct observation**.

Although there are serious ethical questions involved in participant observation, these methods have produced some excellent research over the years, from the classic study by William Whyte, *Street Corner Society*, which looked at the life of Italian immigrants in the poor quarter of Chicago, to a more recent study by James Patrick on gang behaviour: *A Glasgow Gang Observed*. Besides the ethical problems associated with participant observation, there are a number of practical problems that have to be dealt with.

EXERCISE

Suppose you want to join a social group whose lifestyle you wish secretly to observe. Write down how you would go about it and identify any problems you think you might encounter.

As you have no doubt realised, participant observation, though appearing to be a relatively easy and exciting sociological method, makes great demands on the sociologist both in terms of skill and commitment. Some of the problems you have identified will be similar to those experienced by one young sociologist who recalls his problems in his fieldwork notes:

FIELDWORK NOTES (participant observation – concealed)

Day 1

I joined a group of 'dossers' at the back of the bus station. I thought I looked suitably scruffy but I spent a lot of time just standing about waiting for someone to talk to me. Eventually one of them came over and asked me if I had any money. I said yes and he then asked me for the price of a cup of tea. I gave him the money. This I soon realised was my first mistake. Suddenly all of them approached me and asked me for money. They must have thought I was a soft touch. One of them called me a mug-punter. I wasn't sure what that meant.

Day 6

If someone had told me that sociological research was this hard I might have studied physics instead! These last few nights I've slept in derelict houses and washed myself in public toilets. The food I've eaten has been terrible but I have to do everything they do or else they'll become suspicious of me. I think they accept me although I'm sure that they are still a little wary of me. The good thing is that we spend a lot of time during the day in the reading room of the public library – in search of warmth rather than books – and this gives me a chance to write up my field notes. But I try not to be seen doing it. I keep my notes in my tatty old bag with my other bits and pieces. I'm surprised how knowledgeable some of them are – I expect it's got something to do with all the newspapers they read. This surprised me. Reading habits might be an interesting thing to observe.

Day 17

Last night was tricky. We were all in this derelict building and it was freezing. There was ice all over the inside walls! God knows how people manage to survive this life, but they do. A new face appeared and he was well known to the lads. He'd been up north but had returned – hitching lifts mostly on the back of trucks (modes of travel might be worth observing) – to get away from the bitter climate up there. To everyone's delight he produced a bottle of some sort and the lads in turn started to drink from it. Then it was my turn. I'm not sure what it was but it burned my guts. I was sick. Some of them laughed at me but one or two gave me funny looks. I got the feeling that THEY WERE OBSERVING ME! (Could I risk a study of drinking habits?)

As we can see from these fieldwork notes the sociologist encountered a number of problems. One problem, which he doesn't go into deeply, is the difficulty of joining a group and becoming accepted. What usually happens is that he has to make preliminary observations – a sort of trial run – before carrying out his detailed research. Exactly what research is envisaged by this researcher is not stated in these extracts but it might be anything from the study of reading or drinking habits to modes of travel.

For the research to be successful the sociologist has to attract as little attention to himself as possible. As an actor playing a part he has to put on a convincing performance. He must be familiar with the type of slang used by the particular group – what the sociologist refers to as **argot**. When our fieldworker stumbled over the meaning of the word 'mug-punter' (it means a fool, somebody who doesn't understand what's going on) it could have led to problems. To get information the sociologist must communicate with the group under study and if he doesn't understand their argot he will get into trouble.

Another problem that can distort accurate observation is called **observer bias**. When this happens the researcher allows his own views and opinions to affect his judgment. In our example, the researcher came very near to this when he expressed surprise that vagrant men should enjoy reading newspapers. Fortunately he didn't allow this to prejudice his observations. He also tried his best to be objective by not being too involved in taking the lead or by being excessively sympathetic. If a researcher does become so involved in the group activity he loses his sense of objectivity, this is known as **going native**.

Unfortunately it sometimes happens that the group under observation gets suspicious of their new member. This happened to our researcher when he sensed he was getting 'funny looks'. Once suspicions are aroused the group members may cease to act naturally and so undermine the whole purpose of the research. Even the most experienced researcher would have problems under these circumstances. Perhaps the most unpredictable aspect of all participant observation concerns **out-of-sight events** which obviously remain unrecorded yet may themselves be of crucial importance. After all, researchers are only human and can't be in two places at once. Consequently if a few people become separated from the group under study the researcher will have to decide which part of the group to study.

Case studies

So far we have discussed social surveys, questionnaires, interviewing and observation as means of gathering information about social behaviour. These are the main but not the only research tools employed by researchers. The case study technique is also used by sociologists who wish to conduct research into an individual problem (the cause of stress within a particular family) or within an institution (the causes of a prison riot). The researcher will make full use of all the available data, personal and official records and conduct in-depth interviews with many or all of the people involved, before presenting the results in the form of a case study.

Primary and secondary sources of information

Most of the research techniques described secure what is known as **primary source information**, which means that the sociologist is responsible for collecting the information at first hand.

Secondary source information is material that already exists, usually in published form. Records of births and death rates, government statistics, letters, newspaper articles, diaries, journals, national surveys and the published findings of other sociologists are all examples of secondary source materials. Other rich secondary sources available are publications in other disciplines, such as medical, psychology and economics journals and the case studies of social workers. For instance, economic statistics might show us an increase in unemployment, medical statistics an increase in alcohol addiction and the case-work of social workers an increase in alcohol-related child abuse and wife battering. Novels and plays can also provide useful insights into social behaviour, especially of historical times. Generally speaking, most sociologists use both primary and secondary sources of information in their work. The advantages of secondary source information to the sociologist are that they

- show details of work already done in the area
- are a source of new ideas and techniques
- may act as a stimulus for further research
- provide information
- show trends and patterns.

What would you say are the disadvantages of their use to a sociologist embarking on a research project?

EXERCISE

Make a list of possible sources of information available to a sociologist researching into the

- attitudes towards the enemy of British front-line trench fighters during the First World War
- academic performance of immigrant girls in a large comprehensive school
- the incidence of poverty on a local housing estate.

Present your list under the two headings of **primary** and **secondary** source information.

In your study of sociology you may read a study that interests you. If you do, please pay close attention to the methods used to gather information. Most studies will include, usually at the back of the book, a section on research methods. For example, Willmott and Young's famous study, *Family and Kinship in East London*, tells how the sociologists used a variety of methods ranging from social survey techniques, interviews and participant observation. For a fascinating look at how inventive researchers can be we strongly recommend Stanley Cohen's *Folk Devils and Moral Panics*. As a sociologist you not only have to be logical and clear in the way you organise your work but also creative.

EXERCISE

As a social scientist you are asked to recommend the most suitable method of collecting data in the following research areas:

- The life-style of gypsies
- The likelihood of children from working class homes going to university
- The effects of fluorescent lighting on employee performance
- The incidence of glue sniffing in a large school
- The causes of poor industrial relations in a small factory
- Regional differences in consumer spending
- How inmates adjust to long-term imprisonment
- Personal interactions between residents in a drug rehabilitation centre

You are to select your method of research from one or more of the following:

- Social surveys – personal interviewing or postal questionnaires
- Participant observation – open or concealed
- Non-participant observation – explain the circumstances
- Case-study techniques
- Secondary sources of information – mention sources

Explain the reasons for your choice of research method(s) and indicate the kinds of problems that are likely to arise in each case.

Sociological concepts and theories

You will recall that in a previous section we introduced the word **culture**. Your immediate understanding of the meaning of this word may be different from the one used in sociology. The everyday use of this word is usually linked to the world of arts, to literature, drama, music, books and ballet – all of which are forms of artistic culture. Culture for the sociologist refers to the way of life of a social group. In other words this concept, like many others you will be asked to think about, has a precise meaning which helps the sociologist in his analysis and description of social behaviour.

For the sociologist, **concepts** are essential tools of the trade. For example, if a sociologist asks you to describe the culture of your school or college you would know instantly what he meant. So though we sometimes accuse sociologists of using jargon – and to be fair some of them do use too much – the use of concepts is both necessary and practical in sociological work. When you have worked through this book you will have mastered some concepts which will be useful in your own sociological observations and discussions.

As well as concepts, sociologists also make use of what is called **theory**. By theory we mean the body of ideas which make up sociological thought. To appreciate theory we will mention 2 of the founding fathers of sociology whose theories are still of great importance.

Sociology itself developed during a time of rapid social change in Europe during the 18th and 19th centuries. In France great changes took place during and after the French Revolution, and in Britain a developing industrial society was bringing about important social changes. Sociology developed as a response to these changes. The early sociologists were interested in scientifically studying how social groups would react to change and what would happen to society itself.

From these pioneering days we can identify some important names and influences. Emile Durkheim and Karl Marx stand out as their influence is still widespread today. No doubt many of you will have heard of Karl Marx and it is enough to say that his political writings have been so influential that a third of the modern world's political systems are based on his ideas. Marx saw himself first as a political thinker but his work has immense importance for the sociologist.

Durkheim and Marx saw the organisation of social life in industrial societies differently. For Durkheim, society is usually in a state of consensus, that is in general people are in agreement on how society should be run. Durkheim also sees society as being composed of different parts, with each part working efficiently if society is to survive and prosper. For example, an important part of any industrial society is the education system.

How does the education system help society to survive and prosper?

In Durkheim's view the education system is responsible for the training of young people to prepare them for their participation in another section of society, the economic sector. Take the present emphasis on the teaching of computer skills in schools. Durkheim would say that the decision to introduce computer education wasn't made because the education authorities thought it would be an interesting subject to study, but because we need a workforce that can understand the use and practical application of computer technology. It would make no sense at all to introduce the study of Ancient Greek into schools because an ancient language does not help us to deal with the problems and developments in modern industry.

Durkheim would also see the role of the Church and the beliefs that dominate our religious life as having a key part to play in maintaining consensus within society. Religion instructs us in what is moral and immoral – that is what is right and wrong. This provides us with codes of conduct which serve to guide our behaviour in our everyday world of work and leisure. According to Durkheim all major social activities, whether they are within the family setting, the mass media or the political system, are essential in maintaining a consensus in a stable society. This is what we mean by having a theory about society. Karl Marx offers us a completely different theory.

Marx saw society in terms of conflict between groups that have economic power and groups that do not. For Marx it is the ownership of wealth – money, property, industrial and commercial buildings, land – which gives wealthy people power over others. The mass of the population is controlled in every facet of their lives by these powerful economic groups.

Unlike Durkheim, Marx argued that the subjects taught in schools are basically the ideas of the ruling economic class. Children are encouraged to accept the values of this class through their teachers and textbooks. This leaves them uncritical of society and ready to accept the control and ideas of the class who oppress them. Instructing children in computer skills would be to invest the workers of the future with a skill that can be exploited for profit by the employing class. Religion too plays a part in controlling our behaviour. Marx called religion 'the opium of the people' which means that religion offers us only the morality of blind obedience (thou shalt not) and vague promises about the future (when the meek shall inherit the earth). Political parties, local government, newspapers, television, radio, all conspire to oppress us and present a one-sided view of the dominant wealth-owning class.

Durkheim then sees a society based on general agreement between the various social groups and Marx sees such groups in perpetual conflict. These are 2 theories of society and it will be for you to judge which one (it could be a bit of both and there are others of course) you think most adequately describes how people and social groups experience the world in which they live.

You may be wondering how these concepts and theories fit into the study of sociology. You remember that sociology involves us in a scientific approach, and as all science is based on theory and concept, both of these are necessary tools used in sociological investigation. In order to focus our minds clearly on this, let us examine the way of life of a minority group in our society: the gypsies. This is how one of them describes his experience:

When you're on the road like we are you soon find out that you're at the very bottom. You're the lowest of the low. You've got no permanent home and you've got no friends except other gypsies. Most people think we're dirt. The law are always comin' round and asking you to move on. We're not wanted. We're outcasts in society. No one realises that our way of life goes back thousands of years. They think we're just slobs and louts.

Think of the concept of culture. How would it explain the way of life of the gypsies? How would Durkheim and Marx analyse the gypsies' role in society?

The concept of culture would be used to explain the gypsies' traditions, habits and way of life which have evolved over hundreds of years. Sociologists influenced by the work of Durkheim would ask questions about the contribution this social group makes to society and might suggest that as they are outside *normal* society they contribute very little. In other words if everyone adopted their lifestyle society would no longer be possible in the way we understand it. A Marxist would suggest that gypsies, with little property or wealth, will be dealt with severely by the police for failing to comply with the rules of society. The police action is a punishment because they refuse to conform and the police would be seen as acting in the interests of the economic dominant classes. Because the gypsies do not work and refuse to involve themselves in production, the economic position of the ruling class is being threatened.

To take your thinking a little further, and to bring it into line with your own experience, try a Durkheimian or a Marxist analysis of something which strikes you as sociologically interesting. By working through problems like this you should become more at ease with sociological theories. Whatever theory we favour it finally provides us with a view of the world we live in. It gives our ideas form and helps us to understand more clearly what is happening around us.

EXERCISE

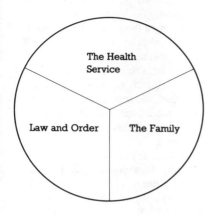

	Number	Proportion of all names drawn
Moved	299	10%
Dead	23	1%
Not eligible	34	1%
Interviewed	1928	64%
Refused	533	18%
Too ill, deaf or senile	57	2%
Always out, not traced	126	4%
Total	3000	100%

Source: The Symmetrical Family M Young and P Willmott

Taking each of these institutions in turn explain how Durkheim and Marx might interpret its function in society.

QUESTIONS

1 *a* What is sociology? (8 marks)
  b Explain how sociology can help us to understand society. (12 marks)

2 (Survey sample from *The Symmetrical Family*)

In order to study family life, the authors of *The Symmetrical Family* took a sample of 3000 people to be interviewed. They said:

'We did not succeed in interviewing all of them . . . The losses were large. Were they so much so that, together with biases in the sample of areas or inadequacies in the electoral lists themselves, they made our sample unrepresentative of the population? There is no sure answer.'

a According to the passage, why were the authors concerned about the losses of people from the original sample? (1 mark)
b According to the above table, what percentage of the 3000 people chosen to make up the sample were not interviewed? (1 mark)
c Define the term **sample** and explain why sociologists often take a sample when carrying out a survey. (4 marks)

d What steps would a sociologist take in order to obtain a representative sample? (6 marks)
e Young and Willmott use the interview method in '*The Symmetrical Family*'. Suggest an alternative method of collecting information about family life and indicate the strengths and weaknesses of your chosen method. (8 marks)
Source: AEB O Level, 1983

3 *a* Explain what is meant by the term *sociological theory*. (5 marks)
  b Describe 2 contrasting theories of social behaviour that attempt to explain the social world. Illustrate your answer with examples. (15 marks)

Lord Harry's Fall

From the files of our crime reporter **Sally Thirkettle**

Harold George Trotter was released from Leicester prison at 8am on Thursday after serving 2 years of a 3 year sentence for illegally importing pirated videos. At his trial he was described by 'smiling' Judge Parker as the 'most evil and corrupt' criminal he had sent down that session.

Lord Harry's celebrated criminal exploits began when he made his first fortune on a £50 000 consignment of ladies' shoes he unlawfully imported from the Far East, which he marketed under the slogan 'Smart 'n' British'. Masquerading as a West Country footwear manufacturer he persuaded the giant footwear retailers Softshoe to purchase the consignment for three-quarters of a million pounds. They later discovered to their horror that all the shoes were left-footed rejects. When the ruse was discovered Lord Harry had absconded to the Costa Brava, well out of reach of the British police and the courts. His family continued to live comfortably in Britain.

It was in Spain that he became known as 'Lord' Harry because of his fast living and luxurious lifestyle. He frequently invited admiring British holidaymakers to his 5-star hotel to join him pool-side for a drink and a game of poker with his crooked British expatriate pals. His guests were expected to pay for the drinks by losing at cards.

The police finally caught up with Lord Harry for the first time when he attempted to return to Britain with some extra luggage – a suitcase full of hard-porn videos. In court the prosecution read out charges relating to 38 other offences ranging from petty theft, fraud, unlawful distilling of 500 gallons of whisky and soft drug trafficking.

'That was the end of my career as an international operator,' Harry told reporters with some pride on his release from prison. 'Going to prison has destroyed me completely. I had a large detached 6-bedroomed house in an exclusive part of Warwickshire and my kids went to expensive private schools. We had four cars, one a Rolls with our family crest on the driver's door, a large indoor pool, memberships of several top-class golf clubs and friends in high places. People in the neighbourhood really looked up to us. We were class. Now they call me "Poor Lord Harry".'

'Prison is the worst thing that can happen to anybody, believe me. All this talk about it being a holiday camp is crap. I spent 2 years banged up with two pimps in a cell that was designed for 1 prisoner. We were locked up for 23 hours a day. We could only send 1 letter a week and have 1 visit a month. That was the worst part of it. All my fancy friends and neighbours – I never saw or heard from them. Even my wife stopped visiting me after 6 months. She said it was bad for the kids. The sanitary arrangements were disgusting.'

'Now I'm out things look even blacker. The bank has called in the mortgage and sold my house and all my possessions. My wife has gone off with a gambler and my 2 kids are in care. The kids live in a children's home on the other side of the city. They're only 12 and 13 years old. They said I can't see my kids until I get permission from the court. Can you imagine that?'

'Don't get me wrong. I don't blame them for sending me to prison, but it's not right when they punish my kids as well. My eldest lad is already in trouble with the law for stealing

from cars. Taking away our home was diabolical.'

Lord Harry enquired about the location of the nearest Salvation Army hostel and asked me for some money. I gave him 2 pounds. He said that wasn't enough for a taxi. I suggested that he might travel by bus. He apologised for his rudeness and went sauntering towards the city. Poor Lord Harry.

QUESTIONS

1   Contrast the range of cultural influences likely to have been experienced by Lord Harry's children before and after the prison sentence.

2   'Prison culture is designed to be a grim alternative to the culture of society.' Using as many examples as you can think of, explain why this statement might be true.

Can you think of any circumstances when a prisoner might find prison life satisfactory?

3   How would Durkheim and Marx understand the purpose of prisons in our society?

Points for discussion

- Prisons help to preserve civilised society.
- Much more should be done to improve prison life to help prisoners adapt to society.
- Criminals with growing families should be given shorter prison sentences.

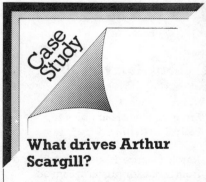

Case Study

What drives Arthur Scargill?

1   Arthur Scargill is sitting behind an iron-framed oak desk in primary

school in wartime south Yorkshire. He is only six but already he stands out among his 50 or so classmates.

2   Some of them call him *brussen* – cocky – always needing to be right, always verbally outsmarting them. Others admire his superior ways and he has already acquired a small but devoted following in the playground at Worsborough Dale school. They think he is something special. They are right.

3   Like many of the other boys, he will begin his working life at 15 at the pits. But he will soon escape. He will travel the world, discussing its future with Khrushchev in the Kremlin, Castro in Cuba; go on lecture tours of America; rap out orders in snazzy offices where his portraits hang on the wall; debate in the Oxford and Cambridge unions; stay in a flat in London's fashionable Barbican, close by Tory cabinet ministers.

4   He will be an important visitor to 10 Downing Street: have a chauffeur, luxury cars, Airedales, ponies, smart suits, a large salary and generous expenses. His verbal smartness will swell into forceful political rhetoric. His enemies will be some of the most influential people in the land. His devoted followers will be members of one of the country's most powerful unions.

5   Forty years on from the time the blue-eyed little boy sat behind that desk, he will be locked in a conflict that stretches the nation's political system, its method of maintaining law and order and its economy. He will be one of the most important, most admired, most hated, most feared men in the country.

6   How did he become so special? The most obvious clues lie in his parents. Arthur was an only child. His father, Harold, still alive at 78, was a miner but went into the RAF in the war, so Arthur's mother, Alice, had her young son largely to herself. She doted on him. Years later, when he came home from work, his dinner would be on the table, his slippers

waiting; if they weren't, Arthur would be upset. But mother didn't mind: to her Arthur was always on a pedestal. He was devastated when she died when he was 17.

7　The vital input from his father was political. Although the family's material circumstances were by no means bad – when Arthur was three, the family moved from the basic industrial cottage where he had been born to a comfortable crescent home with two bedrooms and a bathroom – Harold Scargill was a devoted member of the Communist party.

8　The newspapers that came into the home were the *Daily Worker, Reynolds News* and *Tribune*. The pamphlets and tracts were on subjects like starvation in imperialist, capitalism-infested African countries. The books were *The Iron Heel*, or *People of the Abyss* by Jack London, or *The Ragged Trousered Philanthropists* by Robert Tressell. Not surprisingly, they coloured young Arthur's view of life. In Tressell's 633-page 'story of 12 months in hell', about a group of oppressed industrial workers, the hero Owen concludes that public ownership of land, mines, railways, canals, ships, factories, and all other means of production, was the only solution to life's problems.

9　The boy the mother had placed on a pedestal became an ideologically well-educated young Communist dedicated to overthrowing the capitalist system. It was a potentially explosive combination.

10　It was natural that he should join the Young Communist League. In those days the YCL had discipline. Stalin was still a wonderful example. Not just anyone could join: it was decided whether you were suitable. You had to have the correct ideas, socialist ideas, and be willing to develop your ideology in a disciplined manner. Because mining dominated the area, much time was devoted to how the industry would

play its part in overturning capitalism: after all, miners clearly would benefit by Marxist policies.

11　But they didn't necessarily *know* that it was capitalism that was holding them back. Strikes, disputes – *struggles* – could educate them.

12　Soon Arthur won a place on the national YCL committee, with special responsibilities towards industry. He had become one of Britain's leading young Communists, and his father was proud of him.

13　By now Arthur was working. Although his mother had wanted to protect him from it, Arthur had gone to the pit at 15. It was a traumatic experience for him: the noise, the dust, in the screening sheds (on the surface) and later at the coalface itself were almost too much. Yet the job made sense for anyone who wanted to change the face not just of industry but of Britain too. Increasingly sophisticated automation meant that the number of men needed was certain to decline, just as many pits where sooner or later stocks would be geologically exhausted were doomed. These constant threats or fears simply strengthened the miners' powerful sense of loyalty to both their industry and their union.

14　And at the busy Woolley pit, north of Barnsley, the young Arthur found plenty of reasons for struggle, straightaway becoming a self-appointed leader of the apprentices who, he insisted, deserved better treatment.

Source: The Sunday Times

*QUESTIONS

1　Explain, in your own words, the meaning of
- forceful political rhetoric (paragraph 4)
- to her Arthur was always on a pedestal (paragraph 6)
- public ownership (paragraph 8)
- Marxist policies (paragraph 10)
- traumatic experience (paragraph 13)
- sophisticated automation (paragraph 13)

- miners' powerful sense of loyalty (paragraph 13)

2　According to these extracts, what were the most important cultural influences in Arthur Scargill's life?

3　In paragraph 5 Arthur Scargill is described as 'one of the most important, most admired, most hated, most feared men in the country.'
a　Which social groups or institutions are most likely to admire or hate him?
b　Explain how Marx and Durkheim would analyse this description.

*Do not attempt these questions until you have read the whole of this chapter.

Points for discussion

- Most of what we think comes from our family home.
- Reading doesn't influence anybody.
- Communism is a superior social system because it restricts individual liberties for the benefit of society as a whole.

Fieldwork notes

TYPE OF RESEARCH Participant observation (concealed)
GROUP UNDER STUDY Typing pool of 5 females in small office
SUBJECT OF STUDY An aspect of social behaviour of female workers
NAME OF RESEARCHER Kathy Lawson*
MODE OF ENTRY Arrangements made with manager, Mr Dutton
DATE AND TIME Day One/Monday 2nd February/8.30am

8.30am Arrived early to get myself sorted out and make final arrangements with the manager. Mr Dutton failed to turn up – he phoned in to say his car had broken down. I had to ask the cleaner to take me to the office. New electronic typewriters! The manager told me they were IBM electrics. Two girls arrive, Tracy and Fiona. They know about me and tell me where to sit and show me the place. Talked to Tracy. She's 19 and has worked here for 2 years. She said she liked Mandy but not Anne. She asked me about my last job. I wasn't expecting that question. I told her I worked in an office in another town.

9.00am Boss still not arrived. Now I won't get the chance to look through the girls' personnel files for information. All the girls have now arrived. I introduce myself. Two of them (Mandy and Maria) couldn't understand why I've been employed since the work is so slack. Of the 5 typists, Mandy and Maria are married. Mr Dutton arrives in a sweat at 9.20am.

9.30am Mr Dutton gives each of us a pile of typing and winks at me. Fiona complains about the typing she's been given. She said she's always getting hand-written invoices to type. Anne disagrees. Argument ensues, but nothing serious. Mr Dutton asks Mandy to make him a cup of coffee. Why do men always expect women to make them coffee? This typing is difficult for me. Fiona asked me where did I do my training. I said I wasn't used to these electronic machines. She said I can always come to her for help if I wanted to, but she advised me that Anne was usually too busy to help. These women are so catty!

10.30am Coffee break at last. They have a kitty of 50 pence a week each. I join the kitty of course. We take turns to make the coffee and tea. All stop work and pull chairs round to face each other for a chat. Mandy is reading The Sun and said 'I wonder where they get these girls from to pose like that'. Tracy said they were all actresses and they get about 90 pounds if their photo is published. Fiona said they used invisible wires to prop up the girls fronts. I said that women shouldn't let themselves be used like that - it's demeaning. Fiona said she has to work 2 weeks to get 90 pounds. Mandy said that they don't use invisible wires but sticky Sellotape. Everyone laughs. Mr Dutton sticks his head out of his office door and asks Fiona to bring him another cup of coffee. Later Maria said we shouldn't have to make coffee for someone else in our breaktime. I suggested that

Fiona should tell the boss to make his own coffee. Silence. Well, back to work.

12 noon My typing is definitely improving. Mr Dutton calls me into his office to take some notes. Then he apologises for coming in late. We have a long chat about the form my research might take. He made a few useful suggestions. Interesting that it never occurred to him that my research might include him! Got back to my desk in the middle of an altercation. Someone had opened the wrong window and papers had blown all over the office. Chaos. Interesting that Anne (the youngest?) seems to have taken over sorting out the mess. I thought one of the older married women would have taken charge. It's a pity I missed most of this.

1.00-2pm Lunchtime Problems. Maria and Tracy go to the pub for lunch and Mandy, Anne and Fiona lunch in the office. I decide to stay in the office since there's 3 of them here. At least I can catch up on my fieldnotes. Both Anne and Fiona are eating incredibly thin wafers spread with cottage cheese. They are both on a 1000 calorie diet, whatever that is! I ask Anne why is she dieting. She said she's always on a diet. She hates being fat. Her boy friend doesn't like fat women either. I asked her whether he likes her for herself or her body shape. She said she wasn't sure what I meant. Fiona sees me reading The Guardian and asks me why don't I wear make-up. I said it makes my face spotty. Mandy said she only buys The Sun for her husband. She'd buy The Guardian if she had her own way. She stuffed her paper into her handbag as though she was embarrassed.

3.00pm I've definitely got the impression that Mr Dutton and Maria are on more than friendly terms. Maria told me that she had a ploughman's lunch and a lager in the pub. I said I might join them tomorrow. She said it was quite expensive and that I ought to stay in the office for lunch until I got used to things. Mr Dutton comes into the office and puts the kettle on for the girls' tea. Mandy said that miracles do sometimes happen, even in this office!

4.00pm In terms of friendships there seem to be 2 distinct groupings. Group 1: Maria, Tracy

and Mr Dutton. Group 2: Anne and Mandy. Fiona seems to be the odd one out - not reticent but ignored in general. The atmosphere is happy and relaxed but there are undercurrents. Rumours exist about the introduction of a word processor. One or two of the women fear for their jobs. Mandy asks nobody in particular what she ought to buy her old man for his tea when she does her shopping after work. 'Fish and Chips' pipes in everybody in chorus. It must be an old joke. Then Maria says that husbands should do their own cooking. Mandy said she would rather do the cooking herself than be poisoned. Maria asked me who does my cooking. I said I do. Then I explained that I lived on my own in a flat, I am divorced, and I'm 32. This interrogation came as a shock. They know more about me than I know of them! I should have been prepared for it. I underestimated them.

5.00pm The end of a very long day. Perhaps I haven't come out too badly after all. My interrogators seem satisfied. But it is going to take a lot of effort before I become part of the furniture.

*Kathy is a mature sociology undergraduate. She has been asked to conduct research into an aspect of social behaviour at work and to produce a report. These field notes are the first step in gathering information and impressions. Kathy has had some limited part-time experience working in an office.

QUESTIONS

1 Outline the problems experienced by this researcher. Organise your answer to include points about
- gaining acceptance
- communication difficulties
- observer bias
- 'going native'
- out-of-sight events
- unnatural behaviour in the presence of an observer.

2 As a researcher, how would you have prepared yourself for this particular type of investigation?

3 Concealed participant observation has certain advantages and

disadvantages over open observation. What are these?

4 Suggest an interesting area of research that this sociologist might pursue in the typing pool. Give reasons for your suggestion.

Points for discussion

- Concealed observation is unethical.
- It is not possible to learn anything worthwhile from such a small group of people.

Important Points

- Sociology provides us with the opportunity of taking a more logical and objective view of the social world.
- Sociology gives us a scientific framework by which we can systematically measure and understand the range of complex social behaviour in society.
- Sociologists use the concept of culture to describe the whole way of life of a group or a society.
- Cultural influences are potent factors in the development of the individual.
- Most sociological research requires a representative sample group for the purpose of investigation.
- The use of social surveys, questionnaires, participant observation, case studies and secondary sources of information are the standard tools of sociological investigation.
- Sociological theory is what we call the body of ideas that attempts to explain the social world.

2 Social stratification and social class

When you have worked through this chapter you should have a clearer understanding of

Life chances · **Systems of stratification** · **Ascribed and achieved status** · **Objective and subjective assessments of social class** · **Class consciousness** · **The theories of Marx and Weber** · **The proletariat** · **The bourgeoisie** · **Forces of production** · **Status position** · **Social mobility** · **Embourgeoisement** · **Sponsored and contest mobility**

What is social stratification?

Sometimes sociologists are accused of discussing society in a way that appears remote from our everyday experiences. We can partly explain this by realising that a sociologist's perspective of the world can lead people to challenge their own confidently-held views, which make them feel uneasy. Occasionally the jibes directed at sociologists are an attempt to cover up this unease. If sociologists discuss the rich strata in society they are accused of jealousy. If they turn their attention to the groups which form the poorest strata they are seen as patronising. None of this, of course, is true. A prime task of sociology is to study social behaviour objectively and to account for the existence of different social groups in society.

This should give you an idea of what is meant by **social stratification**. The term describes the way things are arranged in layers, rather as a geologist would understand a rock face as being made up of separate horizontal layers of material. When sociologists talk of stratification they are referring to social stratification, which means that some people occupy what are seen as the top positions, and others the bottom positions. This does not mean that the people in the top positions are superior to those at the bottom, or vice versa.

Look at your classroom colleagues. If we were to take body height as an indication of difference, it would be fairly easy to sort out the whole class into 3 groups of tall, medium and small pupils. We could even divide the class into male and female to find out if there is a relative difference in height between the sexes. But these are physical and not social differences. Sociologists are interested in slotting people not into physical but into social categories, on the basis that certain groups share common patterns of social behaviour which make them different from other groups.

We are all aware that in our society some people live in large, warm houses while others shiver in cold, damp tenements, and that some people consider £100 spent on a dinner for 2 as part of their normal experience when most of us find it hard to think how such a large amount could be spent on just 2 meals. We also know that great social and economic differences exist in our society. Even so, because we are so close to these differences and so familiar with them as social phenomena within our multi-cultural society, we tend to take them for granted. We forget that a person's economic position within the social hierarchy has a great bearing on every aspect of his or her lifestyle. Social stratification can be seen as the houses we can afford to live in and how they are furnished. It can be seen in our shopping baskets and by the type of food we eat. It exists in our attitudes towards law and order, nuclear disarmament, politics, eduation, work, and will influence which religion we choose to believe or not to believe in. Our position on the social ladder will give some indication about the type of television programmes we enjoy watching and the kind of newspapers we buy and the type of person we will marry. It may even tell us something about the illnesses we will endure and when and how we will die!

Life chances

15 September, 1984 was a day you may not remember. It happened to be a Saturday. In some parts of the country people were enjoying the sunshine, whilst in other parts they were cursing the rain. Some people had a good day and some not so good. Over 2000 couples got married.

Two women in particular had a special reason to remember the date. They both gave birth to bouncing baby boys. Although both babies were healthy and born at exactly the same moment in the same country, they entered different social worlds. The one boy, who later would be known as Prince Harry, was welcomed not only by his parents but by the whole nation. His birth created great excitement, with TV and radio bulletins constantly informing us of the progress of mother and child. Presents and cards arrived from all over the world and church bells were rung throughout the land.

Prince Harry was born in a hospital which charged a fee for the use of its facilities. Finding the money was no problem for his parents. The other child, Jonathan, was born in a hospital in the north of England. Although Jonathan's parents were both overjoyed with the latest addition to their family, they were nevertheless worried about the future. There would be children's clothes to buy and extra food. It's difficult to be confident about the future when you've been on strike for months and you have no idea when you'll next see a wage packet. It's difficult to even consider the future seriously as jobs in the community will be lost when the Coal Board shuts the mine.

But for now, Jonathan's parents are happy enough to buy flowers and a small box of chocolates with their last fiver. Why shouldn't the birth of their son be celebrated too?

On day 2 the media had a lot to say about Prince Harry and the miners' strike. They had nothing to say about Jonathan. It was difficult to believe that both children were born into the same world, that they shared the same planet.

Although we have taken examples from the extreme ends of the social stratification system, we nevertheless hope that you take the point. From the moment of our birth we are socially and economically located within a social world and whatever happens to us throughout our lives our social position at birth and in childhood will exert a dominating influence on our future life-chances.

EXERCISE

Take a copy of the following social experiences which form part of all our lives and write a few notes to predict the life-chances for Prince Harry and Jonathan.

We now have some idea of what is meant by social stratification and we appreciate how our position in the social hierarchy is important in terms of educational opportunities, future employment prospects and social and economic success. However we need to go further if we are to understand the importance of sociological work in this area. There are many different systems of social stratification and whilst we can identify differences we should be aware that the very existence of social stratification means that some social groups are always at an advantage over others.

EXERCISE

Most people regard themselves as belonging either to the middle class

	Prince Harry	Jonathan
The type and location of family home and facilities enjoyed		
Financial security of parents		
Health care available		
Educational prospects		
Leisure pursuits		
Job or career prospects		

	Position of my parents	
Social factors	Middle class stratum	Working class stratum
Type of education received	☐	☐
Level of income	☐	☐
Money saved or invested or available to spend	☐	☐
Size or condition or value of family house	☐	☐
Type of locality in which the house is situated	☐	☐
Ownership of valuable possessions (cars/videos/jewellery)	☐	☐
Leisure pursuits and friendship groups	☐	☐
Type of occupation or status at work	☐	☐
Power or authority exercised at work/community	☐	☐
General political or social attitudes	☐	☐
Level of respect or admiration received from others	☐	☐
General appearance	☐	☐
Accent or vocabulary range	☐	☐

Now compare your order of priorities with other people's. Is there a high level of agreement? Why should there be so much disagreement?

stratum of society or to the working class stratum. In which stratum would you place your own parents? On page 21 there is a list of social factors that are connected with social class. In your notebook, first rearrange this list of factors in descending order of importance. If you think that 'general appearance' is the most important factor in determining a person's position in the social hierarchy, then this would be at the top of your list. When your list is finished, complete the exercise by indicating your parents' class stratum for each factor by ticking the appropriate column on the right.

Some systems of social stratification

Apartheid

South Africa is a country that is socially, politically and economically organised on the basis of the colour of people's skin, and the social significance of skin colour. The system is known as apartheid (Afrikaans for *apartness*). The important feature of apartheid is that the black and coloured people in South Africa are not treated in the same way as white people because they are regarded by the ruling white minority as inferior. This division of society by racial segregation means that apartheid is a system which gives social meaning to the physical fact of skin colour. As black is inferior to white, the whole political, economic, legal and social organisation of South African society must take this 'fact' into account.

The personal and social implications of apartheid are very real. To be black in South Africa is to be at the bottom of the social hierarchy. It means living in the worst housing conditions, receiving the poorest education

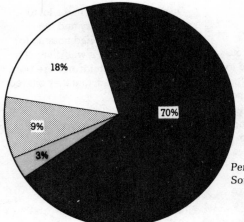

Percentage distribution of races.
Source: National Census, 1970

■ Blacks   ▨ Coloureds
□ Whites   ▨ Asians

South African population

Total population 21.5 millions

and experiencing the bleakest employment opportunities. It means living in a society which entertains separate laws for whites and blacks and being racially excluded from huge areas of the country. To be black means not having a vote, being told which bus to travel on, which park bench to sit on and which public lavatory you can and cannot use. Although the South African government is beginning to modify some of the more extreme forms of its race laws (blacks and coloureds are now allowed to marry whites), the deep-rooted social attitudes that prop up apartheid remain. For most of us in Britain it is difficult to appreciate the full horror of apartheid.

The rumour

Henderson decided to drive to the black township. He had wanted to interview Uma Kumari, their black spokesman, at the hotel but the only blacks who were allowed to come into this part of the town were the kitchen porters who were kept out of sight in case their presence upset the white guests.

There was one black guest in the hotel, an American tennis player. He had been invited to play in a tournament, and while the laws prevented blacks and whites competing together the government was trying to attract black foreign sportsmen and women to improve South Africa's international image. Usually these people would come if the price was right. The tennis star told Henderson in the hotel lift that he was officially defined as an 'honorary white'. He had documents that gave him white status for the 14 days he was allowed to stay in the country. They allowed him into places normally reserved for whites only. Henderson smiled at the thought of how funny it would be if the black player forgot his pass and got himself arrested having dinner at the hotel. How embarrassing that would be. It would serve him right. To Henderson he was a traitor to his race.

Henderson started to drive out of the city. He passed the high-class shopping areas and the tree-lined suburbs that represented the trappings of wealth of the white community. Then the rain started. He drove past a woman running in the middle of the road. He slowed down and asked her her destination. As she was heading towards the same township, he offered her a lift. She looked uneasy but got into the car.

She told him that she was a maid and worked in a house back down the road. Her day started at 5 in the morning and she got home at 8.30 in the evening. A long day, Henderson thought, a very long day.

On the road ahead there had been a traffic accident. He slowed down as a police officer approached his car to ask him where he was going and to produce his papers. There was something menacing about the way the officer asked his questions and how he looked at his passenger.

'You're a journalist then,' he said checking through the papers. 'I suppose when you go back home to Britain you'll write about how we treat our black brothers and sisters.' Then the officer smiled. 'Put the pretty black lady in the back of the car, please Sir,' he said softly 'blacks and coloureds aren't allowed to travel on the front seat with white drivers.'

Henderson did what he was told, but not without clamping his jaws together to stop himself from screaming.

'You can go on,' the officer said finally, 'unless you want a story.'

'A story?' Henderson's journalist ears pricked up.

'Yeah, there's been an accident here. One of the stupid blacks got run over by a lorry. But don't worry, we'll look after him.'

'Have you called an ambulance?' Henderson asked.

'No, we haven't. There's no need. He's dead, we think. We'll put him in the boot of the car and take his body back to town. We don't want to leave him here. Someone might accuse us of brutality.' The officer laughed and waved Henderson on.

When they arrived at the township it was getting dark, but not dark enough to hide the squalor and deprivation. The woman got out of the car and thanked Henderson for the lift. Her long day was now over. He got out too and walked towards the house where he had arranged to meet Uma Kumari. As he

approached he saw a group of people jostling outside the tumbled-down dwelling. There were women and children crying and a dog whining. It was difficult, almost impossible, to make out what was happening.

The rumour was spreading that Uma Kumari had been taken away for questioning. Henderson must have passed them on the way in, Uma's wife suggested.

EXERCISE

1   Note down the differences between the social experiences of black people and white people on the basis of the information in this story. Can you think of other situations in which black people are disadvantaged?
2   How do the attitudes of the police officer reflect the system of social stratification?
3   Why do you think apartheid persists in South African society? Do you think as a system of social organisation it will survive into the 21st century? Explain your views.

Caste

One system of social stratification that interests sociologists is the caste system of India. This system has attracted research because it has managed to survive more or less complete for 3000 years despite recent attempts to change it. Although it is too complex to explain fully in a limited space we can provide you with enough information to allow you to understand its central features so you that you can compare and contrast it with other forms of social stratification systems.

Caste is a social system that is closely linked with the Hindu religion. Hinduism, which is by far the largest religion in India, is practised by 83% of the population. In its purest form, members of particular castes (or classes) are restricted from moving

from one caste into another, except in the exceptional circumstance of a woman moving into her husband's caste. This movement is known as **hypergamy**. This is, however, unusual as most people marry within their own caste. In fact the caste system not only locates a person within the social hierarchy but also dictates the type of work members of each caste may carry out in Indian society. It is this restrictive nature of caste that has led the government to reduce the influence of caste, and, in turn, of Hinduism, over some aspects of Indian social and economic life.

When a person is born into a particular social group and is given the status of that group it is known as **ascribed status**. To understand what this means let us first list the main castes. Like all systems of stratification there are social groups at the top and groups which occupy the lower positions:

The Brahmans
The Kshatriyas
The Vaishyas
The Sudras

Outside of these 4 main groups there are about 50 million of the poorest members of Indian society. Although part of the caste system, they are regarded as 'outcastes' or 'untouchables' and form the lowest class in Indian society.

The social barriers between these groups are rigid and impassable. Those at the top, the Brahmans, occupy the most prestigious economic and social positions. Originally they were the priest caste and given the importance of religion in Indian society it is easy to understand how those who controlled the religious institutions would wield the most power. The next group, the Kshatriyas, provides people to fill high-ranking positions in the administration and the military, and the Vaishyas, those for the trading and manufacturing sector. Finally we have the Sudras who are the main labour force. The untouchables are the least privileged group in which are found the vast majority of the poor and unemployed. For most Hindus, to touch an untouchable is to be defiled.

It is not suggested that if you are a Brahman or a Kshatriyas you automatically become a priest or a general, but that those who do become involved in religion or who enlist as army officers are drawn from these castes. It is a rigid system and certainly an untouchable has no opportunity of moving out of his or her caste. The importance of caste is not that it defines occupational groups but that it gives a specific social status to everyone in Hindu society. Everyone has a place and knows where he or she stands in relation to other members of society, and Hinduism teaches that there should be as little physical contact as possible between the castes. The system is sustained because the ascribed social position of an individual has been defined by a higher order than man, Hinduism. Protest against what might be regarded by some as injustice is seen not only as an attack against the ruling political order but against the teachings of Hindu religion itself.

It is difficult for people in the West to understand why the caste system is accepted, especially by the outcastes at the bottom of the pile who experience the worst of the poverty we associate with Indian society. However, before we smugly dismiss the Hindu system we should remember our own Christian ideas of heaven and hell and the resurrection. The caste system is strange to us because we are in a different culture. If we were socialised into the norms and values of Indian society we might think the social organisation of Western culture equally odd.

EXERCISE

1   How would the concepts of culture and socialisation help us to explain the persistence of the caste system in Indian society?
2   What role would the family play in maintaining the caste system?
3   Find out about the culture of one other religious group in Indian society and on an outline map of India, indicate the geographical locations of the main religious groups.

We have examined the broad features of South African apartheid and the caste system of India. These are both examples of what are known as **closed** systems of social stratification. They are closed because an individual cannot easily move from one social group to another. A black person cannot become white and a person born into a caste will remain in that caste throughout his life. This ascribed social position, which exists from birth, will be instrumental in determining where a person will live, whom they will marry, how much they will earn in an approved occupation, where their children will be educated and the degree of respect they will command from the dominant group in society.

In Western Europe and North America, however, stratification is understood in terms of social class. We call this an **open** system of social stratification. Although the social class system is in no way as rigid as either the caste or the apartheid system, it does not allow or freely encourage easy movement from one social class to another.

The social class system

What we now understand as social classes emerged during the industrial revolution. This is not to say that before industrialisation social classes did not exist. They existed under a system of stratification known as the Estate or the Feudal system. The elements of this system were a monarchy, an aristocracy who owned vast tracts of land, a variety of small traders and artisans, skilled and semi-skilled labourers and an agricultural peasant labour force. It was essentially a closed social system and while a degree of movement between the classes may have been possible it was a rare occurrence.

The industrialisation of Britain not only changed the economic landscape but also the social landscape. New manufacturing industries were developed by a new economic group, the industrial class, who employed huge numbers of urban workers who became known as the working class. This emerging class was recruited from the ranks of agricultural workers who had been made unemployed by improvements in agricultural machinery and new methods of farming. They had the choice of either starving in the countryside or working in the developing industries in the new towns. This industrial working class often worked in appalling conditions and their houses, built near the factories and owned by their employers, were damp and squalid.

An excellent account of the conditions faced by the working class can be found in the classic work *The Condition of the Working Class in England* by Friedrick Engels. Engels looked not only at living conditions, but at the general health of the working class. He reported on persistent chills due to inadequate food, clothing and heating, and on malformations of the spine which were common amongst millhands. Although the horrors described by Engels are not in evidence today it would be incorrect to imagine that sections of the working class do not suffer hardship. We will be dealing with aspects of class hardship in another chapter.

If you think that social class has little to do with you, you should remember that we are all located in social and economic groups by the government, based on information in the *Census* form which is completed by every household in the UK. You take the social class given to the head of your household. This method of classification is based on the following 5 occupational groups:

educational experience (a doctor's education and training is much longer than a postman's). This is not to say that postmen are socially inferior to doctors, but as sociologists we know that given certain information it is possible to make assumptions about people's behaviour, attitudes and even their spending habits. It is our job that defines to a large extent our social position or role in society and the responsibilities and rights that accompany it.

The division of the whole of society into 5 or 6 social classes based purely on occupation leads to difficulties of interpretation. For example, it ignores the question of wealth and ownership. Although doctors and university lecturers might rightly occupy

classification. If they are not included, then we have the right to ask why this particular social group has been omitted from a major index of social classification. *Class 2* occupations create similar problems of definition. To be a manager or a teacher simply defines an occupation. It does not distinguish job status or position of power within either the employing organisation or the community. Should a works manager or a headmistress, each responsible and rewarded for the managing of 150 staff, be put into the same social class grouping as the manager of a supermarket employing 5 staff, or a newly qualified nurse?

Registrar General's social classification			Social group	Percentage of population
Middle class	Class 1 Professional	Lawyer, doctor, accountant, dentist, university lecturer, director, scientist, etc	A	5
	Class 2 Managerial and technical	Manager, teacher, librarian, nurse, laboratory technician, pharmacist, owner of small business, etc	B	14
	Class 3a (non-manual) Clerical and minor supervisory	Clerk, shop assistant, policeman, sales representative, typist, secretary, etc	C1	10
Working class	Class 3b (manual) Skilled trades	Electrician, tailor, printer, bus driver, cook, hairdresser, etc	C2	44
	Class 4 (manual) Semi-skilled	Farm worker, postman, barman, machine operator, bus conductor, etc	D	17
	Class 5 (manual) Unskilled	Labourer, porter, office cleaner, window cleaner, messenger, etc	E	7
	Not classified			3

The Registrar General's social class groupings are based on a person's occupation because the type of job a person does will tell us about his or her level of income (we know that doctors earn more than postmen) and about a person's

Class 1 this does not necessarily mean that they are the most wealthy group in society or that they exercise great power. It is not possible to know whether or not the most wealthy and powerful are even included in the

Can you discover any other inconsistencies in the Registrar General's classification?

Despite the limitations of the Registrar General's classification and of similar systems introduced as alternatives, there is no social classification system based on occupation that is completely satisfactory. Sociologists accept that social class is probably the sum total of a cluster of related variables. In *Social Mobility in Britain* F. M. Martin found that most people understood social class as a host of factors including educational attainment, income level, job or profession, type and situation of residence, accent and family background.

However it is to the Registrar General's classification we must return, because this type of class analysis not only helps us to understand society but provides practical help to many organisations. For example, those who want to sell goods and services to us take full account of class divisions, as we can see from this advertiser's brief on the launch of a monthly magazine:

You can get an idea of the social classes newspapers and magazines are aimed at by looking at the type of advertisements, articles and news stories they present to their readers. Look at this list of national newspapers and make a note of the type of worker likely to buy the newspaper and the social class to which he or she belongs:

buys or reads *The Times* or that teachers never read the *Sun*, but there are powerful class and educational influences that make it unlikely. Of course, given the type of work most people are involved in there isn't the time or the opportunity to read *The Times*. If you work on an assembly line or down a mine there is little chance to read an article which

Newspaper	Type of worker likely to purchase	Registrar General's social classification
The Times		
Financial Times		
The Daily Telegraph		
Sun		
Daily Mirror		
Daily Express		
Daily Mail		
Morning Star		
Daily Star		
Guardian		

No one is suggesting that an unskilled manual worker never

deals in depth with present government policies or a military

---

Lifestyle products

35 THE MALL, LONDON

Information for advertisers, copy writers and graphic artists

Agency:	LENNARD, McGOVERN AND PARTNERS
Product:	*LIFESTYLE* A monthly colour magazine published on the first Friday of the month. Size A4. Launched with 128 pages.
Distribution:	National UK distribution network including major commuter points. Price range £1.25.
Target groups:	Social classes 1 and 2, with predominantly female purchasers and readership.
Content:	The magazine will be aimed at those income groups that have disposable income to spend on expensive furniture and clothes and who are resident in the more fashionable and exclusive suburbs of towns and cities.
	The typical reader will be educated up to university standard and will like to see himself/herself as well informed in social, economic and political matters. Readers will be interested in music, art, literature, fashion, expensive transport, wine, travel, etc, and will be particularly interested in current trends in the arts. Advertisements will be based on quality goods directed primarily at high income groups A and B.
Market research:	This indicates that some readers will be drawn from Class 2 & 3 (C1). As these readers may have Class 1 or Class 2 aspirations, they may buy the magazine in order to identify with higher income groups. It is therefore the intention of the editorial staff to include general interest features to cater for this wider market.

coup in Peru. It is far easier to do that if you are a sociology lecturer, although market research tells us that this occupational group is more likely to read the *Guardian*.

We know from the vast amount of research into people's social behaviour that class divisions still exist in Britain. Although we can assess a person's class position objectively on the basis of educational qualifications and income, there is more to class than this. We also have attitudes and feelings about our position in society and this is known as **class consciousness**.

EXERCISE

Here are six variable social factors that have a part to play in determining a person's class:

1 Explain to what extent each factor has contributed to your own class position.
2 Of the 6 factors, which factor do you think is the most important in influencing a child's eventual class position as an adult? Explain the reasons for your choice.

Class consciousness

Here are 2 individuals who have no doubt about their social class position:

1 I feel that I have an important position in society in that one's family has lived in the old country for generations and though our money is no longer tied up in banking and land – actually we're pretty poor these days – I think one has a responsibility not only to one's class but to the people who live in the village. Years ago families depended on the estate for employment and village traditions are still linked with the family and the house. We have this sort of open day every August and we lay on a bit of a spread and it's all terribly great fun. When I go into the local pub or the village post office the folks have a certain respect for me. My family have always been seen as good sorts and I think that's exactly how they see me.
2 I would say I'm working class because all my life I've been aware that life has been something of a struggle.

I'm not saying that my life has been harder than anyone else's. But I know that when I clock on for work at 7 in the morning there are some buggers who won't arrive until after 10 and they'll be off for a 3-hour lunch at 12.30 leaving me to my sandwiches and brew. I've always been aware of the value of money. You tend to value things when there's not much of it around. I'm better off now than my father ever was. He knew some hard

times, but deep down not much has changed. I remember when he retired – or rather when he was forced to retire because of ill health – I asked him what he liked best about retirement. He said going down the pub, just on opening time, to have a couple of pints and read the evening paper. Just sitting there, he said, in clean clothes, having a drink at a time when he normally would be on his way home from work. That was great, just being clean with no oil on his hands. He said it was like Sunday lunchtimes every night. It made him feel great.

We can see that the 2 people have clear ideas about their social class position. They have particular attitudes about class and what it means to them. This subjective aspect of class – it is called subjective because it is difficult to measure a person's attitudes and feelings – is known as **class consciousness**.

The subjective nature of class consciousness is important because it helps us to understand how we feel and think about our class position in the social world. Social class is based not only on an objective assessment of factors such as family, friends, education and occupation, but also on our perception of our own social class. This is because what others think of us and what we think about ourselves will alter our behaviour in the social world:

I've never thought of myself as working class. I might be a brickies' labourer and live in a council house but I've always felt different from other working class people. My mates at work call me 'Davros' because I read *The Times* and do the crossword and because I'm a Conservative party voter at elections. But I'm not a snob. I really do like reading *The Times*. I like classical music, too, and Shakespeare, and I like playing chess. You might laugh, but I regard myself as a middle class person.

Under the Registrar General's classification 'Davros' would be firmly placed in social *Class 5*, although he obviously regards himself as middle class because he thinks that his social behaviour is more middle than working class. This contradiction suggests that neither an objective nor a subjective method of defining class is completely satisfactory, and that both must be taken into account if we are to begin to grasp class as a social phenomenon.

EXERCISE

How would you describe your own class consciousness? What experiences have influenced your awareness of your own social position?

We have examined social class from a descriptive viewpoint. We are now ready to move on to theories of social class and to the relationship between social class and social experience.

Theories of class

Karl Marx (1818–1883)

Marx is one of those writers whom many people have heard of and talk about but few have actually read. In fact most people read books about Marx's work rather than read the original texts because they think his work is too difficult to understand. However at least some of his books are easy to follow with a little effort although you should never be afraid to attempt to read a writer's original work if you get the opportunity.

Marx argued that the different groups in a capitalist society are in conflict over the ownership of resources available within society. In Western industrial societies he saw 2 opposed groups stratified into 2 distinct classes. At one extreme there is the working class or the proletariat who are subordinate to and exploited by the dominant ruling class, the capitalists or bourgeoisie at the other extreme (bourgeoisie = boorzh-wa-zee). According to Marx this dominant class has control over the 'means and forces of production', including the labour force, through the ownership and control of factories and the raw materials used in manufacturing. This ownership not only gives the bourgeoisie economic power but ruling power through the control of governments, the legal system, education and the mass media. These important institutions are then allowed to foster and maintain the status quo in society. In other words, the bourgeoisie exercises complete economic and social control over the lives of the vast majority of working people throughout the whole of their lives.

Critics of Marx argue that while this analysis may have been applicable to the early stages of industrialisation, it is no longer relevant in present day industrial societies. Marxism, the argument goes, has simply underestimated the resilience of the bourgeoisie in their successful attempts to bridge the gap between the 2 classes. The working class has won big political battles (eg getting the vote for all classes) and has gained major concessions from the bourgeoisie (allowed to form trade unions). Free compulsory education has further helped to break down class barriers by giving working class children the chance to join the middle classes. Critics also point out that societies which experience even greater extremes of social and economic inequality, such as caste, have not been subject to class conflict of any major kind.

However we do know that social

The Proletariat
(the working class)

- Ruled
- Wage slaves
- Alienated
- Non-owners
- Sellers of labour
- Powerless
- Socialism
- Exploited

The Bourgeoisie
(the capitalist class)

- Rulers
- Buyers of labour
- Owners and controllers of the means of production
- Political power
- Influence and wealth
- Profit
- Toryism

Conflict
- Class consciousness
- Class struggle
- Revolution

A Marxist model of society

class is real enough and the fact that we may not agree with Marx might itself be a measure of the power of the economic interests that attempt to influence us. An example of this is the way present day governments have introduced laws to control and regulate the activities of organised labour. The trade unions' attempts to organise and represent the interests of the working class often come into conflict with the government, the courts and the police.

We can also examine the way industrial issues are presented in the mass media. Most newspapers are highly critical of trade union policies and industrial action, although we have to take into account that newspapers are owned by a few people who have other economic interests. If Marx were alive today he would tell us that newspapers, radio and TV news and current affairs programmes broadcast a cleverly doctored one-sided view of society, a view that represents the interests of the ruling class. He believed that all history, all human development, is characterised by struggle and conflict between the haves and the have-nots. He predicted that this class struggle would first result in increasing class consciousness and eventually to violent revolution, with the proletariat taking power from the ruling class to create a fairer society based on the collective ownership of wealth and power. The production of goods and services would be for the benefit of society and not simply for profit. This will lead to a classless society.

The writings of Marx are controversial partly because they amount to a condemnation of capitalist societies and because of the way such societies exploit their largest group, the working class. Of course, Marx is not the only thinker to comment on the social organisation of society. Another major figure is Max Weber.

EXERCISE

Closure warning to Lucas factories

Lucas chiefs have told management of Midland plants: 'Make money – or else.'

Heads of the firm which made £32 million last year have issued instructions to factories that they must make profits or face up to closure or being sold off.

In a stark, no-nonsense message, Lucas chairman Mr Godfrey Messervy revealed that top executives have drawn up competitive action plans – known as CAPs – for every aspect of Lucas business.

And in a newspaper interview, Mr Messervy said: 'Those chunks of business which can't produce credible CAPs will be either dismantled or sold off.'

The chairman's statement will do much to kill the post-profits joy that last week swept through the massive components business, which has suffered 35 plant closures and 20 000 lost jobs in just four years.

Despite the best financial results for five years, Mr Messervy promised that it will still take another two years to get the lucas Industries group into shape.

'There is more grief and pain to come,' he said.

The chairman's statement backs up union fears that lucas plants in the West Midlands still face a massive shake-up.

At the heart of the changes could be Lucas's Birmingham-based Electrical group, which is already losing 700 jobs in a £15 million modernisation programme.

But Mr Messervy's weekend comments did nothing to allay fears that the electrical business will be pruned down to just two factories in the next five years, with hundreds more lost jobs.

Mr Ernie Hunt, the engineering union's Birmingham south district secretary, said today: 'The workforce is being made to pay for Lucas management's inability to secure sales in Europe.'

Source: Birmingham Evening Mail

1   In one paragraph, summarise the main points contained in this article.
2   How would a Marxist explain these events at the Lucas factories?
3   How might a non-Marxist explain them?
4   Using the same statistics contained in the article, rewrite a slightly shorter article based on a marxist viewpoint. You may rewrite the headline if you wish.

Max Weber (1864–1920)

Although Weber agreed with Marx that society is divided between those who own and control the means of production and those who do not, he introduced a further factor to help us to understand the nature of class in industrial societies. In *Class, Status and Party* he suggested that status is also an important factor in the analysis of social class. Weber argued that the formation of social groups depends on their **status position**. He uses the term **status** to refer to the prestige social groups enjoy and their degree of social influence. For example, certain occupational groups have high social status, such as doctors and surgeons. This high status gives them both influence and power and they will probably share similar interests and lifestyles. However, doctors and surgeons may not be the highest wage earners in our society and they do not own the hospitals they work in, but as an occupational group they enjoy a certain social prestige and admiration. Their control over life and death and their skills and knowledge give them status, and this status gives them influence. In fact many doctors will be members of the British Medical Association which is a powerful pressure group that has enormous influence over the government's health policy. (Weber uses the word **Party** to include such pressure groups.)

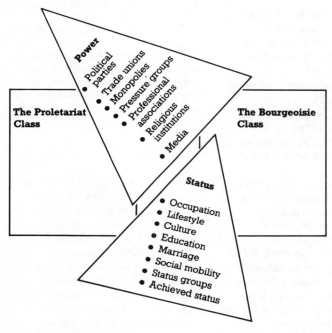

A Weberian model of society

Although Weber accepts that social classes do exist, what is more important to him is that we distinguish between class and status. Status is more important than class because it defines a person's social position and therefore his or her ability to benefit from society's rewards. For instance, black people tend to have less chance of getting a job or getting promoted in a job than white people from the same social class, and a teacher can get a mortgage more easily than a

printer who may receive a higher salary.

Weber also argues that class divisions are less rigid than Marx proposed because **status distinctions** can cut across class solidarity. For instance, many employed working class people regard themselves as 'respectable', or a cut above 'lower class' people who 'scrounge' off the state or just 'doss' around. If these 'dossers' happen to be Irish or gypsies, blacks or Pakistanis, then these

create even more status distinctions within the same class grouping and a growing source of internal class resentment. Class groupings, according to Weber, are not as stable or as powerful as Marx imagined.

This blurring of the edges of class solidarity with status distinctions is further eroded by the possibility of promotion through the class hierarchy. After all, it is not impossible for the child of a labourer to become a doctor or even a Prime Minister. This opportunity to climb the status ladder through hard work,

skill, ingenuity or even cunning is known as obtaining **achieved status**.

While we might accept Weber's arguments about the importance of status, it remains fairly obvious that the members of high status groups will be recruited mostly from the ranks of the better-off social and economic classes.

EXERCISE

Study the following occupations and award points on the basis of social class, status and power. Award between 0 and 5 points for each factor and total to a maximum of 15 points based on the following:

High					Low
5	4	3	2	1	0

Then enter the ranking group based on:

Totals	Ranking group
13 – 15	A
10 – 12	B
8 – 9	C1
6 – 7	C2
3 – 5	D
0 – 2	E

Definition of headings:

Social class stratification based on occupation, income and wealth
Status social position as judged by other members of the community
Power the capacity to influence the behaviour of others. (Weber's ideas about the nature of power are more fully explored in the chapter *Power*.)
1 Compare your ranking positions with the Registrar General's classification system. To what extent does your ranking agree and disagree? Are there any glaring inconsistencies?
2 Compare and discuss your ranking with a friend's. Are they similar? Is it possible for you both to come to a compromise to produce a common ranking? How does your common ranking compare with other common rankings in your group?
3 On the basis of your discussions, what recommendations for improvement (if any) would you make

Occupation	Social class	Status	Power	Total	Ranking group
Dustman					
Bank manager					
Member of Parliament					
Vicar					
Rock star					
Nurse					
Advertising executive					
Shop assistant					
Beautician					
Cleaner					
Computer programmer					
Teacher					
Painter and decorator					
Professional gambler					
Dentist					

to the Registrar General's classification?

Social mobility

We know that caste and apartheid are examples of **closed** systems of social stratification and that the social class system is an **open** system. This means that in our society it is possible to move from the bottom rung of the social ladder to the top rung. In fact some people in the public eye will tell stories of how they were born into the poorest and most deprived sections of society and with hard work rose through the ranks to command lofty social positions. While no one is denying that these rags-to-riches stories are true, the very fact that we are made aware of them is an indication of their news value. If such social movements were commonplace they would not be of general interest.

When sociologists discuss social mobility they are referring to the movement of individuals or groups from one section of the social hierarchy to another. This movement can take 2 forms:

Horizontal mobility describes the movement from one social position to another without promotion or demotion to another

social stratum. An example of this is a works manager who changes his job to take up full-time teaching. Of greater importance to sociologists is vertical mobility, which describes movement either upward or downward in the class strata.

Vertical mobility is usually upward. The most common way to achieve upward mobility is through a change in employment associated with educational success. Marrying into a higher social class is also a possible route, but less likely. Thus, the bright son of an unemployed steel worker who gets a university degree before winning a parliamentary seat would be an example of this. Eventual marriage to the daughter of a high court judge, followed by rapid promotion through the political hierarchy to become Prime Minster, would complete the process.

The question of social mobility first arose in sociology in the 1950s and early 1960s. At that time there was a general increase in the living standards of most people in Western societies. It was thought that the working class in particular were earning higher wages and enjoying a lifestyle and economic security similar to that of white collar workers who were traditionally regarded as middle

class. This led certain commentators to suggest that we could no longer realistically accept that a working class existed. This idea developed into the **embourgeoisement thesis** which argued that Britain was becoming a middle class society. Evidence of increasing affluence and opportunities for working class people was summed up in a famous catchphrase of the time 'you've never had it so good'. Full employment, high wages, marvellous white collar job opportunities in the South East and the Midlands, money to spend on TVs, washing machines, home ownership and family cars, all pointed the way to the embourgeoisement of the working classes. Soon everybody would be middle class.

EXERCISE

In what way is the material lifestyle of your parents different from the lifestyle of your grandparents? What have been the social consequences of these changes?

A major study, *The Affluent Worker*, was carried out by a team led by John Goldthorpe and David Lockwood. Their research was based on a sample of manual car workers and white collar workers living and working in Luton. Luton was chosen because it was a prosperous area of modern industry employing young mobile workers. If traditional social class divisions were being challenged it was likely to be taking place in towns such as Luton.

While the study showed that many manual workers owned their own homes (this was unusual at the time) and had a high standard of living, the researchers found that to maintain their income levels they worked longer hours than their white collar counterparts. They also found that their attitudes about work were unchanged. Many manual workers cultivated what sociologists call an **instrumental approach** towards work, that is work was seen simply in economic terms and offered little job satisfaction. There was also minimal social mixing between the two groups and social attitudes were slightly different. For example, a manual worker saw a car or a washing machine as a status symbol while his middle class counterpart took ownership of such items for granted. There was also a difference in political attitudes. The Labour Party was regarded by the manual workers as representing the interests of the working class, a political party to which they strongly associated to the extent that 80% of them voted Labour at elections.

The Goldthorpe and Lockwood research suggested that social changes were taking place within Luton's working class community, but that these changes were superficial. They found some evidence that the values and aspirations of working class families were becoming more middle class. They were experiencing what sociologists call notions of **class convergence**, but the idea that social classes were disappearing or merging because of increasing affluence was rejected. Class still existed in the social landscape of Luton as it did in every other part of the country.

An American sociologist, Ralph Turner, researching into the relationship between education and class (*Education, Economy and Society*) drew up a neat model to explain social mobility in Britain. He argued that there were 2 types of mobility:

Sponsored mobility. The classic British system of achieving high status on the basis of family background, the 'right' kind of education, and on the

recommendation of top people who are prepared to *sponsor* the upward mobility of their protégé whom they expect to have similar values as themselves. Sponsored mobility is a form of ascribed status. A child, usually a boy, is filtered through the best schools and colleges that privilege can buy to become, in his turn, a member of the 'élite' and a sponsor himself.

Contest mobility. An American-type system of open competition. A fairer and freer system of allowing all children from an early age to compete or to *contest* on equal terms to reach the higher social and economic levels. Many more children from all classes are fed through the university system to fight it out for a share of the limited number of top positions society can offer.

Turner's analysis is interesting because he saw the possibility of increasing social mobility – and therefore a way of undermining class advantage – through the education system. However in the chapter on education in this book you will see that class privilege and family background are themselves important in determining educational success. In British terms, Turner might be putting the cart before the horse!

Another important piece of research was published in 1980 called the *Oxford Mobility Study*. This study was based on a sample of 10 000 men. For research purposes the authors identified 7 classes in society and simplified these into 3 main groupings:

The Service Class. People with well paid jobs and career prospects: managers, teachers, doctors and solicitors
The Intermediate Class. People with routine non-manual jobs: clerks, sales personnel, typists and laboratory workers

The Working Class. Skilled, semi-skilled and unskilled manual workers: printers, lorry drivers and labourers

The aim of the study was to see how open the British class system had become and in particular how easy it was to move from the working class into the service class. The researchers found that while the chance of this type of social movement taking place had increased by about 7% overall, the research indicated that whatever the chances a working class boy had of getting a job in the service class, the intermediate class boy had 4 times the chance. So while there has been some change in social mobility patterns, the change has not necessarily benefited the working classes.

However there is an important point to be made when discussing the question of social mobility. As industrial societies develop, it will be necessary to recruit more highly skilled workers. Although this will create changes in the occupational structure of society, this does not mean that the actual class structure will be affected. The class structure is like league football: although individual teams get promoted and demoted, the major league divisions remain unchanged.

EXERCISE

1 Do some research on your own family background and complete as much as you can of the family tree. Explain if there have been any great changes in the class of occupation between the generations. If there had been changes, this is known as **inter-generational mobility** (mobility *between* generations). Can you go back any further?

2 Now choose one of your relatives who started off his or her working life in a working class job and climbed the occupational ladder into a middle

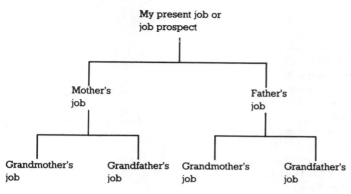

```
              My present job or
              job prospect
                    │
        ┌───────────┴───────────┐
     Mother's                Father's
       job                     job
        │                       │
   ┌────┴────┐             ┌─────┴─────┐
Grandmother's Grandfather's Grandmother's Grandfather's
   job         job           job           job
```

Family job tree

class occupation. Explain in detail how this new status was achieved. When an individual is socially mobile it is known as **intra-generational mobility** (mobility *within* one generation).

Social class is still with us. The idea that we live in a society that has glaring social and economic inequalities is usually dismissed or ignored by those who live in the more prosperous areas of our society and who enjoy the largest share of the nation's wealth. Whatever we think of the work of Marx or Weber or the embourgeoisement thesis, we have to accept, realistically, that while the social class system is not as rigid as apartheid or caste, it nevertheless results in misery and hardship for some sections of the population.

QUESTIONS

1 Social class is the description applied to social stratification in modern industrial society. It differs from other forms of stratification in that it does not have any official basis, nor is it legally enforced. In fact, definitions of social class in industrial society still vary: the Registrar-General's scale which is frequently used in government statistics is a socio-economic scale based on occupation, whilst Marx's view of social class is very different.

Other forms of stratification, such as caste systems, and the feudal systems, tend to be *closed* in that people cannot easily move from one stratum to another. In theory at least, Britain's social class system is 'open' and vertical social mobility is possible.

Some sociologists have suggested that there is extensive mobility between social classes. It has also been suggested that social classes are gradually disappearing from the structure of our society. Others have argued that the differences between the social classes are more difficult to identify.

   a Give one example from the extract of a closed system of stratification. (1 mark)
   b What is the difference mentioned in the extract between '*open*' and '*closed*' societies (systems of stratification)? (2 marks)
   c What is meant by embourgeoisement? (3 marks)
   d Briefly describe Marx's view of social classes in industrial societies. (5 marks)
   e What evidence might sociologists offer for the persistence of social class stratification in modern Britain? (9 marks)

Source: AEB O Level, 1982

2 What is the relationship between class and culture? (20 marks)
3 *a* Name 2 forms of social mobility. (2 marks)
   b Describe the most common way by which a person can become socially mobile in Britain. (3 marks)
   c Discuss the proposition that upward social mobility in modern Britain is much more common now than it was 20 years ago. (15 marks)

Cadogan Square four times which is about a mile. It's kinda silly to bathe before you exercise, isn't it? I do shower but I prefer a bath. Here in England I use an avocado soap, what's it called Sarah? ('Savon à l'huile d'Avocadat by Crabtree & Evelyn in Kensington'). I shave with an electric razor, and I use a variety of after-shave scents, Monsieur Givenchy, Revlon's 'Shaz'.

I read the papers just before I get dressed – *The Mail, The Telegraph, The Herald Tribune* and also *The Express* and *The Times.* Very often I'll have people come over here for breakfast meetings around 8.00am. Today, someone came at 7.00. No! I don't eat breakfast, we only had dinner at four o'clock this morning. I'll just have some coffee and orange juice and sometimes grapefruit juice. My barber? He is a she, Lee has The Barbershop in Clarges Street.

There's Missy at the Bay Hill in Orlando, Florida, but mostly it's Lee here in London. Manicure? No! No! I bite them! (Sarah shrieks with horror 'That's letting the side down, how can you bite your nails after all the wonderful PR I've got you!' she exclaims. 'My area is Europe across to Japan. I don't travel with Mark, he has another English lady, Judy Stott, who looks after him in the States.')

'I'm sorry you can't photograph my wardrobe the bedroom is in chaos. I'm leaving in half an hour to catch the flight to Hamburg. Yes! I'm here for Wimbledon.

WARDROBE

Hats and Gloves. No! Never wear hats. I have golf hats but I never wear them. Yeah! I know it's bad for a fair skin.

Overcoats. I have seven or eight raincoats, I think you call it a 'mac', that one over there it's very light – a Harrod's special made in Western Germany. I leave a lot of clothes around at different places all over the world. I have six homes where I spend a lot of time at, and the other

two, I own but don't go to too much. I have this London mews house, my home in Cleveland, Ohio; an apartment in New York; a condominium called 'Kapalua' on the island of Maui, in Hawaii; and another condominium in Palm Springs, California. Arnold Palmer and I have a country golf club in Orlando, Florida called 'Bay Hill'. That makes six, the two I don't go to much, is one in the Fijian islands in the Pacific and 'La Manga' in Spain, a development which didn't do as well as everyone thought it would, but it's being revitalised now by somebody else.

Suits. I have a lot of suits which are made for me all over the world; various clothing companies that we do business with, like Nino Cerrutti, Lanvin in New York.

Shirts. I have many many shirts. I buy them all over the place and I keep them forever. I don't get my shirts made.

Ties. I buy my ties from Cerrutti or they're given to me as presents. Some of our clients are top designers. I have a lot of ties. I like conservative ties, like the striped one I'm wearing.

Shoes. I have cupboards everywhere full of shoes. I prefer browns and blacks. I get them from Johnston & Murphy, a shoe manufacturer in Tennessee. I prefer loafers to lace-ups. I wear long woollen Byford socks. No! they're not clients. My sports shoes for jogging and tennis are mostly Wimbledons. I wear a belt sometimes, I have maybe twenty.

Jewellery. I wear a gold Rolex watch, yes! they're clients, and a gold bracelet, a Cartier, I bought in 1973. I saw someone with one on and I liked it. In my pocket I carry a gold Cross pen, 3 × 5 card-hold, a calendar (diary), money clip, keys and credit cards. I do wear reading glasses but I've no idea what make they are.

Source: Avantgarde, November 1984

QUESTIONS

1 At what social stratum of society is the *AVANTGARDE* magazine largely aimed?

2 'I believe in success. Successful individuals in business are the risk-takers who create employment for the rest of us. They work harder than everyone else and they deserve greater rewards when they succeed.'

   a What evidence is there in the article to support this point of view?

   b Using examples from the article, briefly explain Marx's theory of class conflict.

3 Discuss the relationship between class and status. Illustrate your answer by referring to the theories of Max Weber and to the more important status symbols contained in the article.

4 In contrast with children born into *Class 5* families, what life-chances and social experiences can the gentleman in the article provide for his children?

Points for discussion

- In Britain, people are poor because they choose to be.
- In our society everyone has the chance to become a *Class 1* person.
- Social class should be abolished in Britain and complete Marxism introduced.

Class & leisure

British TV (4 channels/ evenings only shown)

CENTRAL
5.45 News.
6.00 Crossroads.

6.25 Central News.
7.00 Name That Tune hosted by Lionel Blair.
7.30 Coronation Street.
8.00 This is Your Life.
8.30 Mike Yarwood in Persons.
9.00 Travelling Man.
10.00 Party Political Broadcast the Conservative Party.
10.05 News At Ten followed by Central News.
10.35 Midweek Sport Special.
12.05 Closedown.

BBC 2
5.35 Fast Forward.
6.00 The High Chaparral.
6.50 The Phil Silvers Show.
7.15 Cameo.
7.25 Ebony with Juliet Alexander and Vincent Herbert.
7.55 My Music with question master Steve Race.
8.20 Harry Ferguson: Inventor.
9.00 Oxbridge Blues.
10.05 Out Of Court.
10.35 Party Political Broadcast. Conservative Party.
10.40 Newsnight.
11.25 Top Gear Rally Report.
11.35 Buongiorno Italia!
12.05 Closedown.

CHANNEL 4
6.00 Silents, Please.
6.30 The Living Body.
7.00 Channel 4 News with Peter Sissons.
7.50 Comment. Frank Dobson, Labour MP for Holborn and St Pancras.
8.00 Scotland's Story. David Hayman narrates this penultimate episode of the story of Scotland.
8.30 Diverse Reports. Undermining the Industry? Steve Hewlett and Barbara Evans reveal the vital role that new technology plays in the Coal Board's plans.
9.00 The People Show In 'Starwashed'.

10.05 Black Hollywood. This documentary tells of a struggle against persistent stereotyping.
11.30 Close.

BBC 1
6.00 News.
6.30 Midlands Today.
6.55 I've Got A Secret.
7.30 Sharon and Elsie.
8.00 Dallas.
8.45 Points Of View with Barry Took.
9.00 Party Political Broadcast by the Conservative Party.
9.05 News, Weather.
9.30 In At The Deep End. 'Auctioneer'. Chris Serle can't afford any mistakes when he tries his hand at Sotheby's as an auctioneer.
10.20 Sportsnight.
12.10 News, Weather.
12.15 Closedown.

From the 4 TV channels, select 5 programmes that you believe might be of interest to mainly *Class 1* and *Class 2* (A + B) viewers. Select a further five programmes that *Class 4* and *Class 5* (D + E) viewers might watch. Set them out under these headings:

Programme title   TV channel
Social class of viewer

Complete a similar exercise on the 3 radio stations and compare and discuss your results with others in the group. What general conclusions can you draw about class, TV viewing and radio listening?

As a social observer, on what commercial TV programmes would you recommend these product advertisements should appear to reach the appropriate audience?

The *Sun* newspaper   *The Times* newspaper   A strong lager   A cold water soap powder   An industrial robot

Radio

RADIO 2
4.0 David Hamilton. 6.0 John Dunn. 8.0 European Soccer Special. 9.30 Listen To The Band. 10.0 The Golden Years. 10.30 Hubert Gregg. 11.0 Brian Matthew. 1.0 Bill Rennells. 3.0 Broadway Babes. 3.30–4.0. Vernon and Maryetta Midgley.

RADIO 3
5.0 Mainly For Pleasure. 6.30 Debut. 7.0 Scottish Season: Macbeth. 9.10 BBC Singers. 9.35 Six Continents. 10.0 Ferdinand Ries. 10.45 Ladies Lost And Found. 11.0 Salomon String Quartet. 11.57–12.0 News.

RADIO 4
5.0 PM. 6.0 The Six O'Clock News. 6.30 Top Of The Form. 7.0 News. 7.5 The Archers. 7.20 Checkpoint. 7.45 The Reith Lectures 1984. 8.15 In Business. 8.45 Analysis. 9.30 A Talent To Amuse. 9.45 Kaleidoscope. 10.15 A Book At Bedtime. 10.30 The World Tonight. 11.15 The Financial World Tonight. 11.30 Today In Parliament. 12.0–12.15 News. 12.33 Shipping Forecast.

Explain, sociologically, the reasons for your recommendations.

QUESTIONS

1 a What is the meaning of the term **social stratification**?
  b What form does social stratification take in British society?
2 Using illustrations from your analysis of British TV and radio programming, what evidence is there to suggest that the organisation of mass media entertainment is strongly influenced by factors of social class?
3 'There is no relationship between class and participatory sport in British society'. As a sociologist, what do you think of this statement? Explain your point of view.

South African TV (2 channels/available evenings only)

TV1
TONIGHT

5.53 CROSS QUESTIONS

6.19 THE WONDERFUL WORLD OF DISNEY. Smoke. The second and final episode of this story of a teenager's reluctance to accept his mother's new husband, following the tragic death of his father. starring Ron Howard and Earl Holliman.

7.08 KRUIS OF MUNT. Bedrog Loop sy Meester. Pete Ryan is suspected of having stolen $1 million. He asks Pete to help him find the real thief and clear his name.

8.00 NEWS

8.28 WEATHER REPORT

8.41 THE A-TEAM. Tonight's episode of The A-Team is titled Bloody Day At Bad Rock.

9.30 SWEET CHARITY. A New York dance-hall hostess dreams of true love, but always falls for the wrong man. A colourful musical based on a play by Neil Simon, directed by Bob Fosse. Starring Shirley Maclaine, John McMartin, Ricardo Montalban, Sammy Davis Jun, Chita Rivera, Paula Kelly and Stubby Kaye.

11.45 TEACHERS ONLY. Cooper's Arrangement. Diana's attempts to revive the principal's social life after three years of widowerhood, uncover the affair he has been having with his secretary, Shari.

11.10 NEWS

12.25 EPILOGUE. The Rev Tony Louch.

TV2
TONIGHT

6.00 OPENING

6.05 ENDULO IZILWANE ZISAKHULUMA

6.32 UMUNTU AKALAHLWA. Path Of A Man. Bomba's group have a water shortage and it seems there will not be tranquility among the terrorists for long.

7.00 NEWS

7.13 NDIKHU MBUZE. The 10th show in this big prize series.

7.41 OPERATION KHANYISA. A very unfavourable report on Mandla Sikhakhane's secret trips appears in the newspaper. The code 6 agents are locked up by the Cubans while Koos is freed. At night Koos and Bani try to release the locked-up code 6 men.

8.09 PROMOS

8.14 SATURDAY SPECTACULAR

9.00 NEWS

9.28 WEATHER REPORT

9.31 IPHUNGA ELIMNANDI

QUESTIONS

1 What evidence is there to suggest that South African TV programming reflects the apartheid system?

2 *a* Why is apartheid regarded as a closed system of social stratification?

   b What is meant by the term **ascribed status**?

3 Describe briefly one other form of closed social system.

Important points

- Social stratification describes the process of ranking the members of a society into social groups on the basis of shared patterns of behaviour.
- Virtually all societies experience social stratification of one form or another.
- Apartheid, caste and feudal societies are examples of closed social systems. In closed systems, a person is born into an ascribed social position from which it is difficult to leave.
- The class system in Western societies is an example of an open social system. In an open system it is possible, though difficult, to move from one class to another to obtain achieved status.
- The most common and useful form of social class grouping is based on the Registrar General's 5 occupational classes.
- Social class will determine a person's social behaviour and cultural activities.
- A person's awareness of his or her own class is called class consciousness.
- Karl Marx believed that there are two classes in industrial societies, the bourgeoisie and the proletariat. These two classes are in perpetual conflict.
- Max Weber regarded status and power as important factors in class difference.
- The movement of individuals from one class to another is called social mobility. Sponsored mobility and contest mobility describe two ways of being socially mobile.
- Recent studies suggest that social mobility might not benefit the working classes as much as the middle classes.

3 The Family

When you have worked through this chapter you should have a clearer understanding of

Kinship · **Family structures** · **The family in other cultures** · **Functions of the family** · **The family as a unit of production** · **Conjugal roles** · **Stages of family life** · **The nuclear family** · **Role conflict** · **Marital instability**

What is a family?

Throughout history people have lived in communities and these communities have been based on some form of family structure. We say *some form* of family structure for although sociologists agree that the family unit is common to all societies, there is great difficulty in arriving at a precise definition of the family which would meet with every sociologist's approval.

EXERCISE

Which of the following do *you* think is a family? Make a list of your selection in your notebook:

- An unmarried man and woman living together as man and wife
- A divorced woman living at home with her 2 children
- A single woman bringing up her 2 children
- A married couple with one child
- Two divorced men, one with a child from a broken marriage, sharing a flat
- A widow living with her divorced son-in-law
- A widowed grandmother living with an unmarried mother and her son
- Three students sharing a house

- An old woman living alone with her pet poodle
- An unmarried man and woman living together with the man's son from a previous marriage
- A divorced woman sharing a flat with her elderly mother
- A married couple living with an adopted child

You can see now why it is so difficult to define a family. If you were to describe your own family circumstances, for example, what would you say?

You would probably describe the people living in your own family house, such as your parents or guardians and your brothers and sisters. You could explain how you get on together and how you carry out your respective roles in the household affairs. You might mention the times when all the members of your family and all your relatives get together at weddings, Christmas parties and christenings.

Nevertheless in our society it is difficult to arrive at a description of a family which fits in with everyone's circumstances. We know that the popular view of the family is of a mother, father and children. However there are one-parent families and childless couples and unmarried couples with children, all of whom think of themselves as members of a family. No matter how we define the family we know that it is a very important institution within our society.

Before we explore aspects of the family in detail, let us define what we mean, sociologically, by the family. We have already suggested that sociologists often disagree over the meaning of words, but we can take as a working definition Burgess and Locke's definition in their book *The Family*:

The family is a group of persons united by ties of marriage, blood or adoption, constituting a single household, interacting and intercommunicating with each other in their respective social role of husband and wife, mother and father, brother and sister, creating a common culture.

Patterns of kinship

An important term sociologists use when discussing the family is **kinship**. We can define kinship as the social relationships which exist between the members of a family. Kinship may describe the immediate relationship we have with our parents, brothers and sisters or it can refer to a wider kinship network which would draw in our aunts, uncles, cousins and nieces.

Think of the cards we might send at Christmas. At the top of the list we have the names of our 'close kin', and then a longer list to include the names of our wider kinship network. We choose to send cards to our relatives because we want them to know that we are keeping in touch and thinking of them during the festive season. We also like to receive cards from them. Occasionally we send cards to the members of our wider kinship group simply because they have sent cards to us – a sort of social blackmail – and this has the effect of bonding the kinship network.

In order to understand complicated kinship networks, sociologists have introduced some special terms:

The nuclear family. This is usually the smallest and most common family unit found in Britain and consists of 2 generations, a mother and father (first generation) and their children (second generation). However, a nuclear family is not necessarily always a small family. A family of 14 – mother, father and their 12 children – is still a nuclear family.

This type of family lives separately from its relatives, sometimes in a different part of the country, and is usually economically independent and self-supporting.

The extended family. This type of family is either a horizontal or a vertical extension of the nuclear family. Whereas the nuclear family contains two generations (parents and children), the vertically extended family contains three or occasionally even four generations who share the same household. The typical extended family in Britain consists of grandparents, parents and their children.

A household may consist of a nuclear family, plus aunts, uncles and cousins. This type of family structure, consisting of 2 generations, is a **horizontally extended family**.

A family unit may at the same time be horizontally and vertically extended, but the main point to note about the extended family is that it contains family members other than those who make up the nuclear family, all of whom rely on each other for economic and social support.

The modified extended family. This is a term used to describe the typical family in modern industrial society. It is a structure where separate nuclear families, related to each other, live separately and remain independent of each other, but rely upon each other for important services such as childminding or home repairs. In the event of a crisis, these separated families will turn to each other for assistance.

EXERCISE

Using appropriate symbols and names, construct a family tree of your own family, or any family whom you choose to study. Identify what type of family structure it is.

Although nuclear and extended families or their variants are by far the most common family structures to be found in human society, there are others:

A matrifocal family is one in which the family unit consists of a woman and her dependent

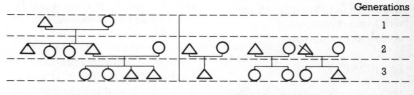

Generations
1
2
3

Vertically extended   Horizontally extended

△ = Deceased

The extended family

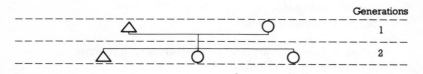

Generations
1
2

△ = Male

○ = Female

The nuclear family

children, sometimes with the addition of the woman's mother. This type of family structure is common among black families in the USA and the West Indies and to a limited extent in urban areas in Britain.

Family structures are also affected by different forms of marriage:

Monogamy allows one wife to one husband and is the only permissible form of marriage in

Britain and in countries where Christianity is the dominant religion.

Polygamy allows more than one marriage partner at a time. The two forms of polygamy are called polygyny and polyandry.

Polygyny which allows a man to have more than one wife at the same time is common in some parts of the world. It was practised by Mormons in Utah in the USA during the last century, and by many present-day Muslims.

Polyandry which allows a woman to have more than one husband at a time, is less common than polygyny. It has been found to exist in the Marquesas islands in the Pacific and in parts of Tibet.

Group marriage is an extremely rare form of marriage where all the individuals regard all others of the opposite sex within the group as marriage partners.

EXERCISE

Construct a kinship chart similar to those drawn up for nuclear and extended families to illustrate a matrifocal and a polygamous family structure.

Why is the family important for the individual?

Our earliest experiences of the world take place within the family and we know that these family experiences have a great influence on our lives. In this example a young person describes the influence his family had over him regarding politics:

All my family voted Labour in the elections. In fact everybody in the mining village voted for the Socialists except me. I voted for the Conservatives but I hadn't the nerve to tell anyone. Even now, 5 years later and living in London, I still feel as though my family are looking over my shoulder when I put my cross against the Tory candidate.

Although we can understand how the family might influence us in matters of politics we should be aware that our experiences within the family can affect us in other ways as well. This article was published in a newspaper some years back:

House of shame

A local doctor was amazed when he discovered a 9-year-old boy imprisoned in a cellar. Dr John Tolley of Hattington in Northumberland said that the child had been kept locked up and hidden in conditions of unbelievable squalor since birth.

The police, interviewing the child's unmarried mother at a large terraced house on the outskirts of town, unearthed a 9-year-old mystery. Apparently the child had been secreted and reared in the cellar since birth by the mother's elderly parents who were unable to face the local community with the scandal of an illegitimate birth. Since the death of both parents, the mother could no longer cope and called in Dr Tolley to attend to her sick child.

'I couldn't believe what I found,' the doctor told us. 'The boy had been locked in a damp and poorly lit cellar no bigger than a garden shed. He was unable to speak properly, he was grossly underweight, filthy, his skin was covered in sores, and he walked with a semi-erect gait because of the low ceiling. He was animal-like in his behaviour. He had never been outside in the fresh air.'

Dr Tolley, who takes a special interest in community health care, explained that the child's medical problems were not nearly as serious as the social and psychological consequences of such deprivation. 'It is unlikely that this child will ever catch up on what he's missed socially. We can't just turn on a tap and replace all those childhood experiences. It is most unlikely that the boy will recover completely.'

The mother, who has not been named, is presently helping the police with their enquiries. Her child is receiving medical attention in hospital.

As the article suggests, the boy could hardly speak, he had difficulty in walking, and he certainly would have had problems dealing with people in the community. He would know little of the world outside his cellar room. In fact we can say that his cellar room *was* his world. What he would have been deprived of is what sociologists call **primary socialisation**. This means that the child would not have learned how to communicate, mainly through language, with others. He would not know how to interact with people, and he would be ignorant of the world as we understand it. He would be a complete stranger in the social world.

EXERCISE

Make a copy of the table on page 40 in your notebook and draw up a list of 10 social experiences of which the child in the article has been deprived, and indicate with a tick what in your opinion is their degree of importance for normal childhood development. The first 2 have partly been done for you.

We can see that much of our behaviour, our ideas, our ways of coping with the world, are shaped by our earliest experiences within the family setting. Within this setting a child can learn about the cultural attitudes and values of our society and get some ideas about how to behave within a gender role in order to feel confident about his or her identity. Think about yourself for

Social experiences	Degree of importance			
	1	2	3	4
1 Playing with other children				
2 Shopping with mum				
3				
4				
5				
6				
7				
8				
9				
10				

Compare and discuss your results.

a moment. You know, more or less, exactly who you are, what you are doing, and where you fit in. If you are a young person, the chances are that sooner or later you will return today to the protection of some form of family unit.

This is why the family is important. It provides a limited but secure social and economic environment in which children can mature successfully in preparation for the adult world with its more complicated and demanding social structures. The family setting may also provide a structure in which parents themselves gain a sense of security and purpose by bringing up children. The notion that children serve a purpose for adults as well as vice versa is known as **legitimate regression**.

The idea that family life offers us this kind of stable and supportive structure in which to develop has been argued by Talcott Parsons and R. Bales in their book *Family, Socialisation and Interaction Process*. This letter, published in the agony columns of a woman's magazine, goes some way to support this view:

How could that reader who calls herself 'Disenchanted' possibly think so badly of family life? I owe everything to my family. Despite lack of money and border-line poverty they managed to bring up us 5 children in

a happy and creative atmosphere and encouraged all of us to go to university.

Maureen Warilow

Not everyone would agree with this optimistic view of family life. R. D. Laing in *Divided Self* and David Cooper in *Death of the Family* argue that the family is just as likely to be a source of conflict and oppression and the cause of much unhappiness. Back to the agony column:

Family life is best? – don't make me sick! I spent the first 15 years of life being bullied by a selfish drunken father. He forced me and my mum to obey his every will and command. He was so friendly with people outside the family home, but inside he became a petty tyrant. I spent most of my childhood in the kitchen with my mum while he got drunk watching the telly. My mother finished up in the looney bin and I ran away from home.

Disenchanted

EXERCISE

Discuss these two extreme views of family life. In what way do you agree and disagree with them? Suggest possible alternative ways of organising society to the traditional nuclear and extended family structures.

Why is the family important for society?

The family performs certain

functions for other institutions as well as for the individuals that make up society. The sociological use of the term **function** differs from its everyday use. When sociologists focus their attention on the functions of an institution such as the family or the school they examine the contributions that are made by these institutions and also the links they have with other parts of society.

What are these functions that the family performs for society?

First, there is the **reproductive function**. The family provides society with new members and so enables society to continue to exist. For many, one of the main reasons for getting married is to start a family. Although the number of one-parent families is increasing, there are still strong social pressures to keep childbirth within a family. We cannot ignore the problems a single parent may face in bringing up children alone.

This leads to the second function that the family carries out – the **maintenance function**. Parents are expected to care and provide for their children and if they don't welfare agencies intervene to make sure that someone else does. The rise in the school leaving age (or job starting age) has meant that children are economically dependent on their parents for much longer than they used to be.

So not only does the family provide society with new members, it also protects its members, socialises them (in conjunction with the education system) and provides for them (with the assistance of welfare schemes such as the Child Benefit Allowance). It also provides a source of leisure and recreation, especially for important occasions like Christmas, birthdays and marriages.

The family also functions as an agent of social control by supporting and reinforcing society's standards. The role of parents in teaching their children how to become decent, law-abiding citizens is often emphasised by teachers, politicians and leading figures in the Church. There is also a very real way in which children themselves act as a social control over their own parents. Some parents may feel that by not going on strike or by delaying or abandoning divorce proceedings, for example, they are reducing the risks of disrupting family life (therefore causing fewer social problems).

As we shall see, the family in pre-industrial Britain was a unit of production and performed an essential economic function for society. Ronald Fletcher argues in his study *The Family and Marriage in Britain* that although this function has been lost with the process of industrialisation, the family in modern times has an **economic function** as a unit of consumption. Think of the many things that you have in your home – the carpets, furniture, television and washing machine. How many of these commodities belong to you personally and how many were bought for family use? Industry needs a market for its goods and the family provides this market. There are many industries whose products are aimed at the family rather than at individuals.

Industry also needs a workforce that is motivated to work. According to Fletcher, the family provides this motivation through its demands for consumer goods that wages will buy. How many of these needs for consumer goods are real and how many are created by advertising techniques has been questioned by other sociologists.

Other institutions can and do

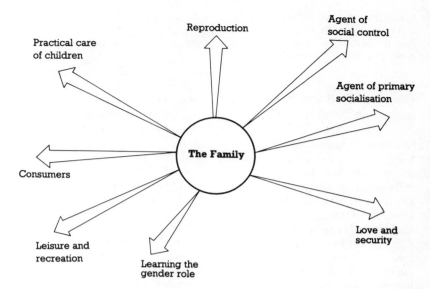

The functions of the family

perform many of the functions that have been carried out by the family which has led sociologists to question the necessity of the family in modern society. As Margaret Mead explained in her study *Male and Female*:

Almost every human need that has historically been met in the home can now be met outside it: restaurants serve food; comics, movies and radio provide amusement, news and gossip; there are laundries and dry-cleaners and places that mend one's socks and store one's winter coat, wash one's hair and shine one's shoes. For sex satisfaction it is no longer necessary to choose between marriage and prostitution; for most of those without religious scruples sex is available on a friendly and amateur basis and without responsibility. When one is sick, one goes to a hospital, and when one dies, one can be buried quite professionally by an undertaking establishment. The old needs of food, shelter, sex and recreation are all efficiently met outside the home – and yet more people are married today than ever before in the country's recorded history.

The suggestion here is that the family may not be all that it is cracked up to be. As we have seen,

the social value of family life as a happy, secure and mutually rewarding experience is questioned by many sociologists, some of whom point to rising divorce rates as an indicator of increasing family strife. They make the point that we are all so used to accepting family life as 'normal' and 'proper' that we are prejudiced against the possibility that there may be more satisfactory ways of organising society to better suit the individual. However, we can sum up with a diagram the important functions of the family in society. (See above.)

EXERCISE

You are a member of a research team. After discussion, choose one of the topics within the wheel and find out

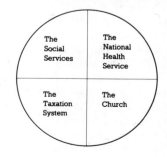

Research wheel

as much as you can about how the institution attempts to preserve and help the family. Each team is to produce a full set of notes.

Comparative and historical aspects of family life

It is difficult to think about the family in an objective way because our attitudes have been influenced by our own family experiences. However, the structure of the family does change over time and it can vary from society to society. This is how one woman recalls her experiences of family life in the west of Ireland in the early 1900s:

Interviewer: How many people lived in your house?
Oona: Thirteen of us lived in the house and the house wasn't all that big. My father, who was a fisherman, my mother and 8 brothers and 2 sisters.
Interviewer: You said your father was a fisherman. Did you help him?
Oona: I never helped him on the boat but I did learn how to mend the nets. All the girls did, and we would go to the nearby town on a Friday and sell fish. My brothers all worked with my father, although there really wasn't that much work for them all, and three of them went off to America and two went to England looking for work.
Interviewer: What about schooling?
Oona: We didn't bother much with that. All you needed to learn would be taught in the family. The girls learned all about cooking and looking after the house and the men, and the men did all the hard work on the boat and out at sea. I can read and write, but not very well. There was no need for it.
Interviewer: Didn't you ever want

to read a book in your free time?
Oona: Free time?
Interviewer: When you weren't working.
Oona: There wasn't much time like that! People would gather round sometimes and tell stories and sing songs. Some of the men would drink poitin . . .
Interviewer: What's poitin?
Oona: You would know it as whiskey. The men would make it, although you had to watch out because it was illegal. But no-one really bothered about it. There was no real harm in it. You made all your own amusements. You see it's hard to imagine what life was like in a house where you had no running water, no lighting or any of the modern conveniences. There was nothing like supermarkets or anything like that. I mean, I used to have to walk a quarter mile to the nearest tap to draw water . . .

From this conversation we can see that family life in the west of Ireland was different from family life today. Think about your own family experiences. Although you spend some time at work or school, think of the non-work time you have and how you spend it.

Oona's family was large, 13 in all, living under one roof in a rural community. Families in modern urban industrial societies are much smaller and live in a less stable, more mobile society. The average British family in the 1980s can expect to move house about once in every 7 years. Again, compare your family life with the extended family life of an African tribe described by Isaac Schapera in *Married Life in an African Tribe*.

Schapera found that the families of the Kgatla tribe produced the bulk of their domestic needs. The family worked at cultivating corn and

other crops, breeding livestock, hunting animals and collecting edible plants. In all these activities everyone except the infants took part, with the men, women and children having specified jobs according to their ages. If a particular job was too big for one family to handle, they asked for help from other families and paid for this work by giving meat to the helpers. Because of the difficulties in getting foodstuffs and cultivating the land, the different families were all willing to help one another in times of crisis. In other words, the families formed a close community, with each family being able to depend on others for help when the need arose.

Even though the family is the basic social unit in society, this does not of course mean that the family itself is not altered by a changing society. We return to the interview with Oona to see what is meant by this:

Interviewer: When did life change for you?
Oona: It changed for all of us when the big boats started fishing in the waters where our families had fished all their lives. There were smaller catches and the canning companies bought off the big trawler owners. Many people had to move away and find work in the towns or move to England or America. The older people stayed but the younger ones moved on. I went to Dublin and worked in domestic service. I haven't seen one of my sisters for 10 years.

We can see that the family can change as society itself changes and this can lead us to consider what sociologists see as an important influence on the structure of the family and a person's experiences within the family. This important influence is known as **industrialisation**.

EXERCISE

Working as a member of an oral research team, you are to conduct a survey to compare certain aspects of family life before the Second World War with the present day. You will need to interview an elderly person, possibly a grandparent.

In preparation for your oral report to the group, you are to take notes to explain the differences and similarities you find in relation to:

- housework
- at-home leisure activities
- holidays.

The family and industrialisation

Industrialisation has had a major influence on all aspects of social life. Before we examine how the family was influenced by industrialisation let us first consider what we mean by industrialisation. The word describes a series of technological, economic, social and cultural changes that have taken place over the last 200 years which have transformed Britain from an agrarian to a mainly industrial society.

Before industrialisation, people made their living from the land. Our society was mainly a rural society. The process of industrialisation came about as the production of goods moved away from the rural areas into the factories which were located in the expanding towns. As jobs became scarce in the countryside families moved to the towns in search of work, and most found living accommodation close to the workplace. Initially these new townspeople were strangers to one another but as time passed communities became established, as this writer noted on a visit to

a northern town in the middle of the 19th century:

It would be impossible to describe these communities as pleasant. The first thing you notice as you approach the town is the awful stench and the black acrid smoke billowing from nearby factory chimneys. Then you notice the rows of drab, overcrowded houses and the dirty children and you begin to wonder how people manage to survive in these conditions. Yet though the squalor is self-evident you also get a sense that the hardships experienced by these people bring them closer together. They will help each other by sharing what meagre things they have. It is as if they have been united by sheer poverty and the brutality of their lives.

Although we may not agree with all the observations made by this writer, he does touch on something which has been identified by sociologists as the community spirit. This community spirit has persisted within working class communities to this day. One such community has been described in some detail by the sociologists Michael Young and Peter Willmott in *Family and Kinship in East London*, which is a classic study of working class life in the 1950s.

They found that families tended to work and live in the same area and relatives lived close by. The pub on the corner was a favourite meeting place for the men and people knew one another because the same families had lived in the same area for generations.

Willmott and Young also considered relationships inside the family home. They found that the work men and women did within the home was clearly defined. There were activities which were seen as men's work and activities which were seen as women's work. The sociological term they used to describe this aspect of social behaviour was **conjugal role**, and as the men and women tended to carry out

specific tasks on their own, they referred to this as **segregated conjugal roles** (sharing tasks in the home would be called **joint conjugal roles**). Of course, ideas about what is a man's job and what is a woman's job are still the subject of comment. On a local radio phone-in one gentleman said as recently as 1984:

It really makes me sick when I see blokes helping their wives with the shopping and going to the launderette. This is women's work. I don't expect my missus to service the car and I don't want her to expect me to do the ironing.

While no-one expressed themselves quite like this in the Willmott and Young study, this view highlights how some people see conjugal roles within the family. You may think that the type of life described by Willmott and Young is not typical of your experiences. This is because society is changing. In fact the same sociologists found that the patterns of family life altered when younger families were rehoused on new housing estates. Instead of living in a close-knit community, families found themselves amongst strangers, and much of their free time was spent within their new house or flat. Men and women changed their ways of behaving in the light of new circumstances. This phenomenon was not just found in East London. One married woman summed up her experiences after moving away from an area she had lived in for most of her life:

I lived in an area where everyone knew everyone else. We were always in and out of each other's houses. My mum would stay at home looking after us and my dad would be off down the pub with his mates. Dad and mum went out together a couple of times a year – on her birthday and Christmas Eve. My brothers all got fixed up with the firm my dad worked for. When I moved out of the area with my husband things were different. People on the new estate kept themselves to themselves. My husband spent more time at home helping out in the house. We did more things together like shopping and going out for a quiet meal. Even the way my husband deals with the kids is different – he takes more of an interest in them. My dad left everything to my mum. I suppose it's got something to do with the estate itself. We've all got really nice homes so we spend more time and money on them. No-one around here would dream of just popping in for a cup of sugar.

The changes the woman is talking about didn't simply occur because she moved house to live in another area. They were the result and influence of other changes taking place in society. The role and expectations of women, for example, were undergoing modifications and more women were going out to work. Attitudes towards marriage and childbearing were also changing and couples were having smaller families.

Nevertheless we should accept that there are still divisions of labour within the family home which are based on notions of what is men's work and what is women's work.

EXERCISE

Consider your own experiences within your family and then make a copy of this list of household tasks and indicate in the spaces who does what in your family circle. You might like to compare your results with a colleague's. What does it tell you about your family?

We have suggested that the family has undergone various changes as a result of industrialisation. The modern family, or the nuclear family, differs from the larger extended family group we would have found in the cities and towns of 70 years ago.

Conjugal roles within your family household

Household tasks	Segregated conjugal roles		Joint conjugal roles
	Mostly done by women	Mostly done by men	A shared task
Cleaning the house			
Ironing			
Painting and decorating			
Shopping for foodstuffs			
Washing-up dishes			
Cooking main meals			
Washing clothes			
Tending the garden			
Looking after the children			
Organising holidays			
Household repairs			
Sewing and repairing clothes			
Clearing drains and gutters			
Making beds			
Handling the family budget			
Changing fuses and wiring plugs			
Vacuuming			
Organising the TV viewing			

Is there a link between the kinds of work men and women do in the home and in paid employment?

A large Victorian middle class family. The photograph does not include servants, gardeners, cooks and kitchen maids who helped to 'run the house'. Nor does it show other members of the family, such as grandparents or aunts who may have shared the same household to create an extended family unit.

QUESTIONS

1 Identify for yourself these family members:
- the head of the household and his wife
- the family 'Nanny'
- the children's favourite uncle.

2 Describe what you are likely to see on a photograph of a present-day family.

We can now look at another study by the sociologists Willmott and Young *The Symmetrical Family* which attempts to trace the development of the family from pre-industrial England to the present day. This study will give empirical support to the points we have raised in this section and to the observations made in the extract. The study suggests that the family has moved through several important stages:

- **Stage 1.** This is the **pre-industrial family.** The family is placed in an agricultural community. It produces its own goods and provides most of what it needs. This is the family as a unit of production.
- **Stage 2.** This family structure begins with the **industrial revolution**. Members of the family become wage-earners and the family group is no longer a single unit of production. In response to the poverty experienced by the industrial working class, the kinship network extends to include people beyond the immediate family. This provides a safety net and security against the problems of poverty. (Notice the similarity with the Kgatla tribe living in a completely different culture.)

For Willmott and Young, women were very important in establishing these networks. This led to the establishment of strong female groups within working class communities, all helping out in time of crisis. This weakened the bond between husband and wife, and men, feeling excluded from these female groups, sought each other's company in the nearest pub. The **Stage 2** family survived well into the 20th

century as was documented in their earlier study *Family and Kinship in East London*.

- **Stage 3.** This family is home-based and free time is often spent within the home doing a variety of chores and watching television. This **nuclear family** is somewhat cut off from its extended kinship network. For Willmott and Young this family structure is typical in modern industrial societies, especially amongst the working class.

Although the nuclear family is the most common family structure in Britain, they point out that there are differences to be found between nuclear families, and these differences are related to social class. For example, sections of the middle class are more work-centred and less home-centred. They noted in their studies of 190 directors that the directors were less likely to involve their wives in leisure activities, for example, than working class families. The authors suggest that this is because work is interesting and demanding for the directors, whereas working class husbands get little satisfaction from the work they do and so derive satisfaction within the family home. The wives of the directors had a specific role which was to look after the children and the home, and they did this without much assistance from their husbands who might be playing golf with work colleagues.

Not all sociologists would agree with this analysis. One sociologist, Ann Oakley, sees the role of women within the family differently and we shall discuss her work in detail when we look at women in society. However there is no doubt that *The Symmetrical Family* provides us with a useful framework with which to analyse the changes which have taken place within the

family from pre-industrial times to the present day.

EXERCISE

What would you say are the main advantages for children in being brought up in a family with a wide kinship network?

The family today

Although extended family structures and large nuclear families still exist in Britain, it is the small closely-knit nuclear family that is by far the dominant family structure. Why should this be so? What have been the social and economic influences that have encouraged the growth of the nuclear family and the decline of the extended family? It is possible to identify 3 major trends.

1 Many sociologists, especially the American sociologist Talcott Parsons, see the emergence of the nuclear family as being the direct result of industrialisation. According to Parsons, a pre-industrial or rural extended family was basically a unit of production. It was a family capable of producing goods for its own needs. With industrialisation, society itself produced these goods in factories and so the economic reason for the extended family diminished. The present-day nuclear family is not basically a productive unit but a unit of consumption.

2 A second important reason for the decline of the extended family was the increasing tendency of the State to carry out some of the traditional functions of the self-supporting extended family. Because of the relative isolation of smaller urban families in an industrialising society, the State was obliged to get more involved in providing such things as educational facilities, health care,

and the financial and social care of the old and infirm. The caring functions of the extended family therefore decreased in importance. An example of a large family providing its own education is described on page 42.

As society began to provide better health care, transport facilities and educational opportunities, young people's expectations rose. Rather than being satisfied with the age-old custom of marrying and bringing up a family in the village of their birth, even perhaps in their parents' own house, young single people and newly married couples tried their luck elsewhere. Getting a job in a distant town had for the first time become a possibility. Improving education in particular had widened horizons and was an important factor in encouraging this new **social mobility**.

3 The third reason for the emergence of the nuclear family is associated with the more liberal attitudes found in today's society. A modern family is generally more open and democratic, with certain family members enjoying more freedom than before. In today's nuclear family the wife and older children will, in general, have more control over their lives than their counterparts in the extended family, which tended to be patriarchal (father dominated). In the early 1920s, for example, only 4% of wives did full-time paid work compared with about 20% today.

This greater equality for women, and probably for older children too, leads to greater freedom of action. Although not all sociologists agree, women now have more opportunities to pursue activities outside the family home. The availability of simple, safe and cheap contraception has also given women more control over the timing of their pregnancies and the final size of

their families. Children of smaller nuclear families also expect a greater degree of independence. In Victorian times it was common to find 3 or 4 children of large working class families sharing the same bed. Today's older children not only expect a bed but a bedroom of their own. All of this

suggests that during this century the small nuclear family has become associated with what we might loosely summarise as 'the good life'.

How the families compare

The increasing isolation of the

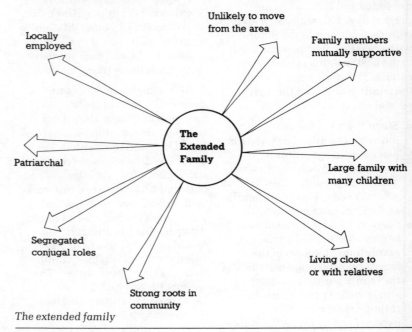

The extended family

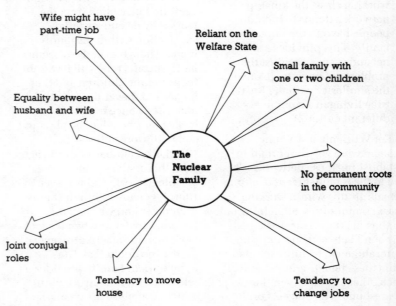

The nuclear family

small working class nuclear family has the effect of turning the family home into the major centre of social activity at the expense of external activities such as attending cinemas, pubs, theatres and visits to friends and relatives. In the nuclear home the individual family members are drawn closer together in their social relationships. When this internalising process occurs, the family is described as becoming **privatised**.

EXERCISE

Although sociologists believe that the modern family relies on the State to provide many of its essential needs, there are some who argue that this is not as simple as it appears. In your own words, explain how your own family made or makes a contribution to your personal development in respect of:

- recreation and entertainment
- educational achievement
- health care
- religious or political development.

Marital instability

This is the final part of a radio talk given by the Reverend Scott on *The Decay of Britain*:

Daily I lament the gradual erosion of the moral foundation on which our society is built, but now it seems that the bulldozers have come in. They come in the form of soaring illegitimacy rates, rising numbers of abortions and dramatic increases in the numbers of divorce petitions being filed. Does not the drastic rise in the divorce rates in this country suggest an impending demolition of that most sacred and valuable haven – the family? Are the marriage vows, undertaken in the House of God, no longer to be respected?

Whether or not morals are deteriorating is a question that

can best be dealt with by the Church. The Reverend Scott, however, does raise a few points which interest sociologists. For example, does the rise in divorce signify the breakdown of the family as we know it, and is society changing in a way that is challenging the need for marriage? Sociologists are also interested to know *why* divorce rates have risen and if there are marriages that are particularly **divorce prone**.

But first we shall examine Reverend Scott's statement and ask a question. Has there been a 'drastic rise in the divorce rates' as he has stated? What he means precisely by a 'drastic rise' we do not know, but here are some statistics taken from *Social Trends*. Look at them carefully and then answer the questions:

EXERCISE

	Great Britain		
	1961	1971	1981
Marriages (thousands)			
First marriage for both partners	331	357	255
First marriage for one partner only	%	%	%
Bachelor/divorced woman	11	21	31
Bachelor/widow	5	4	3
Spinster/divorced man	12	24	36
Spinster/widower	8	5	3
Second (or later) marriage for both partners			
Both divorced	5	17	44
Both widowed	10	10	7
Divorced man/widow	3	4	5
Divorced woman/widower	3	5	5
Total marriages (*thousands*)	387	447	388
Remarriages[1] as a percentage of all marriages	15	20	34

[1] Remarriage for one or both partners.
Source: Office of Population Censuses and Surveys.

1 How many first marriages for both partners were there in 1961 and 1981?
2 What percentage of all marriages were remarriages in 1971 and 1981?
3 What do these statistics tell us about remarriage for partners who are
- both divorced, and
- widows and widowers?

4 Do these statistics support the view that marriage is on the decline? Explain your answer.

In the 19th century, divorce was so expensive that only the wealthy could afford it. Charles Dickens' story *Hard Times* tells us about the problem of getting divorced before 1857 (Note: a suit is a legal document used in divorce):

Why, you'd have to go to the Doctors' Commons with a suit, and you'd have to go to a court of Common Law with a suit, and you'd have to go to the House of Lords with a suit, and it would cost you (if it was a case of plain sailing) I suppose from £1000 to £1500. Perhaps twice the money.

So what happened in 1857?
The **Matrimonial Causes Act** of **1857** enabled divorce to take place if the 'matrimonial offence' of adultery had taken place. Divorce was made cheap but not cheap enough for many. It was not until **Legal Aid** was made available in 1949 that divorce became possible for the majority of couples. In the 1950s the grounds for divorce were

extended to include cruelty and desertion.

You may have noticed that so far a matrimonial 'crime' had to be committed before a marriage could be legally ended. The **Divorce Reform Act** of **1971** changed this, making divorce possible simply because the marriage has irretrievably broken down.

These changes in the law have reflected changing attitudes to divorce. There is now no longer the stigma attached to divorce that there once was. Consider this statement made by Emily who is 92-years-old and who has witnessed a great many changes in her lifetime:

Divorce? It was unthinkable except in the direst of circumstances. It would have meant being rejected by my own family as well as having to put up with all the tongue-wagging in the neighbourhood. Anyway, how could I have managed on my own with five children to bring up?

Today, various welfare benefits enable single-parent families to exist without the financial support of a second parent. Also many women are now wage-earners which means that their economic dependence on their husbands has been reduced. When Emily was a young wife and mother this was not the case. It may be that marriage partners now feel less responsible for their children knowing that severe economic hardship will not follow their separation. There are also more childless couples and smaller families than there used to be, as the table below shows.

EXERCISE

In what way do these statistics give support to the argument that divorce is less disruptive to family life than it used to be?

The rise in divorce has prompted the fear (as expressed earlier by the Reverend Scott) that marriage and the family are redundant in modern society. For Ronald Fletcher marriage and the family are alive and well. The divorce rates indicate that marriage is now valued more highly than before. In *The Family and Marriage in Britain* he puts forward the argument that marriage partners now have higher hopes for their future than previously, and if their marriage does not live up to expectations they are likely to end it.

The high rate of remarriage (34% of all marriages in Britain in 1981 were remarriages) supports Fletcher's view that marriage is highly valued and that the search is for a more suitable partner rather than an alternative style of family life.

Other sociologists, however, take the view that marriage cannot fit in so comfortably in modern society. Nicky Hart, in her *When Marriage Ends* points to the role conflict experienced by married women in industrial societies. Many women are required to go out to work in order to provide the comforts and necessities for their families *and* are expected to be good wives and mothers. Marital strain is, she argues, a consequence of this conflict of roles between worker, wife and mother. It is significant that 70% of all divorce petitions are now brought by women but only 7% rely on maintenance from their ex-husbands as their main source of income.

Statistics do not tell us the whole story of marital breakdown. It is important to ask what the statistics on divorce do not tell us as well as what they do. They tell us about the numbers of marriages which have ended in divorce but they do not tell us about the **separations** that have taken place by partners who are still married. Nor do they tell us about so-called **empty-shell** marriages in which the unhappy partners still go on living together. These two groups – separations and empty-shell marriages – must be taken into account when examining the extent of marital breakdown. It is not possible to say whether marital instability is now more widespread than it used to be because we have no way of knowing how many unstable or unhappy marriages existed before legislation made divorce easier.

Even so, sociologists are able to identify factors which make a marriage more prone to divorce than others:

- **Age at marriage.** The younger the partners are when they get married the likelier they are to get divorced.
- **Number of children.** Divorce rates tend to decrease with larger families and remain high

The size of British households 1961–1982

	Percentages					
	1961	1971	1976	1980	1981	1982
Households by size						
1 person	12	18	21	22	22	23
2 people	30	32	32	32	32	33
3 people	23	19	17	17	17	17
4 people	19	17	17	18	18	17
5 people	9	8	8	7	7	7
6 or more people	7	6	5	4	4	3
Total households	100	100	100	100	100	100
Average household size (number of people)	3.09	2.89	2.76	2.68	2.71	2.64

for childless couples.

- **Social class background.** In Britain, divorce rates are high amongst those in the lower middle class and the lower working class. There is also an increased likelihood of divorce if the partners come from different social classes.
- **Religious differences.** Jews and Roman Catholics are less likely to get divorced than people of other religious or non-religious groups. 'Mixed marriages' are also prone to breakdown.
- **The marital status of parents.** There is an increased likelihood of divorce if one or both of the partners' parents have experienced divorce themselves.
- **Occupation.** It has been found that those in occupations that involve excessive absences from home or a high degree of work involvement are more divorce-prone than others.

As a sociologist, you will appreciate that we have been looking at trends in marriage and divorce. We know, of course, that marriages can and do succeed even when the odds are against their success.

EXERCISE

These wedding reports were taken from local newspapers. In each case, assess the divorce-proneness of the newly-weds, giving reasons for your assessment:

JONES–COOK
Linda Jones and Darren Cook were married at the Heybrook Registry Office on Thursday. The bride, aged 18, is a packer at the local biscuit company and the groom, also aged 18, is an unemployed pattern-maker. The couple will live with the bride's mother after a brief honeymoon in Blackpool.

BENNETT–COURTENAY-SMYTHE
The marriage took place between Anthea Bennett and James Courtenay-Smythe on Saturday at Saint Augustin's in Cirencester. The Reverend Masterson officiated. The bride, aged 25, is a bilingual secretary for a large finance company at which the groom, aged 28, is Chief Administration Manager. Following a honeymoon in Moscow, the couple will live in the newly-converted cottage on the Courtenay-Smythe estate.

MILOWSKA–DAWSON
Janina Milowska and Stephen Dawson were married at Saint Catherine's Roman Catholic church on Saturday. The bride, aged 21, is a receptionist in a dental surgery, and the groom, aged 20, is a trainee long-distance lorry driver. The couple will live in Thornby Road.

HONIG–COHEN
Ruth Honig and Benjamin Cohen were married at the May Lane Synagogue on Sunday. Ruth, a university lecturer and Benjamin, a company lawyer, both in their late twenties, will live in Pimlico after a honeymoon in Rome.

We have tried to explain how the family has changed within our society and why the family is such an important social unit in all societies. We all have had experiences of some sort of family life and although there can be problems – tension between individual members, wife battering, child abuse, divorce – the family unit has persisted reasonably well over time despite the many social pressures of a changing society.

QUESTIONS

1 a What is the difference between an extended and a nuclear family? (8 marks)
  b Explain why the extended family has declined in Britain. (12 marks)

Have a bet on the marriage stakes!

Bookie gambles on 7-year itch
A bookmaker wants couples to bet with him on how long their marriages will last.

Those who survive the seven-year itch will at least double their money – before betting tax.

Bookmaker Willy White, 34, is offering these odds:

Couples 30 or over: Even money on the marriage lasting another seven years without a break-up or either partner having an affair.

Aged 26 to 29: 6–4 against.

21–25: 2–1 against.

16–20: 5–2 against.

In his betting shop in Monks Road, Lincoln, a poster challenges couples:

'We don't believe your marriage will last another seven years without either horse or jockey having an affair or the complete breakdown of the marriage . . . prove us wrong.'

Willie, who is single, said: 'This is not a cynical bachelor's view of marriage.

Safe
Willie is promising the first 50 gambling couples to stay together for seven years candlelit suppers as a bonus.

The first five winners who gamble £1000 are promised a two-week second honeymoon.

'It's a very good investment,' said Willie.

He added: 'This scheme could save a few marriages.

'If couples get into a sticky patch they might say: 'Let's stick together, Darling, and we'll be on Easy Street.'

But the scheme was attacked by the Marriage Guidance Council.

'No sensible person should touch it,' a spokesman said.

'Regretfully, however many couples go into marriage wondering exactly how long it will last . . .'

Source: Daily Mirror
By FRANK PALMER

2 a Explain why the bookmaker is offering different betting odds to couples of differing ages (3 marks)

b What factors in marriage are associated with an increasing risk of divorce? (6 marks)

c What do we understand by the term 'empty shell marriages'? (3 marks)

d Explain why the increase in divorce is not matched by a corresponding decrease in the popularity of marriage. (8 marks)

3 What purpose does the family have in society? (20 marks)

Case Study

Sad times for the families

The changing face of family life in Britain is catalogued today in a vast series of facts and figures on the way we live.

They are the result of a government survey which shows that values are declining and attitudes changing.

There are more people living together, more divorces and more one-parent families. Among all this the birth rate is falling.

The trends are revealed in the 322-page General Household Survey, 1982, released by the office of Population Censuses and Surveys.

About 21 000 adults were interviewed for the survey which gives a spot of advice to men hoping for a large family.

They should marry a bride under 20 because girls of that age continue to have the greatest number of children. There is a snag ... they are more likely to have a divorce too.

Life in Britain 1984 has its consolations. More people own their homes, and families have more freezers, colour TVs, washing machines, tumble driers, telephones and central heating.

There are lighter moments in the survey report, too. Drinking, it tentatively suggests can improve your health.

More lone parents

There are more one-parent families, the survey report shows.

Just over 12% of all families with dependent children were headed by a lone parent compared with 8·3% in the 1970s. The proportion headed by a mother alone rose from 7·1% to 10·7%.

And 64% of one-parent families lived in rented council accommodation; compared with 27% in owner-occupied homes.

The biggest group of single lone mothers was in the 16–24 age range. The largest number of widowed lone mothers was in the 40–44 age group.

More living together

More couples are living together before they marry and more marriages are ending in divorce.

Fewer children are being born. The survey says that even if the birth rate rises after the age of 30, women born in the 1950s are unlikely to reach the average two children per woman necessary to replace their own generation.

Women whose husbands were in manual rather than non-manual occupations tended to be more fertile, the survey reports.

The level of fertility was also higher among women who had not obtained qualifications equivalent to GCE O Level than for other women.

The survey also suggests that there may have been higher fertility within marriage among daughters of manual workers.

Seventy-one per cent of women aged 13–49 were legally married at the time the survey was taken, excluding those who were separated.

And among the remaining women – those who were not legally married but including the separated – 12% had a live-in lover.

Around 21% of first-time brides and grooms lived together before their wedding, and as many as 67% of couples in cases where at least one of the partners had been married before.

The time spent living together tended to be longer among couples where at least one of the partners had been married before.

More than 40% lived together for 2 years or more before marrying, compared with 24% of couples marrying for the first time.

Divorce rates increased over the 1970s and early 1980s, and the probability of a first marriage ending in divorce or separation was greater for girls married before they were 20 than for women who married later.

Daily Mail comment

Family decay

The picture of Britain presented in the latest General House Survey is disquieting in the extreme. It shows that the conventional family consisting of a married couple with children at home is now in the minority.

On the increase are households consisting of a lone adult, those with couples without children, or single parent families, while the number of families with unmarried mothers has doubled in the last decade.

These are surely the signs of a dissolving society. And it is hard not to link the decay of the family with the rising rate of crime. This hardly seems the right time for legislation to make divorce easier and quicker than ever. Perhaps these figures will make the politicians think again.

Source: Daily Mail, 26 June 1984

1 On what survey are these extracts based?

2 What evidence is there to suggest that the number of single parent families is increasing?

3 What kinds of people tend to have more children?

4 Under the heading *Daily Mail Comment* the writer describes the survey as 'disquieting in the extreme'. What sociological evidence is there to support or contradict this point of view?

5 As a sociologist, explain to the author of *Daily Mail Comment* the relationship between easier divorce, the rising rate of crime, and the decay of the family.

Points for discussion

- Couples should live together before marriage to improve their chances of successful marriage.
- The increase in single families proves that traditional family life is on the decline.
- Much more should be done to encourage poor and uneducated people to practise birth control.

Fear haunts tower block

City tower block families have become prisoners in their own homes after threats of violence from rowdy neighbours following a spate of all-night parties and drunken orgies.

They say neighbours have threatened to beat them up and pour paraffin through their letter boxes when they have complained to the police about the noise.

City tower blocks.

Already this year tenants have had to petition the city council about broken lifts, stairways being used as lavatories, unruly neighbours, excessive break-ins and smashed-up children's play areas. Last year an unemployed father of 3 threw himself from the eighth floor.

But now a new horror of horrors is haunting the residents of City tower blocks: the all-night party with wild screaming youths hurling cans and bottles from top floor windows.

A 25-year-old mother of 2 young children said that she had been forced to split up her family. She said: 'We have to put up with loud music day and night. My children cannot sleep. I have had to send my younger child to live with my mother. I want to leave the flats. I don't think I can take any more. How do they expect us to have a normal family life in a place like this.'

An elderly widow said she did not dare leave her flat, she was petrified. Another said: 'I have written to the council about nuisance neighbours, their language is atrocious. One night they were throwing their furniture about, but I was too frightened to go out for the police. I'm so grateful that I'm not bringing up a family here. Parents can't control their kids here.'

A council spokesman said: 'A second petition has been received by the housing committee who have referred it to the tenancy sub-committee. Officers will investigate the complaints and report back.'

QUESTIONS

1 According to this newspaper article, what problems are being experienced by some tenants? Are there any problems that might exist that are not mentioned?

2 In what way is living in a tower block likely to influence family life in respect of

- bringing up children
- the entertaining of friends and relatives
- the enjoyment of social amenities?

3 Now that you are formed into a housing committee, discuss solutions to the problems experienced by families in the City tower blocks. Organise your recommendations under these headings:

- What we think can be done to help families under the existing circumstances, and
- To what practical use can we put the tower blocks if we decide to rehouse all the families?

Points for discussion

- Council tenants who get

subsidised accommodation shouldn't complain about anything.

- Separate facilities should be provided for young people so that they can hold parties without disturbing anyone else.

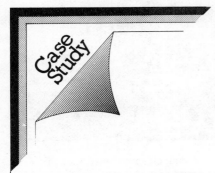

Case Study

Danny McIntyre joined a commune in late 1969. The commune members owned 12 acres of farmland and a small farmhouse in North Wales. Danny bought a share of the farm and land and went to live in the commune with high hopes. The commune itself was largely self-supporting, mainly by producing vegetables and wooden toys for sale in the local markets. What follows are extracts from Danny's diary.

QUESTIONS

1 Explain, in your own words, the meaning of

- commune (introduction)
- job rota (day 1)
- wholesaler (day 1)
- ego trip (day 19)
- heavy in the evening (day 19)
- sexists (day 33)
- moral dangers of communes (day 43)

2 Using some sociological terms, explain

- *a* in what way was the social organisation of this commune different from your own family life, and
- *b* in what way was it similar.

3 How did influences outside the commune influence behaviour within the commune itself.

Day 1

Had breakfast and met some people. I was given my job for the day. I was told that after a month I would be involved in working out the job rota. It was all very democratic. It made me feel good. Later in the morning I went to the town to sell vegetables to a local wholesaler. Everything was OK but I felt we were given a bad deal. Anyway who needs a lot of money. All you need is love and just enough to get by on.

Day 3

As I'm a carpenter by trade I've been up on the north boundary mending fences. Some local kids knocked them down last night. Tony told me some locals didn't like us living in the area. Sometimes it's hard to understand why people are so hostile. But I'm feeling good

and things can only get better!

Day 7

Not a good day. The local police paid us a visit. They'd been tipped off that some of us had dope. No one had – it's one of our rules. Anyway after a couple of hours they left empty-handed. They said they were only doing their job. It proved to me that people still want to cause us pain. That's so sad.

Day 19

I spent most of the day digging trenches. I don't mind my share of hard work but sometimes it appears to me that it's always the same people who get dirty jobs. I mean Cal – he's the commune's founder member – he spent most of the day talking to journalists from some London papers. He really liked it. I suppose he's on a bit of an ego trip, but it just gets me. Things got a little heavy in the evening. One of the

4 Why do you think people want to live in communes? What experiences are they seeking?

Points for discussion

- Leaving home is freedom.
- Human beings are basically selfish and greedy. Communal living is bound to end in failure.
- There is no satisfactory alternative to the family in Britain.

Important points

- The family is the basic social unit within society.
- Our earliest and most crucial experiences of the social world take place within the family. This is called primary socialisation.
- These early family experiences will have a powerful influence in determining our behaviour and our attitudes in adulthood.
- Patterns of kinship are important in all societies.
- The typical nuclear family in our society is only one kind of family structure. In other societies the family may take on a different structure, usually determined by social and economic factors.
- Industrialisation describes the process of change from an agricultural society to a predominantly industrial society.
- Since industrialisation the family has changed from an extended unit to a nuclear unit.
- As the structure of the family has changed, so too has the relationship between members within the family, in particular the conjugal roles between men and women.
- Some factors in a marriage tend to make it more divorce-prone than others.
- Although divorce and illegitimacy are increasing, this does not necessarily mean that the family is in decline.

reporters asked us when were we going to get the dope out, and later made a suggestion to Jenny that didn't go down too well. He was so uncool. I really thought he imagined he was in for some orgy or something.

Josh told him not to believe everything he read in the newspapers! We all broke up at that. It was just too funny!

Day 20

Cindy joined us yesterday. She'd hitched from Newcastle in less than 5 hours. Difficult to believe. That makes 17 of us all told, and a cat. Roughly speaking there's 3 couples with 5 kids — they more-or-less stick together. Then there's 6 more of us, 4 girls and 2 fellas. With only 5 rooms in the farmhouse this makes sleeping arrangements a bit complicated. There's an old barn I've had my eye on — but it needs repairing. I wouldn't mind shacking up in there.

Day 38

Problems. Problems. Why can't people just relax and be cool? The women got together today and said that some of us are sexists. Things got a little 'political.' They said that they were being treated just like 'straight housewives.' Maybe they've got a point. There's too much tension in the air.

Day 35

Cal has been using dope. We had an emergency meeting late last night. Some people wanted Cal to leave the commune as he had broken one of our main rules. Cal then said that if he left there would be problems as he owned a large amount of the land. Josh said he was blackmailing us. The meeting broke up and it was clear that people were on edge with one another.

Day 36

On top of the problems with Cal we had a visit from someone from the local education department. They wanted to know about who was providing education for the 3 kids of school age in the commune. We said we provided it but apparently that wasn't good enough. They said that we didn't have the proper facilities. Cal said we would have to take legal advice on all this.

Day 43

I've decided to leave. With one thing and another nothing is turning out as I imagined. There is a lot of hostility between people. The dream is over for me. This morning our commune was made famous in one of the Sunday newspapers. All lies. They described us as a dope-infested love-nest and warned parents about the moral dangers of communes for their children. It made me spew. I've decided to move on. Maybe communes like this will never work until there are more like-minded people. We are too much in the minority. It is all very sad.

4 Education

When you have worked through this chapter you should have a clearer understanding of

Formal and informal education · **The tripartite system** · **The comprehensive system** · **Streaming** · **Elaborated and restricted speech codes** · **The transmission of civilisation** · **Gender socialisation** · **Feminist sociology** · **Social interaction** · **Sociology of the school** · **Pupil identities** · **The self-fulfilling prophecy** · **The formal and hidden curriculum** · **High and low status subjects**

Why have education?

When we consider the amount of money, time and effort spent in educational institutions it is not surprising that sociologists see education as a very important area for analysis. In our society education is seen as a basic right – by law we are all compelled to spend a certain amount of time being educated – and because of this we may fail to realise that the right to be educated is a relatively recent development. In fact the State only took on the responsibility for providing elementary education for everyone in 1870, and it was 10 years later, in 1880, that school attendance was made compulsory, but only for children up to the age of 10. **The Fisher Education Act** of **1918** made school attendance compulsory up to the age of 14, and in 1947 the school leaving age was raised to 15. The current minimum leaving age of 16 came into effect in 1973.

We can see that our society has placed more and more emphasis on education over the last 100 years or so. The questions that spring to mind are: Why did the public education of children suddenly become so important? Why has our society placed more and more emphasis on education since the last quarter of the 19th century?

To understand this we need to think about what happened to our society during this period. We know from other chapters in this book that there have been enormous changes during this time and this change we know as **industrialisation**.

Industrialisation meant that the growth of the factory system required a labour force that had the skills to practise the new forms of production. One way of understanding the importance of this change is by examining the field notes of a sociologist who undertook a study of a nomadic tribe that had no experience of the industrialisation process. The way the members of the tribe organised their lives had changed little in the last 3 centuries:

Within this small, non-literate tribal group there is no need for formal education. The young people learn all they need to know from their parents and the tribe's elder members. They learn about hunting, fishing and crop growing – in fact all the skills necessary for a productive life – from the adult members of the group. This is achieved not by sitting them down in one spot for a period of instruction but by allowing the children to imitate the work carried out by adults. The boys accompany their fathers into the bush and to the river banks and the girls stay in the village with the women to carry out a wide range of tasks from sewing, thatching and preparing food. Education is a very practical experience and is designed to equip all members of the tribe with the skills necessary to be both productive for the group as a whole and efficient enough to satisfy each individual's needs and wants.

In what way is this form of education different from your own? Are there any similarities?

To begin with, in our extract most of the education is imparted by practical example. Knowledge and skills are acquired through actually carrying out tasks. We call this an **informal** system of education. There are no classrooms, no textbooks, no written examinations, no notes to make and no teachers! In fact there are no schools. Yet there are similarities with our education system. The purpose of education in our society, which is a **formal** system of education, is to provide the skills and knowledge to enable each child to succeed in our society. So you can see that although the type of education required by children to succeed in each society is quite different, the reason for having education is the same.

You might think that the level of education and learning experienced by the tribe's children is so basic that these children are by our standards uneducated, but the knowledge we all have and need has to be assessed within a social context. This means that we have to judge the value of what people know by taking into account the needs of wider society. You may be able to operate computers and mend car engines but what do you know about hunting, crop-rotation and building your own house? Probably very little. Yet the knowledge and skills you have are those that are relevant to the historical and economic period in which you live.

This is the answer to our question about why education has become more important in an industrialising society. As society becomes more complex, so new skills are required to meet the demands of that society. By the middle of the 19th century expanding industry and commerce required a labour force that could at least read and write. Today's educational demands are much more complex than this. Take computer technology as an example. You are probably the first generation of school pupils and students who have been given instruction in computer studies. The reasons for this are clear enough. Computer technology is becoming more and more important in the modern world; computer literacy is a useful skill

and essential for many different occupations.

Another important element associated with the introduction of mass education in the last century is what we might call the political influence. The late 19th century saw the growing importance of trade unions, the right to vote, the emergence of the Labour Party, and a general feeling that the working classes ought to have a greater share of the cake in a fairer society, and that included the right of children to a free basic education. Education, in this atmosphere of political change, would also help to maintain a stable society by providing the reading and writing skills to introduce young people to the values of society.

We have suggested that the provision of education is important because we need to ensure that the individuals who make up society acquire the skills and knowledge necessary both to understand and to deal with the demands of a modern society. But understanding this is just to scratch the surface of education as a topic for sociological examination. For instance, we mustn't think that pre-industrial societies educated their children using only an informal system of education and industrial societies only a formal system. Obviously much of what you yourself have learnt today, perhaps most of it, has been learnt informally outside the classroom – breakfast TV and radio at home, conversations with members of your family and school friends, reading the newspaper on the bus, have all made a tiny contribution to what we understand as your education. However it is to the formal system we must direct our attention if we want to know more about the functions of education in our society.

In the following sections we will

look closely at the key areas of interest, and as you work your way through them and become acquainted with the research you can ask yourself how they stand up in the light of your own experiences. This is one area of sociology where you have a direct interest.

EXERCISE

Here is a definition of education: education is a learning process by which we transmit the culture of a society from one generation to the next. By culture we include knowledge, skills, language and the values we think are important.

Take a copy of these 2 headings and make lists of as many formal and informal learning experiences as you can:

Formal education. What you have learnt this week at school or college.

Informal education. What you have learnt this week outside school or college.

The 1944 Education Act

Although the expansion in the provision of education was in response to the growth of industrial society, the great landmark in education was the Education Act of 1944. In the 18th century education was a privilege that only the sons of the aristocracy and wealthy enjoyed. In the 19th century, even though many more children experienced some form of education, there remained great educational inequality. This inequality had nothing whatever to do with a child's ability but was the result of certain groups being better placed economically and socially to make the most of the then available education. However not only was there inequality between social groups but also inequality between the sexes. Education, the argument went, was wasted on women – after all, most women would soon be married with children, a home and a husband to look after.

We can justify calling the 1944 Education Act a landmark because it aimed to bring about equality of opportunity in education which had previously been absent. The Act laid down that local education authorities were to provide free state education for all children at 3 levels: Primary, Secondary and Further Education. Education authorities were also required to set up three different types of schools in the secondary level. These were grammar schools, technical schools and secondary modern schools. It became known as the **tripartite system** of education.

The tripartite system was based on an examination taken at 11 years of age called the 11-plus, and a pupil's performance in this examination determined which school he or she would attend. Grammar schools recruited children who displayed academic ability, technical schools pupils who showed skills in technical subjects, and secondary modern schools children who failed to progress to either the technical or grammar schools.

Although we can accept the 1944 Education Act, and the organisation of secondary education that followed it, as a noble attempt at bringing about equality of opportunity we can see that the way this system was organised was related to the needs and demands of the economy, and particularly to the needs of industry and commerce. The grammar school was ideally suited to prepare pupils for university and so for entry into the professions, and the technical school pupil would follow a path that would lead him or her (more often than not him) into an apprenticeship to learn a trade. This left the secondary modern school pupil available to take up one of the then numerous unskilled and semi-skilled jobs in industry. Although there were many young people who did not neatly fit into these categories, such links between the 3 types of schools and the needs of the employment system did exist as this extract illustrates:

I failed the 11-plus and found myself at Wood End Secondary Modern. I didn't have that bad a time there but I always felt I could have done much better for myself. Like my brother Frank. He was the clever one in the family. He passed his 11-plus and went to the grammar. He got a job in a bank when he left school. I think that my horizons were narrowed by what the teachers told us. I remember we were taken to this factory – it was part of a careers lesson – it was a terrible place, hot and dirty. The teacher kept saying what a great place it was to work in. Then one kid asked him if it was that good why didn't he work there. He couldn't answer that question – or maybe he didn't want to answer. You see, he had the choice – we didn't.

This helps us to understand why the tripartite system was not looked upon favourably by everyone. Despite undoubted advantages, it appeared to many to be unfair and socially divisive, with its 3-tier system of educational opportunity favouring certain children and disadvantaging others on the results of a single written examination at the age of 11.

It was also wasteful in terms of exploiting the full range of human resources by failing to give large numbers of children the best start in life. The 11-plus was open to the criticism that it attempted to assess a child's intelligence to a degree that was not shown to be accurate or fair. Not all children who went to grammar school did well on academic courses, and some able children, who may have been late developers, did not get the chance to gain academic qualifications at secondary modern schools. There was also unequal regional availability of grammar school places. For instance, if you happened to live in certain parts of the country you might have a 40% chance of getting a grammar school place, while in another part of the country only a 10% chance. Pupils who might have benefited from a more technically slanted education were also to be disappointed. Very few technical schools were ever built or opened.

Not surprisingly, by the 1960s things began to change. Many secondary modern schools introduced CSE examinations for the first time in 1964 and some began to feed their brighter children into newly created O Level courses. Two important government reports of the time, however, the *Crowther Report* (1959) and the *Robbins Report* (1963) suggested that the triparitite system was still failing badly to give all children equal opportunity of gaining paper qualifications and thus access to higher education. Research also highlighted the effects of low status schools in branding the individual child as a 'failure' just because he or she happened to attend a particular school in a run-down locality.

EXERCISE

The 11-plus was (and still is) a test designed to assess a child's level of intelligence. Children who registered the highest scores were judged to have high IQs and were offered grammar school places. The remaining children (perhaps over 80%) were directed to secondary modern schools. What follows are a few examples of the kind of questions set for the 11-plus examination:

Pick out the correct word and underline it:
1 Help means the same thing as (hinder, assist, warning, agree)
2 Gift means the same thing as (Christmas, joy, present, package)
3 Rare means the same thing as (scarce, common, valuable, beautiful)

Pick out the word or number most unlike the others and underline it:
4 1, 3, 5, 6, 9
5 Beautiful, ugly, plain, unhappy
6 Cow, dog, bird, cat
7 Bucket, spade, cup, jug

Stephen is 8 years old and his mother is 30 years old:
8 What will Stephen's age be when his mother is 35?
9 How old was his mother when Stephen was born?
10 When Stephen is twice as old as he is now what will his mother's age be then?
11 How old will Stephen be when his mother is 4 times as old as Stephen is now?
12 In how many years will his mother be 3 times as old as Stephen?
13 Draw in the missing shape in the blank space:

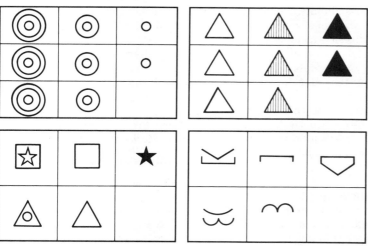

These questions are for *you* to answer:
1 Do you think a test of this kind measures a person's intelligence? Are there other kinds of ability that it does not measure?

2 Children from working class backgrounds and from ethnic minority groups tended to do less well in the 11-plus than children from the middle classes. Can you suggest reasons for this?
3 What would you say are the main problems in attempting to assess the intelligence of an 11-year-old child?

The comprehensive system

Under this barrage of criticism, the tripartite system started to crumble and many education authorities began to look at a new type of school that seemed to offer hope of a more satisfactory education for a greater number of pupils between 11 and 18 years of age. It was called a comprehensive school. In a comprehensive school, that might house over 1000 pupils, it was possible to provide a wide range of educational opportunities to satisfy the needs of most children in a locality.

The advantages of a large school quickly became apparent. The 11-plus could be abolished at a stroke and pupils had a wide range of subjects to choose from in a single well-equipped school. It became

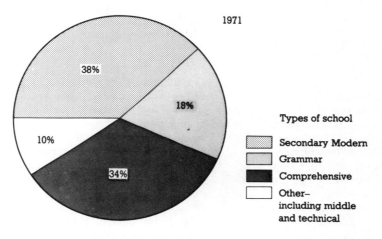

1971

Types of school

- Secondary Modern
- Grammar
- Comprehensive
- Other– including middle and technical

Pupils receiving State secondary education in England

possible for the first time to provide a decent education for slow learners and late developers as well as able pupils, and much of the failure associated with attending secondary moderns could be swept away. It was even possible that class divisions in society could be challenged on a vast scale as a result of merging a 'classless' population of secondary schoolchildren in just one type of school. The success of the comprehensive as the most popular form of school was inevitable, as the diagram on page 58 illustrates:

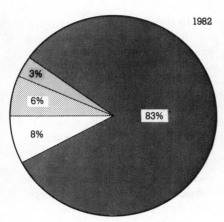

1982

Note: These statistics do not include secondary pupils attending private or independent fee-paying schools. Approximately 6% of all eligible children in the UK received their education in this way in 1982.

Despite the popularity of comprehensive schools in England (similar trends occurred in the rest of Britain) doubts began to surface to challenge the high hopes associated with this new type of school. Extremely large schools could not only provide a comprehensive education but also an impersonal atmosphere in which children might feel insecure, especially if their school occupied several sites. The idea that any type of school could create an ideal social mix of pupils was called into question when it became clear that most comprehensives recruited pupils from well defined geographical areas. Rather than challenge social divisions in society, comprehensives were reinforcing already existing social patterns of behaviour and class difference. Many parents, too, expressed disappointment in having no real alternative when it came to choosing a different type of school for their children.

In order to deal with the problems of teaching children of mixed abilities together in one school, comprehensives introduced the practice of streaming. This means that pupils who have the same level of ability in a subject are put into the same class. This allows brighter children to progress at a faster rate than less able children who progress at their own pace in their own classes. Critics are quick to point out, however, that streaming is just another form of selection not unlike the 11-plus.

EXERCISE

Can you think of any more advantages and disadvantages of streaming? Do you think that streaming is a satisfactory way of organising a school? Explain.

Although the schools made possible under the Education Act of 1944 were a vast improvement on what had previously existed, sociologists soon began to see that much of the hope associated with the tripartite system and the new comprehensive schools was never fulfilled. It became clear that other social factors have to be considered when looking at education in society. Even though the 1944 Education Act was egalitarian in intent, giving every pupil an equal chance of a 'good' education irrespective of the financial and social position of his or her parents, research began to indicate that education was still reinforcing the inequalities which exist in society. This is because the type of school a child attends is only one factor that can affect how well that child performs there.

As a sociologist, what social factors would you consider important in predicting likely success or failure at school?

Problems resulting from living in poor housing conditions, the educational experience of a pupil's parents, type of diet, cost of school uniform and equipment, the economic and social status of the pupil's family, are all factors that can influence a child's performance in the classroom and determine a parent's choice of school. Social research suggests that working class children are still at a considerable disadvantage when it comes to educational opportunities, even within a comprehensive school system. Later in the chapter we will be in a position to examine some of this research, but first we will look at the work of one researcher who believes that the way we use language is crucial in influencing progress at school.

The importance of language

Basil Bernstein, a sociologist who has written several books on the importance of language in education, including *Class, Codes and Control*, argued that there is a relationship between a child's home life, speaking skills and academic success at school. He put forward a theory that there are basically 2 patterns of speech which he called **elaborated** and **restricted** codes. These codes identify 2 ways of speaking learnt by children as a result of living in different home environments. Here is an example of what is meant by this:

Scene: Breakfast time at home.
Cast: Mother, and child of 8

Family using a restricted code

Mother: Eat it!
Child: No, I won't!
Mother: Eat it! I haven't got time to mess about.
Child: No! I won't. It's runny.
Mother: Look, shut up, and eat it! What are you doing at school today?
Child: Swimming.
Mother: Right, I'll put your things in your bag.

Family using an elaborated code

Mother: Eat your breakfast!
Child: No, I won't!
Mother: Why not?
Child: I don't like this egg. It's too runny. I like my eggs nice and soft.
Mother: Why don't you dip your soldiers in it, and then bite their heads off. What have you got at school today?
Child: We're going swimming.
Mother: So what do you want to take with you when you go swimming?
Child: I don't know.
Mother: Well, what do you need when you go to the swimming baths?
Child: Money ... oh ... yes ... my trunks and my towel. I can swim on my back.
Mother: Of course you can. And you can eat runny eggs. Look, it's all gone.

Can you see the difference between these conversations? Can you work out the relationship between speaking patterns at home and success at school?

In the example of the restricted code, the mother and her child are having a conversation that is much shorter than the other example. Both are using fewer words and simpler expressions, and they obviously do not feel the need to 'elaborate'. When the mother asks: 'What are you doing at school today?' the child replies; 'Swimming'. The mother immediately understands this and responds with: 'Right, I'll put your things in your bag'. Bernstein suggests that this restricted code relies on shared meanings and assumptions that need not be expressed in words. A lot of the communication remains unspoken. The speaker and the listener understand each other perfectly without the use of

elaborate explanations and descriptions.

The elaborated code example describes a similar situation. This time both mother and child are using a greater number of words in more complex sentences to achieve more or less the same results – getting the child to eat his breakfast and ready for school. However when mum asks: 'Well, what do you need when you go to the swimming baths?' she of course already knows the answer, but she forces the child to respond with a long-winded reply. Bernstein argues that this form of conversation is more democratic than the abrupt language of restricted speech in the sense that the child is encouraged to participate in the decision-making process, unlike in the restricted speech example where the child is expected to do what he is told.

What has all this got to do with education?

Simply this, that schools are organised in a way that tends to favour children who have been brought up in home environments in which elaborate speech codes are more commonly used. When a teacher asks a class of 8-year-olds: 'Why is it a good idea to learn to swim?' he too, like the mother in the elaborated code example, knows the answer already, and a child with a large vocabulary who has been encouraged to think for himself might just have the right answers compared with a child of equal ability who has had no such encouragement. Taking this argument further, it is easy to see how children who have experienced elaborated speech codes tend to be successful in examinations, including the 11-plus, especially in subjects demanding language skills in the form of essays. Teachers, who are themselves largely recruited from

similar backgrounds, also prefer teaching youngsters who are capable of handling words in this particular way.

Bernstein argued that restricted speech codes are used mostly in working class homes and elaborated codes in middle class homes, thus giving middle class children an advantage at school over children from the working classes. Of course this doesn't mean that only middle class parents invite their children to 'discuss' problems and only working class parents tell their children to 'shut up'. Neither is it suggested that working class children can't speak and write elaborated speech codes when it suits them, nor that a restricted speech code is an inferior way of speaking. He was simply trying to show us how language is influential in educational success and failure, especially if we continue to organise our schools to favour this particular form of language skill.

EXERCISE

Scene: Two 15-year-old school friends discussing TV horror films

Caroline: Did you see it?
Pete: Rubbish!
Caroline: It was great!
Pete: Get lost! It wasn't as good as last week's.
Caroline: That *was* rubbish!
Pete: It was great! Did you see when he twisted his head all round?
Caroline: That's a trick.
Pete: It scared you.
Caroline: I've had more frights shopping at Woolies

1 How would Bernstein define this type of speech?
2 Generally speaking, in what way is this conversation different from the conversation of children using an elaborated speech code?
3 Rewrite the passage with Caroline and Pete using an elaborated speech code. You will

have to use your imagination for this.

4 Explain in your own words why Bernstein believed that elaborated speech is associated with success at school.

The functions of education

As we have discussed, a prime function of education is to **serve the economic life of the country** by sorting out and grading young people's knowledge and skills in a systematic way in preparation for a working life. Generally speaking, as pupils progress in school, and sometimes through to college and university, their education becomes increasingly specialised to match the type of employment they are likely to pursue when they complete their education. However we are now in a position to study schools as they function as a social institution.

An individual pupil will experience school not only in terms of acquiring knowledge but as a **social activity**. He or she will be a member of a social group called a class. Although we accept the role of the teacher as important, a great deal of learning occurs informally within the class and between pupils belonging to peer groups of friends. The effects of these social interactions are often so far-reaching that they can remain in our memories for years, as this reminiscence reveals:

What I can't understand is why I was so eager to leave school when I was 16. Now I'm 21 I realise what a great life it was. In fact most of my friends I now have I met at school. I'm actually getting married soon to a girl from my class, although at that time I didn't even like her. Actually, she's been complaining about me playing football at the weekends instead of seeing her – come to think of it, most of the kids in the team I knew from school.

From this we can see that school provides a setting in which a child can learn to cope with living and working with other people through the acquisition of social skills.

Another important aim of education is that it acts as an **agent of socialisation and social control**. If primary socialisation takes place within the family, we can expect the school to provide what is called **secondary socialisation**. This means that the education process is instrumental in giving guidance to pupils in what society considers as acceptable and unacceptable forms of behaviour. Children are expected to develop into law-abiding, hard-working citizens who know the difference between right and wrong. For example, most schools regard it as an important part of their job to encourage pupils not only to work hard at their studies to gain qualifications, but to develop responsible attitudes towards such things as regular attendance, punctuality, dress, personal cleanliness and respect for the school rules. When the rules are broken or challenged, sanctions are available to protect the authority of the institution (caning, reprimand, suspension or expulsion by the headmaster) and the authority of the individual teacher (lines, detention or extra homework).

A further element of socialisation has been described by some sociologists as the **transmission of civilization**. Put simply, this means that commonly accepted values that our society regards as important, such as loyalty to one's friends and country, a belief in the democratic process and the importance of fair play in human activities, are built into the teaching programmes and into the way school life is organised. For example, school sports and team games, religious education, morning assembly, communal eating and the organisation of pupils into 'houses' (read country) are partly encouraged for this purpose.

An often unrecognised function of the school system is what we might call its **custodial value** to the family. This newspaper article will give you an idea of what is meant by this:

Mad mums tangle with teachers

Rush hour traffic was blocked for up to three hours yesterday by a demonstration of angry parents outside the Dame Wilmot Junior and Infant School. Striking teachers, protesting parents and exasperated motorists had to be separated by the police to avoid an ugly incident.

Banner waving Mrs Lucy Edwards explained: 'These teachers haven't got the right to go on strike in the children's dinner break. They just don't seem to understand the hardship they're causing by sending the kids home. Most of the mums here rely on the school to look after the kids in the daytime so they can go out to work. I've got a part-time job from 10 till 4. How can I look after an 8-year-old child at lunchtime and earn money to pay the rent?'

Jenny Cowley, a 35-year-old divorcee and night sister at Hadden Maternity hospital, said: 'I really sympathise with the teachers. How else can they fight for a better salary? But they shouldn't just send the children home at lunchtime. I need the daytime to get my sleep in. I can't cope fetching my little girl when I should be sleeping. I'll have to give my job up and go on the dole.'

No teacher representative was available for comment.

As you can see, a school not only provides an education for children, it also provides a social facility on which many families depend for their economic well being. A school may also be important in **preserving stability in family life** by providing a refuge for children from unhappy or stressful homes, as well as allowing many parents valuable time to recover from the strains of bringing up children.

EXERCISE

This form is used by some employers in the garage trade to assess the progress of their trainees at 6 monthly intervals:

Trainee Appraisal (please indicate progress by ticking appropriate box)

Factor	High ⟶			Low
Time keeping	Always punctual ☐	Occasionally late ☐	Fairly often late ☐	Regularly late ☐
Attendance	Always present ☐	Occasionally absent ☐	Days off regularly ☐	Numerous days off ☐
Talking and Listening	Can communicate effectively with a wide range of people ☐	Can follow and give simple descriptions and explanations ☐	Can hold conversations and take messages ☐	Can make sensible replies when spoken to ☐
Reading	Can understand a variety of forms of written materials ☐	Can follow instructions and explanations ☐	Can read straightforward messages ☐	Can read words and short phrases ☐
Writing	Can write reports describing work done ☐	Can write instructions and explanations ☐	Can write straightforward messages ☐	Can write words and short phrases ☐
Interpreting Signs and Drawings	Can interpret and use technical drawings unaided ☐	Can make use of technical drawings, with help ☐	Can make use of simple drawings ☐	Can recognise everyday signs and symbols ☐
Number and Cash Handling	Competent to handle cheque and credit enquiries ☐	Can handle customer money and complete receipts ☐	Can solve problems by adding and subtracting ☐	Can count objects accurately ☐
Standard of Work	Takes pride in excellent achievement ☐	Good achievement with few errors ☐	Work acceptable but room for improvement ☐	Poor quality work, lacks pride ☐
Attitude to Work	Always keen, interested and industrious ☐	Interested and trying to improve ☐	Accepts all tasks and performs adequately ☐	Lack of interest and enthusiasm ☐

Dealing with each factor in turn, or with convenient groups of factors, explain how the school system contributes to a trainee's progress in the garage trade.

The persistence of inequality

Some social factors that have led sociologists to argue that educational inequality persists are to be found in this short story:

Old promises never die . . .

Williams watched the well dressed man on his TV screen spout about the opportunities available for young people. Nothing much changes, Williams thought, the same old lies, the same old rubbish.

He remembered his form teacher, Mr Baker, saying the very same thing years ago. He always took the opportunity to tell his class how everyone was enjoying a good standard of living, how people were buying cars and household gadgets and taking holidays under a Mediterranean sun.

Mr Baker had droned on about an affluent society. Williams remembered being puzzled about where this affluence was. The world beyond the school gates was for him one of overcrowded houses, of being sent to the corner shop to get bread, milk and bacon on tick. It was a world of paper-thin walls that allowed no privacy. There was no opportunity for homework because there were little brothers and sisters to look after, and no time just to sit and think. If he picked up a book to do his homework, an interruption was never far away. 'If you can't work at home, go to the local library', Mr Baker advised. Williams asked him if this is what he had done when he was at school. 'Of course not, my parents were concerned about my education. They didn't let me run wild.' Funny how casual remarks can hurt – even after all these years.

Williams had left school, unqualified, at 15. His uncle had fixed him up with an apprenticeship in the shipyard. It was a job for life. Yet even then he had wanted to say, just once, that maybe he should have stayed on at school. But an education beyond 15 was a luxury in his street. An extra wage packet, no matter how small, eased the financial burden and helped with the household budget. Now, many ships later, the yard had closed down and he had joined the army of unemployed. Plenty of time now to sit and listen to politicians talk about the great opportunities which lie ahead in the bright new technological age.

Williams managed to pull himself together. Time to switch channels he thought.

What this story helps us to understand is that we cannot seriously discuss equality of education without considering education within a wider social context. This is exactly how sociological research was to be conducted over the years.

Research carried out by Floud, Halsey and Martin in their *Social Class and Educational Opportunity* looked at the performance of pupils in two areas of the country, South-west Hertfordshire and Middlesbrough. In Middlesbrough, where incomes were low and housing poor, the educationally successful pupils tended to be the children of better-off parents. The economic standing of pupils' parents in the relatively affluent South-west Hertfordshire was less important in terms of their children's educational achievement.

The importance of the material environment in which a child grows up was further emphasised in the late 1960s in the study *Poverty – the Forgotten Englishman* by Coates and Silburn. Similarly, this study looked at the relationship between economic and social factors and a pupil's achievement in school. The research was carried out in the St Ann's area of Nottingham, an area noted for damp, draughty and underheated housing. The children were smaller and frailer than children from the more prosperous parts of the city. They lacked adequate diet and were more likely to be ill, having more time off school than their better-off peers. At school they were found to have a limited vocabulary and were unfamiliar with the use of crayons and paints. Coates and Silburn pointed out that due to social and economic circumstances these children were at a distinct disadvantage from the very start of their schooling. It would make little difference to them or their parents to know that grammar schools existed. Coates and Silburn detected a certain 'hopelessness' in the St Ann's area and much of this hopelessness was carried into the classrooms by the children. Statistics from the study indicated the results of such deprivation. Less than 10% of the children were average readers for their age group, the vast majority being below average, and only 1.5% obtained grammar school places compared with 60% of children from the middle class suburbs.

The results from these and other research enquiries suggest that no matter how legislators attempt to bring equality of opportunity to the education system, we have to accept that the inequality experienced *outside* the classroom has a significant bearing on the achievement level of pupils within the classroom. The studies carried out in the 1950s and 1960s showed that while many working class pupils did indeed attend grammar schools, the opportunities provided by the tripartite system of education overwhelmingly benefited the children of middle class family income groups.

What problems do you think a working class pupil would encounter at a grammar or comprehensive school which mainly recruited pupils from middle class backgrounds?

A study by Dale and Griffith *Downstream: A Study in Failure* found that many working class pupils experience a **culture clash** when attending grammar schools. By culture clash they mean that there is a conflict between different value systems. This extract from a play contains an example of this:

Scene: School cloakroom. Pamela, Susan and Carole are discussing the forthcoming school trip to the Loire Valley in France.

Pamela: It's about the only thing to look forward to – that and the long summer holidays.

Susan: I'm going to try and get round my dad for some extra spending money. I think he's got some francs left over from last year's holiday in Brittany.

Pamela: I have to work really hard on my dad. But he always gives in in the end. He's always pretending to be mean. He likes me to fuss round him. What's your dad like Carole? Is he mean?

Carole: No, he's OK. Anyway, it doesn't matter. I won't be going on the trip.

Pamela: What! Everyone's going.

Carole: I'm not. My parents can't afford it.

Susan: Meanies.

Carole: No they're not. It's just that they've got to spend their money on more important things.

Pamela: What's more important than the school trip? My dad says it's educational. You can practise your French there. That's much better than boring lessons with Mrs Peters.

Susan: You hate French. You're hopeless at it.

Pamela: That's not the point. Carole's the best in the class. Old Mrs Peters is always saying that you have an aptitude for languages. Doesn't your dad realise the opportunity you're missing?

Carole: If he could afford to send me, he would. We don't all have rich parents.

Susan: But we're all going. I think your dad is a little old meanie.

What we have here is a conflict of values as a result of the girls' socialisation within their own family groups and through growing up in different social and economic worlds. Susan and Pamela take going on the school trip for granted. Going abroad is what people in their social group enjoy from time to time. Carole's experiences in her social world are affecting her chances of improving her French by preventing her going on the trip to France.

EXERCISE

Steven Moffat
I live with my mum and my older brother on the Endwell Estate. We have 2 bedrooms in our 4th floor flat which is owned by the council. I think my mum is on social security. Anyway my mum and my brother are out of work for the moment. The flat's terrible. All the walls are damp and the people next door are always drunk and shouting at one another. I like watching TV when I'm not out with my mates.

David Fairweather
My mum and dad are both teachers. Naturally, they're both dead keen about my education. We live in a big semi-detached house with a long garden. They bought the house because it was near to my school. I think they have a mortgage. I have my own room to escape to. As long as I get good reports from school they leave me alone. When you haven't got any brothers and sisters, having teachers

for parents can be a real pain.

Explain in what practical way the social backgrounds of these two 13-year-old schoolboys might affect their performance at school.

If social factors are important in influencing success at school it will come as no surprise to find their influence extending into post-school education. During the 1960s and 1970s there was an expansion in the number of places available in colleges of further education (technical colleges) and in higher education (universities and polytechnics). Without suggesting that a further or higher education is essential or even desirable, there is no doubt that paper qualifications improve an individual's chances of employment. From this table you can see that the number of university graduates from all social classes has increased, although the proportion from each social class has changed little:

class group 8 who gained university degrees has risen from 0.9–1.8 at the same time as the percentage of members from group 1 has risen from 15–27%. This table is taken from a study by Halsey and Karabel, *Power and Ideology in Education*, which suggested that there is no clear evidence that demonstrates a marked reduction in class inequality in education. Given the present unemployment levels of young people it would be interesting to see which sections of the social strata have been hardest hit. It would be reasonable to assume that the group would come from the working class sector of the population.

EXERCISE

Study and understand the chart on page 64 before you begin the questions:
1 Approximately what percentage of students had fathers in the professional and employers and managers groups?

Social origin and university degree
Men in England and Wales aged 25–59 in 1972. Total sample 6700

Percentage gaining university degree by class of origin

| | Class of origin | | | | | | | | Total % of |
Born	1	2	3	4	5	6	7	8	population
1913–1931	15.0	7.4	3.8	3.0	1.5	1.3	0.9	0.9	2.6
1932–1947	27.0	17.6	5.8	5.1	3.6	2.3	2.4	1.8	6.0

Source: Oxford Mobility Study

Key to class groupings
1 Professional, high managerial
2 Lower professional and managerial
3 White collar
4 Self-employed, including farmers
5 Supervisors of manual work
6 Skilled manual workers
7 Semi-skilled and unskilled
8 Agricultural workers

The percentage of members from

2 Approximately what percentage of young people in the general population had fathers in the top 2 groups?
3 What single most important conclusion do you draw from your answers to questions 1 and 2?
4 Briefly provide a few social reasons why the children of skilled manual and non-professional fathers have fewer opportunities for higher education compared with children from the professional and managerial groups.

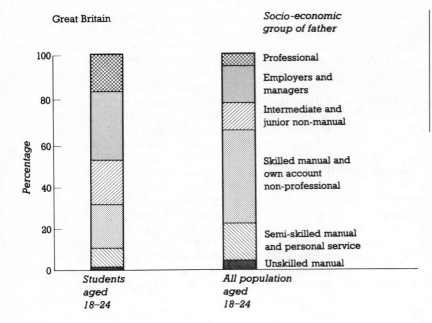

Great Britain

Socio-economic group of father

Professional

Employers and managers

Intermediate and junior non-manual

Skilled manual and own account non-professional

Semi-skilled manual and personal service

Unskilled manual

Students aged 18–24

All population aged 18–24

Full-time and sandwich course students attending university or college by social group of father 1981–82 Source: General Household Survey 1981–82

Women and education

Lost chances

Another long empty day lay ahead. Ann went over to the window. From the 14th floor in the high-rise she could see across the city. People were out there doing all sorts of things. She thought of the day ahead. It would be the same as yesterday and tomorrow – collecting the children from school and preparing an evening meal for her husband. But there were many hours between now and then, too many hours.

Ann reflected on the what-might-have-beens. What would have happened if she'd stayed on at school? What if the teachers had encouraged her to develop her potential? What if her parents had believed that education was just as important for her as it was for her brother? If only she had spent less time reading those trashy magazines that told her that falling in love and being the perfect wife was the ultimate aim in life. She had had her children and was a good wife and mother. Now she lived in a rabbit hutch and did her best to make it homely. She turned to gaze at the TV screen. It flashed an advertisement of a mother telling her daughter how pretty she was compared with her rough little brother. She could see the same thing happening to her own daughter. 'Mummy-can-I-have-a-Sindy-doll', Elizabeth would repeat endlessly, 'Mummy-am-I-pretty-Mummy-is-it-true-that-sugar-and-spice-and-all-things-nice-are-what-little-girls-are-made-of?'

There were times when Ann had wanted to help her father out with jobs around the house. She was told to go and help her mother – girls weren't allowed to do men's work. There had been many subjects she was interested in at school, but the teachers encouraged her to concentrate on subjects 'more suitable for girls'. Now she could

cook and sew and look after her home. But Ann wanted more. She wanted the chance to use that part of her which had never been used. Maybe she had been born a generation too soon. Maybe things are different now. She looked out over the sprawling city and wondered ...

Ann's experiences point to the problems faced by many women in both the education system and the family group. Although progress has been made regarding the position of women, research indicates that women do not always enjoy the best opportunities within the education system. As far back as 1963 the *Robbins Report* showed that 3 times as many girls left school at 15 as boys and only one third of A Level students and a quarter of university students were women. In 1974 women made up 36% of university entrants and over 30% of polytechnic students, but by 1981–82 women occupied 41% of all full-time places at universities. Of course, no-one is suggesting that there is a conspiracy against women in the education system. Like the question of social class, we have to consider the position of women in the wider society.

As sociologists, how do we explain the difference in school achievement between men and women?

In 1962 Thelma Veness, in her study *School Leavers*, looked at the attitudes of 600 female school leavers in two English southern counties. Almost 300 saw their main 'job' in life as looking after their husbands, and they all imagined that they would be married by the time they were 25 years old. Veness argued that the girls were far less ambitious than the sample group of boys, who were themselves more interested in jobs and careers. For the girls, marriage was their main goal in life.

EXERCISE

Look at this list of life ambitions. If you had to rearrange them in order of priority, in what order would you put them?

A job	Love
A husband	Marriage
A career	Children

Now compare your list with a friend's, preferably of the opposite sex. Can you explain to each other how you arrived at your decisions?

In a study by the sociologist Sue Sharpe in 1974, *Just Like a Girl: How Girls Learn to be Women* she found that working class schoolgirls saw their priorities in terms of: love–marriage–husbands–children–jobs–careers in descending order of importance. She suggested that the reason for this can be found in the girls' experiences of school. Although changes have taken place in school curricula, girls are still directed to arts subjects, including cookery and needlework, and steered away from scientific and technical subjects. In other words, the way schools are organised leads girls to think that homemaking and being a good wife and mother are the only goals open to them. This is part of what is called **gender socialisation**.

However, we must not neglect social class. Women from middle class homes are likely to achieve far more in terms of educational qualifications. For example, we have already seen the substantial increase in the recruitment of women into higher education. Again it is the girl from the working class home who tends to lose out. Taking the evidence we have discussed, as well as the vast amount of data being made

available through **feminist sociology**, we know that women underachieve in the education system, and this can partly be explained by the experiences of women in the school system and the subordinate position of women in society generally. We will return to this subject in the chapter *Women*.

EXERCISE

Draw up a questionnaire based on Sue Sharpe's list of priorities. Conduct your research on sample groups of girls and boys in your school or college. Present your findings in a short report.

Education and ethnic minorities

In our multi-racial society it would be foolish to pretend that we do not discriminate against certain ethnic minority groups. In his *Schools and Race: Five Views of Multi-Racial Britain* Alan Little supplies us with some data to give us an idea of the extent of a 'problem' experienced by one minority group in the education system:

Before you continue, are you sure that you understand the terms 'placed in the upper quartile' and 'Indigenous'?

We can see that the performance of pupils of Asian origin is similar to that of indigenous pupils but that children of West Indian origin perform badly. However, recent research, especially by the National Children's Bureau, indicates that second generation British West Indian children have improved educationally although they still lag behind both Asian and white pupils. Even so, as recently as 1985, the *Swann Report*, enquiring into the education of children from ethnic minority groups, confirmed that West Indian children still perform badly at school despite recent improvements. (See below.)

The report argues that the underachievement of black children is not the result of low IQ, nor the fault of teachers, but is associated with:

- low social and economic status of the majority of black families
- racial prejudice against ethnic minorities
- discrimination in society in

Percentage of pupils fully educated in the UK placed in the upper quartile on transfer to secondary school

	English	Mathematics	Verbal Reasoning
West Indian origin	9.2	7.4	7.2
Asian origin	19.3	20.2	21.2
Indigenous	25.0	22.9	19.8

Source: London Education Authority

How West Indian children perform in their education (percentages)

	O Levels 5 or more passes	O Level or CSE English	O Level or CSE Maths	A Level 1 or more passes	University entrance
West Indian children	6	15	8	5	1
Asian children	17	21	21	13	4
All other leavers	19	29	21	13	4

Source: Swann Report 1985

general and in the education system in particular.

An interesting question arises here. Since the Asian community experiences similar social deprivation and racial prejudice, why do Asian children achieve such relatively good results? The report suggests that this is because Asian communities keep a 'low profile' in white society, and exercise greater educational control over their children in tightly-knit family units. However, not all Asian children do well at school. An important group, the Bangladeshis, perform little better than West Indian children, despite low profile tightly-knit family units. The *Swann Report* does not attempt to explain this inconsistency.

In his study *Endless Pressure* Ken Pryce points out that West Indian parents have great aspirations for their children and see success in the education system as one way of achieving status in white society. So why do black children experience a learning problem? Again we have to look at the social and economic environment in which children are brought up. Many black children live in decaying run-down areas of cities and suffer the same deprivation as some poor white sections of the working class population, whose children also do badly at school. A tendency to bad health, faulty diet, overcrowded living conditions, unsatisfactory social amenities only add to the difficulties West Indian parents have in taking a proper interest in their children's education. In fact we can say that West Indian communities generally experience worse unemployment and poverty than any other social group. It would be surprising *not* to see this reflected in poor school performances.

EXERCISE

Explain in what way poor health and overcrowding are related to success or failure at school.

Much has been written about speech patterns of West Indians. We should be aware that these speech patterns are associated with the individual's social class as well as the geographical area of the West Indies from which the child or the child's parents originate. Some educationalists argue that one reason for the failure of West Indians in school is that white teachers do not understand them; but this is too simplistic. The natural language of most West Indian school children is an English-based creole. Put simply, a creole is a language system which has been developed in a particular social setting, in this case the West Indies. It is a simplified version of a source language, English, that was brought to the West Indies during periods of colonisation. Work started as a *Schools Council Project* at the University of Birmingham points out that many West Indian children are bidialectal in creole and standard English. What is important are the attitudes of teachers towards the dialects of their pupils. It is often the case that the use of a particular dialect or speech pattern is regarded as a sign of a lack of intelligence, and it is this misunderstanding that has created problems for the children of some West Indian parents:

When I'm at home I can follow what my parents say and they can follow what I say. And with my mates there's no problem either. It's just at school. You sometimes get the idea that the teacher thinks you're stupid and you can't help feeling that this has nothing to do with your ability but because you're black.

In other words, failure to conform to the teacher's views on 'correct

English' can lead pupils to be perceived as unintelligent.

We can also say that since racism has persisted within our society a West Indian sub-culture has developed and this has led many young black people to employ their distinctive linguistic forms to distance themselves from white society which they identify as hostile. This feeling of alienation is very real and is not only a feature of life in schools but a feature of West Indian life in general.

EXERCISE

Inglan is a bitch is written by Linton Kwesi Johnson, a British black sociologist, poet and recording artiste. The poem is written in a rhythmic dialect style and describes the bitter experiences of a first generation black person in Britain:

Inglan is a bitch
w'en mi jus' come to Landan toun
mi use to work pan di andahgroun
but workin' pan di andahgroun
y'u don't get fi know your way aroun'

Inglan is a bitch
dere's no escapin' it
Inglan is a bitch
dere's no runnin' whey fram it

mi get a lickle jab in a bit 'otell
an' awftah a while, mi woz doin' quite
   well
dem staat mi aaf as a dish-washah
but w'en mi tek a stack, mi noh tun
   clack-watchah!

Inglan is a bitch
dere's no escapin' it
Inglan is a bitch
noh baddah try fi hide fram it

w'en dem gi' you di lickle wage packit
fus dem rab it wid dem big tax rackit
y'u haffi struggle fi mek en's meet
an' w'en y'u goh a y'u bed y'u jus' cant
   sleep

Inglan is a bitch
dere's no escapin' it
Inglan is a bitch fi true
a noh lie mi a tell, a true

mi use to work dig ditch w'em it cowl
    noh bitch
mi did strang like a mule, but, bwoy,
    mi did fool
den awftah a while mi jus' stap dhu
    ovahtime
den awftah a while mi jus' phu dung
    mi tool

Inglan is a bitch
dere's no escapin' it
Inglan is a bitch
y'u haffi know how fi suvvive in it

well mi dhu day wok an' mi dhu nite
    wok
mi dhu clean wok an' mi dhu dutty
    wok
dem seh dat black man is very lazy
but if y'u si how mi wok y'u woulda
    sey mi crazy

Inglan is a bitch
dere's no escapin' it
Inglan is a bitch
y'u bettah face up to it

dem have a lickle facktri up inna
    Brackly
inna disya facktri all dem dhu is pack
    crackry
fi di laas fifteen years dem get mi
    laybah
now awftah fifteen years mi fall out a
    fayvah

Inglan is a bitch
dere's no escapin' it
Inglan is a bitch
dere's no runnin' whey fram it

mi know dem have work, work in
    abundant
yet still, dem mek mi redundant
now, at fifty – five mi gettin' quite ol'
yet still, dem sen' mi fi goh draw dole

Inglan is a bitch
dere's no escapin' it
Inglan is a bitch fi true
is whey wi a goh dhu 'bout it?

1 To get a clearer idea of this language form, write out the first 5 verses using standard English.
2 What evidence is there in the poem to support the argument that many black people in Britain experience social deprivation and alienation?
3 Using Bernstein's theories, explain

why some West Indian children experience disadvantage at school.

Life in the classroom

We have so far discussed the persistence of inequality in education in terms of social class, gender and race. We are now ready to move into the classroom itself to see if the social action taking place there has a bearing on educational performance:

Schooldays

John was late again. The papers were an hour late arriving at the newsagents so he was rushing to finish his paper round. He wasn't worried about being late for school, but he was worried about his homework. He had wanted to see his mate, Barry, to copy his. They had an arrangement. They each did homework on alternate nights and copied from each other, and the teachers hadn't copped-on. This convinced Barry and John that teachers didn't bother much with marking. If their class was doing A Levels it would be different, but in the words of one teacher, their class was full of no-hopers. Well, if that was what they wanted, that's what they would get. If the worst came to the worst you could always give Billings a sob story. He was the Maths teacher who always told the class that he was on their side. He said he understood them. He tried to talk their language and he liked to discuss the latest bands. He was OK in his way but he was soft, an ageing hippy. The best thing about Billings was that you could easily get him off the subject. He'd played in a band in the 1960s and he would tell the class boring stories from his hippy past. He still had long hair, but now it was receding. He looked a mess. You'd think with his money he would do something about his clothes! He

said clothes didn't matter that much, but he was lying. He was a real poser. He was so easy to set up.

This story shows that pupils have conscious images and ideas about their teachers. It also shows that pupils, as no doubt you are aware, are not just sitting in class passively listening to the teacher's words of wisdom. They are actively responding to a wide range of stimuli, some of which, perhaps most, have little to do with what is actually being taught. In other words, a classroom provides a setting in which complex social interactions are constantly taking place.

Teachers also have ideas and attitudes which they bring to their classes. This is how one teacher saw some members of his class. The notes on the following page were written by Mr Billings at the start of term.

The attitudes of teachers towards their pupils, as well as the pupils' attitudes towards teachers and towards each other, can have a significant bearing on social behaviour in the classroom.

This is what sociologists call the **sociology of the school** and it highlights the way pupils' identities are constructed as a result of classroom experiences. For example, John and his classmates in the story *Schooldays* were seen by their teachers as no-hopers and they tried to live up to this definition of themselves. Sociologists call this process **labelling**. Labelling has been investigated in a number of interesting studies. Before we examine one of these, David Hargreaves' *Social Relations in a Secondary School*, let us explain what is meant by labelling. If a teacher thinks that a pupil is unintelligent he may reinforce this view on every occasion he meets the pupil. Eventually the pupil accepts the teacher's

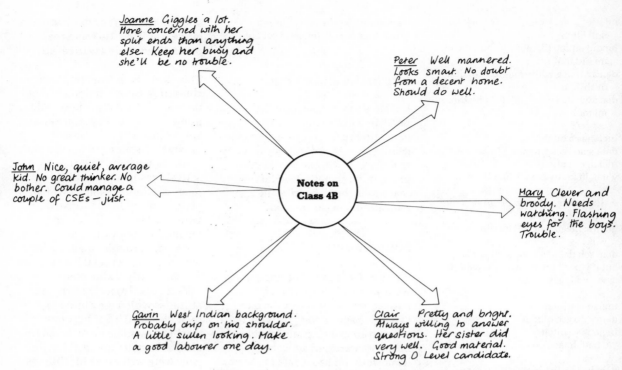

Notes on Class 4B

Joanne Giggles a lot. More concerned with her split ends than anything else. Keep her busy and she'll be no trouble.

Peter Well mannered. Looks smart. No doubt from a decent home. Should do well.

John Nice, quiet, average kid. No great thinker. No bother. Could manage a couple of CSEs — just.

Mary Clever and broody. Needs watching. Flashing eyes for the boys. Trouble.

Gavin West Indian background. Probably chip on his shoulder. A little sullen looking. Make a good labourer one day.

Clair Pretty and bright. Always willing to answer questions. Her sister did very well. Good material. Strong O Level candidate.

definition of his abilities and behaves in a way that corresponds to the teacher's negative views. This process of becoming what another person wants you to become is known as a **self-fulfilling prophecy**.

The interesting point about self-fulfilling prophecies is that pupils will respond to both positive and negative prophecies of their abilities. Think of your own abilities. The subjects you are best at now will probably be those where you have had the most encouragement as a result of a good relationship with a teacher. You are responding to his or her high expectations of you. Hargreaves' study showed how certain pupils were labelled as troublemakers and these pupils were mainly found in the schools' lower streams. The teachers had written them off as failures. Hargreaves found that in order to cope with these negative

definitions the pupil would seek out other troublemakers and this, in turn would lead to an informal group or subculture within the school. The troublemakers would gain prestige from one another by disrupting lessons, cheeking teachers, and generally getting noticed for the wrong reasons. Membership of this subculture usually leads to failure in the more legitimate school activities.

This research underlines how complex social life is within classrooms, and how teachers' attitudes, biases and prejudices might exert a powerful influence on how pupils judge themselves and their abilities. The girls in Sue Sharpe's study saw love, marriage, husbands and children as main goals in life mainly because their school and home experiences gave them fewer opportunities to explore other possibilities. This approach to the sociology of the school shows us that pupils themselves have an important influence in the classroom. When sociologists refer to **pupil**

strategies they are referring to the way pupils can manipulate the teachers. Copying from each other, steering teachers off the subject, not answering questions and disruptive behaviour are just a few examples of the stratagems pupils adopt to influence the course of events in the classroom.

EXERCISE

Can you think of any examples in your own school history where a teacher made a vital contribution to your success or failure? What pupil strategies have you experienced? Why were they employed and what was the result?

The transmission of knowledge

The school curriculum

As we have discussed the function of education in society, we can now look at the school curriculum. By curriculum we mean the official course of study followed by pupils at school. Each schoolchild will experience the curriculum through a weekly timetable. Every subject on the timetable tells the pupil that he or she will experience what sociologists call **knowledge transmission**. In simple terms, this means that after each lesson a pupil should know more than he or she knew before the lesson.

A reasonable question to ask is: What factors determine the choice of subjects or activities on the timetable? If you think about it, there are many subjects that could be included but usually are not (first-aid and politics). Some pupils may receive a bigger dose of some subjects (maths and English) than other subjects (history and geography) and many may not receive any tuition at all in particular areas (foreign languages). The only topic that must by law be taught to pupils in Britain is religious education. However, as we have shown earlier in the chapter, the social and economic forces that permeate our society reach far into schools and universities and exert an influence on the content of school and college curricula.

In a 1984 poll, *Britons observed*, conducted by the **Harris Research Centre** on behalf of *The Observer* newspaper (1084 respondents) mathematics was the subject that respondents thought the most important, with English running a close second and computer studies and science in third and fourth places. Social studies was well down the list. This perception of education in the general population is clearly reflected in the curricula of most schools.

The social divisions that exist in society are also reflected in the way school life is organised. It has to be remembered that schools are themselves organisations with management structures where status and power are held in the same high regard by staff as they are in other areas of society. The secondary school curriculum can be seen in similar terms. Schools tend to place high and low status values on subjects according to their degree of supposed worthiness. Here is a list of subjects that are taught in most schools. Rearrange them in 2 columns in what you believe are high and low status subjects:

Physics
Woodwork
French
Industrial craft
Mathematics
English literature
Physical education
Technical drawing

In general, high status subjects tend to be those that are more academic (usually involving a form of writing skill) and low status subjects those that are more practical (hand and eye skills). Thus parents and teachers tend to regard schools that are successful in academic subjects in greater esteem than schools which produce poorer academic results. Here are more details from the Harris survey:

Question a Which three of these subjects are the most important at school nowadays? And *b* which are the least important?

Most important		Least important
		Less than
81%	Mathematics	0.5%
79%	English	1%
29%	Computer studies	4%
22%	Science	4%
15%	Foreign languages	17%
10%	Business studies	10%
8%	Technical subjects	5%
8%	Religious education	37%
7%	Sex education	28%
6%	Home economics	16%
6%	Social studies	19%
6%	Economics	6%
6%	History	14%
6%	Physical education	18%
3%	Geography	8%
3%	Woodwork/ Metalwork	12%
2%	Peace studies	49%
1%	Art	35%

EXERCISE

The subjects we like best at school may not be the subjects that our parents would prefer us to like. Using the Harris survey as a guide, conduct a survey in your school to find out which subjects are thought by pupils to be the most important. Offer an explanation (if required) as to why the results of the 2 surveys should differ.

The hidden curriculum

If it is true that an important function of education is to give children instruction or guidance in acceptable social behaviour – what sociologists call secondary socialisation – then where does this appear on the timetable? In fact it does not appear. It is what is called the **hidden curriculum**. Here are some comments from pupils:

- The teacher always goes on about my dress. She thinks I'm not smart just because I dress in a different style. I bet I spend more time thinking about my appearance than she does ...
- The geography teacher told us that only morons watch *Crossroads* ...
- I'm grateful to Mr Harris because he helps me to keep out of trouble with the law. He runs the school's football team at the weekends. Next week he's giving me a chance in goal ...
- One of our teachers keeps going on about nuclear disarmament. She keeps telling us that we should ban all nuclear weapons in Britain. When I told my dad about it, he

went mad. You see, my dad believes in the nuclear deterrent. When I told the teacher that I thought having nuclear weapons stops other countries using them against us, she told me to shut up and get on with my work.

Examples of this kind are common school experiences but they are unlikely to be written down in the teacher's lesson notes. This does not mean they are unimportant. In fact they are vital ingredients in the whole process of what we know as education. They are powerful teaching tools. Combined with the **open** curriculum, the **hidden** curriculum performs an important role in shaping a child's view of the world.

Sociologists who understand society in terms of conflict take a critical view of the way the school curriculum is organised. They argue that the curriculum serves the interests of powerful economic and political groups in society by helping to keep young people 'in their place' by controlling their behaviour and by political bias in the selection of information. Knowledge is packaged in such a way that the views of the dominant system prevail (it might be capitalism or communism). For example, the facts relating to the history of the Second World War might be interpreted differently in a London school from how they would in a school in Washington or Moscow. What type of education children should receive, what subjects should be taught, and how they should be taught, are the kinds of critical questions these sociologists ask. A pupil hints at these criticisms in a poem he wrote for the school magazine. The poem was considered to be unsuitable by his teachers:

The kid who asked a question

There was a kid who asked a question
in school

Like why were some people rich and
why were some poor
The teachers told him to shut up and
stop
Playing the fool.

He went on to work in a sweatshop
He was covered in grease and grime
He asked about improving working
conditions
And the gaffer told him not to waste
his time.

He was put on the scrapheap
Just another old fool
But he found the answer to his
question
That he had asked back in school.

This poem may have been rejected because it is a bad poem or because it appeared to be critical of the way society is organised. The latter reason would fit in nicely with the arguments of the sociologists Pierre Bourdieu and his colleagues working in the Centre for European Sociology in Paris. Bourdieu argues that schools in Western societies process not knowledge but a culture based on the norms and values and accepted ways of thinking of the dominant classes. He goes further in his criticism. He argues that the education system has a major role in what he calls **the social function of elimination**.

By this he means that the majority of working class children are eliminated from higher levels of education. He points out that many working class pupils realise this from their experiences in and outside scshool. When they fail to show any great interest in what is taught they are being realistic because they know their chances of academic success are slim. Whatever we feel about these and other ideas one thing is clear: the time and money spent on education and the rewards given to those who succeed within it make it a crucial topic for study. But we cannot study education without reference to wider society. If we argue that the education system is still characterised by inequality for some social groups, we have to realise that these groups are subject to the same kinds of inequality in wider society.

EXERCISE

Explain in your own words what is meant by the term **hidden curriculum**. Give some examples of how some subjects in the **open curriculum** might be influenced by our social and political system.

QUESTIONS

1

The change in ability test scores of children between the ages of 8 and 11 years

Measured ability at 8 years of age – test scores	Children in an upper stream Average change in test scores between 8 and 11 years	Children in a lower stream Average change in test scores between 8 and 11 years
41–45	+5.67	−0.95
46–48	+3.70	−0.62
49–51	+4.44	−1.60
52–54	+0.71	−1.46
55–57	+2.23	−1.94
58–60	+0.86	−6.34

(+ indicates improvement in score. − indicates deterioration in score)
Source: *The Home and the School*, J. Douglas

a Using the previous table, state what average change occurred in the test scores of children in the upper stream whose test score at 8 years of age was 49–51. (1 mark)

b Using the table, state which ability group, in which stream showed
  i the greatest improvement in test scores
  ii the greatest deterioration in test scores. (2 marks)

c What does the table show about the possible effects of streaming on children? (2 marks)

d Socialisation and social control are thought to be two important functions of schools in industrial societies. Explain how schools carry out these functions. (6 marks)

e How important is the part played by schools in determining the educational achievement of a child? (9 marks)
  Source: AEB O Level 1983

2 Explain how the curricula of British schools may be related to the wider society. (20 marks)

3 Discuss whether the introduction of comprehensive schools has succeeded or failed to bring educational equality. (20 marks)

Case Study

Thank God for the holidays ...

These extracts are from a play set in a shabby 15-year-old comprehensive school in a city suburb. Mr Dobbs, the history teacher, is concluding a rowdy lesson on the Industrial Revolution with the mixed form 5B. Dobbs is a youngish, genial, and slightly incompetent teacher.

Mr Dobbs: Right, shut up you lot and close your notebooks. I'm going to test your memory to see how much you've taken in. Johnson, tell us all about the importance of the Bessemer process in steel making.

Johnson: I don't know Sir ... I've never heard of it. Isn't it time for a break (*shuffling of feet*) ... I'm bursting.

Mr Dobbs: You'd better not burst in here Johnson. You lot are wet enough already (*cheers*). Come on, what's the answer? You're supposed to be doing the steel industry for your CSE project.

Johnson: But I wanna pee, Sir.

Mr Dobbs: You'll have to wait. You can't just walk away from a problem by going to the toilet. That's what tea breaks are for.

Franklin: (*seeking an audience*) I prefer to drink beer myself.

Mr Dobbs: You would. Vanessa (*who is admiring herself in a mirror*) put those things away. You know the school rules about wearing make up.

Vanessa: Rules are stupid, Sir. Why can't we wear lipstick if we want to? What's wrong with make-up? Everyone wears it these days.

Franklin: Even Johnson! (*uproar*)

Johnson: Shut yer face, Franklin, you're all mouth.

Franklin: Vanessa's seeing Johnson tonight at 8 o'clock. What do you think of that, Sir?

Mr Dobbs: Give it a rest Franklin. (*To Vanessa*) What have I told you? Put it away. This is a classroom, not a boudoir.

Franklin: What's a boudoir, Sir?

Mr Dobbs: It's a ladies bedroom, Franklin. Something that you've had no experience of. (*laughter*)

Vanessa: Are you married, Sir?

Mr Dobbs: What's that got to do with anything?

Vanessa: I bet your wife wears make-up, don't she Sir?

Mr Dobbs: No, she doesn't, because I'm not married.

Franklin: Ooooh – I'm free – shut that door – shut that door ... (*whistles and uproar as school bell goes*).

Mr Dobbs: All right, you rabble, off you go. And not all at once.

Scene: staff room
Smith: Coffee for you Mike?

Dobbs: Thanks Ruth. My God, what a lesson! That lot in 5B want chucking out, the lot of them. Thank God for the school holidays on Friday.

Smith: Surely not all of them?

Richards: How do you find Franklin?

Dobbs: A pain in the posterior. Can't we do something about him? Can't we recommend him for expulsion or something? What about remedial education?

Richards: I think he should be put down into 5C. That'll teach him.

Smith: He'll probably enjoy the notoriety. He was bragging in my lesson about how many uncles he's got in prison. I understand he's been taken into care. Actually, come to think about it, he's a lot cleverer than he pretends. He's bright enough in biology to do an O Level.

Dobbs: He isn't clever in my class. Anyway, being clever isn't enough, is it? You've got to apply yourself in this world to be successful. He's too busy playing to the gallery.

Smith: Perhaps you're right. I'll be sorry to see him go down to 5C, all the same.

Scene: school canteen
Johnson: What have we got next, Dave?

Franklin: I dunno. I lost all my notes last night, didn't I? Some geezer broke into my room and nicked my bag when I was round the pub. Can you lend me a quid?

Vanessa: Why didn't you tell Dobbs about your bag being stolen? It would have saved you that argument with him. Oh, you are stupid, Dave.

Franklin: Dobbs is a dodo.

Vanessa: What's a dodo?

Franklin: I dunno. But it sounds good, don't it?

Johnson: Yeah, I like that. Dobbs is

a dodo. Yeah, we'll have to make up a saying for Miss Miles ... What about Miss Miles is vile ... Yeah, great ... What about old Hurd?

Franklin: Old Hurd is a ...

Vanessa: Leave off, will you ... he's sitting behind us.

Johnson: Dobbs has really got it in for you, Dave. He'll kick you out of this place if you don't watch it. You're getting a reputation son. We're leaving school in May. Don't you want your CSEs?

Franklin: What's the point of a few CSEs? I'm gonna finish up on the rock and role anyway. I think an uncle of mine might fix me up with a nice little number down the market. No tax or insurance or nothing. I might as well have a good time while I'm here.

QUESTIONS

1 Explain, with reference to the extracts, what sociologists mean by the terms:
  a labelling; and
  b pupil strategies
2 Describe some of the social experiences in the lives of working class children that are likely to affect their education for the worst.
3 'A primary aim of education is social control.' Explain the meaning of this, using examples from the extracts.

Points for discussion

- Children learn much more from each other than they do from teachers.
- There is no such thing as bad pupils, only bad teaching.
- The wearing of school uniforms should be compulsory.

Case Study

The government's view

In September 1984 the government published a paper entitled *The organisation and content of the 5–16 curriculum* which made some recommendations about how the school curriculum should be organised. Here are a few extracts:

This paper is concerned with what all pupils should be offered during the compulsory period and what some pupils should be offered additionally. The purpose of this paper is to raise questions and to invite comments on them, with a view to establishing as wide a measure of agreement as possible.

5 Important elements of the curriculum which should be offered by schools are not subjects. Examples are the opportunity to develop personal qualities, to learn desirable modes of behaviour, to acquire study skills, or to become familiar with the broadly shared values of our society. Such elements may be taught in the course of teaching subjects, or by combining elements from several subjects to make a specific course.

The primary phase (5–10)
8 Children develop very quickly during their time in primary schools. The primary phase should help pupils to get the most out of the process of growing up and should build on their natural enthusiasm during this period of rapid change. To this end, the skills and knowledge acquired in the primary phase should help pupils to learn to understand themselves, their relationships with others and the world around them; should stimulate their curiosity and teach them to apply it purposefully and usefully; and should develop those personal qualities and attitudes which, if acquired during the primary phase, provide a sound foundation for what follows. The primary phase should:

- place substantial emphasis on achieving competence in the use

of language and in mathematics;
- introduce pupils to science;
- provide worthwhile offerings which develop understanding in the area of history, geography and RE;
- offer a range of aesthetic activities;
- provide opportunities throughout the curriculum for craft and practical work leading up to some experience of design and technology and of solving problems;
- offer physical and health education;
- introduce pupils to computers; and
- give them some insights into the adult world, including how people earn their living.

The secondary phase (11–16)
11 It is government policy that the 11–16 curriculum for all pupils, in addition to RE, should contain English; mathematics; science; a worthwhile offering of the humanities; aesthetic subjects; practical subjects; and physical education; and a foreign language for most pupils.
16 The following paragraphs set out, in summary form, some provisional views on the place of the main subjects in the 11–16 curriculum.
17 There can be no question that *English* and *Mathematics* should be compulsory for all pupils.
18 *Religious education* is the only subject which has a statutory place in the curriculum.
19 *Science* at school is generally thought of as, at least, three subjects – physics, chemistry and biology. Government policy is that all pupils should be introduced to each of the three.
21 Some of the least able pupils should not study a *foreign language*; that a large majority of pupils should study one for 3 years; and that some should study one for 5 years and a second for 2 or 3 years.

22 Some pupils are bound to devote less time to the *humanities* than others. During the 5 secondary years, every pupil should study history, geography, and principles underlying a free society and some basic awareness. But choices will have to be made in years 4 and 5. Is it acceptable that any of these, 3 elements can be dropped in these 2 years?

23 *Aesthetic subjects.* Each pupil should have at least either music or art or drama in his programme, and every pupil's 5 year programme should contain all three.

24 Attention needs to be given to the *application of knowledge and skills.* This objective is relevant to a wide range of subjects, notably mathematics and the sciences. The growing availability of computers to schools provides the opportunity for applying some of the knowledge and skills acquired in a wide range of subjects. The removal of clutter, for example in the form of knowledge which is less essential, from many existing syllabuses would help to make room for the practical applications of what is learned.

25 *Design and technology* is the subject in which practical applications are fostered. Throughout the 5 year period all pupils should have in their programme this subject which requires them to study and solve problems involving the use of materials and which entails some element of designing and making things.

26 *Home economics* should be included in all pupils' curriculum during the course of the first 3 years. Thereafter it should continue to be available as an option.

27 *Pre-vocational studies* which specifically seek to assist young people to prepare for the world of work.

28 *Physical education* is widely believed to be a compulsory subject in the curriculum.

29 In addition room is commonly found for a number of areas of varying importance. *Social education, environmental education, computer studies, careers education* and *health education.* Other topics, such as the issues of peace and war, do not normally have time specifically devoted to them but arise naturally in various parts of the curriculum. Some of these areas, such as careers, health and social education, are essential ingredients of a broad and relevant curriculum.

QUESTIONS

Read and understand *The organisation and content of the 5–16 curriculum* thoroughly before you attempt the questions.

1 In what way are these proposals for changes in the curriculum different from the more traditional curricula in secondary school education? You may illustrate your answer by referring to your present timetable if you wish.

2 Using extracts from the paper, show that the government acknowledges the social function of education.

3 'Education is mainly a preparation for a working life.' Quoting details from the paper, explain whether the government is moving towards or away from this way of thinking.

Points for discussion

- These proposals prove that the government is really trying to provide a more practical education for the majority of pupils.
- Education is something more than a preparation for work; it is a preparation for life.
- Most school work is boring.

Important points

- Education is a process by which we transmit the culture of a society from one generation to the next.

- Formal education mostly takes place within a school or college classroom. Informal education is the process of learning through experience.
- The 1944 Education Act introduced free state schooling under a tripartite system of education based on an 11-plus examination.
- Comprehensive schools, which were introduced in the 1960s, accepted all children from primary schools without selection.
- The success or failure of a pupil at school under any system of education is largely determined by external social factors.
- There are fewer educational opportunities for working class children than for middle class children.
- The kind of speech pattern used by a child's family and peers might be influential in determining the degree of academic success or failure.
- The main purposes of education are to provide the skills and knowledge in preparation for a working life, instil the accepted moral values of society, encourage the development of social skills, act as an agent of social control and provide social and economic amenities.
- Poverty and deprivation are associated with failure at school.
- Despite greater educational opportunities, the proportions of working class and middle class students attending university have not substantially changed in the last 70 years.
- Although the social and economic position of women has improved, women from working class backgrounds tend to underachieve in the education system.
- Educational inequality within ethnic minority communities is

associated with language difficulties and poverty.
- The social pressures that teachers and pupils exert on each other in the classroom will affect a pupil's educational performance.
- The choice of subjects in the school curriculum is related to the social and economic needs of society.

5 Work

When you have worked through this chapter you should have a clearer understanding of

The division of labour · **Intrinsic job satisfaction** · **Extrinsic job satisfaction** · **Facets of alienation** · **Patterns of leisure** · **Inequalities at work** · **Work deprivation** · **Extreme occupations** · **Mechanisation** · **Automation** · **Aspects of trade union influence and power**

What is work?

If we think carefully about the nature of work in society we might understand that the activity we call work is a very important part of human behaviour. Not only can we spend a lot of our time at work but we also depend on the work of others if our lives are to run smoothly. We rely on a vast unseen army of people to provide the goods and services that enable us and the world we live in to function effectively. The people who produce these goods and services in exchange for wages are called workers. In fact we can define work as a paid activity based on a contract of employment between an employer and an employee.

Work in a society like ours, an industrial society, is mainly based on what is termed the **division of labour**. By this we mean that an individual worker is expected to concentrate his or her skill in a limited or specialised area of work. For example, in the mass production of motor cars there are few workers who are solely employed to produce complete cars. A so-called car worker is

more likely to be working as a body or engine assembly worker, a welder, a paint sprayer, or a car salesperson. (See also pp 204–5.)

EXERCISE

Draw up a list of some of the workers who have provided the goods and services which you have used today. Set down your information under these headings:

What activity have I been involved in today so far?

Types of job or workers who have made this activity possible

You may have been woken this morning by an alarm clock, washed, dressed and listened to the radio while you ate breakfast. You may have used public transport to get to school or college so that you can read this book! All of this involved workers such as clockmakers, water and sewage workers, clothing and electronic assembly workers, milkmen, farmers, bus drivers, teachers and printers. The air you are now breathing has probably been altered by the work of someone. It will have been heated, cooled, filtered, blown or polluted

in one way or another. We can now begin to see how important work is for us as individuals and for society as a whole.

Availability of work

Those who do not or cannot work full time are children under the age of 16, students completing full-time education and those who are too old or too sick to work, who may receive some form of pension. Many women prefer to remain temporarily or permanently out of the labour market to have and to raise children or to care for the family home. In any practical sense, work is simply unavailable to a large section of our society. Can you identify any other non-working groups?

For those who want to work but cannot, the most potent factor is the availability of jobs. During 1984–85 recorded unemployment levels hovered around 3 million. Most job losses have occurred in manufacturing industries in specific areas of the country. Engineering-based industries, steel, shipbuilding and coal-

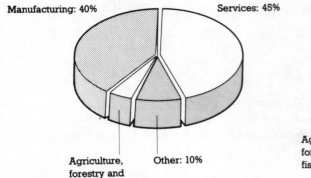

1955

Manufacturing: 40%

Services: 45%

Agriculture, forestry and fishing: 5%

Other: 10%

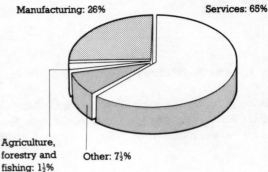

1984

Manufacturing: 26%

Services: 65%

Agriculture, forestry and fishing: 1½%

Other: 7½%

The changing patterns of employment, 1955 and 1984
Source: Employment: The Challenge for the Nation

mining are badly affected, and if you happen to live in one of the areas coloured black on the following chart of Britain, you will be aware of the limited job opportunities available.

Generally speaking, however, over a 30-year period between 1956 and 1984 there has been a substantial shift in employment patterns from the manufacturing to the servicing industries, as this extract from a White Paper shows:

Types of jobs

Of the 26½ million people in the labour force, over 23 million are in work. This is not very different from the total in work 30 years ago; but the similarity masks big changes in the nature and location of jobs.

In 1955 manufacturing accounted for 40% of employees in employment; in 1984, 26%. But the service sector has grown from 45 to 65%.

The sectoral shift has been matched by an occupational shift: even within manufacturing industry a much higher proportion of people are in non-manual occupations, particularly scientific, technological

and professional ones.

The number of self-employed has grown markedly too – from 1·7 million in the 1950s to 2·4 million now.

With the change in the industrial balance, there has been a change in the geographical balance, hitting hard those regions most dependent on the older industries. But other regions meanwhile have profited from the growth of new services and high-technology manufacturing.

Source: Employment: The Challenge for the Nation.

Can you name 5 manufacturing jobs and 5 servicing jobs?

As a sociologist studying areas of heavy unemployment involving perhaps whole communities, you would expect to find many social problems associated directly and indirectly with unemployment.

EXERCISE

This chart shows the likelihood of remaining unemployed during the winter of 1982–83. Study it closely and answer the following questions:

1 Generally speaking, which geographical regions have the most and the least unemployment?
2 Regarding types of industry and population density, what do areas of high unemployment have in common, and what do areas of low employment

have in common?
3 Identify 6 cities experiencing high unemployment (with Atlas).
4 In a city or large town with a high and long-term unemployment record, what kinds of social problems are you likely to find? Make a list.

Family influence

Having established how important the availability of work is in our society we can now consider how people choose particular jobs. As sociologists we know that people's behaviour and attitudes are influenced by a number of social factors.

What could influence a person in choosing a job?

An important influence is the family. Think for a moment how your family may have tried to influence you. In this extract one worker recalls his experiences:

Both my parents are teachers and they really encouraged me to enter the teaching profession. When I was a kid they spent more time with me than other parents might because they had longer holidays. Eventually I became a teacher myself. I think their influence was really important. It seemed natural for me to follow in their footsteps.

We know that families represent a

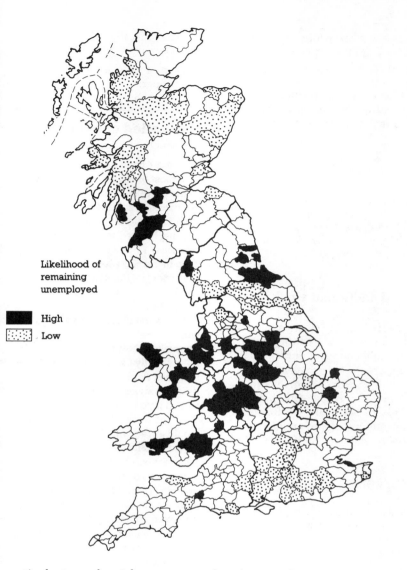

Likelihood of
remaining
unemployed

■■■ High

[:::::] Low

particular type of social group within the structure of society and we also know from the chapter on social stratification that the family in the extract is middle class. So we can say that a family, and in particular the social class of an individual's family, can have a great influence on how a person chooses a job. Of course we might think that if someone is really determined they can achieve almost anything in terms of a career, but as sociologists we are careful not to make a statement such as this. We can turn to the evidence provided

by other sociologists to help us understand the importance of family background in determining job choice. In a study carried out by Halsey, Heath and Ridge, *Origins and Destinations*, the relationship between social class and education was explored.

Why should social class and education be related to choosing a job?

We are right to think that the more qualifications a person has the better the job he or she can apply for. This factor is even more

crucial during times of high unemployment. The study *Origins and Destinations* looked at 8529 males educated in England and Wales and found that the pupil from the middle class had a much better chance of getting qualifications from the education system than a working class pupil. For example, it showed that a young person from the middle classes had 8 times more chance of being at school at the age of 17 compared with a person from the working classes, 10 times more chance at the age of 18 and 11 times more chance of entering university. If we accept that education opportunities and qualifications are related to employment prospects, we can see how useful the findings of these sociologists are.

We have shown the complex but nevertheless very real relationship between family background, education and work. Given the importance of educational and training qualifications in our technological society, we can see how family background, education and choice of employment combine to provide clear advantages to the child of middle class parents.

EXERCISE

How much influence would you say your family is having in forming your attitudes about work or job choice? You must take into account their influences regarding the kind of education you receive and the subjects you are encouraged to study.

Social class and education

We have established that to understand how people choose their jobs and careers we have to take into account the influence of social class and education. Of course we would be foolish to imagine that no-one from the working classes goes to university and gets a highly paid job. There is, as we know, a certain amount of social mobility in our society, which means that there are opportunities to move up the social ladder. But getting the right qualifications is only part of the story. Again we can return to the family and its influence:

Actually it was all rather easy for me when I came down from university. I wanted to work in finance and an uncle in the City put in a good word for me with an American finance house. Naturally I got the job. Yes, I suppose I was lucky, but that's part of it isn't it – knowing the right people and having family connections?

Although not everyone who goes to university will have this kind of experience, there does appear to be many examples of it nevertheless. Phrases such as 'the old boy network' and 'it's not what you know but who you know' are examples of this. Of course some people might say that those who believe this sort of thing are simply jealous and are making excuses because they themselves have failed to get to the top. But two writers, Ralph Miliband in *The State in Capitalist Society* and Anthony Sampson in *The New Anatomy of Britain*,

suggest that the 'old boy network' exists and it is often the way in which people are recruited into the top jobs.

Let us sum up the most important influences in choosing a job in the form of a diagram. (See below.)

EXERCISE

In the diagram you can identify 4 fairly important factors which influence our job prospects. Make a copy of this and add any other factors that could influence a person's choice of jobs.

Satisfaction at work

We are likely to spend a lot of our time at work and while getting enough money for our efforts is important – a fair day's pay for a fair day's work – many people want to enjoy the work they do. This leads sociologists to look at the amount of **job satisfaction** people get from their work.

EXERCISE

Make a list of 5 jobs which you think might give you satisfaction, and indicate if the jobs have anything in common. Then make a second list of

jobs that you just couldn't do no matter how much you were paid.

This article appeared in a local newspaper:

A satisfied couple
by Pam Freely

John and Alison Roberts are happy. Like most of us they could do with a little more cash, but running their hairdressing salon 'Curls' they wouldn't swap their jobs with anyone. I talked to John during a very busy Friday afternoon at his shop in the High Street.

'It's not just that I'm my own boss,' he told me, 'it's a number of different things. First of all I like meeting people and talking to them. You wouldn't believe some of the things people tell their hairdresser! But the thing I really like is that I can use my initiative. People will ask me about different styles. They see me as an expert if you like.'

At this point Alison chipped in. 'I would agree with that. I like the responsibility that goes with the job. It's great when you've finished styling someone's hair and they tell you how pleased they are. You get a feeling that you have actually achieved something.'

'Yes,' John added, 'at the end of the day you think that you've made someone feel better. You've been creative and the job gives you the chance to use your imagination. You might be rushed off your feet but you don't mind. At least you feel fulfilled.'

After John had used his imagination on my hair I left the shop. I wondered how many people were as satisfied with their work as John and Alison. In many ways they are lucky, not only do they own their shop, which gives them a certain amount of control over what they do, but the type of work they do, as they both point out, gives them the opportunity to be creative and to use their imagination. In short, they are using their talents to the full.

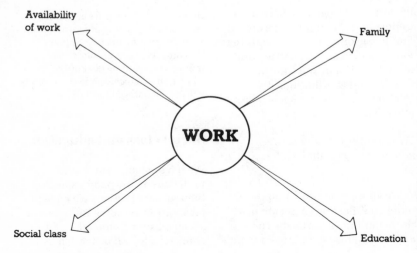

Availability
of work

Family

WORK

Social class

Education

Make a few notes about what John and Alison found satisfying in their jobs. Compare their views with the points you made in the previous exercise. In what way are your views similar to theirs?

The attitudes shown towards work by John and Alison are part of what sociologists call **intrinsic job satisfaction**. This means that they both feel that their jobs are worth doing, that they are providing a useful service, and that they genuinely like what they do for a living. Of course not everyone at work is in this position. Because of the various social factors operating within our society many people have the opposite attitude to that expressed by John and Alison. A great number of people at work have little or no interest in their jobs, and work is simply a means towards an end. These workers find enjoyment mainly in their non-work time, as this worker explains:

All I think about is getting out of this place as soon as I can. The job is really boring, and to be honest, a trained monkey could do what I do each day. I just think of the money at the end of the week and what I'm going to do at the weekend.

Sociologists such as J. H. Goldthorpe have called this an **instrumental attitude** towards work (or **extrinsic job satisfaction**). Some sociologists have argued that this attitude is experienced by many workers in industrial societies and may lead to a state of mind known as **alienation**.

EXERCISE

Draw up a list of 5 jobs that you think most people would find boring. Produce a similar list of jobs that are likely to provide a high degree of job satisfaction. Make comments about what the jobs in each list have in common.

Alienation

One writer who has tried to deal with this subject is Robert Blauner in his book *Alienation and Freedom*. What does Blauner mean by **alienation** and **freedom**?

Think back to the hairdressers, John and Alison. Let us try to imagine their working day. They open up shop and the first customer arrives. They talk to the customer about what he or she wants done. While as skilled hairdressers they have a rough idea of how long the job will take, nothing is written down which says 'you must complete this job in 25 minutes' – how long they spend with each customer is decided by them and them alone. They can chat to the customer and when they have finished they can discuss the results. As John says, at the end of the day he feels satisfied. This is what Blauner is getting at in his book. He is saying that John and Alison are experiencing 'freedom' in the way their working lives are organised.

Let us take this a little further by looking at a worker who has an instrumental attitude towards work:

Monday is the worst day of the week – I dread it. I arrive at twenty-five past seven and go straight to my machine. and dead on half-seven I start working. My machine drills holes in metal strips and I've done this job now for 5 years. At quarter past nine we get a 15 minute break and after that we work till 12.30. Then everything stops for 3 quarters of an hour, and at 1.15 we start again. The same old strips and the same holes! At 3.00 we have another break for 10 minutes and I work on to the 4.30 finish. I'm glad to see the back of the place. I can't get away fast enough. I never talk about work at home. I mean, what can I say? Every day is exactly the same. I'm like a machine myself. Sitting there at my bench punching holes in metal strips. A mate of mine was transferred to the packing department after working in

my section for 12 years. All she did was pack machined parts into boxes. I asked her if she liked her new job and she said she was over the moon with it. She enjoyed the responsibility. Can you imagine that? A child could have done her job. Sometimes my husband asks me about the people I work with. I hardly know any of them. It's not as if you can have a chat with the noise from the machines. I just think about the end of the week when I get my wages. When I'm not thinking about that I'm daydreaming or thinking about the programmes on last night's telly.

This account describes a situation where a worker gets very little job satisfaction. Her job is repetitive and she certainly isn't involved in any decision-making. In fact we can see from her description that her work-day is controlled minutely, and even the noise in the factory makes it difficult for her to talk to her workmates. For Robert Blauner this worker would be experiencing alienation at work. Her job offers almost nothing in the way of satisfaction.

Blauner uses the term **alienation** to describe people's attitudes towards their work. Of course he didn't go to them and say: 'Excuse me, are you alienated?' He had to decide first how he would approach the issue of satisfaction at work. From the previous two accounts we probably have some idea ourselves of what we would look at. Blauner suggests that different jobs produce different attitudes towards work. He argues that when we look at people at work these guidelines are a useful measure of job satisfaction:

- **Powerlessness.** How much control does a worker have over his or her job? What decisions is the worker allowed to make for himself, for example?
- **Meaninglessness.** How much does the individual worker feel he has achieved? Does the work have any real meaning? Is there a recognisable final product?

- **Isolation.** How much personal involvement is there? Does the worker see himself as part of a team, or does he feel cut off?
- **Self-estrangement.** Does the worker feel debased by what he is doing? Does he feel as though he is letting himself down by involving himself in trivial or limiting activities?

EXERCISE

As an experiment, try to discover for yourself a particular worker's attitude towards his or her work. (It might be better to choose someone you know personally.) Using your own ideas draw up a short questionnaire of about 10 questions designed to find out what the person feels about his or her job.

Produce a short report to indicate the degree of alienation you have found.

Blauner did not look at every job but he did try to identify aspects of particular jobs which could then be applied to others. For example, he found that printers were the least alienated and most satisfied workers he came across. He suggested that this was because they used their unique skill in deciding for themselves how particular jobs should be carried out. The work they did was varied, there was never a set routine, and there were different kinds of printing jobs available. He also pointed out that printers often work in a team and have a lot of pride in their work.

The least satisfied workers were those who worked on an assembly line, like the woman in our extract. The work involved repetition and the workers had little control over what they did. There was little skill involved and often they felt cut off from their workmates.

The most important feature of Blauner's work is that he gives us some points to think about when we look at satisfaction at work. He also gives us questions to ask if we want to find out if a particular job offers satisfaction or not.

EXERCISE

Take a copy of this chart and, using Blauner's guidelines, estimate the degree of alienation experienced by these 10 workers. In each of the 4 columns following every occupation record a score up to a maximum of 4 based on these categories:

4 = experienced to a high degree
3 = experienced to some degree
2 = experienced, but only slightly
1 = not experienced
0 = the opposite is experienced

Occupation	Powerless-ness	Meaningless-ness	Isolation	Self estrangement	Totals
Nurse					
Garage mechanic					
Production-line worker					
Coal-miner					
Waiter					
Schoolteacher					
Check-out assistant in supermarket					
Typist					
Police officer					
Lorry driver					

Compare your totals with other people's and discuss your results. A score of 16 will indicate a maximum degree of alienation.

Work and leisure

Although we have looked at the attitudes people have towards their work, sociologists are also interested in the relationship between work and leisure. The first problem we have to deal with in understanding work and leisure is what exactly do we mean by these terms? Where do we draw the line between the two? For example, which of the following do you consider to be work and which do you consider to be leisure?

First take a copy of this chart

Tick box

Activity	Work	Leisure
Housework	☐	☐
Travel to work	☐	☐
Childcare	☐	☐
Personal care	☐	☐
Shopping for food and clothes	☐	☐
Eating	☐	☐
Sleeping	☐	☐
Visiting relatives	☐	☐
Mending the car	☐	☐
Attending classes to study sociology	☐	☐
Meals and breaks during paid work time	☐	☐
Being unemployed	☐	☐

Don't be surprised if you had second thoughts about which column to tick. Whether you chose column 1 or 2 will probably have more to do with your attitudes towards the subject rather than a choice based on undisputed facts. Whether or not we get paid for the activity or whether it is a duty or a pleasure are the sorts of questions that we might have asked ourselves. Generally speaking, we can define leisure as an unpaid activity, not involving any contractual obligations, that we usually enjoy during our free time.

Returning to our simple definition of work as being a paid activity under a contract of employment, many sociologists have shown that the work we do has a powerful influence on our leisure activities. This is how work affects one young worker:

I work in a large city centre store and I have to work all day Saturday which is our busiest day. I get time off in the week but it's not the same. I used to follow the local football team even when they were playing away, but now the only time I can get there is when they play evening games. It's not that I miss the football so much – I also miss seeing the old crowd who go to the games ... especially the darts game before the match in the *Black Horse* ... but that's how it is with my kind of job.

EXERCISE

Can you think of any other ways in which work can affect someone's leisure time? You can start your list with weekend working (shop-work) You must also take into account different wage levels.

One sociologist who has studied the way work affects leisure is Stanley Parker in his book *The Future of Work and Leisure*. Parker argues that if we look carefully at jobs we can see the relationship between work and leisure falling into patterns.

First there are the jobs that extend into leisure time. Here work is very important to the workers involved and they might find that when they get home, instead of forgetting about the job, they will continue to think about it and possibly do some work at home. Workers who find themselves in this position see their jobs as one of their main interests in life. Parker calls this arrangement of work and leisure the **extension pattern** because work activity extends into non-work time and becomes itself an ingredient of leisure time.

This extract is taken from a personal letter written by an oil executive to a job-hunting university graduate:

Don't imagine coming into my game gives you an easy life. Sometimes I'm at it for 16 hours a day, and I hardly ever get a chance to see my family from one month to the next. Last week I was in the Middle East and tomorrow I'm flying to the States. My salary is enormous of course – and there are other compensations – but there's a price to pay. I live, eat and sleep oil.

A second and possibly larger group of workers tends to make a clear distinction between what they do at work and what they do in their non-work time. This type of worker would see his outside activities as his main interest in life. This is how one worker expressed her point of view on work and leisure on a recent radio phone-in programme:

Caller. I work in this small office and I don't think I'd say my job was that interesting.
Interviewer. Well why do you work there then?
Caller. That's easy. I work for the money. I mean it's not a bad job as jobs go. I could do with more money, but then who couldn't? My working conditions are pretty good and I've got a great social and family life. I just work

for the money.

This worker doesn't dislike her job, it's just that there are other things in her life which she thinks are more important. Parker calls this mix of work and leisure the **neutral pattern**.

There is a third group of workers who do dangerous or unpleasant work in conditions that most of us would hate. Coal-miners, deep-sea fishermen and sewerage workers are examples. Parker suggests that such workers use their leisure-time to make up for the danger and unpleasantness of their jobs. Leisure is a way of getting completely away from distasteful work and is often spent relaxing with mates in a pub or working men's clubs. Work and leisure have become totally separated and mutually exclusive into an **opposition pattern**. Sometimes this leisure takes on extravagant forms with a 'I-work-hard-and-I-play-hard' attitude. Back to the phone-in:

Interviewer. Did you say you were a brickie's labourer? And what do you get up to in your spare time?
Caller. I go crazy. Nothing better than an all-night party for me, or a big booze-up with me mates. Then I like going to the night clubs in town with me mate. You know, pick up a couple of girls like and back to his flat and then ... hello ... have we been cut off?
Interviewer. Er ... well ... getting a bit strong there ... Do you have any hobbies or anything?
Caller. I don't have any real hobbies. I like drinking and the horses. I never read or anything like that. Sometimes I work every day for weeks on end, and then I might get laid off.
Interviewer. Do you like your job?
Caller. No. I hate it. I couldn't go to work at all if I didn't have a blow-out in town now and again.

Although we can see that Parker's theory is a very useful way of understanding the relationship between work and leisure, we are wise enough to know that an individual worker is unlikely to fall completely within any one of the 3 categories, and is more likely to experience an unequal proportion of each.

EXERCISE

Working in pairs, make a copy of this table and suggest 3 jobs you think should fit into each category. Explain clearly the reasons for your choice.

Work and leisure

Relationship between work and leisure	Type of job	Reasons for choice
Extension pattern You take the work home with you.	1	
	2	
	3	
Neutral pattern Work is just a place to earn money.	1	
	2	
	3	
Opposition pattern Leisure is a compensation for a lousy job.	1	
	2	
	3	

influence their leisure time. We can now take our examination of work a stage further. Peter Townsend has looked at what he calls **work deprivation** in his study *Poverty in the United Kingdom*.

What do you think he means by the term work deprivation? What is it?

Townsend does not mean by this that we are deprived of work (ie unemployed) but that many working people might suffer from **deprivation at work**. In order to develop this concept of work deprivation, Townsend, in his

get an idea of the extent of work deprivation found in the 1979 Townsend study. On the left of the table are job descriptions which might indicate undesirable features of a particular job:

Percentage of men and women experiencing different kinds of deprivation at work

	Men %	Women %
The character of the job		
Working mainly or entirely outdoors	31	4
All working time standing or walking	57	42
At work before 8am or working at night	36	15
Working 50 or more hours a week	24	4
Security		
Unemployed more than 2 weeks in last 12 months	5	4
Subject to 1 week's notice or less	44	51
Conditions and amenities		
Working conditions poor or very poor	23	15
Welfare or fringe benefits		
No wages or salary during sickness	37	35
Paid holidays of 2 weeks or less	56	61
No meals paid for or subsidised by employer	76	69
No entitlement to occupational pension	43	61

EXERCISE

1 Examine this table carefully. What general conclusions can you make about job deprivation as experienced by these workers? Can you explain the similarities and differences between the work of men and women?
2 In the following table, Townsend's main headings have been placed alongside 5 occupations. After group discussion, make some brief notes in the appropriate spaces to show that you have a rough idea of the differences between the jobs.

Inequality at work

We have established that work is vitally important for the smooth running of our society and we are aware of the different social factors which lead people to choose particular jobs. We know also from the work of Blauner that certain workers derive satisfaction from their jobs, and from Parker that the work people do can

study of 2000 working class households in the United Kingdom, examined the following factors:

- the job itself (what the person actually does)
- the security of the job
- the conditions the worker experiences at work
- the welfare and fringe benefits which go with the job.

From the following table we can

Set out your table like this. Leave plenty of room for your written answers.

Occupation	The job itself	Security	Conditions	Welfare
Production line worker				
School teacher				
Fashion designer				
Bricklayer				
Sales assistant				

In a recent newspaper feature article this is how one managing director described his work. Ask yourself: What work deprivation does he experience?

I've got responsibility for the overall running of the company, which is demanding, but I really enjoy it. In fact my wife says I'm married to the company and not to her! The job is very secure and I don't have any serious financial worries. Should I ever have to leave this job then I'd expect a very good golden handshake. We've recently moved to new premises which are very plush indeed. I've even got a shower unit in my office and I keep a couple of suits there in case I have to go straight out in the evening for dinner with an overseas client. My two children are away at boarding school and the company has been very good in that they help to pay the school fees, and each year I get a bonus based on the overall profits of the company. I've got a company car – a new Rover actually – and also a couple of credit cards which I use for company expenses. I know I'm lucky but I think I deserve to be.

Although there might be an element of truth in the final comment, the experiences of the managing director are somewhat different from the experiences of many of the working class employees in Townsend's book.

We can see that for a number of reasons the actual experience of work is not pleasant for many people. Townsend also shows that manual workers generally work longer hours than non-manual workers. In fact, he found that 38% of non-manual workers worked less than 40 hours a week. He also shows us that work deprivation can be related to bad health. In the sample a significant number of manual workers had to have 3 weeks or more off work during the year due to illness. Townsend points out that the farther you move up the occupational hierarchy, or the social class ladder. the less time you are away from work due to bad health.

The importance of the Townsend study is that it highlights the inequalities at work in showing the various deprivations many manual workers have to face. The sociological study of deprivation in work has tended, in the past, to concentrate on extreme occupations. Extreme occupations are those which involve a high degree of danger, physical effort and skill. Tunstall's study The Fishermen and Coal is Our Life by Dennis, Henriques and Slaughter are examples of this. These studies look at the dangers involved in mining and deep-sea fishing and how this work can affect various aspects of the workers' behaviour. The men working in these industries experience such a high degree of danger that it makes their work significantly different from many other types of occupation.

EXERCISE

What other examples of extreme occupations can you think of?

Changes at work

The way we are organised at work, the kind of work we do, and the length of time we spend doing it, are constantly changing. This is how one farm labourer describes his work on the farm. He is, of course, discussing a time long since gone:

Come harvest time most of the farm workers would stop doing their normal work and help bring in the crop. Sometimes extra labour would be hired from the village to help us out. It was hard work and long hours but we all pulled together. Nowadays one man and a machine can do the work of 20 men in less than half the time. When the machines came to the farms many of us had to find work away from the land.

We know that as industrial societies developed, fewer people were required to work on the land because technology played an ever increasing role in farming. Workers and their families moved away from their villages to seek work in the towns in the newly-built factories. The factory offered a different way of producing goods. Individual workers were employed in producing or assembling sometimes only parts of a product using highly specialised machinery. This system of production led to what we now call mass production which usually means that goods could be produced more efficiently and therefore sold more cheaply to the consumer. This mechanisation of the workplace has been the most important feature throughout the 20th century and has been responsible, along with the growing influence of trade unions, for the changing social conditions at work.

A significant change is now taking place within the industrialised world and this change will have a great effect not only on the type of work which will be available but also on the numbers of people needed within many industries. The changes envisaged have led some observers to suggest that we are about to see, in the last years of the 20th century, the most dramatic reorganisation of work since the Industrial Revolution.

What is the reason for this change?

The change is based on the introduction and development of the microprocessor and the application of microelectronics to almost every area of human activity. Think for a moment about the pocket calculator. We all know how small they are and the many different mathematical problems they can solve. Twenty years ago without microelectronics, a device carrying out similar functions would have been about 100 times larger, not as reliable, and more significantly, so expensive as to be unavailable to most of us.

The application of microtechnology has led to the very real possibility of maintaining and expanding industrial output and greatly reducing the workforce. This has led many workers to be suspicious of the new technologies being introduced, as this newspaper report illustrates:

Robots at Reagons

The robots are coming! The robots are coming! Maybe they are not like the ones we have all seen in science fiction films – they don't look like metal men – but they are here and they can do amazing things. In fact a 'welding robot' introduced last week at the Reagon Power Press Plant on the Hilton industrial estate can do the work of 15 welders.

Great news for those with shares in the company. Lower labour costs and increased output mean more profit. But what about the workers? Terry Hall, a union official, put it like this: 'While we can all marvel at what these machines can do, we must be aware that the more we see these welding robots in factories like ours the less you are likely to see workers. These new developments in technology are threatening our livelihoods.'

One can appreciate the fears expressed by Mr Hall. He also talked about something which may get overlooked: 'I know most of my members take a great pride in their work. They've learnt their trade and are proud of their skills. Many of the developments we are seeing in industry remove the need of these skills and this turns the workers into machine minders. Who wants to work in a situation like that? This new technology is turning the men into robots themselves.'

Whatever the arguments and the fears, both management and workers alike are in agreement over one crucial fact of industrial life. The robots are not only coming but they are coming to stay!

We can see that the application of technology can affect the numbers of people at work – leading either to new jobs being created in the 'sunrise' industries or to unemployment and all the misery associated with it – as well as the level of job satisfaction experienced by those in employment. Of course it is not only factories and blue-collar workers that are experiencing the effects of the new technology. Many people believe that white-collar jobs in particular will be even more affected.

A survey on office technology carried out by the **Association of Professional, Executive, Clerical and Computer Staff (APEX)** has looked closely at the impact of office technology on the work of office staff. In terms of employment prospects the survey suggests that job losses were running at the ratio of 50–to–1 against jobs being created. In terms of de-skilling, 30% of those answering the questionnaire said they had direct experience of this, and 40% argued that the new technology increased skills in certain jobs. What is clear from the survey is that the way people experience work is changing and, as the report suggests, there is a strong possibility that industrial societies may well be characterised by 2 widely different groups of workers: those who are highly skilled technologists and those who are simply machine-minders.

Although many jobs will still have to be carried out by people, we should realise that the nature of work is going through important changes. Perhaps the question we should be asking is how will this influence our leisure time? Another important question is whether we will be able to get satisfaction from our work if machines are going to be more and more involved. We are not at the moment able to answer these questions with any degree of certainty, but it gives us plenty to think about.

EXERCISE

Some kinds of human activity in the workplace are more easily carried out by machinery. Other kinds of work do not so easily respond to automation. Take a copy of these headings and enter at least 10 appropriate jobs under each heading. Explain whether or not there are any special features about the jobs in the first column that are different from the jobs in the other column:

Jobs or skills that are being affected or will be affected by automation	Jobs that are less likely to be affected by automation
1	1
2	2
3	3
continue with your list	

Trade unions

A trade union is an organisation whose purpose is to promote the interests of its subscription-paying members. In 1983 over 11 million workers (over 50% of workers) were members of about 400 trade unions in Britain. Generally speaking, the power of unions is based on their capacity to exert collective pressure and influence on employers and the government primarily through negotiation. Only occasionally do unions resort to industrial action in an attempt to get what they want. The activities of trade unions as pressure groups are also explored in the chapter *Power*.

Why should a worker join a trade union?

EXERCISE

Below are 10 reasons why an employee might join a trade union. Read them carefully, and in your notebook rearrange them in descending order of importance to reflect what you believe to be the priorities of an average trade union member.

Workers join unions because unions:

Attempt to redistribute national income and wealth more equally in a move towards a fairer society

Give workers more say in the planning and control of industry

Improve the working environment – heating, lighting, health and safety

Provide financial and legal support during illness, accidents, redundancy and unemployment

Improve conditions of employment – better wages, shorter hours and longer holidays

Fight for full employment at government level

Attempt to influence government policy regarding cost of living, health, housing and education policies

Take an active interest in promoting job satisfaction, job training and retraining

Support the Labour Party financially and politically

Actively resist workplace closure and fight for job security

Although all of these are acknowledged as trade union functions, most trade unionists would agree that the main functions of a trade union are to negotiate higher **real** wages and shorter hours and to improve the conditions under which people work. Resisting workplace closure and promoting job security would also be high on their list of priorities. The redistribution of national wealth, support for a political party, promoting job satisfaction, giving workers more say in the planning and control of their industry are still important to trade unionists, but they would occupy a lower position on their list. (It is important that you know the meaning of the phrase **higher real wages**.)

How does your order of priorities compare with this?

How are unions organised?

In Britain, the trade union movement is a mixture of different types of unions. There are, however, 4 broad strands of trade union organisation that can be identified: **craft, industrial, general** and **non-manual** unions.

Craft unions. These are unions whose members have usually served an apprenticeship to achieve a high level of skill in a specific field. Train drivers and the workers who have printed this book are members of craft unions. Membership of craft unions is generally declining.
General unions. These were formed originally when traditional craft skills were being replaced by semi-skilled or unskilled labour. General unions are often extremely large because they recruit membership in many industries. The **Transport and General Workers Union** (TGWU) has over 1.6 million members working in a whole range of industries.
Industrial unions. These were formed to enable the employees in a single industry to gain more worker control over the planning and organisation of their industry. **The National Union of Railwaymen** (NUR) is an example of a union that operates only in the railway industry.
Non-manual unions. Non-manual or white-collar unions are the fastest growing of the four main types of unions. Workers in this group regard themselves as professional people, usually employed in a service industry. Your teacher will probably be a member of a white-collar union (either the NUT, NASUWT, PAT or NATFHE: find out what these abbreviations stand for).

EXERCISE

Job Description	Craft Union	General Union	Industrial Union	Non-manual Union
Welder	Job requires high degree of skill. 3 or 4 year apprenticeship training. College attendance to get craft or technician qualifications.			
Lorry Driver				
Computer Programmer				
Car Assembly Worker				
Post Office Worker				
Shop Assistant				
Electrician				
Coal-miner				

Make brief comments in the appropriate column to show that you know the type of union the worker is likely to join. The first example has been done for you: set out your table like the example above and leave plenty of space for your written answers.

The key people in trade union organisation are the full-time officials employed by the union and the unpaid trade union representatives or shop stewards. Shop stewards are ordinary working employees earning normal wages who have been elected by union members in the workplace to represent them in negotiations with the employer and to help with problems on the spot, such as safety matters and overtime queries.

When an employer and a union agree that all the workforce must be members of a trade union they are said to be operating a **closed shop**. Power workers, coal-miners and TV actors are examples of workers who operate a closed shop.

QUESTIONS

1 'The work we do may influence many aspects of our non-work life.' Describe and explain how our work may affect leisure, family life, voting behaviour and status. (20 marks)
Source: AEB O Level 1983

2 How do sociologists explain why some workers dislike their jobs whilst others enjoy theirs? (20 marks)

3 *a* According to the tables below, what percentage of unions have a membership of less than 100 members? (2 marks)

b What percentage of unions have a membership of less than 1000 members? (3 marks)

c What was the total membership of trade unions in 1976 and 1982? (2 marks)

d What would you say are the most significant reasons for the decline in trade union membership between 1979 and 1982? (3 marks)

Table 1 Trade unions – numbers and membership, end 1982

Numbers of members	Number of unions	All membership (thousand)	Number of unions (percentage)
Under 100	78	4	19.5
100– 499	101	25	25.2
500– 999	46	33	11.5
1 000– 2 499	48	74	12.0
2 500– 4 999	37	127	9.2
5 000– 9 999	22	147	5.5
10 000– 14 999	3	44	0.7
15 000– 24 999	16	330	4.0
25 000– 49 999	15	546	3.7
50 000– 99 999	13	983	3.2
100 000–249 999	11	1 868	2.7
250 000 and more	11	7 265	2.7
All members	**401**	**11 445**	**100·0**

Table 2 Trade unions – numbers and membership, 1976–1982

Year	Number of unions at end of year	Total membership at end of year (thousand)	Percentage change in membership since previous year
1976	473	12 386	+3.0
1977	481	12 846	+3.7
1978	462	13 112	+2.1
1979	453	13 289	+1.3
1980	438	12 947	−2.6
1981	414	12 106	−6.5
1982	401	11 445	−5.5

Source: Department of Employment Gazette, January 1984

e Discuss the reasons why workers join trade unions. (10 marks)

The Saturday morning man

I remember him because he was the first customer we served after we took over the Olde Oak Inn. We opened on a Saturday morning. David and I thought we would never get the place ready in time, but we did, and we waited with great excitement for our first customers. We had always wanted our own business and the money we had saved over the years meant that we were in a position to buy a nice little pub in the country. I had never worked as hard as I did the week before we opened. But as David said, you don't mind hard work when you are actually enjoying yourself, and I agreed with him.

He came in and ordered a pint of lime and bitter. He looked shy, and when he got his drink he went over to the table by the fire and took out a large notebook from his rucksack. I saw him making notes and drawing sketches of what looked like trees. He became a Saturday morning regular. He always arrived at the same time, bought one drink, took his seat by the fire, and made some notes in his big notebook. It wasn't until much later that I discovered he had been walking in the woods for hours. In fact he usually arrived on the early bus which dropped him off at about 7am. He was, I began to think, an eccentric. A friend of mine in the village who knew him quite well told me about him. Apparently he lived in the city, right in the centre, you could almost call it a slum, and he'd worked in the same chemical factory for over 20 years.

'Funny old bloke,' my friend had said, 'he's interested in the natural history of the area. That's what he writes and draws in his book. There's not much he can't tell you about the plants and animals, and everything else for that matter, in this part of the world. I can't see why he bothers actually. I've lived here all my life and I wouldn't know one tree from another or a goldcrest from a blue tit.'

I decided that next time he came in I would ask him about his walks in the woods. I didn't want to pry but I was interested, and a good licensee should take an interest in her customers. He came in one drizzly Saturday morning and whilst pulling his pint I asked him about his activities.

'Oh,' he said, 'I suppose people have noticed me over the years. It's not surprising really when you think about the number of times I've been round here.'

'You find this part of the world interesting then?' I asked.

'Well yes I do,' he said, and I could see he was willing to hold quite a long conversation. 'It's not just the fresh air but the woodland plant life and birds.'

'I suppose we take it for granted,' I said, just for something to say.

'I don't know about that. It's all a matter of what interests us really. I mean I can see that you and your husband like your work a lot. You've made a few improvements here and you keep a drop of good beer. I don't dislike my job, it's just that I get very little from it. I turn up every day – it's a chemical works actually – and I get my money at the end of the week. There's no challenge there and no chance for me to get on. When I come to this part of the world I'm interested in what goes on. I'm always seeing new things, unexpected things. I love it. You never know where you are with the countryside, so much happening all the time.'

He smiled softly and finished his beer. 'It's my hobby you see. My family thinks I'm obsessive about it – they think I'm mad – but they don't mind. When I get out here I can forget about the grimy factories and my job. Ideally I'd like to be a game warden or something like that, but it's too late for that now. So the nearest I can get to it is through my hobby. What's the point of sitting in front of the telly all day? I'd rather do something interesting.'

'I see what you mean,' I said, thinking how I felt when I worked in dead-end jobs. I remembered the worst job I had. I was a farm girl. I couldn't wait to get away from that pig farm. Funny how people feel differently about their jobs.

QUESTIONS

1 What does the Saturday Morning Man dislike about his work? Why does he think that it is too late to change jobs?

2 Explain the differences in attitudes towards work highlighted in the story in respect of:

   a intrinsic job satisfaction, and

   b instrumental or extrinsic job satisfaction.

3 How might the man's interest in the countryside compensate for his lack of job satisfaction? Mention a sociological study from either this chapter or from your general reading to support your answer.

Points for discussion

- The Saturday Morning Man is just a story. In real life, people like this don't exist.
- All this talk about job satisfaction is rubbish. Give workers a choice between high wages and job satisfaction and they'll go for the money every time.
- As the computer age advances we will become a nation of 2

classes; the haves and the have-nots.

Lost weekend

Sandra wasn't looking forward to telling David about the change in plans. They were both expecting to spend a weekend on the coast. They had chosen a quiet hotel and had planned long walks on the cliffs overlooking the bay. That was until Sandra heard the bad news. A colleague at work had gone down with the 'flu and she would have to attend a computer data conference in London in his place. She had told her boss that it was difficult having to change plans at such short notice, but she realised that the conference was important and she knew that she would have to spend some time away from home when she took on the job. But none of this was going to please David. He had already accused her of spending too much time on her work. She remembered the last row they had had over this.

'I wouldn't mind,' he had complained, 'but you bring so much work home with you. Everything seems to centre around computers and your precious little job.'

In a way he was right. She was involved in her work but he knew that when he married her. She had a responsible job with good career prospects and she was successful and happy at work, even though it made heavy demands on her time.

As she drove the car into her garage Sandra realised that she had forgotten to go to the supermarket at lunch time. She simply didn't have the time to go shopping. She had spent the time discussing the London trip with her boss. With no groceries and a lost weekend it was on the cards that tonight she and David would have an almighty row. She wasn't to be disappointed.

'You know how we both looked forward to the weekend away!' David shouted, furious at hearing the news.

'I'm sorry, but there's nothing I can do about it,' Sandra explained, 'I'm just as disappointed as you are. But it's part of the job.'

'I bet you are,' David said with sarcasm.

'Look, I know you're upset, but tell me what would you have done in my place?'

'That's different.'

'Why is it different?'

'Because I'm the main bread winner. I've got rights too, you know.'

'For God's sake, David, this is the 1980s. Grow up. Look, I've got a job that is demanding but I enjoy it and it does give us a good standard of living.'

'Are you saying that I can't support you?' David asked, reddening.

'I'm not saying that at all. But I'm entitled to a career just as you are.'

'OK,' he said 'I'm sorry. Let's leave it. At least we can have a quiet weekend at home.'

Sandra braced herself. 'I didn't manage to get to the supermarket. I didn't bring back any groceries ...'

'That's great that is! Now your job stops us eating!'

Sandra decided that she would spell out some home truths. 'Listen David what time did you finish teaching?'

'Half three.'

'Right. Couldn't *you* have gone to the supermarket? The tea could be on the table now if you had bothered.'

'You know I've got exam scripts to mark. I got home early and I've been marking ever since. You're beginning to get on my nerves.'

'OK. So it's all right for your job to get in the way of our home life, but it's not OK if mine gets in the way. Is that the picture?'

'Point taken,' David said, relieved that a new idea was growing in his brain. 'I'll tell you what, why don't we go out for a meal? We've lost a weekend so let's have a night out instead. We could go to that new Italian restaurant.'

Sandra thought of the papers she was expected to read for the conference. In the circumstances they could wait. That is the trouble with work. Sometimes it gets in the way of what really matters.

QUESTIONS

1 In what way is work causing problems in David's and Sandra's marriage?
2 Indicate other areas of family life where work could upset the lives and plans of David and Sandra.
3 How might an understanding of attitudes towards women throw light on some of David's views?

Points for discussion

- Sandra should be prepared to give up her job if David expressed a desire to start a family.
- One of the main reasons for the increase in divorce is because people like Sandra and David are too selfish and are not prepared to make sacrifices.
- If both partners in a marriage are working during periods of high unemployment, the government should pass a law to discourage one of them from working.

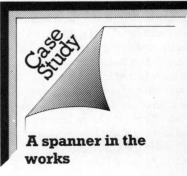

A spanner in the works

A production line at a large car making company in the West Midlands has come to an abrupt halt because a spanner has been deliberately jammed into the mechanism. The foreman responsible for the line reports the incident to management who immediately suspend the 25 workers on the line. All 1500 assembly-line workers in the plant down tools in sympathy and walk out, bringing car production to a stop.

Despite prolonged negotiation both management and unions fail to come to an agreement to enable car production to restart. The management insist that all employees are to go back to work immediately whilst enquiries are made to discover the persons responsible for the sabotage, who will then be dismissed. The unions argue that management behaviour is dictatorial and does not take into account the reasons for the workers' behaviour. The union negotiators insist that all workers be allowed to return to work without victimisation.

Both management and unions finally agree to call in an independent professional arbitrator, Margaret Jennings, to help to bring the 2 sides together. Miss Jennings' first action will be to interview representatives from each side in the dispute.

You are to play one of the following parts:

Margaret Jennings Arbitrator
Henry Fox Production manager
Dave Masterson Shop steward

Margaret Jennings' brief
You know that the most important point for an interviewer is to allow the interviewee to do most of the talking. But first you must prepare a set of questions for each side to answer. You feel that if at the end of the interviews you have established a few facts, defined the problem, got each side to admit to a few mistakes,

and perhaps found some areas of agreement, you will be well satisfied. Your objective is to get the 2 sides to agree to a course of action that will end the dispute and get the men back to work.

The manager's brief
The same old story. Some maniac throws a spanner in the works and brings the whole factory to a stop, and I've got to explain why I want to sack him! What's the point of having management if you can't get rid of saboteurs who threaten everybody's livelihood? Unless we get the line rolling again our competitors will roll over us and we'll all be out of work. If I can't win this one, God help us! I'm determined to argue my strongest case.

The shop steward's brief
This management can't see the wood for the trees. All right, somebody dropped a spanner into the gearing. Big deal. Why did they have to over-react and sack the whole line? Why didn't they call in the union to help sort out the problem? Why can't they see that 15 hundred line workers just wouldn't walk out and lose their pay unless there was something seriously wrong with working conditions? I'm going to tell them a few home truths – if I get the chance.

This information is available to both management and unions:

- The line men cheered when the line stopped
- The family car being produced is in fierce competition with imported models
- Overtime has recently been cut
- The line speed has been increased without consultation with the union
- Yesterday a man caught his arm in the fast moving rollers under the belt and broke a bone
- The company is anxious to secure a lucrative overseas contract based on a no-strike agreement

with the workers
- A bonus scheme is to be introduced, linked to the line speed
- There is a shop steward, Dave Masterson, working on the line
- The line has traditionally high rates of absenteeism
- The local unemployment rate is 21%
- The company has plans to replace some line-workers with robots
- The company increased profits by 18% last year
- The average take-home pay for the line workers is £95 for a 40-hour week
- Every minute's stoppage on the lines loses the company £3000.

Using the case study as a role play
1 The manager and the shop steward should prepare their arguments in writing in preparation for the interviews.
2 The arbitrator will have prepared appropriate questions in readiness for a separate interview with each side.
3 A third three-way discussion will take place involving all 3 participants during which a statement in writing will be drawn up to indicate the final position reached by both sides.
4 Observers are to make notes of the proceedings, particularly noting gains, losses and compromises experienced by each side, in preparation for a follow-up discussion.

Using the case study as an exercise
Both sides in the dispute eventually accept that worker dissatisfaction was an important ingredient that led to the loss of production. After further discussions, several plans are put forward to tackle this problem:

- Replacing the workforce with robots linked to a central computer
- Using robots controlled by line

workers for uncomfortable jobs (for example, working on the underside of car bodies)

- Rotating jobs so that nobody does the same job for more than one day a week
- Enlarging the job so that workers get a chance to fit a whole engine, for example, rather than just a few parts
- Taking the assembly away from the line and, working in teams, construct the car from components brought to the central area
- Leave the production system as it is but increase the rates of pay.

QUESTIONS

1 Which plan would you choose if you were
  a a car production-line worker, or
  b the production manager?
  (Give your reasons)
2 Suggest any plans of your own for dealing with worker dissatisfaction.
3 What would the consequences be of turning the car plant over to robot automation?
Make a list of the points both in favour of the idea and against it.

Important points

- Work is a paid activity based on a contract of employment between an employer and an employee.
- Work in industrial societies is based on the division of labour.
- The work people do is often a direct result of their social class and educational background.
- Some people really like the work they do. Sociologists call this intrinsic job satisfaction.
- For others work is just a means of getting wages. Their main interest is not their work but their non-work time. We call this an instrumental attitude or extrinsic job satisfaction.
- The type of work people do is associated with the degree of alienation they experience.
- There are strong relationships between the work a person does and their non-work time activities.
- Just as there is inequality within society there is also inequality at work.
- Many people experience extreme forms of deprivation at work. This deprivation is strongly related to the type of work carried out by the working class.
- It is still not possible to be sure about how computer-based technology in the workplace will affect job satisfaction or influence the way we spend our leisure time.
- Trade unions are important organisations representing the interests of the majority of working people.

6 Women

When you have worked through this chapter you should have a clearer understanding of

Sex and gender · **Gender messages** · **Prejudice and discrimination** · **Primary and secondary breadwinners** · **Gender socialisation** · **Gender divisions in employment** · **Sexual stereotypes** · **Egalitarian marriages** · **Dual roles** · **Women and education** · **Teacher expectations**

Are women socially inferior to men?

Yes, women *are* socially inferior to men because they generally

- earn less money at work and are employed in low-status and low-pay jobs
- gain fewer educational qualifications and own less property
- have less say than men in how the country is run
- do not share equal status with men in wider society

The question many sociologists like to ask is: why do these important inequalities exist in our society? How is it possible, for example, that in 1986 there were only 25 women Members of Parliament compared with a staggering 625 men? Let us examine some of our assumptions about men and women. In your notebook indicate whether you agree or disagree with each of these statements:

1 Men and women are born with different intellectual capacities.
2 Women are inferior because of the way they've been brought up.
3 Men are naturally stronger than women – women are the weaker sex.
4 Women have achieved equality with men – the fight's over.
5 Girls and boys have the same opportunities at school. If girls don't take science subjects, then that's their choice, and their fault when they can't find jobs that need science qualifications.
6 Young children need their mothers at home.
7 Housework's a doddle.
8 Women are abandoning their domestic responsibilities by going out to work.
9 Husbands and wives now have equal say in how the house is run.

In this chapter we will examine how some of these statements stand up to scrutiny. We will also discuss why sociologists are interested in knowing about the nature and extent of sexual inequality in our society, and why the inequalities faced by women in particular tend to persist.

Women and work

Do you think that the following jobs can best be done by men or by women, or do you think they can be done equally well by either? Take a copy of the table, and tick the appropriate column.

How did you decide which jobs can best be performed by either

	Men	Women	Either
Bricklayer			
Nursery nurse			
Gardener			
Welder			
Dentist			
Motor mechanic			
Beautician			
Electrician			
Primary school teacher			
Miner			
Typist			

men or women? Did you use any of the following criteria?

- Physical strength – believing men to be stronger than women
- Natural aptitude – believing that men and women are naturally more suited to different things
- Formal qualifications
- What women or men would prefer to do

Your reasons may have been based on natural differences between the sexes or you may have considered that socially created differences between the sexes lead to greater suitability for certain jobs. You might have thought that all the jobs can be performed equally well by both men and women. But in the real world of work, what jobs are done by men and women? Look carefully at the following table which indicates the distribution of employment in Britain:

Socio-economic group of people in employment in 1977

| | Distribution of employees | |
	Male %	Female %
Professional, managers and employers	22	6
Other non-manual	18	53
Skilled manual	39	8
Semi-skilled manual	13	24
Unskilled manual	8	9

Source: Social Trends

1 In which categories of occupation are there significant differences between the percentages of males and females?
2 What kinds of jobs done by women would you expect to see included in the 'other non-manual' category?
3 What generalisations about women's employment can be made from this table?

EXERCISE

Make a list of the names of 3 men and 3 women you know well who are either in full or part-time employment. State their job titles and explain the differences (if any) between the jobs they perform. Present your answer under these headings:
1 Pay   **4** Promotion
2 Hours of work   prospects
3 Status   **5** Fringe benefits

Although women form a sizeable chunk of the working population (over 40%), they tend to be concentrated within a narrow range of occupations. The 1971 Census showed that two-thirds of women in paid employment belonged to only 3 out of 27 occupational groupings. The 1981 Census, which reduced these occupational groupings to 18, shows that women continue to be concentrated in certain areas of work. These are clerical jobs (33%), service sector jobs (23%) and professional jobs (14%).

The 5 most typical female occupations in Britain are nursing, primary school teaching, factory work involving packing and producing domestic products, secretarial and low-grade clerical jobs and shopwork. These jobs are seen by many sociologists as an extension of women's domestic roles. What women do at work in many ways mirrors their duties

and responsibilities within the family home. This point is illustrated by Mackie and Patullo in their *Women at Work*:

The woman employed outside her home is much more likely to be making biscuits than cars, serving coffee than building ships, doing the dry-cleaning than dock-work.

EXERCISE

Here are 4 common domestic chores. Suggest at least 3 equivalent jobs that are found in women's employment for each chore:
1 Caring for   **3** Serving meals
young children   **4** Shopping
2 Tidying up

Mary Benet, in *Secretary: An Enquiry into the Female Ghetto*, argues that there are similarities between office work and housekeeping. She sees office work as the business equivalent of housework as 'both jobs are custodial, concerned with tidying up, putting away and restoring order rather than producing anything'. A woman's domestic child care role may also find its equivalent in primary school teaching. Although over half of all teachers in Britain are women, three quarters of them work in primary schools. This leads us to an important point about women in the professions.

Few women workers are to be found amongst the high flyers, especially within the ranks of top white-collar professionals, managers and employers. Generally speaking, women tend to be employed in the minor professions such as teaching and social work, whereas men occupy the high-status professions such as dentistry, medicine and law. However, even where men and women are engaged in the same work, there can be marked differences in opportunities. The following table illustrates this point:

Selected NHS hospital consultants, England and Wales, 1977

5 feminine and 5 masculine specialities

Speciality	% women	% men
Most women		
Child and adolescent psychiatry (mental illness)	32.7	67.3
Mental handicap	19.6	80.4
Medical microbiology	14.8	85.2
Dermatology	12.6	87.4
Radiology	10.9	89.1
Most men		
Infectious diseases	0	100.0
General surgery	0.9	99.1
Neurosurgery (brain and nerves)	1.2	98.8
Plastic surgery	1.3	98.7
Cardio-thoracic surgery (heart and chest)	2.6	97.4

Source: DHSS Statistics and Research

Ann Oakley makes the following comment on the gender divisions within the NHS:

Among hospital consultants, the medical specialities where most women are to be found are those relating to children and mental disorder. They also put people to sleep, chart the behaviour of microbes (microbiology), concern themselves with people's skins (dermatology) and take pictures of people (radiology). None of these areas has high status within the medical profession, whereas the majority of surgical specialities, which men control, command much higher respect.

Women are also more likely than men to be working part-time. Approximately 65% of women in the labour force are employed part-time, and being a part-time worker usually means that there is less chance of training and promotion, greater job insecurity, reduced fringe benefits, and lower rates of pay than full-time colleagues receive for identical work. Women's full-time pay is also less than men's. The *Low Pay Unit* estimated that in 1979, out of 150 000 homeworkers mostly involved in sewing, more than half were earning less than 40 pence per hour. A more recent comparison of men's and women's pay levels can be found on page 114.

In essence, there are 3 important features of the work women do which make it different from the work men do:

- Women are engaged in a far narrower range of jobs in low status positions

- Women earn less money and receive fewer fringe benefits
- Women are likelier to be in part-time jobs and are therefore not covered by many important employment protection laws.

Women are also no different from men in the way they are expected to share the burden of unemployment. Class and particularly ethnic factors are equally important for women in determining whether or not they will get a job or remain unemployed, and young Asian women and West Indian men are the groups most at risk. The following chart is taken from the 1981 *Labour Force Survey*.

EXERCISE

1 Which age group suffers most from unemployment?
2 What percentage of 16–24 year old

Female unemployment rates in Britain, by age and ethnic origin

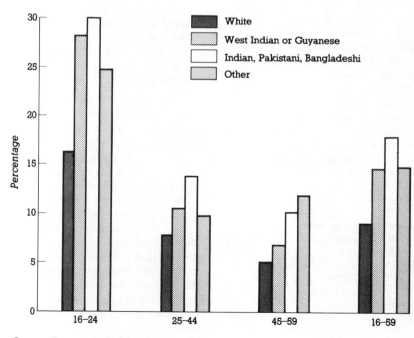

Source: Department of Employment Gazette, June 1984

Asian women experience unemployment?

3 Suggest a few reasons why Asian and black women experience greater unemployment than white women.

4 Why does the percentage of unemployed women fall with increasing age?

Why do women experience disadvantage at work?

One reason is that employers tend to select employees on the basis of certain notions they hold about the suitability of men and women for particular jobs. A survey entitled *Management Attitudes and Practices Towards Women at Work* revealed that more than one-third of managers in 223 establishments believed that women belonged at home, and were inferior employees because of high absenteeism and turnover rates (they changed jobs faster than men). The survey also found that managers rated men more highly than women in every important area in the selection procedure, such as 'personality', 'education' and 'salary required'. The *Sex Discrimination Act* and the *Equal Pay Act*, which came into force in the mid-1970s, made it illegal to discriminate against a person because of her (or his) sex. Although employers can now be made to consider women for jobs which have previously been performed only by men, Acts of Parliament cannot in themselves get rid of prejudice, as this exercise shows:

EXERCISE

Here are some questions that have been put to women in job interviews:
• How long have you been married?
• Do you have children or do you plan to have children?
• What will you do if your children are ill?
• What arrangements do you make for your children after school or during school holidays?
• Does your husband mind you working?
• What does your husband do?
• Why do you want to go out to work?

What prejudices against women workers are contained in these questions?

One reason why men and women do different jobs might be because men are stronger than women. However, Kate Millet, in *Sexual Politics*, notes that although men naturally have bigger muscles than women, they are encouraged as children to develop their strength whilst girls are usually discouraged. Even so, the argument to justify **gender divisions** in employment on the basis of women's inferior strength is weak because:

• Women are capable of doing heavy work. In the Soviet Union and the USA women work alongside men in the coalmines and steel-making plants.
• Most men are not involved in work that requires exceptional human strength.
• Superior physical strength is not a basis for superior rewards in our society. In fact the physical strength required for the high-status and high-pay jobs is negligible. Women need not be excluded.

Ann Oakley argues that the main reason for the subordination of women in the labour force is that the mother-housewife role is regarded as the most important role for a woman in our society. Paid employment is seen as less important than her duties and responsibilities in the home and towards her husband and children.

Sociological studies have revealed that family factors are crucial in women's decisions to take up paid employment. Viola Klein's *Britain's Married Women Workers*, a study conducted in the late 1950s and early 1960s, found the main reason for women taking up paid employment was to supplement the family income. A more recent survey, the *Family Formation Survey*, shows women taking up paid work between the births of their first and second children because they needed the money (47%) and because they wanted 'extra things' (27%). Furthermore, success at work is difficult to achieve alongside success in the mother-housewife role. Women professional workers have been found to be 3 or 4 times less likely than their male colleagues to be married because of the incompatibility of the mother and worker role.

The American sociologist Theodore Caplow provides a useful guide to help us understand why so many women experience disadvantage at work. In *The Sociology of Work* he suggests that:

• Being or becoming a mother interrupts careers as women must leave work temporarily to give birth and to bring up children. This makes employers less willing to invest in training programmes for women or widen promotion prospects.
• Women are regarded as **secondary breadwinners** which encourages the idea that men, as **primary breadwinners**, ought to be paid more.
• Women are less geographically mobile than men because of their ties to husbands and children. When a family moves house, the reasons for the move are more likely to be connected with the husband's job rather than his wife's.
• The supply of female labour exceeds demand. Employers are not under any great pressure to attract female labour with high wages or favourable conditions.
• There remains a great number of written and unwritten rules and regulations which restrict

women's work or bar them from certain occupations. In Britain today you are still unlikely to bump into women sailors, mineworkers, 'firemen', construction workers and 'dustmen'.

The processes of socialisation and education may also be important in preparing girls for the sexual inequalities which persist in employment, and we will look at these in more detail. Although most sociologists accept that there have been improvements made in the employment prospects of women, huge obstacles still remain. These can be summarised as:

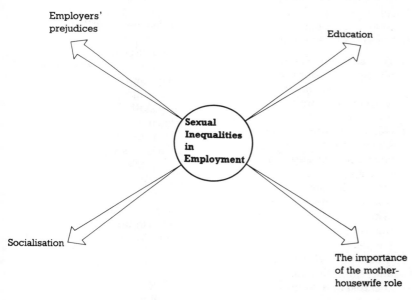

Inequalities in the employment of women

EXERCISE

This letter appeared in a local newspaper:

Talkback

Sir,
It was with interest and indignation that I read your recent article about

women going out to work.

Isn't it about time that the ladies in our society were given some positive encouragement to return to their traditional role as housewives? My own wife left her clerical post upon marriage to me some 30 years ago and has been a happy and contented housewife all her married life. Her being at home is an arrangement that has suited all members of my family.

Is it any wonder that we have soaring unemployment rates when women are taking men's jobs away from them?

The time has come for MPs and councillors to consider the issue of working women carefully. If

wives will not listen to reason and continue to behave in this morally reprehensible fashion by depriving men of work, then we need laws to prevent women from working if their husbands are employed. After all, women only go out to work for the cake money – money that is frittered away on unnecessary luxuries for themselves.

Should we allow women this 'cake' whilst many families are deprived of bread?

JS

Write a letter to *Talkback* in response to the objections raised by JS. Use as much sociological data as you can from this chapter to help you with your arguments.

Gender socialisation

In what way are women socially different from men?

Here is a list of personal qualities. Which of these qualities do you think tend to apply more to men than women? Rearrange the words in 2 columns under the heading of either male or female, and compare your results with others in the group to assess the overall level of agreement:

Sensitive	Bitchy
Aggressive	Enterprising
Active	Gentle
Kind	Warmhearted
Sympathetic	Cautious
Confident	Talkative
Bullying	Sly
Brave	Pushy
Adventurous	Sentimental
Ambitious	Tough
Logical	Squeamish

Although it would be foolish to argue that we can slot all men and women into such simple categories, you should be able to see from your assessment that there can be an amazing level of agreement in the way we perceive sex difference. This is largely because the differences are determined by the sorts of role each sex is expected to take up as an adult. Personality differences between the sexes have been proved to exist by research as well as being suggested by our own observations.

Are these differences natural or are they learnt?

Some researchers argue that

differences between men and women arise from basic biological differences between the sexes. Men, it is argued, are physically stronger than women, so naturally they should and do dominate. Women, who are less strong, are submissive, because they produce children and have a natural caring instinct. Although a considerable amount of time and effort have been (and still are) spent on research aimed at proving that males and females have naturally different abilities, personality characteristics and potentialities, no conclusive evidence has yet been produced.

In her book *Male and Female* Margaret Mead described how different personality characteristics predominate in different primitive tribes. She found the Arapesh tribe sociable, compassionate, loving and passive – characteristics regarded as feminine in our society. The Mundugumor, by contrast, were masculine in their treatment of each other – harsh, violent and quarrelsome. She went on to describe how work was organised by women and men in the Pacific island of Samoa:

Both men and women do heavy exacting gardening and tiring fishing. Both men and women cook, both men and women do handwork . . . work is primarily scaled to age and status rather than sex. Both men and women are strong and muscular.

She pointed to other societies in New Guinea where:

Women share in the heavy, exacting spurts of work . . . so men share in the small routines of everyday life: care of children, fetching small things from the bush.

It is not necessary to look far afield to find examples that challenge the idea that men are physically stronger than women. Female bricklayers in the Soviet Union, women coalminers in the USA,

front-line girl soldiers in Israel and Lebanon, the competent performance of women in traditional male areas of work in our own society, all suggest that women may not be weaker than men. After all, statistics reveal that women live longer and are generally healthier, and no-one can prove that there is any basic difference between the intellectual capacities of women and men.

It is difficult to separate those characteristics of ourselves which we inherit at birth from those we have acquired. Sociologists, of course, are mainly interested in the social forces that determine differences between the sexes.

How then do women and men become socially different? We must first draw a distinction between sex and gender:

- The **sex** of a person is biologically determined. Sexual differences are natural and universal and are more or less unalterable.
- **Gender** is culturally and socially determined. Ideas about appropriate behaviour for men and women are not universal – they can change from one culture to another. Whereas sex describes the difference between male and female, gender describes the difference between masculine and feminine, and **gender socialisation** describes the process whereby masculine and feminine behaviour are learnt.

Gender socialisation begins at birth. When a nurse in a hospital wraps a blue blanket around a baby boy and a pink blanket around a baby girl, a sexual identity has been imposed on the baby. Later, boys and girls are conditioned or socialised to become typical boys and girls. They are treated differently by their parents and those around them, and different things are expected of them.

Sara Delamont in *The Sociology of Women* describes an experiment in which a film of a 6-month-old baby, dressed in yellow, crying, crawling, smiling and generally behaving as we might expect a baby of this age to behave, was shown to a sample group of professionals such as child doctors, psychologists and nursery nurses. Half the group were told that the baby was a boy, the other half a girl. They were asked to describe what the baby was doing at each stage. The results were clear. Different motives were attributed to behaviour, according to the sex of the baby. If they thought it was a boy, they described it as 'angry' when it cried, but if a girl, as 'frightened'.

Differences are further emphasised in later childhood. Boys and girls practise their roles through their toys. Toys are not just playthings. They enable young children to develop a wide range of skills and aptitudes, and they encourage the development of masculine and feminine characteristics.

EXERCISE

Which of the following toys are likely to be given to girls or to boys? How do you think these toys enable girls and boys to acquire feminine and masculine characteristics?

Sindy doll	Construction set
Racing car	Dumper-truck
Teddy bear	Cosmetic set
Football	Cleaning set

It has been said that boys, through their toys, learn to manipulate objects, explore and do practical things, whilst girls learn to bring up children, to be quiet, to keep clean and be decorative. As a further exercise you might like to look through a mail order catalogue to find examples of toys that prepare children for their gender roles.

The world conjured up by toys represents different present and future roles for boys and girls. It has been found that girls' toys are simple, solitary and passive, whilst toys for boys are more varied, more expensive, complex, social, and activity based.

Gender socialisation and the media

Children are also influenced by mass media products, which tend to reinforce **sexual stereotypes**. These influences have been discussed in several recent studies, and the general consensus is that the world presented to children in the mass media is unreal, biased and reliant on excessive sexual stereotyping. Women are often left out of stories and where they do appear they are frequently presented as frightened, passive or domestic bores. In a recent analysis of the content of children's programmes in Britain it was observed that boys are usually the interesting characters – the ones who have adventures, who have the leading roles and who tend to succeed.

A survey at Princeton University in the USA in 1975 found that 75% of all leading characters on American TV were male. Although the 1970s saw the arrival of Wonder Woman and Charlie's Angels, these heroines could never get away with being fat (like Cannon), paralysed (like Ironside), bald (like Kojac) or scruffy with a glass eye (like Colombo). Nor on British TV can we imagine female equivalents of Patrick Moore and Magnus Pyke, let alone a Terry Wogan or a Jimmy Saville!

Gender messages are transmitted in a great deal of adult literature and broadcasting. Most tabloid newspapers and TV soap operas feed on culturally-enhanced differences of masculinity and femininity. Gender emphasis is thought to be a vital component in commercial success. And not without justification. The most widely read newspaper is the *Sun* (over 4 million copies per day), and the most popular TV programme at the time of writing is *Dallas* (13 million viewers). The naked page 3 girl and the ruthless JR are constant reminders of the 'sexy' woman and the 'macho' man. Of course, it is to women, particularly homely-vulnerable-attractive women, to which most newspapers, magazines, advertisers and TV programme makers turn to provide them with prime material. Here is a typical article that was published in the *Daily Mirror:*

Miranda makes it big [but stardom hasn't changed her – yet]

by PAULINE McLEOD

Miranda Richardson, pert and pretty in a Fifties dress over frothy petticoats, let out a ladylike little yelp of horrified surprise.

It wasn't loud enough to stop the traffic . . . but that's what happened.

Miranda, the 26-year-old little-known actress who has become an overnight success with her film portrayal of Fifties murderess Ruth Ellis, had been waving her arms about to emphasise her embarrassment at sudden stardom.

Suddenly a bracelet flew off her wrist and vanished under a passing delivery van.

Miranda beamed a big smile at the driver – who promptly braked and reversed, causing a mini jam.

Miranda, originally from Southport Lancs, is a bright, bubbly, sunny-side-up character.

The depression which she felt while playing Ruth Ellis, the last woman to be hanged in Britain, has lifted.

'I got to like Ruth tremendously,' she says. 'She was a real show-off, you know. She loved to dance and it was a real joy for me to have to take ballroom dancing lessons.

'I sing the title song of the movie, though I still am not quite sure if my voice is any good.

'Filming was depressing at times – it's not a particularly happy subject. I had a laugh as well on the set, but it was very tiring.'

Once, she went to the pub in Hampstead, London, outside which club hostess Ruth shot her lover David Blakely.

'When I first saw a picture of Blakely, I thought, what a wimp, a chinless wonder,' says Miranda.

'I can imagine he was a real big kid, capable of being charming in his weakness and vulnerability.

'I don't really think he could ever have been good at anything.

'It's such a shame Ruth wasted so much energy on him.'

What we have here is a fairly average media write up of an 'unknown' actress who has played the leading part in a newly-released film. However, before the actress is allowed to voice her own opinion, we are fed a substantial diet of female gender cues in case we are tempted to take her opinions too seriously. Here are just a few:

pert and pretty
frothy petticoats
ladylike little yelp
beamed a big smile

and although the first half of the article attempts to portray a rather silly and trivial person we can see that Miranda is anything but silly and trivial. In fact she is an intelligent and perceptive woman who is only allowed to express her opinions and ideas about her work in the last 4 paragraphs.

But are we being too serious about all this? What does it matter anyway, the argument runs, since everybody knows that the tabloids are fun-loving comic-like throwaways. What's the harm in them? After all, they treat men just as badly as women. Think of the way they treated Boy George and Ken Livingstone, and look at what they said about Prince Andrew's escapades. Nevertheless, if you thumb through almost any tabloid or colour magazine, you will see womanhood exposed in its stark nakedness, voluptuous, glamorised, painted in amazing colours, and sprawled across cars and settees selling anything from jewellery to cigarettes. You can read numerous feminine-interest articles on dieting, skin care, dress sense, make-up, hair styling, unwanted body hair and 'how-to-get-your-man'. It is the sheer volume of material on woman-as-the-sex-object that gets across the gender message to both boys and girls and to men and women. It is an irresistible force.

Sue Sharpe in *Just like a Girl* discusses the potent gender messages that are transmitted to boys and girls through the mass media and concludes that:

throughout the media, girls are presented in ways which are consistent with aspects of their stereotyped images ... the chance is seldom given to boys and girls to see girls and women doing things which require strength of character and initiative. Finding a man, looking after him, helping others and solving personal problems are the only activities women are allowed to undertake.

No sociologist would ever suggest that toys, comics, magazines and other mass media products enable girls to learn their sex roles, or that girls turn to these sources for guidance in appropriate behaviour. However, the influences of the gender messages that are transmitted are significant. They reinforce and perpetuate sex role stereotypes and ideas of socially acceptable masculine and feminine behaviour.

GROUP EXERCISE

1 Get hold of a range of comics that are widely read by boys and girls. Taking the girls' comics first, work through them carefully and make some observations about the following:

a Practical activities engaged in (eg helping mother)
b Concerns and interests shown (eg an interest in boys)
c Roles presented (eg mother or nurse)
d Stereotyped images (eg contented or nagging housewife)

Now complete the same exercise on the boys' comics. What conclusions can you draw from your findings?

2 Choose a male and a female character from the cast of either Coronation Street or EastEnders (or any other current TV soap opera) and analyse the degree to which the script writers and the actors have interpreted sex roles in a particular episode. It would be helpful to you if you could acquire a video recording of the programme under analysis. You may be asked to report your findings to the rest of your group for critical comment.

Coronation Street
This week's cast:

Nicky Tilsley	Warren Jackson
Gail Tilsley	Helen Worth
Brian Tilsley	Christopher Quinten
Ivy Tilsley	Lynne Perrie
Vera Duckworth	Elizabeth Dawn
Jack Duckworth	William Tarmey
Terry Duckworth	Nigel Pivaro
Kevin Webster	Michael Le Vell
Curly Watts	Kevin Kennedy
Connie Clayton	Susan Brown
Harry Clayton	Johnny Leeze
Sue Clayton	Jane Hazelgrove
Betty Turpin	Betty Driver
Andrea Clayton	Caroline O'Neill
Wilf Starkey	Jim Bywater
Alf Roberts	Bryan Mosley
Emily Bishop	Eileen Derbyshire
Deirdre Barlow	Anne Kirkbride
Phyllis Pearce	Jill Summers
Martin Platt	Sean Wilson

EastEnders
This week's cast:

Ali Osman	Nejdet Salih
Sue Osman	Sandy Ratcliff
Lofty Holloway	Tom Watt
Lou Beale	Anna Wing
Pauline Fowler	Wendy Richard
Michelle Fowler	Susan Tully
Arthur Fowler	Bill Treacher
Mary Smith	Linda Davidson
Pete Beale	Peter Dean
Kathy Beale	Gillian Taylforth
Angie Watts	Anita Dobson
Tony Carpenter	Oscar James
Sharon Watts	Letitia Dean
Ian Beale	Adam Woodyatt
Ethel Skinner	Gretchen Franklin
Dr Legg	Leonard Fenton
Andy O'Brien	Ross Davidson
Debbie Wilkins	Shirley Cheriton

Women and the family

It has been suggested that husbands and wives now practise joint conjugal roles as equal marriage partners in sharing the load of domestic responsibilities. However, many feminist writers have been critical of this egalitarian notion of modern marriage, and in *The Sociology of Housework* Ann Oakley claimed that:

Only a minority of husbands gave the kind of help that assertions of equality in modern marriage would imply.

From her sample, Oakley discovered that only 15% of husbands had a high degree of participation in housework and about 25% participated in childcare. Although she found a degree of sharing in regard to decision-making and leisure pursuits, the prime responsibility for the home and children still rested with the wife. Oakley rejected the idea of 'symmetry' suggested in the Willmott and Young study (see page 45) for 'as long as the blame is laid on the woman's head for an empty larder or a dirty house, it is not meaningful to talk about marriage as a joint or equal partnership'.

Angela Coyle, in her 1984 book *Redundant Women* suggests that some women have acquired a **dual role** in which they combine paid work and unpaid domestic work. Women are not abandoning their housewife roles – they are fitting the roles of housewife and paid worker together. Coyle is one of many feminist sociologists who see most marriages as an exploitative relationship in which husbands exert economic power over their wives. Being the chief breadwinner, the husband is in a position to set the standard of living for his family and decide how much of his income his wife may use. She becomes financially dependent on him.

EXERCISE

Housework
Monday ain't no funday
I get the blues so bad
I slave from dawn to sunset
I think I'll end up mad.

Tuesday ain't much better
The chores they're still the same
I clean and wash and mend and scrub
And my reward's another person's name.

Wednesday, whoopee! my favourite day
A day I love and adore
I don't care what my old man says
The telly ain't no bore.

Thursday ain't so dear to me
The money's all but gone
The only consolation is
I'll get some later on.

Friday morning till evening
I do what I've done all week
He's down the pub with his mates all night
The kids are in bed asleep.

Weekends for some are a time of leisure

For me it's overtime
For me there is no daily pleasure
Only the same old grime.

No holidays, no bonuses, no promotion, no pay
What sort of a job is this?
A job, my dear, what do you say
This is married bliss.

What objections to housework are expressed in these lyrics?

If you were offered a job with the following terms and conditions, do you think you would accept it?

- No pay
- An average working week of 77 hours
- No trade union representation
- No health insurance
- No pension scheme
- No holidays or weekends off
- No opportunities for promotion
- Tedious and monotonous work that has to meet deadlines
- No recognition of the value of the work
- No contract of employment

How many of these factors do you think are applicable to housewives? According to Ann Oakley, in her study *Housewife*, 76% of all employed women and 93% of non-employed women in Britain today are housewives. She characterised the housewife role in this way:

- It is a 'feminine' occupation that is performed almost wholly by women.
- It is regarded as non-work.
- It is invisible (no real goods are produced), privatised and isolated. Housework is usually unsupervised and done in the

absence of family members.
- Housewives are tied to their work by bonds of love and affection, unlike other workers who are tied by contracts of employment.

Can you think of any other ways in which housework differs from other work?

Housework is popularly believed to be a bit of a joke by non-housewives:

Housework – hard work? There's nothing to it. I mean, anyone can do it – a bit of dusting now and again, and cooking a few meals – that's easy enough. It might have been a hard slog in my mum's day but now women have got machines to do all the jobs, like the washing machine and the hoover. They've got nothing to complain about – nothing.

These opinions are not unique, but how accurate or fair are they?

Oakley found that monotony, fragmentation (unconnected tasks) and time pressures are aspects of housework commonly experienced by housewives. Cooking, for example, was reported as being a potentially satisfying task but limits of time, money and having to cope with children make it stressful. The following table compares the monotony, fragmentation and excessive pace (having too much to do) among housewives and factory workers.

Despite modern technology in the home, the amount of time spent on housework has not decreased. According to the Oakley study, in

| Workers | Percentage experiencing | | |
	Monotony %	Fragmentation %	Excessive Pace %
Housewives	75	90	50
Factory workers	41	70	31
Assembly-line workers	67	86	36

1950 the average time spent on housework was 50 hours a week, but by 1971 this had increased to 77 hours. The introduction of labour-saving devices in the home may have eased some of the more physically demanding chores of housework, but women now spend much more time improving standards of hygiene and are more conscious of the need to create what is known as the 'home beautiful'.

The housewife role is usually regarded as traditional. However, in pre-industrial Britain, when the family was a unit of production, women's work was indispensable in the 2 important occupations of agriculture and textiles. The woman's role was always the role of productive worker, whether in the home, on the land, or in the urban workplace. With rare exceptions there were no sexual barriers preventing women from entering an occupation and the choice between work and domesticity did not exist then as it does now. By the mid-19th century the process of industrialisation had channelled women's roles into two separate categories: productive work outside the home and domestic chores within the home.

Ann Oakley identifies 3 stages in the process of industrialisation which mark the emergence of the modern housewife role as the 'dominant mature feminine role':

Stage 1 (1750–1840) The factory began to replace the family as a unit of production. Women and children were commonly employed in factories until a series of Factory Acts restricted the employment of child labour. Women were forced back into the domestic role to look after their children.
Stage 2 (1841–1913) Industrial leglislation further restricted women's employment (in 1842

women were forbidden to work in coalmines) and social and political pressures further eroded employment opportunities for women. Queen Victoria announced: 'Let woman be what God intended: a helpmate for man, but with totally different duties and vocations'.
Stage 3 (1914–1950) The tendency of women to go out to work steadily increased in response to war pressures and labour shortages. It was considered acceptable for women to go out to work as long as the housewife role was given priority.

Today the majority of working women are employed in part-time or full-time low-paid jobs, and it is these 2 categories that account for the marked increase in the proportion of married women at work. The main reason for the

The interior of a turn-of-the-century communal wash-house (exterior photograph on page 125. On the left is a cast-iron bath that doubled as a worktop when the wooden top was folded down. In the centre is a brick coal-heated boiler for washing clothes and heating the bath water, and on the right a 'mangle' to squeeze excess water from the wet clothes before they were hung outside to dry.

concentration of women in part-time work is the expectation that they will continue with their traditional child care role, and contrary to popular belief wives' wages are not set aside to provide frills and luxuries but form a vital part of family budgets.

The proportion of married women employed

Year	Married women in employment
1851	1 in 4
1911	1 in 10
1951	1 in 5
1980	1 in 2

EXERCISE

1 What evidence can you derive from this photograph to suggest that the modern housewife has more time to spare than her predecessors?
2 What do sociologists mean when they say that today's housewives spend much more time on the 'home beautiful'? Illustrate your answer with as many examples as you can think of.

Women and education

Gender divisions in employment

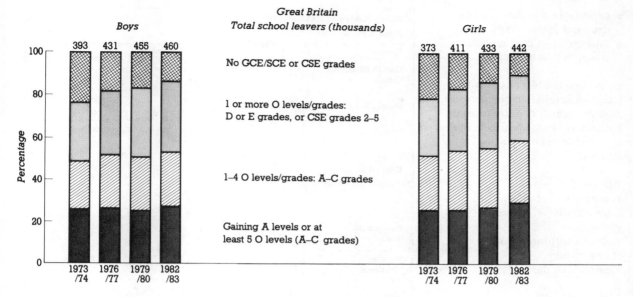

Great Britain
Total school leavers (thousands)

Boys

Girls

Percentage

No GCE/SCE or CSE grades

1 or more O levels/grades:
D or E grades, or CSE grades 2–5

1–4 O levels/grades: A–C grades

Gaining A levels or at
least 5 O levels (A–C grades)

Boys: 393 (1973/74), 431 (1976/77), 455 (1979/80), 460 (1982/83)

Girls: 373 (1973/74), 411 (1976/77), 433 (1979/80), 442 (1982/83)

Source: Department of Education and Science

can be partly explained by girls' experiences at school. One of the main functions of education, as we have already discussed, is that it acts as an agency of socialisation. The schooling process prepares young people for their adult roles and this not only involves the teaching of specific skills and knowledge but also the transmission of values.

The education system does not create gender differences and inequality, although sociologists are interested in the aspects of the schooling process which reinforce and perpetuate gender distinctions. At face value, there is little difference in the educational experiences and performances of girls and boys until the age of 16, except in the area of subject specialisation. Girls tend to specialise in arts subjects and boys in science subjects. Specialisation is important because of its implications for later educational and job opportunities. For example, it is easier to obtain a university place for science than for arts or social science subjects. After 16, however, there are clear

differences between the sexes in educational achievement and opportunities available.

EXERCISE

Look carefully at the chart, and indicate whether the statements that follow are true or false:

1 In 1982–83 girls were more successful than boys in gaining a minimum of 5 O levels (A–C grades).
2 In Britain in 1979–80, 43 300 girls left school.
3 At least 10% of all children in 1982–83 left school without any qualifications.
4 More girls than boys leave school without qualifications.
5 On the evidence of examination results, educational standards are deteriorating.

We will now briefly compare the performances of girls and boys in the education system:

Primary level (5–11)
● girls score higher than boys in tests of verbal ability (word skills). Because of this, the 11-plus examination was adjusted to favour boys in allowing as

many boys as girls to get into grammar schools.

Secondary level (11–16)
Girls
● experience a drop in ability levels
● achieve higher IQ scores than boys but there is a mismatch between IQ and academic achievement
● underachievement begins around puberty and accelerates thereafter

Boys
● IQ scores remain constant
● there is a close relationship between achievement and IQ levels
● underachievement (less frequent than with girls but still considerable) begins before puberty

Post school level (16 plus)
Studies have revealed that women, compared with men:
● are likelier to be found in the *low-status* institutions such as Colleges of Further Education and Teacher Training Colleges
● are likelier to enrol on shorter, low-level courses

- experience a higher level of drop-out at university
- take up fewer post-graduate research jobs as students

According to Margaret Mead's study *Male and Female* there are significant gender differences in both ability and interests between men and women. This is a summary:

Ability

Females are better at
Verbal skills (writing and speaking)
Arithmetic (number skills)
Rote memory
Fine manual dexterity

Males are better at
Spacial tasks (manipulating shapes)
Maths (problem solving)
Mechanical and practical skills

Interests

Females are more interested in activities which are
Musical
Literary
Religious
Aesthetic (artistic)

Males are more interested in activities which are
Mechanical
Scientific
Physically strenuous
Political and theoretical

EXERCISE

As you read through this school report, try to guess the sex of Chris Lovett.

1 How did you reach your decision as to the sex of Chris Lovett?
2 In what way would you expect a school report to be different for a member of the opposite sex?
3 What objections might a sociologist have about some of the comments made by the teachers?

Bishop Fisher Comprehensive School		End of year report: July 1986
Name of Pupil Chris Lovett	**Form: 5C**	

Subject	Grade	Comments
English language **English literature**	D+	Capable but a disruptive influence in class. Could try harder. AR
Mathematics	B	A good year's work - has natural talent. LP
History **Geography**	C	A lively contributor. Produces very untidy work and is easily distracted. P.L.J.
General science	B	Shows interest and ability. Has produced a high standard of work. Reluctant to clear up after experiments. RE.
Art	E	MAKES NO EFFORT. BONE IDLE. A TIME-WASTER. DJ.
Needlework **Home economics**		
Woodwork **Metalwork**	B+	Shows natural aptitude and manual dexterity. Good project results. SR
Technical drawing	B	An able and accurate pupil - has a good head for figures. GN.
Music	E	If I could remember what this pupil looked like I might be in a position to comment. Attendance has been appalling. DR.
Physical education	A	A STRONG STURDY ALL ROUNDER. JJ.

Why is there inequality in educational achievement?

Research findings, particularly from the USA, have challenged the assumption that difference in attainment between the sexes is innate – which means that if girls and boys are not born with different intellectual capacities and aptitudes, then any differences must be socially created. Tessa Blackstone and Helen-Haste, in an article in *New Society*, 'Why are there so few women scientists and engineers?', argue that girls learn to underachieve. Psychologists have explained this as a 'fear of success'. Girls see achievement in intellectual and sporting pursuits as aggressive and therefore as masculine, although this is not a conscious process.

Teacher expectations of a pupil's performances are also important. Blackstone and Helen-Haste point out that these are often unconscious and expressed in various subtle and indirect ways. For instance, the teacher may encourage behaviour differences by allocating different tasks to boys and girls. Boys may be asked or told to do things which require physical strength (such as carrying heavy objects) and technical knowledge (helping to set up a slide show). Girls, on the other hand, may be asked to perform the more social tasks like taking messages, making tea and answering the telephone. These differences serve to reinforce existing notions of masculinity and femininity.

Similar behaviour in boys and girls may also be treated differently by teachers. For example, a girl might be told off for looking scruffy, whereas a boy's scruffiness might be ignored. This highlights a further point. What a teacher does not comment on can be as important as what a teacher does comment on. There is evidence that boys receive far more of the teacher's attention and praise than girls, and that classes are geared more towards the interests of boys. In Michelle Stanworth's *Gender and Schooling: A Study of Sexual Division in the Classroom* it was reported that both boys and girls considered teachers to be more concerned about boys. The teachers themselves thought boys were more conscientious, capable, got on better with them, enjoyed teaching them, and were likelier to consider boys as model pupils. These findings agree with similar studies in the USA which show that boys receive more negative and positive attention from teachers in primary and secondary schools.

Sue Sharpe reports different treatment given to boys and girls, as described by girls in an Ealing secondary school:

Teachers seemed to be more sarcastic to boys and more respectful to girls. (Boys can 'take it' better.) Girls are expected to be more tidy in their ways and in their work. Boys, however, could get away with messy books and untidy behaviour.

School timetables are often arranged around certain taken-for-granted assumptions about girls' and boys' subjects. In a study of British mixed schools in the early 1970s, the employment assumptions shown in the following table were made by both pupils and staff:

Career assumptions of pupils and staff

Girls become
Nurses
Shop assistants
Clerical officers
Typists
Computer operators
Computer programmers

Boys become
Doctors
Managers
Administrative and executive officers
Sales managers
Accountants
Computer engineers or salespersons

Source: Byrne (1975) cited in *Subject Women*

The table suggests that teachers and pupils view the education of boys as being different from the education of girls. This view might affect the way school timetables are organised, in that pupils might have to make certain subject choices. For example, girls might be discouraged or prevented from following workshop-based courses. Sue Sharpe found that even when the opportunity is offered to girls to learn manual skills, they are not allowed access to the more complex tools used by boys to produce advanced work. Her research, carried out in the early 1970s, indicates that the secondary school curriculum is still gender based, though less so than in the past. Girls in her sample were directed towards arts subjects, cookery, needlework, housecraft, typing and commerce. Boys were guided towards scientific and technical subjects.

EXERCISE

Below is a story written by Lucy, aged 8, entitled *What I want to be when I grow up*:

1 In what way could school experiences have contributed to Lucy's ideas about her future?
2 Do you think this story could have been written by a boy? Explain your answer.
3 Write a short story of similar length on the same subject that could have been written by an 8-year-old boy.

The **Equal Opportunities Commission** issued a report in 1983 which highlighted the extent to which subject choice in secondary schools follows sex based divisions. Of a sample group who took craft, design and technology at O level or CSE, only 2.4% were girls. The report suggested that teachers and pupils tended to regard craft, design and technology as boys' subjects. Sexual stereotyping has more powerful effects in mixed rather than in single sex schools where girls are more likely to opt for and do well in maths and sciences. The very presence of boys may have a negative effect on girls' educational performances. An investigation carried out by Smithers and Collings looked at 2000 sixth form pupils in 35 schools in the north of England. They found that more girls were taking science subjects in the single sex schools. The authors,

When I grow up I want to live in a nice big house on the top of a hill with trees all around and swings and apple trees and flowurs in the garden. I will see my best friend Tracey every day because she wants to live in the little house at the bottom of the hill. She can come for tea and her children can come to play with my children. I have decided that I am going to have three children called Lindsey, Paula and Harriet. When my children go to school I'm going to work but I haven't decided what to be yet. I might be a balley dancer or I might work behind the counter at Boots but I don't think I'll do that because I'm not very good at sums.

however, pointed out that girls attending single sex schools tended to come from higher social class backgrounds and have higher ability ranges than their contemporaries in mixed schools.

One other important aspect of socialisation in schools is the stereotyped attitudes of teachers. In primary schools the majority of junior teachers are women who expect from their pupils feminine-associated behaviour such as obedience, silence, passivity and conformity. This probably explains why girls do better than boys at this stage of their education, since younger children like to imitate and identify with parents, teachers and other adults of the same sex.

Schoolchildren can also see for themselves that their own schools are organised along traditional gender lines. As the following charts show, the percentage of women in the top-paid and high-status jobs in teaching is markedly less than for men, while the proportion of low-paid Scale 1 and 2 teachers who are women is high and getting higher. Headships, in particular, are heavily male dominated, even though teaching as a profession employs more

women than men (59% of teachers are women). Gender imprinting does not stop with the organisation of the school; it continues relentlessly throughout a child's school experiences. Male teachers are usually found teaching masculine subjects (physics, chemistry, metalwork, woodwork) and female teachers feminine subjects (biology, music, domestic science, English), and a child's own sex will obviously be an important factor in determining success and failure in particular school subjects.

EXERCISE

1 Approximately what percentages of men and women were primary and secondary school heads in 1983?
2 Can you suggest why there are more men than women head teachers?
3 Approximately what percentage of Scale 1 teachers (lowest grade) were women in primary and secondary schools in 1983?
4 Using data from these charts, explain how the chances of promotion for women teachers have declined between 1973 and 1983.
5 Explain why there are fewer women teachers in secondary schools than in primary schools. Your answer should include references to salary levels and to the nature of the job.

Sue Sharpe concludes in her study of an Ealing secondary school that girls lack 3 qualities which are needed if they are to challenge gender divisions in employment. These are confidence, opportunities in male orientated jobs, and the desire to challenge sexual divisions in the workplace. This desire is hampered by attitudes in general about the accepted roles of men and women.

Although the school does not create gender differences, it can be seen that certain aspects of schooling reinforce and perpetuate these differences. When girls choose girls' subjects they become excluded from a range of possible careers for which the boys' subjects are required. Society, in general, expects less of girls in terms of educational achievement and occupational success. Both Tessa Blackstone and Sue Sharpe's studies reveal how girls have lower aspirations about their careers, and this factor is bound to affect their performance within the education system.

EXERCISE

As a member of a nationwide research

Women as a % of teachers on each scale: 1979 and 1983 primary

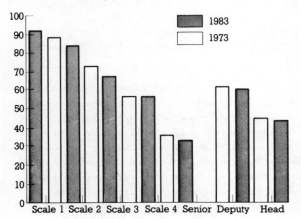

Women as a % of teachers on each scale: 1973 and 1983 secondary

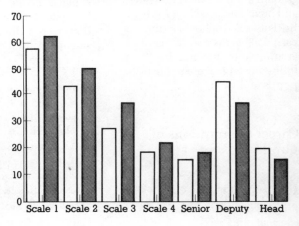

Source: **Department of Education and Science**

team, you are asked to find out what a random sample of boys and girls in your school or college thinks about school and work. Here are 3 questions from the questionnaire that you have been asked to research:

1 In which three school subjects are you most successful?
2 In which subject are you least successful?
3 Taking a realistic view of yourself, what kind of job or training will you be looking for when your education is completed?

When you have completed the interviewing, your next step will be to interpret the data. What you want to know is whether there is a relationship between
- success or failure in subjects at school and job expectations, and
- the sex of the respondent and his or her job expectation.

Present your findings and conclusions in a short report. If you find difficulty in drawing conclusions from your findings, this may be due to faulty methods of interpretation. Social research is never easy.

QUESTIONS

Read this letter which Jane has sent to her friend, Debbie:

Just thought I'd drop you a line to let you know how I'm getting on in my new secretarial job at the record company. To put it mildly, I'm disappointed. You know how I was led to believe that it would be really exciting, meeting lots of interesting people, pop stars and all that? Well, it's completely different. I'm stuck in a dingy office from 9 till 5 all week and I'm at his lordship's (the boss) beck and call all day long – taking him cups of tea, popping to the shops to pick up his newspapers and things, and goodness knows what else!

I spend all day typing really boring letters and answering the phone. The boss is OK, really, but I was a bit put out last week when he asked me to come to work dressed up, as some important blokes were coming, and we had to keep up the company's good image, he said. Sometimes I wish I'd stayed at Pottameats – at least we had a laugh there!!!

How are you getting on with your nursing? Write soon and let me know.
Bye for now,
Jane.

1 Explain the relationship between Jane's job and housework   (8 marks) How do the following predominantly female jobs reflect women's domestic roles:
   a Nursing
   b Teaching in a primary school
   c Shopwork   (12 marks)
2 'The education of girls tends to put them at a disadvantage in the world of work'
   a Explain, using examples, how the school system might contribute to a girl's disadvantage at work.   (10 marks)
   b Discuss the various ways women experience disadvantage at work.   (10 marks)
3 Discuss, with reference to any sociological studies with which you are familiar, the notion that today's women are more liberated than they used to be.   (20 marks)

Bid to give girls a better deal in class
Evening Mail Reporter

New moves are being made in Birmingham to change the old parental belief that it is not worth educating girls and to give girls a better deal in the classroom.

Initial talks were being held today at a meeting between education chiefs and teachers' representatives, on ways of achieving equal opportunity for the fair sex in city schools.

This would involve opening up better career prospects for girls by encouraging them to take up subjects and courses at present dominated by boys, including the sciences, mathematics and engineering.

It would be much more than simply ending the old sex divisions of boys doing woodwork and metalwork while girls do cookery and home economics.

And the review may have to tackle the problem of bright girls including those from ethnic minorities being carried off instead of developing their potential by going on to higher education.

Education officials are proposing to set up a working group between the council and teachers to explore ideas for ensuring that girls get fair and reasonable access to all courses.

A report would be presented later to the city's education committee on how this could be achieved.

The move would be in line with the drive by the controlling Labour group on the city council to promote equal opportunity.

Source: Birmingham Evening Mail

Why it's ladies last at school
by David Lister

Schools are not 'girl friendly'. Teachers give more time and attention to boys, gear their lessons to them, and allow them to hog specialist science and computer equipment. That will be the theme of a national conference in Manchester this week which the Equal Opportunities Commission is organising – for the first time – on girls' education.

The conference, entitled 'Girl Friendly Schooling', will address itself to the fact that, in England, 131 000 boys a year study physics at O level and 42 000 at A level: for girls, the figures are only 45 000 and 10 000.

The researchers and academics at the conference will hear that schools need to make big changes to attract girls' interest and guide them into scientific and technological careers.

A survey of 850 teachers in 50 schools by the North East London Polytechnic shows that half of male and a third of women teachers are opposed to practising equal opportunities. More than 1 in 3 of all the teachers in the survey thought that 'innate psychological differences' between the sexes were responsible for the different career choices of boys and girls.

One of the conference organisers, Mrs Maureen Cruickshank, who is the head of a Leicestershire school, said, 'We haven't begun to scratch the surface of what really goes on in the classroom.' She has video films of lessons showing that the boys sit at the front of the class and the teachers rarely address questions to the girls. In her school, boys and girls taking maths O level are separated, leading to a dramatic increase in the number of girls deciding to take maths at A level.

Dale Spender, formerly of the London University Institute of Education, toured schools to record classroom lessons and found that up to 90% of teachers' attention went to the male pupils.

The Girls into Science and Technology Project, one of the best known research programmes of its kind, says that boys monopolise science laboratory equipment, consistently depriving girls of practical experience.

Researchers from the project believe that if the personal and social side of scientific or technical subjects is emphasised, then girls' interest soars.

They tried a new way of teaching craft, design and technology at one of Britain's largest comprehensive schools, Stantonbury Campus at Milton Keynes.

They asked the children to design a playground, beginning with the safety factors and working back to the technical aspects. This approach led to a significant increase in the girls taking the course.

Source: The Sunday Times

Government statistics

The table below shows percentages of boy and girl school-leavers in England with GCE O Level grades A–C/CSEs Grade 1 in selected subjects. The figures refer to all school leavers irrespective of any A Levels obtained. They relate to 1982–83 and the figures in square brackets show the % increase in girls and boys with this qualification between 1971–72 and 1982–83.

Subject	Boys %	Girls %
English	34[+10]	45[+22]
Mathematics	32[+17]	27[+42]
Physics	22[+37]	8[+110]
Chemistry	15[+32]	10[+111]
Biology	13[+40]	20[+15]
French	11[−14]	19[+7]
CDT and other Sciences	18[+7]	3[−6]
Commercial and domestic	3[+200]	17[+24]

QUESTIONS

1 According to the article 'Why it's ladies last at school'
  a How many girls and boys study physics at A Level?
  b What proportion of male teachers is opposed to practising equal opportunities?
  c What is the meaning of the phrase 'innate psychological differences between the sexes'?
  d What teaching strategy does the 'Girls into Science and Technology Project' suggest to encourage girls to study scientific and technical subjects?
2 What social factors influence a girl's choice of subjects at school?
3 Can you suggest any reasons why up to 90% of teachers' attention went to male pupils?
4 What conclusions can be drawn about the education of girls from the Government statistics?

POINTS FOR DISCUSSION

- Girls have exactly the same educational chances as boys.
- Birmingham education committee is mistaken in encouraging girls to study woodwork and metalwork and other skills leading to dirty jobs.

Case Study

Women at work

The following extracts are taken from case-studies published in *The Other Half of our Future.* All the women were receiving training in carpentry at the Lambeth Women's Workshop (LWW) in London during May of 1984. TOPs are government-sponsored training courses for adults.

Alex

has completed her City and Guilds qualification in carpentry and is working as a skilled carpenter with other tradeswomen. She attended a mixed school where 'there was no woodwork or metalwork for girls'. She found she 'had a block about maths and science' at school but during her City and Guilds training and in her work was able to take a different attitude:

Now I enjoy technical drawing and geometry because I relate it to my work and though I still find some difficulties I can do a lot better than the boys I did City and Guilds with.

She 'always resented the fact that boys did the interesting things at school' but also thought arts subjects were proper for girls and worked for many years in traditional work while considering it wrong that women were 'boxed in' as secretaries, typists, receptionists, etc.

She applied for a TOPs course in carpentry and was rejected on the grounds that she was a woman and did not have the necessary knowledge. 'I went away and did evening classes and read books and did work in jobbing carpentry'. It took 2½ years from first applying for her to obtain a place on a TOPs course. She found evening classes did not teach the fundamental skills she wanted and the supervisor was unsympathetic to her wish to 'learn joints'. She was able to get a day-release course with a woman instructor learning a lot and gaining confidence. She found that at college 'there was neither encouragement nor discouragement, though everything was male oriented'. She has been bombarded with unwanted advice thoughout her studies and training:

Women can't do heavy work/Why don't you do a proper job?/You should be at home having babies.

She would rather not describe the sexual comments made to her as these would read 'like a filthy magazine'. She sums up:

The overriding attitude is that girls/women are either mothers/wives to service men or 'sexy crumpets' to be sexually put down. Whatever class – it's just the ways and words that are different.

Jackie

is in her second year of City and Guilds carpentry and joinery. She took a TOPs course in 1979, worked in partnership with a friend for 2 years and worked for 3 years on building sites.

She attended a mixed school where she says there were 'no opportunities, no encouragement given to girls to take technical

subjects or technical drawing. Science subjects weren't encouraged: academic girls were expected to take arts and languages. If not, then typing and homecraft. Boys' craft subjects were not on the girls' syllabus, though boys could take cooking if they chose to.'

She found an interest in learning carpentry because, amongst the staff of children's playgrounds where she worked, 'the men made the play structures and the women did craft.' She resented the 'sex role divisions' and thought carpentry skills would help her break out of them. Once she started her training 'I found it interesting, realised I could earn a reasonable wage and that I'd have the security of a skill'. Before she started training she was quite good at DIY and she received encouragement 'from friends'.

Though successful in her application for a TOPSs course she was asked questions about her capacity to lift heavy weights which were unrealistic as she found that men on site would not lift such weights without assistance. At the skill centre she was always conscious 'you had to do that little better than the men to be taken seriously.'

She met many arguments against her training on the lines of

Wasting tax-payers' money/she wouldn't be able to get a job/would only want children/not strong enough/couldn't face the conditions (bad weather) on site.

In seeking employment she was told flatly 'we don't want a woman' and at the end of 6 months working on site producing work to a good standard she was told by the site foreman 'that had he been involved in employing me I wouldn't have got the job'.

She records an incident of sexual harassment on site:

I was sent up to the roof (to put architrave round the windows) and I asked the roofers where the windows were. One

said 'could I measure something small for him first'.

In a different way the foreman singled her out by checking her work 'whereas he did not check the other carpenters' work.'

Denise

is a tutor at the LWW. She has passed City and Guilds and did her course at the London College of Furniture. It is clear from her comments that she has experienced racial as well as sexual prejudice:

I attended a comprehensive mixed school. It was unheard of a girl entering a subject reserved for boys but there was no rule . . . so I happened to be the first girl to do woodwork.

A year or two afterwards she was the first girl to do technical drawing.

Her initial ambition to enter the RAF was blocked by her mother's attitude, and she found careers advisers unhelpful. When seeking a job in her chosen skill there were a wide variety of 'discouraging, insulting remarks'. Her first letter of refusal for a job in 1975 said 'We don't employ women.' Other prospective employers commented:

What do you think of your colour?/What does your husband think?/Do you have children?/I will have to ask my wife/I don't think some of the men will like being supervised by a black woman/I really can't imagine . . .

She was told that her hands were not large enough to use a 12 inch pair of scissors.

Her advice to other women who may be starting in the same path is:

If you feel deep down in your heart and mind that you have to do it, do it. Just remember to enjoy it. Some day in the future there may be a few all womens' business companies, whether it be in decorating, electrical wiring, carpentry, plumbing, etc. And the stay-at-home woman might require the services of one of these firms. The woman will be comfortable knowing that someone of her sex is doing a good job.

QUESTIONS

1 Work through these case studies and indicate examples where the education system has failed to provide a satisfactory preparation for a working life or has actually hindered the women's job prospects.

2 *a* From these case studies, select a range of personal experiences that show that some men behave differently towards women workers than they behave towards male workers.

b Can you suggest reasons why men in general have these sorts of attitudes?

c Explain whether you think that male manual workers are more hostile than male professional workers to the employment of women.

3 With reference to any sociological studies you are familiar with, explain why the sexual attitudes of some male workers are based on false and stereotyped ideas of women's capabilities.

4 In general, why do women experience disadvantages at work?

Points for discussion

- Women get the jobs they deserve.
- In times of unemployment, men should get preferential treatment at work.
- Housework is not real work; it's just pottering about.

Important points

- The vast majority of women in Britain experience social and economic inequalities compared with men.
- Most employed women have jobs that are low paid, unskilled, part-time, low in status, short on promotion prospects, unprotected by employment law, and usually within a narrow range of occupations, including shop and office work.
- Many sociologists believe that most employed women are engaged in activities that are essentially an extension of domestic chores.
- In most professional occupations, men, and not women, occupy the high-status positions and are far more likely to be promoted.
- A great deal of prejudice is still directed at women in job selection and promotion interviews, particularly in traditional male-dominated occupations.
- Most research studies suggest that women are disadvantaged at work for social rather than for biological reasons. The potent social factor seems to be the recognition of the mother-housewife role as the most important role for women in our society. Women in paid employment are not taken seriously.
- Female and male personality characteristics are probably socially and not biologically determined.
- We learn to behave like boys and girls are expected to behave from our parents, our toys, the mass media, and the world around us.
- Some research suggests that housework has been socially downgraded compared with paid employment. In fact housework has been found to be more arduous and stressful than many paid jobs.
- Labour-saving devices in the home do not necessarily mean that less time and energy are spent on domestic needs and chores. Gardening and do-it-yourself activities are now more common than they used to be.
- The proportion of married women taking up paid employment has doubled since the last century.
- The education system tends to reinforce and perpetuate gender differences in both students and teaching staff.
- Girls at school tend to specialise in arts subjects and boys in science and technical subjects. This makes it more difficult for girls and women to get technology-based jobs (ie, the better jobs).
- Girls may underachieve in the education system because teachers pay more attention to boys' needs. Sexual stereotyping may also be encouraged through channelling girls and boys into gender-based subjects.

7 Wealth, poverty and welfare

When you have worked through this chapter you should have a clearer understanding of

Social structure · Wealth · Income · Absolute and relative poverty · Objective and subjective poverty · The Welfare State · Functions of poverty · Culture of poverty

Wealth and poverty

We live in a society of different institutions and class groupings making up what we call the social structure. An essential part of the sociologist's work is to identify the objective factors in this structure which make one group different from another. One way of doing this would be to study physical differences. We can observe that some people have blond hair and others black hair and some people are tall and others short. However these physical differences are not of great interest to the sociologist. When sociologists study the social landscape the questions they ask are: Why do some people enjoy great wealth while others are in dire poverty? How is it possible for some people to own villas in Spain and ocean-going yachts while others have difficulty finding their bus fares? How can we spend so much of our money on books, magazines and special foods in order to lose weight when others have to face the struggle to feed themselves and their families? As with many questions relating to wealth and poverty it is possible

to hold strong views. This extract is taken from a speech delivered by an industrialist at a gathering of international financiers:

The point we should never lose sight of is that if you give individual X 100 dollars and you give individual Y the same amount, at the end of the year one individual will have wasted his money while the other individual will have prospered and increased the number of dollars. This, gentlemen, is what we call human nature . . .

What point is the industrialist making?

He is suggesting that the reason some people have wealth and others have none is connected with a quality within people's make-up or personality. In other words, it is a quality or a feature of *human nature*. As sociologists we know that such explanations are unacceptable because life is not that simple. People are neither wealthy nor poor because of some strange quirk of personality. We are all born into families which are themselves a product of the social and economic structure and it is by considering factors associated with this structure that we begin to understand the uneven

distribution of wealth in our society. Of course nobody denies that a person's individual contributions are important in determining the degree to which they will be rich or poor in life, but our life-chances are heavily dependent on our starting position and on our experiences in the world as we grow up. However, before we go any further we must define what we mean by wealth.

EXERCISE

Under the heading **poverty** draw up a list of 10 factors that characterise being poor in British society. You can start your list with **having little money**. Draw up a contrasting list under the heading **wealthy**.

What is wealth?

It will be useful to distinguish between wealth and income. Usually income is spending money coming into the family home and wealth refers to the ownership of fixed assets that can be turned into cash. Although it is true that almost everyone has assets, this does not mean that everyone is wealthy. If you are a house owner, for example, who has a small sum of money stashed in a building society account it would be unrealistic to talk in terms of turning your home into cash because it would render you homeless. Anyway, many people only partly own their homes if they have a mortgage and over 50% of cars on British roads are company owned. Therefore when we talk of wealth, we are not talking about necessary personal possessions that are only partly owned but of the ownership of assets in excess of personal requirements. These **marketable assets** include possession of

- land and buildings
- industrial plant, equipment and goods
- stocks and shares
- large cash deposits and valuable personal possessions.

The diagram shows how this wealth was distributed in our society in 1976.

The distribution of wealth in 1976

We can see that the top 1% of our population owns more marketable wealth than the whole of the bottom 80% of the population. This gross inequality provides the framework on which the social class system of stratification is built. It bestows on the rich a level of prestige, independence and security that is immensely resistant to both change and challenge. The real importance of wealth, however, is not just the comforts it brings to the people who have it but its relationship to the exercise of political power and social control. For instance, by moving shares and capital from one company or country to another a person might increase or

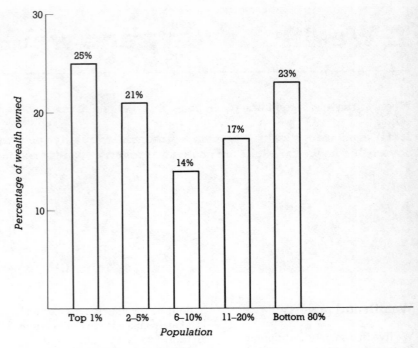

Source: An A to Z of Income and Wealth

Percentage of population owning wealth.

decrease the returns from his investments, and in the Stock Exchange it is possible to see millions of pounds changing hands daily without any goods or services necessarily being produced.

During the 1960s and 1970s investment in Britain was primarily made in property development – note the large and often empty office blocks in your own town – and while this investment gave good returns in rent it had the effect of starving the manufacturing sector of funds. This in turn led British manufacturing to become less profitable as less money was available for investing in new machinery and technology. Today some of the millions of people who are unemployed are aware that the failure to invest in British industry was in part responsible

for the closure of factories and the loss of their jobs.

EXERCISE

With reference to the chart at the top of page 111:

1 Explain in plain English the meaning of the term **dwellings, net of mortgage debt**.
2 How would you describe the trend in home ownership between 1971 and 1981?
3 What particular aspect of wealth ownership has seen the most dramatic change between 1971 and 1981?

The changing distribution of wealth

According to the *Report of the Royal Commission on Welfare and Income* published in 1975 the proportions of very wealthy people in our society have been steadily decreasing throughout the 20th century, as this chart shows:

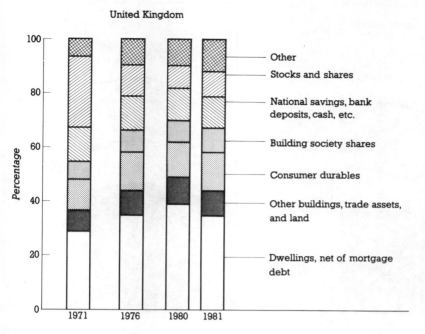

United Kingdom

Other
Stocks and shares
National savings, bank deposits, cash, etc.
Building society shares
Consumer durables
Other buildings, trade assets, and land
Dwellings, net of mortgage debt

Source: Inland Revenue

Composition of marketable wealth of individuals

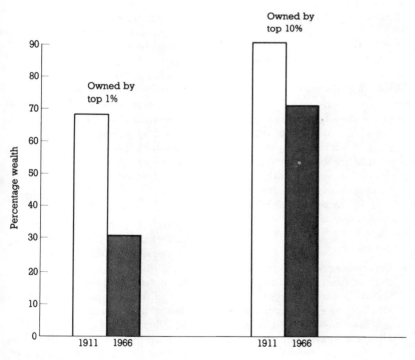

Distribution of wealth in Great Britain, 1911 and 1966

Included in the top 1% very rich are the great land-owning families which still exist in this country and those who have inherited industrial empires or accumulated vast share holdings in major companies. There are, of course, a few self-made millionaires, although the media tend to exaggerate their importance and their numbers.

However, it is to the persistence of wealth that we must turn to understand the consequences of its unequal distribution between the different social classes. Despite the quantitative changes during this century, the qualitative factors remain unaltered. The same small dominant class of people own most of the wealth and maintain the massive differential between rich and poor. The importance of inheritance and class background, and the almost impossible task of becoming rich through personal savings or employment, ensures that the top 10% rich occupy an almost closed social grouping. Even so, between 1966 and 1980 official statistics still show a gradual wealth-levelling process taking place (*see page 112*). Despite these trends, there are some researchers who believe that we are misreading the data. Anthony Atkinson, in his book *Unequal Shares*, doubts whether there has been any significant redistribution of wealth at all. He points out that most wealth derives from sources of income based on the ownership of property and goods such as land and plant. This means that statistics showing the tendency towards a less unequal society might be misleading because they are based on wealth and not on income. In other words, there are many people whose great wealth continues to accumulate because of the income earned by that wealth in the form of rents and

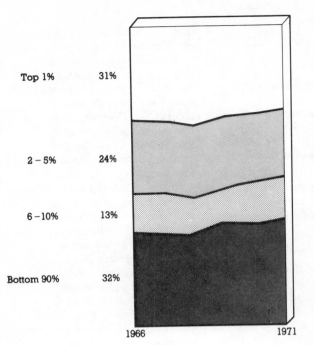
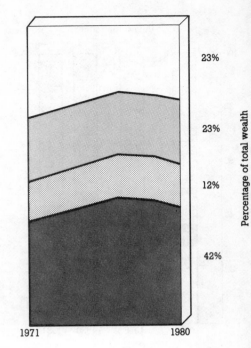

Top 1%   31%

2 – 5%   24%

6 – 10%   13%

Bottom 90%   32%

1966   1971

23%

23%

12%

42%

Percentage of total wealth

1971   1980

(Change in basis of statistics)

Source: Government Statistics

Percentage of population owning wealth.

interest charges. Rather than moving towards the equal distribution of wealth in a classless society, Atkinson thinks that the real distribution takes place between the already rich. Wealth simply begets wealth. The more you have, the greater the opportunities there are to get even more by investing your money in wealth-producing activities.

EXERCISE

Referring to the chart 'Percentage of population owning wealth':
1 What percentage of total wealth was owned by the top 10% of the population in 1966 and 1980?
2 What general trend can you detect in this chart?
3 Draw some comparisons between this chart and the 'Registrar General's social classification' on page 25. Explain which social class groupings are most likely to fit into the four wealth-owning categories on the chart.
4 Taking each wealth-owning category

in turn, describe in one paragraph the kind of person you imagine might occupy that category.
5 Explain, using your own words, why the information on this chart might be misleading.

What is income?

We have already described income as spending money coming into the family home. More precisely it is the disposable money we get from employment and other outside sources after deductions have been made, such as income tax and national insurance contributions. The main sources of income are:

- **Earned income.** This is money derived from employment, taking the form of wages, salaries and company pensions, and may include 'benefits in kind' such as a company car or luncheon vouchers.
- **Unearned income.** This is money derived from commercial

or business activities and property ownership. It includes profits, rents, interest from investments, gambling profits and inherited money.
- **Social income.** This is money derived from the state in the form of welfare benefits. It includes old age pensions, unemployment benefits, child benefits and supplementary benefits for people whose standard of living has fallen below a minimum level set by the government.

Although we have neatly set out the major types of income, it is important to appreciate that an average family in Britain may receive money from all 3 sources, depending on personal circumstances. Many less well off families, for example, will have a nest egg in a building society or a post office earning a little unearned income, and millionaires are as entitled as you are to receive from the state an old age pension and child benefit allowances.

1 My name is Ronald Harvey. I'm 68 years old and I retired from my job as a school caretaker 3 years ago. I live with my wife June in a terraced house which we bought 10 years ago. We collect our old age pension every Thursday from the post office – that comes to £57.55 for the 2 of us. I also get a small pension from my job, about £5 per week. My wife has a part-time job herself in a shop round the corner. She gets £16 per week for that – you know, cash in hand like. We also have a bit of money in the post office. I suppose that's worth about £2 per week in interest. The only other money we get is a rates rebate. It isn't much, mind you, about £1.50 a week, but it all helps. Hold on! You're not from the social, are you? I don't want them knowing about my wife's job.

2 My name is Maureen Johnson. I'm 26 years old and I live in a council flat with my 2 children, Neil and Amanda. My husband walked out on me about 18 months ago and I haven't seen him since. I get £34.80 supplementary benefit and £13.70 child benefit each week, and the DHSS pay the rent of £26.75 a week so I don't have to worry about that. I get one milk token a week for the youngest and I claim free school dinners for the eldest. Making ends meet is a struggle, especially when winter comes – what with Christmas and heating bills – but my dad always gives me 50-odd pounds over the Christmas to help out. I've got a boyfriend, George, although I shouldn't tell you this, he gives me a fiver a week to help clothe the kids. He says he likes them looking nice when we go out – he calls it 'paying the rent'. I also get a few quid when I help out down the *Green Dragon*. At the moment I do 3 nights a week. I get £8 a night and a couple of pounds in tips. George doesn't mind looking after the kids till I get back.

Read through these 2 accounts carefully and under the appropriate headings of **earned income**, **unearned income** and **social income** make a record of each household's weekly income.

Distribution of income

Income, along with wealth, is also unevenly distributed amongst the

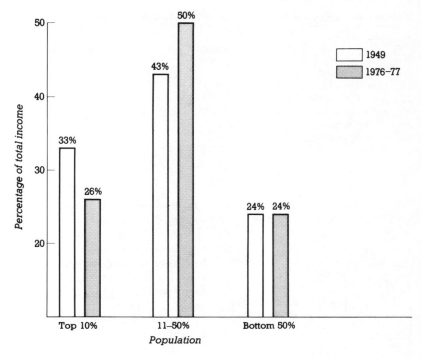

Source: An A to Z of Income and Wealth

Income from all sources over a 30-year period, before tax

population. If we look at the changes in income distribution over a period of 30 years, we can see that the top 10% of the income earning population received more than the whole of the bottom 50%. Although it is true that the top 10% experienced a fall in their share of income over the period, their loss did not help the bottom 50%, but was retained within the top half of income earners:

What do these statistics and trends tell us?

They suggest, in general terms, that although income is unevenly distributed, it is not as unevenly distributed as wealth. They also suggest that for the working class there has been no real opportunity to get a bigger slice of the income cake, despite many promising social and economic trends that seemed to be occurring during the 1950s and 1960s.

There is, of course, more than one way of examining income distribution. A full-time worker's income is likely to be influenced by

* whether they are male or female, and
* whether they are manual or non-manual workers.

According to the *Report of the 1984 Family Expenditure Survey* full-time manual workers earn less than non-manual workers, and women workers are paid substantially less than men workers across the whole spectrum of full-time jobs.

On the basis of information contained in the following table, explain how

* manual workers earn less than non-manual workers
* women do not enjoy equal pay with men for equal work
* wage differentials remain an important factor in the distribution of earned income in British society.

Distribution of gross weekly earnings for full-time adult employees, April 1984

	Male		Female	
	Manual	Non-manual	Manual	Non-manual
	£	£	£	£
10% earned less than	94.1	109.4	62.0	74.5
25% earned less than	115.2	143.3	72.7	89.4
50% earned less than	143.3	188.8	88.6	113.5
25% earned more than	178.8	247.4	108.1	149.6
10% earned more than	220.7	325.2	131.0	185.2

Cost of benefits received as a percentage of wages and salaries

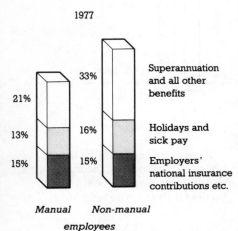

1977

Superannuation and all other benefits

Holidays and sick pay

Employers' national insurance contributions etc.

Manual   Non-manual

employees

Source: An A to Z of Income and Wealth

Generally speaking, the more you earn, the larger percentage of benefit you get on top of pay. We therefore have to think twice before we too readily accept that income differentials are becoming less extreme. It may be that the distribution of income is taking a slightly different form.

EXERCISE

(Refer to table opposite.)

1 What was the average weekly income for a household whose family head was unemployed?
2 What was the gross weekly income for an employed head of household?
3 What source of social income is likely to be available to a household whose head is
   a unemployed, and
   b currently employed?
4 Why is it that the wives of unemployed heads of households tend to earn less than the wives of employed heads of households?

The unequal distribution of income does not stop at wages received. The inequality continues with **benefits in kind** or **fringe benefits** which are becoming more common than they used to be. Many workers receive cash equivalents in the form of superannuation (company pensions), paid holidays, sick pay, travelling allowances, luncheon vouchers and cheap loans. Here again, we find that manual workers do not enjoy the same advantages as their non-manual counterparts.

In fact, as we progress up the social class ladder the **benefits in kind** increase at a substantial rate, as you can see from the following chart:

Poverty and wealth

How much poverty exists in Britain?

There are people in our society who find it difficult to believe that *real* poverty can exist. This might

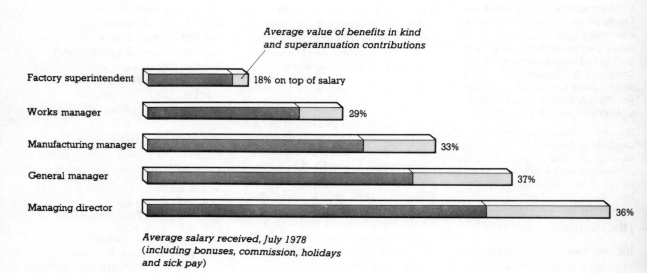

Average value of benefits in kind and superannuation contributions

Factory superintendent — 18% on top of salary

Works manager — 29%

Manufacturing manager — 33%

General manager — 37%

Managing director — 36%

Average salary received, July 1978 (including bonuses, commission, holidays and sick pay)

Average income, by employment status of head of household, 1983

	Employee currently employed	Employee out of job
Average weekly Income (£)	**247.6**	**146.2**
Gross income of household members:		
Head	183.2	98.5
Wife	41.1	28.8
Others	23.3	18.9
Sources of income:		
Wages and salaries	213.0	84.9
Social security benefits	11.8	40.4
Other	22.8	20.9

Source: Family Expenditure Survey

be because their understanding and experience of the social world is limited. We are all, to a great extent, members of our own special communities and it is sometimes difficult for us to appreciate the different kinds of life-experiences that exist in other communities. The following story illustrates this. Although the people in the story have difficulty in understanding how anyone could find themselves living in poverty in present-day Britain, some of us might equally regard their lifestyle as strange and outside our personal experiences.

Dizzy Mrs Simpson

Mrs Simpson was in one of her flaps. Her life was never well-ordered but the unexpected always threatened to bring utter chaos. Her family nickname was Dizzy because of the state she got into when something came along which got her hot and bothered. The telephone call from her daughter was a case in point. Her daughter announced that she would be visiting on Saturday, along with her husband Jeremy. This was enough to send Dizzy into one of her flaps. It was so important to put on a good show for her daughter and her husband because he was a business consultant and on the way up.

Dizzy decided to take them out for a meal. It would be a treat for everybody. They hadn't been in town for ages – she had been much too busy entertaining at home since Bertie had died. A friend, Mrs Henshaw, had mentioned a new French restaurant in Carlisle Street that was simply a 'must'. It was called the *Rue St James* and, according to the well-informed Mrs Henshaw, it provided marvellous food for people who knew how to enjoy themselves. Enjoying food was something Mrs Henshaw knew all about.

Dizzy telephoned the restaurant to make a booking for 3 people. They would sit down at 8, but she planned to be there half-an-hour early for drinks.

'I think Mrs Henshaw must have told everyone about this place,' she remarked on arriving at the *Rue St James*, 'It certainly is very crowded.'

'And they say that people are still living in poverty in Britain,' Jeremy observed as he made his way to the bar to order drinks.

'Well,' said Dizzy, 'you would hardly believe there was a recession. I don't know what people are complaining about.'

The evening went well. It was just as she had planned. They were very pleased with their dinner. They started with mixed *poisson fumé*, then they each tackled three wonderfully melting *cotelilles d'orgneau grillée au ramarin*, laid

carefully on top and not beneath the sauce, just as one likes them. The wine was wonderful. She told herself that the next time she came – and there would be a next time – she would try the slivers of quail breast and tiny quail eggs with a spinach salad. It all seemed so delicious.

'You know,' Dizzy said as she toyed with her lime sorbet.

'I think it's wonderful to live in a country like ours where so many people can afford to wine and dine in places like this.'

Everyone agreed. It was indeed wonderful.

'And I'll tell you something else,' Jeremy added, 'wouldn't life be better if those people who moaned about poverty worked a little harder. You know, I'm convinced that if we could produce more wealth in this country this sort of meal could be enjoyed by everybody. There's plenty to go around, you know, I can tell that from my business experiences. All we have to do is to apply ourselves and get stuck in.'

'Quite so,' said Dizzy, lifting her brandy glass. Jeremy was so intelligent.

They finished their meal. Jeremy offered to pay the bill but Dizzy said it was to be 'her little treat'. After all, she had her own bank account now, and anyway wasn't this the age of women's liberation? She took the bill and after a brief scrutiny decided that £112.67 was by no means unreasonable. What can be more important than to spend one's money on the people who matter most?

They took a taxi home. The cab moved quickly through the inner city on its way to the suburbs. The streets were wet and cold, and the day's litter was being blown about in the strong wind. A few drunks were singing and being sick outside a pub. The taxi sped on. Mrs Simpson didn't look out of the window – she wasn't going to allow anybody to spoil this night for her.

We can see that the people wining

and dining at the *Rue St James* have certain views about poverty. These views are part of a wider perspective of views and attitudes they may have about the social world which can partly be explained by their *own* position within the class structure. You may have found it difficult to understand what they had for dinner because it was probably not within the normal range of *your* social experiences.

We all have what is called **a frame of reference**. The psychologist George Kelly, in *Psychology of Personal Constructs*, argued that each of us perceives the world in a particular way and that we interpret our experiences according to what we regard as important and relevant. In other words, we 'construct' our own view of reality. For example, a person brought up in a pre-industrial rural society might have a different perception of the nature of industrial disputes and trade unions than a person brought up in a modern industrial society. This means that we may all have a limited or blinkered view of society based on our own range of cultural experiences. Unfortunately this can lead us into a trap of believing that other people are just like ourselves, and that the solution to today's problems are solutions based on our own 'common sense' way of thinking (it is called common sense because we rarely question it). Jeremy, in our story, believes that the solution to poverty is linked with our inability to produce more wealth because we fail 'to apply ourselves and get stuck in'. This view might be reasonable or unreasonable. What is important is that we can better understand Jeremy's opinions by taking into account the social world in which he lives.

EXERCISE

Suggest a reason why Jeremy might hold these particular views about poverty. What social factors and circumstances have probably influenced his attitudes? Why does his family approve of his ideas?

What is poverty?

Two of the earliest systematic studies into poverty were carried out in the 1890s by Seebohm Rowntree in York and Charles Booth in London. Booth, in his *Life and Labour of the People of London*, found that up to 47% of the population of London were either poor or very poor and that roughly one-third of the population earned less than £1 a week. Rowntree found similar degrees of poverty in York. Indeed, it was Rowntree who first attempted to define poverty more precisely. He used the terms **primary poverty** (those who couldn't afford a basic level of nutrition) and **secondary poverty** (those who could afford to feed themselves but preferred to spend their money on other things) to distinguish between degrees of poverty. Today we use the term **absolute poverty** to describe a condition in which the basic requirements essential for survival are absent or are in short supply.

What do you regard as the essential needs for survival in our society?

Most people immediately think of the need for adequate food and clothing and the provision of warm shelter. Some people might include the need to be protected from personal danger or for medical care facilities. A few might regard the need to be able to read and write as essential social skills required for survival

in a modern, communication-obsessed society. However, behind all of this there is an assumption that we all require the same basic needs, that there is a sort of common toolkit of needs that we should possess. In a complex, ever-changing society such as ours, this may not be the case. Even food needs, for example, may vary from one person to the next, as the next exercise demonstrates.

EXERCISE

1 Produce a diet programme for all your meals for the forthcoming weekend. Plan what you would like for **1** breakfast; **2** lunch, and **3** evening meal for 2 days. Try to make the meals as varied as possible and include all in-between meal snacks and refreshments.
2 Compare your diet programme with one compiled by a colleague and note any differences.
3 Discuss these differences to find out why food requirements should vary. Record your conclusions in your notebook.

You will have gathered from your results and discussions that there can be marked differences in your food needs. Some of you will like a particular brand of cereal for your breakfast and others will choose not to have cereal at all. Others may prefer to go without breakfast and eat more for lunch. Although the consumption of food is obviously a basic need, the way we interpret this need is not fixed and unchanging. The food requirements of one generation may not be acceptable to the next generation, and the luxury foods of the present can become the basic foods of the future.

In 1950 Rowntree, in his book *Poverty and the Welfare State*, compiled a diet sheet, with the help of the British Medical Association, which set out the recommended nutritional needs for a husband, wife and 3 children for a week. The 1950 prices have been converted into equivalent decimal money. Estimate how much each item would cost today and enter the amount in the last column. Compare the items on this diet sheet with your own nutritional needs set out in the previous exercise and comment on the important differences.

Diet programme for a family of 5 (2 adults and 3 children under 14) in 1950

*All prices shown in decimal pence

Item	Amount	Cost*	Cost Today
Breast of mutton	2½ lb	8	
Minced beef	2 lb	13	
Shin of beef	1½ lb	12	
Liver	1 lb	7	
Beef sausage	1 lb	6	
Bacon	1¼ lb	12	
Cheese	10 oz	3	
Milk	14 pts	29	
Herrings	1½ lb	5	
Kippers	1 lb	5	
Sugar	3 lb	6	
Potatoes	14 lb	12	
Bread	13½ loaves	30	
Oatmeal	2 lb	5	
Margarine	2½ lb	10	
Cooking fat	10 oz	3	
Flour	1¾ lb	2	
Jam	1 lb	5	
Treacle	1 lb	4	
Cocoa	¼ lb	3	
Rice	10 oz	2	
Sago	¼ lb	2	
Barley	2 oz	2	
Peas	½ lb	3	
Lentils	¾ lb	2	
Stoned dates	½ lb	6	
Swedes	6 lb	7	
Onions	4½ lb	6	
Apples	4 lb	2	
Egg	1	7	
Tea	½ lb	8	
Salt and seasoning		3	

Lists of this kind are based on the assumption that we are all in agreement about what the basic

nutritional needs are. However the kinds and amounts of food and liquid intake we demand will often depend on the type of work we do. A big manual steel worker, for example, will need to consume more than a slim office worker to get adequate nourishment for his needs:

When we finish the shift there's nothing better than going straight to the pub to sink a few pints. It's not that we want to drink beer, it's just that when you're dry and hot you need a refreshing drink.

This steel worker believes that buying a few pints of beer at the end of a long and hot day is essential, given the nature of his work. We might ask why he doesn't have a few pints of water instead. However, the local pub also provides cultural support for this particular group of workers where they can relax and unwind after their stint in the plant. This point about cultural support brings us nearer to the kinds of problems we are likely to meet when we try to define exactly what we mean by poverty. If we accept that there can be no general agreement on what are the basic requirements for survival, we can now turn to the *relative* aspects of poverty.

EXERCISE

Which of the following items do you consider essential for a reasonable standard of living in today's society? Set them down under the 2 headings **Essential** or **Less essential**. Discuss whether the items under each heading have anything in common:

Heating for living areas
Meat at least once a week
Warm coat
Bath once a week
Damp-free home
A week's holiday away
Christmas celebrations
Indoor toilet
Bath not shared with other households

Money for public transport
Three meals a day for children
Self-contained accommodation
Two pairs of all-weather shoes
Fridge
Children's toys
Washing machine
Money for leisure or hobby
Two hot meals a day
Vacuum cleaner
Presents for family or friends once a year
Tobacco or alcohol
Television
Evening out once a week
Constant hot water
Newspaper every day
Carpets
Telephone
Garden
New clothes at least once a year
One other item of your choice

Relative Poverty

We can best understand the concept of relative poverty by looking at 2 different views of the world as expressed in a letter and a poem published in a magazine:

Sir,

I read with interest a recently published report that claims people are living in poverty in our major cities. To be blunt, you could have fooled me! Nowadays most people have TVs, cars and indoor toilets, and the State provides plenty of benefits to support the needy and sick. I know that rich people still exist, but to say that a lot of people live in the kind of poverty that I saw and experienced as a young man is ridiculous.

I would like to see how today's younger generation would have coped in my day. Then you made your own entertainment, and the lavatory was in the back yard, and when you had no money you had to try your best without expecting charity from anyone.　　　　*Andrew Hendry*

Everyone's got one

Everyone's got one
I want one too

Don't tell me I don't need it
I wanna be just like you

Everyone's got one
A shiny fast car
All you need is downpayment
Then you travel far

Sick and tired of been
Told the world ain't fair
Ain't asking any favours
I only want my share

Everyone's got one
I seen it on the screen
On the billboards and sidewalk
Everyplace I've been

Everyone's got one
Them people really doin fine
Don't want none of your favours
Only want what's mine.

Dwain

What is the letter and the poem really telling us?

Both writers are contrasting the differences between the haves and the have-nots. The letter writer is using an historical perspective to express the view that the existence of poverty in modern Britain is a myth because of the material benefits that are available to almost everybody, except to the few who are well supported by the state. The poem offers an alternative, present-day view of poverty. It describes an advanced industrial society of fast cars and consumer goods – 'I seen it on the screen' – and an increasing political awareness that such good things should be made available to everyone in society – 'I only want my share'.

The concept of relative poverty implies that in a rapidly changing society what once were luxuries are now regarded as necessities. In the early 1950s families with black and white single-channel TVs were a cultural minority, whereas today the vast majority of the population have multi-channel colour sets. Yet television sets do not contribute to our physical survival, but provide us with entertainment, and conversations about TV programmes are enjoyed by almost everyone. In a similar context, visitors from Britain are usually amazed to see large cars parked outside run-down tenements in American cities. Of course, the USA is very much a car-orientated culture where the limousine is taken for granted. Car ownership in the USA, even by the unemployed, is not regarded as a luxury. Equally those who compare the plight of the poor in the UK with the poor of the Third World may be making a similar error in their understanding of poverty. What is considered a reasonable standard of living in parts of Asia or Africa is not necessarily accepted as reasonable for a modern industrial society. There are also those who, like our letter-writer, attempt to compare today's living standards with those of half a century ago. However they are underestimating the important fact that living standards rise with the social expectations of the population. In effect, we all feel that we have a basic right to share in the material wealth that we see around us in our everyday experiences.

This leads us to another important question. Although to be poor is obviously an objective experience, in that it is linked with hunger, deprivation and early death, it is also a *subjective* experience. In our poem, the hero lives in a modern industrial society which is constantly reminding him, through advertising and personal experiences, of his relative poverty. Yet, because of his social and economic status, he cannot possess what he believes to be available to everyone else. This young mother also makes an interesting point about the subjective nature of poverty:

I don't think I'll ever win the pools. I try to be realistic. What I think about is the day when I'll have some extra money in my purse. You hear about people paying a lot of money for silly things. Well, I'd like to be silly with my money just once in my life. It's knowing that every penny I have is for all the bills and the kids' clothing. That's what gets me down. If only I had enough money, just a little bit extra to play with. It would make all the difference – not in the way we live but in the way I *feel*.

We can see that our experiences in the world influences the way we feel about our own economic situation. We may live in a world of plenty, but the reality of our everyday experiences and our daily round of scrimping and saving underlines the fact that even in a supposedly affluent society we can find ourselves at the bottom of the economic pile.

There are, of course, many families who not only feel poor but who are, in relative terms, actually poor. Even so, subjective feelings can play a powerful role in highlighting particular problems of being poor in today's society, as this unemployed father of 3 explains:

When I watch television with the kids, especially coming up to Christmas, I see all these toys and games being advertised. I know my kids would like them – you see many of their schoolfriends have them – but come Christmas morning they will be disappointed. I accept that we're poor, but when I think of my kids it's another matter. I want money just to spend on them, but I haven't got any – I just haven't – so that's it.

In our discussion about poverty we have examined 3 important factors:

Absolute poverty. This is an unsatisfactory way of looking at deprivation because assessment is based on the assumption that people's basic needs are unchanging.
Relative poverty. This is a much more useful concept because we

can take into account the whole culture of the society in which the poverty occurs. If we experience a standard of living that falls below the general standard, then we are said to be in poverty. Therefore if 90% of households in the UK (Family Expenditure Survey) possess a refrigerator and over 95% enjoy the benefits of electric power and sewerage, then to be deprived of these would indicate poverty in the context of living in the UK.

Subjective attitudes. This describes the way we 'feel' about having and not having. This affects our whole attitude towards poverty and our general social behaviour, particularly if we happen to live in a Western culture that persistently reminds us through advertising of the goods and services we haven't yet acquired!

EXERCISE

Select 3 examples from the following list and discuss how the individuals concerned will experience poverty. Mention the kinds of things they will be deprived of and the particular form the poverty will take:

- a peasant farm worker and his family who are driven from their famine-stricken land to seek refuge in a neighbouring African country
- A young recently-unemployed sales representative and his growing family (social *Class 3a*) living in a salubrious tree-lined avenue (*Class 1*) in North London
- an out-of-work 17-year-old British teenager whose parents are both employed as teachers
- a Jewish inmate in a Nazi concentration camp
- a British single unemployed mother and her 2 children who are receiving supplementary benefit
- a British working class family living on the poverty line in the year 1900.

Who are the poor?

If we accept that poverty is more easily understood as a relative concept, then any individual in our society whose standard of living remains well below that of others is likely to experience some form of deprivation. There are, however, 5 recognisable groups that are particularly vulnerable to poverty:

The unemployed. According to the *Employment Gazette* (January 1985) unemployment had reached over 3.2 million or 13.4% of the working population at the end of 1984, and over 1.25 million workers had been unemployed for over a year. Poverty associated with unemployment is made worse by the uneven distribution of people out of work, with the West Midlands and the north of Britain and Northern Ireland suffering worst of all. Poverty becomes almost endemic amongst families and communities in particular towns and areas when major companies close down.

The low paid. The commonly accepted definition of low pay is a wage of less than two-thirds of average male earnings. According to the *Low Pay Unit* (the official body responsible for monitoring low wages in Britain) this so-called 'decency threshold' is a gross wage of £107 a week in 1984. In their *Cheap Labour* they estimate that 8.3 million workers or 41.1% of the working population of Britain are receiving low pay.

The elderly. Old age can bring poverty to many who have previously enjoyed a reasonable standard of living. According to the Abel-Smith and Townsend study *The Poor and the Poorest*, by 1965 almost half of the old-age pensioners were living below the poverty line. If we take the current estimate of 7.6 million people in receipt of state old age pensions, this means that the elderly form one of the largest and poorest

groups in society, and single pensioners are the most vulnerable of all.

The sick and the disabled. Factors that prevent income from being earned are obviously related to poverty, especially when the chief bread-winner in the family is affected (usually the husband). Government statistics published in 1981 pointed to 3.5 million disabled people in Britain, the majority of whom depend on state benefits.

Single-parent families. This group forms a growing proportion of families experiencing poverty, especially in an age where desertion and divorce are increasing. In Britain, over 40% of single-parent households rely on supplementary benefits, and when we take into account that 1 in 8 births are now to single women this proportion is likely to increase. In 1975 David Piachaud in *The Causes of Poverty* found that 58% of one-parent families were poor. Many single working mothers also have the extra problem of experiencing low wages because of their dependence on poorly paid part-time jobs.

Large families are traditionally included in lists of people who are susceptible to poverty. However, the decline in family size in recent years, particularly amongst the working class, has enabled us to remove this category from the list of social groups experiencing the worst poverty.

The existence of people experiencing poverty originally justified the introduction of the welfare state. Whilst there are people who are sick, disabled, too old to work, or who are genuinely unable to find work or to help themselves, then a caring society is thought to have a duty to support them. Of course, the state also takes on an equal responsibility to identify those who try to take unfair advantage, such as the 'work-shy' and the 'scroungers', and feels duty-bound to employ investigators to root them out. However, this kind of argument has been seriously weakened recently with the discovery of the vast extent of poverty within the ranks of the unemployed and the low-paid section of the population, who can hardly be accused of being work-shy.

EXERCISE

Explain in what way deprivation is likely to affect
- family life
- school performance
- social unrest and delinquency.

Poverty and the welfare state

Our society is often described as being a welfare state. Newspapers publish articles about it and discussions take place on television and in parliament on the 'future of the welfare state'. However, to fully understand why this subject is such a point of interest we need first to define what we mean by the term **the welfare state**.

Write down what you think is meant by the welfare state and indicate how you or your family have benefited from it.

One way of understanding the welfare state is to think of all the rights we believe we are entitled to in our society. If we cannot afford to house our own family we do not see the availability of council housing as a charity but as a right to which we are all entitled, and nor do we live in fear

of being ill or of dying of starvation just because we can't afford the high cost of medical treatment or proper nutrition. In a similar way, although some parents are able to afford to pay for their children's education, the majority of us entrust the state system with the care and education of our children, and we do not expect a second rate education. Basically the whole idea behind a welfare state is to protect us from undue hardship through the provision of an adequate system of social care facilities.

Although the origins of social welfare stretch back into the 19th century, the full-blooded welfare state was not set up in Britain until 1948. It was based on proposals set out in a report called *Social Insurance and Allied Services* which was published in 1942 by a committee organised by William Beveridge. The *Beveridge Report*, as it became known, introduced the concept that the state should play a key role in the economic and social welfare of all its citizens 'from the cradle to the grave'. It laid down the principle that the state should provide the minimum needs for a decent standard of life for everyone through free public education, and the provision of social insurance against unemployment, accident, illness and old age.

Since the Second World War numerous Acts of Parliament have been introduced to give the state powers to intervene in an attempt to eliminate the worst aspects of poverty. Most observers would accept that the state has been largely successful in this attempt, but the financial cost has been enormous. Leaving aside the most expensive item, state education, over 37 billion pounds was spent on the welfare state in the financial year 1984–85. This is how the money was shared out:

The cost of the welfare state 1984–85

Total cost £37,207 millions	Percentage of total cost
Pensions	43%
Supplementary benefit	17%
Child benefit	13%
Sickness/invalidity/ death	10%
Housing benefit	7%
Unemployment benefit	4%
Widows' benefit	2%
Cost of administration	4%

The cost of providing a welfare state places a tremendous burden on the public purse, especially the high cost of unemployment during an economic recession, and some governments have made the *political* decision to reduce spending in the public sector by 'making savings' where they see fit.

What effect has this had on people's lives?

For some people in our society cutbacks in spending on the welfare state will make little difference, but there are many people who will suffer badly because of their dependence on state help. These extracts from a newspaper article illustrate the point:

Waiting in pain

Mrs Henderson, a widow living alone, is just one more casualty of the welfare state. She has been waiting more than 18 months for an operation on her hip – an operation that takes less than 45 minutes but which would give her sleep without pain ... it would enable her to become mobile. She could get out more and start visiting friends again ... Even moving about the house is difficult and the longer Mrs Henderson waits,

the more depressed she becomes ...
After speaking to her I telephoned three local private clinics and asked how long would I have to wait for a hip replacement operation if I went 'private'. My question was greeted with surprise. I could be admitted the following day, I was told ... This was of little comfort to Mrs Henderson. You need a lot of money when you go private – about £1750 for this particular operation ... She hasn't got that kind of money, so she will have to sit and wait for the letter to admit her into a National Health hospital ... In the meantime, the pain and the immobility get worse ...

The kind of problem Mrs Henderson is experiencing is not uncommon in today's health service. In fact the whole range of social welfare services is under such stress that some commentators have suggested that not only are the needy still with us, but that poverty has increased during the 1980s to a point where the poor are worse off now than at any time since the welfare state was set up.

EXERCISE

Working as a member of a research team, find out as much as you can about one of the following welfare benefits. Do not choose a benefit that is already being researched by someone else. You will find it useful to visit your local DHSS office or to write to your local council for up-to-date information. The range of information required will cover these questions:

● What is the purpose of the benefit?
● Who is entitled to receive it?
● What are the benefits available?
● Are there any costs involved for the recipient?
● How are the benefits applied for?
● How are the benefits distributed?

Present your findings as a wall display. Use as many illustrations as you need to aid understanding.

Select one of these benefits for your research:

● old age pension
● supplementary benefit
● family income supplement
● child benefit
● council housing
● unemployment benefit
● widows' benefit and widows' allowance
● health care, involving family doctor services, dentists, opticians and chemists
● the hospital service
● sickness and invalidity benefit
● maternity benefit
● industrial injury and disablement benefit
● housing benefit, including rent and rates allowances

In a report published in 1981 by the **Child Poverty Action Group** it was estimated that there were 15 million people in poverty in the UK. This figure included all households with an income equivalent to the level of supplementary benefit, plus 40%. Their research suggested that over half the children in this group lived in families who had at least one member at work – further emphasising that poverty is not exclusively associated with unemployment. To give you an idea of what it means to be poor, supplementary benefit at the time of the research was £43.50 a week, plus the cost of housing. Unemployment benefit was £27.05 a week for a single adult person and £43.75 for a married couple, plus 15 pence for each child. The **Child Poverty Action Group** pointed out that the number of people living in poverty had increased by a quarter between

1979 and 1981 and would continue to rise as long as the recession continued and the level of unemployment rose.

The previous study was not an isolated piece of research. Findings produced by the **Family Policy Studies Centre** in their *Fact Sheets on the Family Today*, published in 1984, suggest that 3.69 million children were in poverty. The government in 1984 defined poverty and the poverty line at £77 a week for the average couple with one child. The government's definition is based on a minimum level of subsistence, usually expressed as a cash amount, beneath which families are believed to suffer deprivation. However, poverty is not just about money. Without the help of the state, especially without the full support of the welfare services, many families are now having to go without the vital necessities for a successful life. They are becoming impoverished, and so you might think is a society that allows it to happen.

EXERCISE

The **Family Income Supplement** (FIS) was introduced in 1971 for the low paid with children. It takes the form of a cash benefit paid to families to bring them up to a minimum level of subsistence. It is widely believed that 50% of low income families, who are entitled to the benefit, do not apply for it. Now try these questions:

1 How many two-parent families were

Families in the UK receiving family income supplement (thousands)

	1974	1976	1979	1981	1983
Two-parent families: total	42	50	43	77	131
1 child	7	10	7	15	28
2 children	9	13	12	25	47
3 children	9	11	12	19	32
4 children	8	8	7	11	15
5 children	4	4	3	4	6
6 children or more	5	4	2	3	3
One-parent families	39	36	46	65	83

receiving FIS benefit in 1974 and 1983?
2 What evidence is there in this table to suggest that UK families are experiencing increasing poverty?
3 What evidence is there to suggest that poverty in very large families is less extensive than it used to be, compared with poverty in smaller families?
4 How many two-parent and one-parent families were receiving benefit in 1979?
5 Why is poverty more common amongst one-parent families?
6 Can you think of any reasons why families who are entitled to family income supplement do not apply for it?

Why does poverty persist?

Sociologists do not accept that poverty is the result of individual effort; that we are somehow personally responsible for our own poverty. We have all read about the eccentric who abandons his opulent lifestyle to live in abject poverty under a railway embankment, and we may have met well-heeled characters who have drunk, drugged or gambled themselves and their loved ones into appalling deprivation. Although we are all personally responsible for our social behaviour, sociology attempts to stretch out beyond the personal to grasp and *understand* the *general social forces* that are responsible for the existence of poverty as a social phenomenon. For instance, you don't have to be a genius to work out that rich people as a class do not willingly embrace poverty, although sociology can give us insights into the relationship between the rising tide of drug and alcohol addiction and deprivation in inner cities.

Ken Coates and Richard Silburn in *Poverty: The Forgotten Englishmen*, see deprivation in terms of a **vicious circle of poverty**. Once poverty strikes, it locks the poor into an endless circle of deprivation from which it is difficult to escape. Each important point in a person's life circle is connected with another to reinforce the cumulative effects of the poverty:

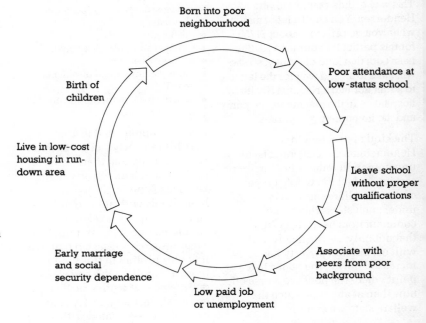

The vicious circle of poverty

The diagram tells only part of the story. The total cost of deprivation will be much higher and may include bad health resulting from insanitary housing and faulty diet, and poor attendance at school and work can lead to even worse academic failure and long-term unemployment. In other words, the all-embracing effects of poverty can sap the will to succeed by undermining self-confidence and encouraging a sense of life-failure. The circle of deprivation is complete.

An American sociologist, Herbert Gans, argues in *More Equality*, that poverty exists because it is of great value to the affluent. Society, he believes, is so obsessed with the 'costs' of poverty that it fails to take into account the kinds of benefits it bestows on the rest of us. He describes 15 functions of poverty that he believes provide advantages to non-poor society. We will look at 5 of them to give you an idea of what he means:

1 The poor provide a reservoir of cheap labour to ensure that dirty and dangerous jobs get done.
2 Poverty creates professional jobs: social workers, police, training instructors, doctors and health workers.
3 The poor give status to the non-poor by remaining beneath them in the social hierarchy.
4 The poor do not have any political clout because they are dominated by superior social groups who hold the reigns of power.
5 Poverty can generate compassion in the rich to make them feel good about 'helping the poor'.

EXERCISE

Taking each of Gans' 5 functions in turn, explain in your own words how these 'advantages of poverty' apply in British society. Can you think of any counter arguments to oppose these functions?

The culture of poverty

The extent of poverty is so great in some industrial societies that social scientists have discussed the possibility of the existence of a culture of poverty. This concept originated from the work of Oscar Lewis in *La Vida*, following his study of the very poor in Mexico, Puerto Rico and New York.

What do you think is meant by the culture of poverty?

What Lewis is suggesting is that extremely poor people develop norms and values exclusively based on the desperate circumstances in which they live. Furthermore, the poor tend to pass on to their children a lifestyle rooted in the culture of the slum. Although children will be encouraged to learn to cope with the pressures of poverty, they will grow up without the conventional social skills and wisdom needed for success in modern industrial societies. For Lewis, life for the poorest is hopeless. They live each day as it comes and survival is an uphill struggle – a relentless round of scrimping and just managing to get by. In many ways poor people are cut off from the rest of society. Advertisers ignore them, politicians are usually unaware of their plight, and 'normal' society tries its best to avoid as much contact as possible. They make us feel uneasy. This story describes an example of the culture of poverty in Britain:

Peter Street

Few people know about Peter Street. Commuters from their rush-hour train windows might catch a glimpse of the shoddy houses as they make their way to and from their city centre offices. Social workers visit the families there, but their words and advice make little impact compared with the harsh realities which dominate the lives of the families they visit.

Kim Brandon had moved into Peter Street 18 months earlier with her 2 young children. After her husband had been sent to prison, the council decided that this was the best place for her. At first she kept phoning the housing department to get something done about her windows, but she soon gave up. The man at county hall said her complaint had been noted and someone would be out to visit her when the department had money for non-essential repairs. Sooner or later everybody got fed up with dealing with the bureaucrats. Peter Street seemed to be at the bottom of everyone's list.

The kids in the street go to the local school and most of them would swear that the teachers always look twice when they tell them where they live. Not that school means much to the children of Peter Street. It is easier to stay at home or to go down to the amusement arcade or sit in the caf and talk to their mates. The last time Peter Street welcomed a truant officer, the story went, German bombs were falling.

Some families had tried to rent their televisions, but most of the rental companies refused to have anything to do with them – they were not considered credit-worthy. It was the same at all the shops and garages in the High Street – nobody wanted to know about giving credit to 'that lot'. The joke was that many people had got themselves into terrible debt by borrowing from the local money sharps at ridiculous rates of interest.

That's the trouble with being at the bottom of the heap. No one wants to know and no one cares. It doesn't take long before you let yourself go and just accept it.

Life in Peter Street reflects some of the hopelessness Oscar Lewis implies in the **culture of poverty**. Of course, Marxist-inclined sociologists would suggest that in a society based on the exploitation of one social group by another, poverty is inevitable. Although the welfare state can make life more bearable for millions of citizens, poverty is the logical outcome of class conflict in capitalist societies. This, Marxists argue, is why the poor find themselves even poorer in an economic recession.

We have tried to point out that we need to be careful about how we define poverty. We have also suggested that poverty is a reality for millions of people not just in Third World countries but in advanced industrial societies. When we discuss poverty we should remember that, as sociologists, we do not blame the individual. It is only by looking at social structure that we will begin to understand that the reasons for the existence and persistence of poverty lie within the social organisation of society.

EXERCISE

Extract from the *Peter Street* story examples of deprivation that contribute towards a culture of poverty. Suggest at least 5 more examples of your own that are likely to be present in this kind of culture.

QUESTIONS

1 *a* Examine the difficulties involved in defining and measuring poverty. (10 marks)
 b How do sociologists explain the persistence of poverty in Britain? (10 marks)

Source: AEB O Level 1983

2 Supplementary benefit

Total number of beneficiaries receiving weekly payments, 1975–1982

	Thousands
1975	2897
1977	3106
1979	2970
1981	3873
1982	4432

Source: DHSS

a What is a supplementary benefit?   (2 marks)

b How many people were receiving supplementary benefit in 1975 and 1982?   (2 marks)

c Suggest 2 categories of people that are likely to be claiming benefit.   (2 marks)

d Why is the level at which people receive supplementary benefit, rather than absolute poverty, used as a measure of defining poverty in Britain?   (5 marks)

e Outline the main causes of rising poverty in Britain.   (9 marks)

3 'The welfare state did not abolish poverty, it redefined it.' Discuss.   (20 marks)

Your View

Your View last Thursday invited you to write in to give your views about poverty in modern day Britain. Today we publish a selection of your letters. As usual, *Your View* is anxious to hear from you folks out there if you have anything to add.

Abolish wealth

The best way to cure poverty is to abolish wealth completely. The government should introduce a law that sets a maximum level of wealth that any individual or family can possess. If this maximum is exceeded, the government will confiscate the excess assets and sell them on the open market in fair competition. The proceeds can then be distributed to the poor to create a fairer society.

I read the other day that the Duke of Westminster inherited over £500 000 000 when his father died in 1979. How ridiculous can it get before something is done about this obscenity! How can any one person be worth so much? How can we allow so many people to suffer deprivation whilst the few wallow in such filthy luxury?

There are a few thousand people in this country who possess vast wealth. There are millions who live in dire poverty. Only a heartless hypocrite would argue that we live in a decent and caring society.

Gavin Newman
Workers Party

Fair shares for all

I work as a shop assistant in a large supermarket. Although I'm 18 I only get £1.60 per hour, so for a 37½ hour week my take-home pay after stoppages is just over £50. Some of my friends who work in small shops get even less than me!

My complaint is that people who get very low wages can't afford to live decently, let alone live well. Unless the government does something about these low wages then you are bound to have poor people, aren't you?

Why can't the government introduce a law about wages? What's to stop us having a maximum and a minimum wage level? On the news the other night, it said that some bosses get over 100 thousand pounds a year income! That's nearly £2000 a week! Can an employee be that valuable?

If it is possible, why can't the politicians bring in a law to tax the top people more and tax people like me a lot less? That way it would be possible to have a fairer spread of wages.

I don't expect to be paid as much as my boss, but I do think that wages could be levelled out a bit in this country one way or another. Fair's fair.

Fiona Anderson

Abolish unemployment

I would like to see unemployment abolished. This is not as daft as it sounds. There is nothing to stop the government introducing a legally enforceable *Right To Work* law. All employers and local authorities would be obliged to find alternative jobs for all employees who would previously have been laid off.

Alan Green

The risk-takers

The correct approach to eliminating poverty is to create more wealth-producing opportunities. I'm sick and tired of listening to the people from the political left whining about the extent of poverty. How envious they are! Why can't these people realise that wealth has to be *created*; it doesn't grow on trees! The people who produce this wealth, after all, are the risk-takers who take chances with their investments and who could lose everything in the process. They also happen to work a damn sight harder than most of us!

Do these lefties seriously believe that if you take away the profit motive, people will work that extra bit harder to produce more? It's human nature to fight to keep in front of the next person. Dole money and social welfare benefits are paid for by the people who produce the wealth. If we take away the financial rewards of risk-taking we would all be on the dole and the economy would collapse.

If we seriously want our society to produce the wealth to pay for all the worthwhile social benefits, then we have to reduce income tax and improve industrial efficiency.

Geoffrey Tree

More benefits

I have been working for the last 5

years at a DHSS office that is situated in a deprived area. It has been my experience that poverty is increasing rather than decreasing, despite the many welfare benefits families can now claim. I believe the reason for this increase in poverty is because whole families are experiencing for the first time since the early 1930s deep-seated deprivation.

Most people believed at one time that they would find work sooner or later. These days unemployment is seen to be more or less permanent. Nobody in the family has a job, clothes, washing machines, TVs, furniture, cars to travel to work, children's toys are all wearing out and the poverty is getting worse.

I genuinely believe that social security benefits should be increased *substantially* to take people out of the poverty trap. This extra money will eventually be spent on goods and services, which in turn will stimulate the economy and create employment.

Asha Bibi

Change the rules?
As a keen government supporter I reckon that the present policy of reducing the real value of wages and welfare benefits is the best method of dealing with poverty.

The simple fact is that we all expect other people to put food into our mouths and money into our pockets. We have to get used to the idea of a slightly lower standard of living in this country.

If we can lower the level at which we define people as poor then we will have fewer people in poverty. There aren't many people in the UK who would be thought of as 'poor' in Ethiopia.

Jason Turner

QUESTIONS

1 Can poverty be defeated? Read through the readers' letters and summarise all the solutions proposed. Add one more solution of your own.

2 Explain what is meant by the terms **wealth** and **income** and describe the changing trends in the distribution of wealth and income during the second half of this century.

3 Draft a letter for publication in *Your View* on an aspect of poverty or wealth. You may develop your own ideas about how you think poverty can be defeated or you can respond to one or more of the published letters. As a student of sociology you are expected to throw some light on the subject.

Points for discussion

- The possession of great wealth is incompatible with a civilised society.
- Technological progress and human invention depend on an unequal society to prosper.
- The people who want to redistribute wealth are usually young people who have no wealth of their own to distribute.

Voices ...

This is a photograph of some of Birmingham's notorious 40 000 back-to-back houses in the early part of the 20th century. As the name suggests, a back-to-back house was a cheaply-built one-bedroom dwelling without a garden that had only one entrance that led straight into a single living room. In the space between each row of houses families shared a communal area called a courtyard or 'yard'. The yard provided an open area, free from traffic, for families to mix and hang up their washing, and it gave the children room to play safely. On the right of the photograph you can see the communal wash-house and toilets. Running water for each house was got from a tap in the wash-house. This type of housing was finally swept away during the slum-clearances of the 1960s.
But what of the people? What were they like? What did they think of their houses and their communities? We will let 2 of them speak for themselves ...

George ...

That's me, George McBride, smokin' m'pipe and leanin' agen door frame. Most folk round 'ere call me Yorkie. I came t'Brum 'bout 40 year ago from Bradford. It were 'bout 1865, I think.

I were 20 year old at the time and I were young 'an rarin' t'go. I could read 'n' write, mind yer. I might tell yer I went t'church school till I were 11. That's more then I ken say fer me 7 older brothers. Not one of um could read or write – but it didn't seem t'bother um.

I were born in Ireland, as a matter of fact, in Cork in 1845. There were 3 girls born before me, but they all died as babbies. Then me ma and pa died when I were 10 and I were sent t'England to live wi me auntie Mary. My God, times were bad in them days. Most of me relations in Ireland died in tater famine in 1846 or emigrated to America. Bradford weren't much better. I started work when I were a nipper in a spinnin' mill, but I were laid off when I were 20. The foreman said I were too expensive.

When I came t'Brum I got job straight away in engineerin' factory, workin' on lathe. I get 2½ pound a week, so I'm not grumblin'. I give most of it t'missus, mind yer. All our kiddies have left home now, two of 'um have married and gone t'America, to Boston. I've got more relations over there than over 'ere. So me and the missus live well now. She pays 7½ shillin' (47½ pence) a week rent to that bastard landlord, Frank Beddows. He owns all the 'ouses round 'ere but he don't never do any repairs. I'd like to get me 'ands on 'im.

I know it's a bit of a dump round 'ere, some people call it a slum, but yer got to count yer blessins while yer can. In Bradford, we didn't 'ave runnin' water, lavs wi a flush and gaslight. All we 'ad were candles and soil privies, that's what we 'ad, and we 'ad t'get water from well. There's still a lot of real poverty in Ireland, mind yer. When I were a bab in Cork, whole families were starvin' t'death. There's a lot worse off than us. Tek a look at folks in the photograph – there's plenty of meat on them kids. Folks is real friendly round 'ere.

and Sarah ...

I'm Sarah Johnson, or at least I was then. I've been called Sarah Miles since 1920, when I got married to Harry. Harry died about 5 years ago. I'm the little girl in the white pinny with blonde hair, third from the right in the row of children. My mum is standing in the doorway of our house, wearing the white apron. She was expecting our Arthur then. He was her sixth and she was only 25! I'm 88-years-old now so the picture must have been taken about 1905. I remember the picture being taken; it wasn't everyday we saw a camera in our yard.

Life was pretty miserable then, and I don't care what anybody says about the 'good old days'. They were very good for those that could afford them – that's what my Harry used to say. Admittedly there was always someone who would help you give birth or lay you out when your time came. In our yard it was old Mother Green, but with the day-to-day living you had to help yourself. My dad could be sent home from work at an hour's notice – he worked at the foundry – and if the work dried up he would be laid off for 2 to 3 weeks at a time. I remember my mother's ashen face if he came home too early. Of course, ordinary married women rarely worked in those days.

We paid our rent every Friday to Mr Beddows. He wasn't a very nice man. He wouldn't think twice about kicking a family out if they were behind with the rent. There was always someone willing to pay the 7/6d for that hovel we lived in. There were no council houses then and there weren't all that many cheap houses you could buy either because the landlords used to buy them for cash and rent them out to mugs like my mum and dad. The landlord never bothered when our tap in the yard or the lav got frozen, or when water poured through the roof on wet days. In the summer we were plagued with rats, mice, and fleas, and we had bed bugs all the year round.

I remember saying to myself when I was about 13 'I'll never live like this when I'm out earning. I'll be out of this slum before you can say Jack Robinson.' I met Harry when I was 16 and we both saved hard for a deposit on a little semi, just like my two boys did in their day.

You don't get poor these days like we were then. There's no need for a dirty house now – not with all the appliances and running water. You imagine having to get all your water from a tap in the yard. Every house has a toilet now. We had to share one up the yard with 2 families. These days, if you have vermin, you can call in the exterminator man. All we had were traps, and getting rid of bed bugs was impossible – they would travel through a row of houses in weeks. People out of work these days can get money from the social security. Then we had nothing but the workhouse, and everybody was frightened of that. It was no wonder my two older brothers joined up when the war was declared. Anything was better than living in a back-to-back and having to share beds. We kids had to sleep head-to-tail and our parents slept downstairs.

My brothers were both killed on the Somme. Half the families in the yard lost somebody in that war. It hit our family pretty hard because my brothers used to send home some of their army pay to mum and she found it a Godsend. If those lovely boys came back into the 1980s they would think they were in heaven.

QUESTIONS

1 From your nearest library find out a little more about

- The Irish potato famine
- the workhouse as a shelter for the destitute
- emigration to the USA at the turn of the 20th century
- the percentage of privately rented and privately owned houses at the

turn of the century compared with today.

Present your findings in the form of notes.

2 What is the difference between absolute and relative poverty?

3 Using examples from the text, explain how George's and Sarah's perceptions of poverty differed. What do we mean by the term 'perceptions of poverty'?

4 Mention a few of the advantages and disadvantages of living in that particular community compared with a similar community of today.

5 Suggest a theory of poverty to explain why the poor tend to remain poor.

6 What do you imagine will be the most striking examples of poverty in today's society to the sociology student of the year 2050?

Points for discussion

- In the UK, every family should have the right to own a decent home with a bit of garden, regardless of the financial cost to the community.
- Today's high rise flats in inner cities are mostly slums.
- No matter what we get, we will always want more.

Old, cold and baffled by benefit forms

Britain's hospital wards this weekend are crammed beyond their normal capacity with old people who are suffering from the effects of the cold weather.

Over a thousand old people have been treated in hospital for hypothermia in the past 3 weeks.

Many more have been taken into hospital because of heart attacks, strokes and pneumonia brought on by the cold. Until this week, the worst cases were in England. Now, with record low temperatures in the north, hospitals in Scotland are filling up too.

'Some 9000 people die from straightforward hypothermia each year. But for everyone who dies of hypothermia many more die of other diseases induced by the cold', says Collins. 'Deaths from heart attacks follow within a day or two of a cold spell. Deaths from strokes occur over the following week, and deaths from pneumonia follow within 10 to 14 days.'

The existing system of means-tested heating allowances, however, is fearsomely complex. Britain has 9m pensioners, but only the 1.6m on supplementary benefit are entitled to help with their heating costs, and usually if they are householders, disabled, or very ill.

Even more confusing are the payments for 'exceptionally severe weather'. They can be claimed when temperatures fall below set points which vary throughout the country, from 0.5°C in Plymouth to −2.9°C in Aberdeen.

To Rose Moreno, a benefits expert with Age Concern, the conclusion is inescapable. 'Old people who claim supplementary benefit are some of the poorest people in the country. Often they suffer from ailments because their homes are in a bad state of repair. They need extra warmth to survive. When they can't heat their homes the end is inevitable.'

The 7.6m people on ordinary state retirement pensions fare little better, according to Age Concern. They say pensions have risen 50% since 1979, but gas has jumped 105% and electricity 74%. This means single pensioners now spend 14% of their income on fuel, and retired couples 11%, compared with about 6% for the rest of British society.

The health department has tried to publicise the supplementary benefits system. But general take-up remains no higher than 71%.

Convincing the elderly to take benefits to which they are entitled is a problem. They are easily confused, and often inhibited by a dignity which shuns the welfare state as 'charity'. Although pensioners' organisations work closely with local authorities all over Britain, and social workers go out of their way to explain the dangers of hypothermia and how to claim benefit, they cannot act for the old. The onus is on the pensioner at every stage.

Even the Electricity Council and British Gas who say 'the last thing we want is to cause old people difficulty by cutting their supplies off' put the onus onto the pensioners.

If pensioners feel they will have difficulty paying their bills it is up to them to approach their local gas and electricity boards to tell them and negotiate phasing the costs over a period of time.

But Mervyn Kohler, of Help the Aged, explained: 'The general problem is that old people do not own up and just let their bills run.'

A long campaign to persuade friends, neighbours and relatives to take an interest in the old during the winter has paid off to some extent. In Coventry, where 1 in 7 of the 350 000 population is a pensioner, there is a pool of blankets, clothes and heaters for those in need, and a fund to help with fuel bills. But John White, the local director of Age Concern, believes at least 15 000 will still suffer.

Source: The Sunday Times

QUESTIONS

1 Write brief answers to these questions:

 a What is hypothermia?

 b How many people in Britain die of hypothermia each year?

 c What is a 'means-tested' heating allowance?

d What is supplementary benefit?
e How many people in Britain receive a state retirement pension?
f What percentage of pensioners who are entitled to supplementary benefit do not receive it?
g The article mentions two voluntary agencies that make a contribution to the welfare of old people. Can you name them?

2 Taking each voluntary agency in turn, explain in your own words their concern about the plight of the aged suffering from the cold.

3 What is the response of the health department and the electricity and gas suppliers to the problems of the old people in need?

4 Old people are just one group in our society who are vulnerable to poverty. Suggest 2 other groups and explain why they are likely to be amongst the poor.

Points for discussion

- In a free society people should be left to fend for themselves.
- The welfare state is admired throughout the world. We should not allow it to fall into decay.
- People who can afford to pay should not be allowed to receive free welfare benefits from the state.

Important points

- Wealth is defined as the ownership of marketable assets in excess of personal needs that can be turned into cash.
- The distribution of wealth in our society is grossly unequal, with the top 10% of the population owning over 50% of the total wealth.
- During this century there has been a tendency towards a more equal distribution of wealth.
- Income is the disposable money we get from employment and other outside sources after deductions have been made.
- Income is also unequally distributed. The top 10% of the income-receiving population receive more than the bottom 50%.
- Income is becoming more equally distributed amongst the top 50% of the population, but the bottom 50% share has remained unchanged.
- Our views and attitudes about poverty and wealth are shaped by the social world in which we live.
- Of the social groups that experience poverty, the low-paid and the elderly are probably the most vulnerable.
- The welfare state is based on the principle that the state should play a major role in the economic and social life of all its citizens.
- Although the welfare state has reduced the worst aspects of poverty, poverty still persists and may be increasing.
- Poverty is not created by individuals; it is a phenomenon that has its roots in the social organisation of society.

8 Population

When you have worked through this chapter you should have a clearer understanding of

Demography · The crude birth rate · The crude death rate · Infant mortality · Perinatal and neo-natal mortality · The fertility rate · The natural increase rate · Migration · Population distribution · Life expectancy · Environmental engineering · An ageing population · A future-orientated society

Why study population?

Can you answer these questions about your own city, town or village?

1 How many people live there?
2 Can you describe the kinds of people who live there in terms of age, social class, ethnic groups and the proportion of males and females?
3 How is the population distributed? For example, can you identify the areas that are overcrowded or underpopulated? Are there clusters of housing near industrial sites?

The scientific study of human populations is called **demography**, and the questions above are therefore of great interest to demographers because:

Question **1** is about **population size**
Question **2** is about **population structure**
Question **3** is about **population distribution**.

However, demographers are not only interested in describing populations. They are also interested in explaining why changes have occurred in the population and the possible consequences of these changes.

Information about population is essential to sociologists too. In order to study the social world properly, it is important for them to have accurate information about the people who make up society and the social forces that influence their behaviour. Like demographers, sociologists are keen to examine both the causes and the consequences of population changes.

What is the nature of the social forces that control our population?

The factors that determine the size and structure of a country's population are:

- the number of babies being born – the **birth rate**
- the number of people dying – the **death rate**
- the number of people entering or leaving the country – **immigration** and **emigration**.

The crude birth rate. The birth rate refers to the number of babies born in each calendar year (Jan/Dec) for every 1000 people in the population. It is called the *crude birth rate* because it gives only an approximate measure of fertility in the population:

Live births in the UK: totals and rates

	Total live births (thousands)	Crude birth rate
1951	768	15.7
1956	796	16.0
1961	912	17.8
1966	946	17.8
1971	870	16.1
1976	649	11.9
1977	632	11.6
1978	661	12.2
1979	706	13.0
1980	725	13.3
1981	704	12.9
1982	692	12.6

Source: Social Trends

In 1982, for example, you can see that for every 1000 people in the UK, 12.6 babies were born. Looking at the crude birth rate over the last 30 years, what overall impression do you get?

To calculate the crude birth rate the following equation is used:

$$\frac{\text{Total number of births} \times 1000}{\text{Total population}} = \textbf{crude birth rate}$$

So, if 672 000 babies are born in 1 year in a country with a population of 56 million, the calculation is

$$\frac{672\,000 \times 1000}{56\,000\,000}$$

giving us a crude birth rate of 12.

Now calculate, to one decimal place, the crude birth rate in a town with a population of 110 000 which produced 1510 babies in 1 year.

The crude death rate. As with the crude birth rate, and calculated exactly in the same way, the crude death rate is defined as the number of deaths for every 1000 people in a calendar year.

The following table divides death rates into age and sex categories. Examine it carefully and then indicate whether the following statements are true or false.

Answer True or False to these statements

1 There are more deaths in the 1–4 age group than in the 5–14 age group.
2 Male deaths mostly outnumber female deaths.
3 There is not a single instance in any year where female deaths exceed male deaths.
4 There are fewer deaths in the 5–14 age group than in any other age group.
5 The number of babies surviving their first year of life has fallen since 1961.

The infant mortality rate is an age-specific death rate which gives us the numbers of deaths of babies under 1 year of age out of every 1000 live births (not out of every 1000 of the population). It is often used as a general indicator of the health of a country. For example, in Britain in the 1870s infant mortality was recorded at over 130 deaths per 1000 live births. By the mid-1970s this death rate had declined to 16 per 1000 live births.

The fertility rate. Comparisons are often made with birth rates, death rates and infant mortality rates not only between different countries but also between different groups within a country's population. A group of particular interest, and one that largely determines family size and hence population size, is the number of women of child-bearing age in the population and the number of babies born to these women.

The fertility rate refers to the number of babies born over a calendar year for every 1000 women in the population of child-bearing age – which is said to be between the ages of 15 and 44:

Fertility rates in the United Kingdom

Live births	thousands
1971	773.3
1981	617.3

Female population aged 15–44	thousands
1971	9441.3
1981	10 395.5

Births per 1000 women aged 15–44	
1971	81.9
1981	59.4

Death rates in the UK

	Age										All ages	Total deaths (thousands)
	Under 1	1–4	5–14	15–34	35–44	45–54	55–64	65–74	75–84	85 +		
1961												
Males	24.8	1.1	0.4	1.1	2.5	7.5	22.3	55.1	125.0	258.6	12.6	322.0
Females	19.3	0.8	0.3	0.6	1.8	4.5	11.1	31.5	89.1	215.9	11.4	309.8
1971												
Males	20.2	0.8	0.4	1.0	2.4	7.2	20.5	51.4	114.7	235.6	12.2	328.5
Females	15.5	0.6	0.3	0.5	1.6	4.4	10.3	26.8	75.2	189.5	11.1	316.5
1976												
Males	16.4	0.7	0.3	1.0	2.2	7.2	20.1	51.4	118.5	250.8	12.6	341.9
Females	12.4	0.5	0.2	0.5	1.5	4.4	10.5	26.6	75.9	203.0	11.8	338.9
1979												
Males	14.4	0.5	0.3	1.0	2.1	6.9	19.2	49.3	113.5	244.5	12.5	339.6
Females	11.3	0.5	0.2	0.4	1.4	4.3	10.2	25.8	71.2	196.2	11.7	336.0
1980												
Males	13.4	0.6	0.3	0.9	2.0	6.6	18.7	47.6	110.3	234.4	12.2	332.4
Females	10.7	0.5	0.2	0.5	1.4	4.0	10.0	25.1	68.1	189.1	11.5	329.1
1981												
Males	12.6	0.5	0.3	0.9	1.9	6.3	17.8	46.2	105.9	228.0	12.1	329.1
Females	9.5	0.5	0.2	0.4	1.3	3.9	9.6	24.5	66.9	180.7	11.4	328.8

Source: Social Trends

In 1981, for instance, for every 1000 women of child-bearing age, 59.4 babies were born. Now answer these questions:

1 How many live births occurred in 1971?
2 In 1981 how many women in the population were aged between 15–44?
3 Between 1971 and 1981 is the fertility rate rising or falling?
4 Work out the percentage difference in births per 1000 women aged 15–44 between 1971 and 1981.

The natural increase rate. The difference between the birth rate and the death rate in a year is known as the natural increase rate (or natural decrease rate if deaths outnumber births). If the birth rate is 12 and the death rate is 9, the natural increase rate is 3, which means that there are an additional 3 people for every 1000 people in the population:

sharply. Can you identify these periods and offer an explanation for the increases?
3 There were sharp increases in the birth rates in 1919–22 and 1946–47. Can you suggest a reason for this?
4 From the mid-60s to the mid-70s the birth rate plummeted. Can you think of an explanation that would at least partly account for this?
5 During the 1920s and early 1930s Britain experienced an economic slump and growing unemployment. From the information contained in this graph, suggest a possible relationship between population growth and economic decline during this period.
6 Taking the graph as a whole, has the population of the UK in the 20th century increased or decreased?

Birth rates and death rates can be calculated locally and regionally and, as we shall see, there are regional and social class variations as well.

can distort the figures.

EXERCISE

1 Rochington had a population of 86 000 in 1981. In the same year there were 1030 births and 845 deaths.
   Calculate the birth rate, the death rate, and the natural increase rate for Rochington for 1981.
2 In 1985 the birth rate in Digby, which had a population of 107 000 was 13 and the death rate 11.
   How many births and deaths were recorded in Digby in 1985?

Population trends

In 1984 the population of the UK stood at 56.3 million, some 20 million more than in 1900. Four stages of population growth can be identified from the year 1000 AD to the present.

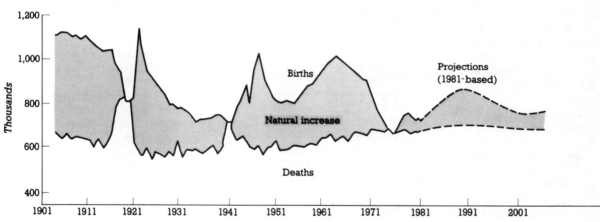

Population changes in the UK

EXERCISE

1 a Approximately how many people died in 1971?
   b Approximately how many children were born in the same year?
   c Approximately by how many people did the population of the UK increase or decrease in 1971?
2 There are 2 historical periods during which time death rates increased

Migration. Factors other than the number of births and deaths can determine the size of a country's population. Migration is a general term used to describe movements of people into a country (**immigration**), out of a country (**emigration**) and from one part of a country to another (**internal migration**). Although an increase in a country's population often resembles its natural increase rate, it is rarely exactly the same. This is because the level of migration

The 4 stages in Britain's population growth

● **Stage 1: Until 1750**. From about the year 1000 AD to 1750 the rate of natural increase in the population was slow. Both the birth rate and the death rate were high. Poor nutrition and lack of medical knowledge, combining with major epidemics and occasional plagues, killed off huge numbers

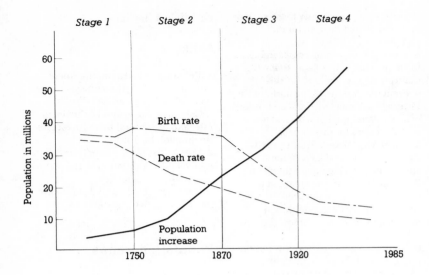

Stage 1 Stage 2 Stage 3 Stage 4

Population growth in Britain

of people to account for the high death rate.

- **Stage 2: 1750–1870**. Britain's population trebled during this period. The birth rate was high and the death rate was falling.
- **Stage 3: 1870–1920**. During this period the falling birth rate and the falling death rate slowed down the rate of population growth.
- **Stage 4: 1920 – Today**. The modern period is characterised by a low birth rate and a low death rate. The introduction of antibiotics and effective birth control techniques have accelerated the trends.

Although the birth rate and the death rate have declined, the population of Britain has continued to grow. As the graph *Population growth* shows, births have consistently outnumbered deaths, resulting in a natural increase in the population.

There is now a greater number of old people in the population than there used to be, but the major cause of this is not the increase in life expectancy at birth (how long you can expect to live) but the decline in the infant mortality rate. According to

Trends in Mortality, a government publication, the life expectancy of people over 45 years of age has hardly changed in the last 130 years, remaining at about 76. What is more significant, however, is that more babies are surviving their first year of life to contribute eventually to the numbers of ageing people in the population.

We will now go on to examine population trends in a little more detail.

The death rate. Epidemic diseases such as smallpox, plague, scarlet fever, typhus and cholera were among the major killers in the 18th and early 19th centuries. The decline in the death rate was due largely to a decline in fatalities from these diseases.

How was the risk of death from epidemic diseases reduced or eliminated?

Howe, in *Man, Environment and Diseases in Britain*, describes two important factors that led to a decline in the death rate. The first is what he called **environmental engineering**, that is the introduction of sewerage control, piped water supplies and other public health measures which

made the transmission of epidemic disease less likely. The second factor was the **improvement in food production and consumption**. In general, epidemic diseases are lethal to badly nourished people. As levels of nutrition improved, so death rates declined.

When demographers break down the overall death rate into age groupings, it becomes clear that the most marked improvement during the 20th century has been amongst babies in their first year of life. The infant mortality rate is often used as a measure of a country's well-being. In general, the higher the standard of living a population enjoys, the lower the infant mortality rate.

The decline in the infant mortality rate has been due to general improvements in living conditions, nutrition and medical science.

The birth rate. To find out why there has been a decline in the birth rate we must look to the family since most children are born into and brought up by a family group. Average family size has declined from between 5 and 6 children for couples who married in the 1870s to just over 2 children for couples who married in the 1970s.

The exact reasons for this decline are not known, but it is linked with the

- introduction of birth control
- improvements in the social status of women
- expectation of rising living standards
- reduction in the infant mortality rate.

Nowadays a couple's relatives or friends expect them to have 2 or perhaps 3 children. Having a large family may be seen as being socially irresponsible. To house,

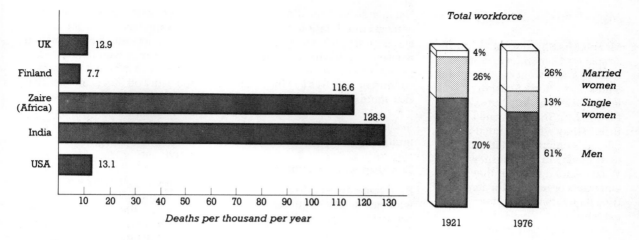

Total workforce

	1921	1976	
Married women	4%	26%	
Single women	26%	13%	
Men	70%	61%	

UK 12.9
Finland 7.7
Zaire (Africa) 116.6
India 128.9
USA 13.1

Deaths per thousand per year

Source: United Nations

A comparison of infant mortality rates between selected 'affluent' societies and Third World countries in 1979

The changing workforce
Source: An A to Z of Income and Wealth

clothe and feed a very large family in line with modern standards of living would in any case be difficult for millions of parents. The expectations of parents regarding family size must also depend on whether they *can* control the size of their families. The present-day availability of contraception has made this control possible.

The social status of women has been important in encouraging family limitation. In the 20th century it has become possible for women to follow careers. Ann Oakley in *Subject Women* points out that marriage is not preventing women from taking a paid job. The numbers of women in paid employment have risen from 1 in 10 in 1911 to 1 in 2 in 1976. In his *Essays on the Welfare State* R. M. Titmuss estimated that the average mother spent 15 years bearing and bringing up her children and that this average has now been reduced to 4 years. This increase in the time available for paid employment is reflected in the right-hand chart.

The biggest change in the composition of the workforce over the last 50 years has been the increase in the number of women, and more particularly of married women, who go out to work. This increase has maintained the size of the workforce as a percentage of the total population despite other changes that tended to make it smaller, such as the increase in the proportion of retired people.

This economic incentive to reduce family size cannot be underestimated. From becoming an asset in the early 19th century, children had become a financial liability by the end of the century. Factory legislation prevented the use of child labour which meant that children could no longer contribute to the family income. Consequently, large numbers of children became an increasing burden on the family's financial resources. (These pressures on the large family group are fully explored in the chapter *The Family.*)

EXERCISE

Are these statements True or False?	True	False
1 Couples today have fewer children then they used to have because they like children less.	☐	☐
2 Advances in medical science were largely responsible for the decline in death rates during the 19th century.	☐	☐
3 The reason for the increase in population growth during the 19th century was the high birth rate.	☐	☐
4 The most important reason for the decline in death rates during the 20th century was the improvement in the infant mortality rate.	☐	☐
5 Good nutrition and improved sanitation have probably saved more lives than doctors.	☐	☐
6 A greater proportion of women go out to work today than before.	☐	☐
7 When families become less poor they tend to have more children.	☐	☐

Migration

Mr and Mrs Sharp went to Saudi Arabia for 18 months to work. Audrey Poole went to Moscow for 6 months to study Russian language and architecture. When Mr and Mrs Sharp returned to Britain they were included in the official immigration statistics, but Miss Poole, on her return, was not. What decided whether they were emigrants or not was the length of time they intended to stay overseas.

According to government rules, an **emigrant** is a person who intends to stay out of Britain for more than 1 year, and an **immigrant** is a person who intends to stay in this country for more than 1 year. So, Britons returning from abroad are included in the immigration statistics just as people returning to their country of origin are included in the emigration statistics.

What effect will these rules have on migration statistics?

Although no precise records of migration were kept until recently, it is certain that up to the 1930s more people left than entered Britain. Overall, it has been estimated that Britain's loss during the period 1871–1931 was 4 million. Apart from 2 periods since 1901, Britain has been a major exporter of people.

Look carefully at this diagram:

*Net migration: United Kingdom
Source: Social Trends*

Net migration is the difference between immigration (inflow) and emigration (outflow). It may be positive (+) in which case more people enter than leave the country or negative (−) in which case more people leave than enter.

*In which 2 periods has immigration been greater than emigration?
Why do people emigrate?*

Read these extracts from people who have left their home countries. What reasons do they give for leaving?

- We were despised and blamed for everything. People who didn't even understand the word 'economy' were blaming us for its failure. I feared for the safety of my family, and when an opportunity arose to leave for the States where, we were told, limited numbers of Jews were being admitted, we packed as much as we could carry. My parents promised to follow us. That was never to be the case. They died in Auschwitz.
- We arrived in Britain one cold February morning, tired and confused but glad to have finally made it to what we believed was our 'homeland'. When they were inviting people in Jamaica to come and work in Britain they told us about the good wages, the good homes, the opportunities for our children. The choice was simple – poverty and unemployment back home or a chance of a reasonable life for ourselves and our children here.

- We emigrated to Australia in 1968 and have never looked back. We're much better off here than we ever would have been in England. Not that we were too badly off, but I can't see that we'd be living in a house with four bathrooms, running two cars and eating steak for breakfast had we stayed in Rochdale.

The reasons you may have noted are persecution, poverty and to seek a better life. Can you think of any other reasons for emigrating?

From 1901 to 1931 the number of people leaving Britain exceeded the number entering. It has been estimated that there were 80 000 more emigrants than immigrants a year during this period. Many Britons emigrated to Australia, Canada, the USA and elsewhere to seek a new life. Those entering were mainly Jewish refugees who came to Britain from Eastern Europe to escape persecution. After 1945 other European refugees came, many of whom were uprooted from and unable to return to their countries of origin.

The period 1955 to 1962 was one of net inflow. About half a million immigrants from the New Commonwealth, in particular India, Pakistan and the Caribbean came to Britain.

The Commonwealth Immigration Act of **1962** placed restrictions on entry into Britain. The previous trend of greater emigration than immigration was then re-established, and apart from a brief period in the 1970s when emigration figures declined, this trend has continued. The **Immigration Act** of **1971** now controls immigration. Only certain categories of people are granted right of abode in Britain.

Many false, extreme and prejudiced comments have been made about immigration to Britain. Between 1967 and 1975

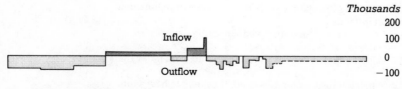

Thousands
200
100
0
−100

Inflow

Outflow

1901 1911 1921 1931 1941 1951 1961 1971 1981 1991 2001 2011

the MP Enoch Powell sparked off a furious political debate by delivering inflammatory speeches about the threat posed by coloured immigrants. It has to be said that over this period there was actually a net migratory outflow of over 400 000 people from the UK. On the whole, the balance between immigration and emigration has not significantly affected Britain's population size.

Migration can be explained in terms of **push** and **pull factors**:

- **Push factors** refer to the conditions that force people to leave their country of origin, such as poverty, unemployment and persecution.
- **Pull factors** refer mainly to the demands made for labour by the host country.

It has been argued that post-war immigration to Britain has largely been due to pull factors. Where a shortage of labour existed, active recruitment took place. This happened in the case of London Transport which advertised for workers in the West Indies in the late 1940s and early 1950s. Many immigrants went into unskilled and semi-skilled jobs in industrial production, often experiencing low pay in unpleasant and dangerous conditions.

At the same time, thousands of doctors and nurses in India, Pakistan and the West Indies were invited to work in Britain's overstrained health service. Official figures show that in 1965 Britain took 1015 doctors from India, 529 from Pakistan, and 182 from other Commonwealth countries. The Health Service provides us with an example of Britain's dependence on the work of immigrants. In 1975, 35% of hospital doctors and 18% of family doctors came from outside Britain.

EXERCISE
Go back to the extracts given by people who have emigrated. Can you identify the push and pull factors? What other push and pull factors can you think of?

Population distribution in Britain

Population distribution describes how a population is spread, the ratio of males to females and the proportion of different age groups in the population. These population facts are important to people other than sociologists. Local and national demands for housing, industry and schools can only be assessed if this information is available, and a company will usually locate a factory within a particular area only after a thorough examination of the statistics relating to the local population.

What information about the local population would the following be interested in obtaining:

- A bicycle manufacturer
- An academic board which is considering establishing a new polytechnic
- A market research organisation interested in testing a new baby product.

Where you live and the density of the population in your region may have far-reaching consequences for you and the community. For example, within the tripartite system of education, the type of schools available for your child's education will depend on the education policy of your region, which could differ from the policy of a region only half-a-mile away. There are also regional variations in the provisions of the National Health Service. This means that the time you have to wait for an operation in Huddersfield might be much longer than in Harrow, or, more drastically, you could die of kidney failure in Dudley but recover in Dover!

Finally, the density and age structure of an urban area or region may have a bearing on your chances of getting a job. Unemployment is not evenly spread throughout Britain. There are marked regional variations. Beatrix Campbell, in her book *Wigan Pier Revisited*, documents an occasion when 5000 people applied for 50 newly created jobs in Sheffield. The competition may not have been as harsh in other parts of the country. In which part of Britain would you say job chances are more favourable?

EXERCISE

Make a copy of the outline map on page 136 in your notebook, and with the aid of an atlas divide the UK into regions. Using the information given, devise a colour code to show how the population is distributed.

England	Thou-sands
North	3 082
Yorkshire and Humberside	4 884
East Midlands	3 779
East Anglia	1 881
South East	16 893
South West	4 343
West Midlands	5 154
North West	6 450
Wales	2 777
Scotland	5 153
Northern Ireland	1 547

Population: social class variations

We can now think about social class variations in birth rates and death rates.

Size is the most marked difference between the Victorian family and the 20th century family.

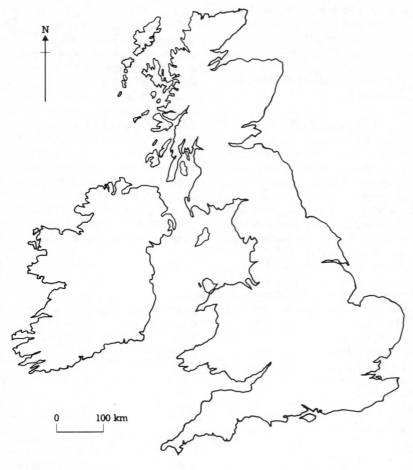

Source: Regional trends

Completed average family size in Britain

Year of marriage	Average number of children
1900	3.4
1910	3.04
1911	2.96
1915	2.5
1925	2.21
1935	2.05
1945	2.2
1955	2.45
1961	2.43 (estimated)
1971	2.39 (estimated)

Source: Office of Population Censuses and Surveys

This table, however, conceals variations between social class groups. In the 19th century, the trend for smaller families was set by the middle class, and working class fertility declined at a slower rate. Recent figures reveal that the class difference in family size has now been reversed. The trend today is for people from higher social groups to have the largest families. The family unit is also important in influencing the nation's health.

Death and morbidity. We often think of illness as a form of bad luck, and we imagine that some people are naturally stronger and more resistant to diseases than others. Although this is of course true, the morbidity (illness) and mortality (death) rates do show significant social class differences. This difference is especially significant for the **perinatal mortality rate** (deaths at birth and in the first week of life) for babies born to the parents of social *Class* 1 and 5.

Perinatal mortality rate

Parents	1978	1982
Social *Class* 1	12	8.3
Social *Class* 5	20.1	15.6
Overall rate	15.5	11.3
		(deaths per thousand)

These figures show clearly that the death rate for babies born to parents in social *Class* 1 had fallen by almost a third between 1978 and 1982, but for babies in social *Class* 5 the fall was less than a quarter. It could be argued, quite simply, that at least 7 working class children had died unnecessarily for every 1000 born. These add up to a lot of pointless deaths. These statistics, along with a wealth of supporting research, suggest that child death is not something that strikes at random. It is a social problem that is more common among the lower social classes.

The adult mortality rates show similar differences between the social classes. Look carefully at the table on page 137. What overall impression do you get about the relationship between social class and death?

Why do you suppose that coronary heart disease has been chosen for comparative purposes? This disease has been chosen because it is affected and possibly caused by smoking, heavy drinking and faulty diet, which of course are largely social habits. As people are not naturally disposed to smoke, drink to excess and overeat, it is reasonable to assume that social

Comparative death rates from all causes and selected cause

	Standardised Mortality Ratio*	
Social Class	Deaths from all causes	Deaths from coronary heart diseases
1	77	88
2	81	91
3a	99	114
3b	106	107
4	114	108
5	137	111

Source: 1981 Census

*Roughly speaking, the use of **Standardised Mortality Ratios (SMRs)** is a way of comparing death rates between the classes. You can see that social *Class 1* deaths from all causes are much less frequent than deaths in social *Class 5*. (Average = 100.)

factors might be of some importance. Heart disease also happens to be the most common cause of death.

Statistics for cigarette smoking show that whilst smoking has decreased for all social classes, there remain important differences between the classes. The working classes are still maintaining their lead. In fact, the social class differences in smoking habits are even wider than before. It appears that the higher social classes are heeding the warnings about smoking and drinking more readily than the lower classes. Similar evidence is mounting to show that higher social groups eat more healthily and take more exercise than the lower social groups.

According to an article, *Death to the Working Class*, published in *The New Statesman* (1980), semi-skilled and unskilled manual male workers in 1972 lost nearly 4 times as many working days as men in the professional and managerial classes through accident and ill health, and in 1976 there were nearly two and a half times as many women suffering from

chronic (long lasting) illness in *Class 5* than in *Class 1*. High death rates among working class adults can be attributed to the hazardous nature of many manual jobs.

Though in general the working classes are less healthy than the middle and upper classes, they make less use of the National Health Service. Under-use of the NHS may be due to factors such as inadequate knowledge about illnesses or to a lack of understanding of how the system works and the range of facilities available. It has been shown that the higher social classes are more likely than others to seek medical help during the early stages of an illness and that they make more demands on the more expensive sectors of the NHS.

Although we are encouraged to look after our own and our family's health, it can be seen that the quality as well as the quantity of our years are influenced by our position in the class structure – a fact that some politicians and social campaigners are eager to put right. The following exercise deals with just one aspect of class difference which may be significant in determining an individual's health: diet.

EXERCISE

The Duckworths and the Marshalls were asked to note a typical weekend's food consumption for themselves and their families:

- Mr Duckworth is a production-line worker in a car factory and Mrs Duckworth is a packer in a biscuit factory. They have 3 children aged 11, 10 and 7.
- Mr Marshall is a lecturer in a sixth form college and Mrs Marshall is a social worker. Their 2 children are aged 9 and 5.

The Duckworth Family	The Marshall Family
Saturday	
Breakfast	
Sugar Puffs with whole milk. Toast (white sliced) with butter and jam.	Muesli (no added sugar) with skimmed milk. Toast (wholemeal) with sugarless jam.
Lunch	
Fried double egg and chips. Bread and butter.	Bread and cheese (Camembert, Cottage and Cheddar). Fresh fruit and yoghourt.
Evening meal	
Steak and kidney pie, with mashed potatoes and mushy tinned peas. Fresh cream doughnuts.	Quiche, baked potatoes and fresh salad. Fresh fruit.
Sunday	
Breakfast	
Bacon and eggs, fried bread and tomatoes. Toast and jam.	Fruit juice. Shredded Wheat. Toast and jam.
Lunch	
Roast pork, roast potatoes and carrots (tinned). Apple pie and custard.	Nut roast, baked potatoes, with green beans (fresh) and carrots. Cheesecake (home-made with reduced sugar).
Tea	
Beans on toast. Biscuits and cakes.	Grilled fish and fresh salad.
Snacks on both days	
Crisps. Biscuits. Chocolate bars and ice-cream.	Nuts. Fresh fruit. Wholemeal crackers and cheeses.

1 To which social class do the Duckworths and the Marshalls belong?
2 What major differences can you detect in the diets of the two families?
3 How do you think factors such as income and occupation might influence the diets of each family?

Sex balance in the population

Take 20 000 newborn babies, equal numbers of boys and girls, and apply current mortality rates; after 70 years there would be 5743 men and 7461 women still alive.

Source: The British Medical Journal

Life expectancy of males and females at birth

	Average age at death			
	Britain now	China	Brazil	Britain 1841
Females	74.8	65.6	45.5	42.2
Males	68.1	61.3	41.8	40.2

Source: Sex, Gender and Society

In every culture and in all recorded periods women have had a longer life expectancy than men. Why should this be so? First, we can identify what we might call biological factors, although social factors play a part in some of these. Can you suggest instances where social factors play a part?

- Out of 7 known causes of perinatal death, boys take the lead in 6, and during the first year of life one-third more males than females die, primarily of infectious diseases.
- Boys and men tend to be more susceptible to infectious diseases at all stages in the lifecycle.
- Boys are more often the victims of childhood accidents both inside and outside the home, and violent accidents (suicide included) in adulthood are likelier to kill more men than women.

- Medical journals have documented how men have a greater chance than women of dying from heart disease, cancer, kidney and digestive disorders. Men are also more susceptible to genetically-based diseases (inherited diseases).

These sex differences in life expectancy cannot be explained solely by biology. Social factors must also be considered. For instance, can you think of a reason why boys are more often the victims of childhood accidents than girls?

Some male mortality and disease are related to occupation. Many jobs that men do are particularly hazardous to health and safety, and it has been suggested that more men die than women and at a young age because they are less willing to seek medical help. Men are also prone to smoking-related diseases, a masculine rather than a feminine habit until recently.

However, present mortality trends are beginning to show a reduced difference between the sexes. Whereas the life expectancy for men is increasing, life expectancy for women has decreased. In certain respects, men's and women's lifestyles are becoming less different as women become engaged in activities once considered masculine. Women now drink more, smoke more, and go out to work more:

- The voluntary organisation **Alcoholics Anonymous** informs us that the ratio of women to men alcoholics has decreased from 1 in 8 to 1 in 3 in the past 10 years. This has put more women at risk of developing alcohol-related diseases.
- The **Office of Population Censuses and Surveys** reveals that whilst cigarette smoking has generally fallen more among men than women, for older women it has hardly fallen at all, and there is growing evidence that smoking is actually increasing amongst young working class females.
- More women are now dying of heart disease and stress-related diseases that once were more likely to affect men.

This narrowing of the male/female mortality gap has been explained by reference to the emancipation of women in modern society. Smoking is no longer considered to be socially unacceptable for women. Indeed, for many women cigarette smoking and social drinking may symbolise the new directions in which women are moving. However, the increase in certain types of 'masculine' behaviour such as drinking and smoking may signify a deep-rooted anxiety and frustration that women have with their roles in society. (This has been more fully explored in the chapter Women.)

EXERCISE

Draw up a list of 10 jobs that are mostly done by men. Make a similar list of jobs for women. From your list of 20, select 5 jobs that you think offer the greatest risks to health and safety, and explain their relationship to the sex of the worker.

Britain's ageing population

We live in an **aged** country. A nation is classified as aged when

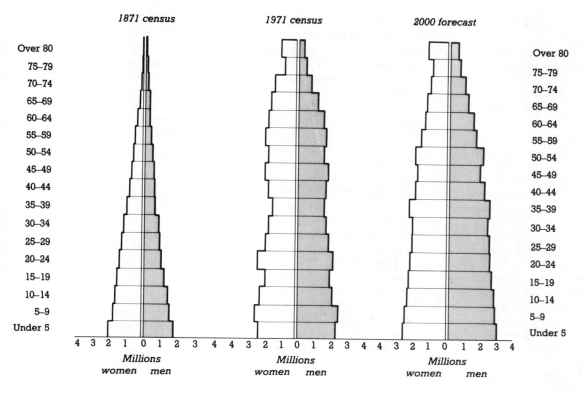

The age structure of Britain in 1871, 1971 and 2000 (forecast)

over 7% of its population are 65 and over. In Britain the aged constitute over 10% of the population. This contrasts with developing countries where between 2% and 5% are over 65, and over half the population are under 20. Examples of these countries are India, Egypt, Brazil and Zaire in Africa.

This table is based on the 1871 and 1971 Censuses and shows how the age structure of the population has changed. The age categories, in 5 year graduations, are divided into the numbers of males and females alive in those categories. To check your understanding of the table answer these questions:

1 Which were the largest age groups in 1871 and 1971?
2 Comment on the differences in sex balance in the population in 1871 and 1971.
3 Can you explain why the 20–24 age

group in the 1971 Census should be bigger than the 15–19 age group?
4 How is it possible to be accurate about the numbers of aged in the population in the year 2000?

Ronald Blythe, in *A View in Winter* (1979), records a series of interviews with old people, and comments:

If a Renaissance or a Georgian man could return, he would be as much astonished by the sight of 2 or 3 thousand septuagenarians or octagenarians lining a south coast resort on a summer's day as he would by a television set. His was a world where it was the exception to go grey, to retire, to become senile and to acquire that subtle blend of voice, skin and behavioural changes which feature so largely in our long-lived lives.

In your own words, summarise in a sentence the main point that is being made in the extract.

Among the major changes that have taken place in the 20th century is the emergence of a

sizable elderly population. Why are there now more elderly people in our society?

First, more adults live longer, largely as a result of environmental engineering and improved standards of living, and medical advances have made a small contribution in extending the life expectancies of old people. The second and more important reason is the dramatic reduction in infant mortality which has allowed a higher proportion of people to survive childhood to reach old age. These 2 factors are dealt with more fully in the section on population growth.

We will now consider the consequences of these demographic changes for both the elderly and for society. One of the effects of old people becoming more numerous is that they have suffered a drop in status. Think of the many unkind remarks that can now be directed at the elderly and the tendency we have to prefix insults to the elderly and the non-elderly with the word 'old'.

Geoffrey Hurd in *Human Societies* describes how in some societies the aged command great respect and power. In traditional societies like Ancient China and India the old had greater power and authority than any other group. They were (and are) respected and their wisdom and experience highly valued.

In order to appreciate why the aged have experienced a drop in status it is important to understand how some of the major social changes that have taken place in this century have affected them. To begin with, we live in a post-industrial society which admires change and innovation and the acquisition of new knowledge and skills. Consider this old person's experience:

Sister Mary Joseph, now aged 84, entered the Saint Vincent de Paul Convent in a small town in the south of Ireland in 1918. She has led a very sheltered life in the convent and she always asks her visitors if they have actually seen an aeroplane. She has heard that it is possible to see pictures of people and places from another country in your own home if you have what she thinks is called a television. It must be pointed out that Sister Mary is not senile – just amazed by the changes that have occurred in her lifetime.

Think of some of the changes and developments that have taken place in your lifetime. Jot some of them down under these headings:

- At home
- At school
- At work
- In entertainment

Taking your own age into account, you can perhaps appreciate the bewildering amount of change that the elderly have to cope with. In what has been called a **future-orientated society**, the knowledge and skills possessed by one generation become quickly outdated. The elderly are considered to be out of touch with the modern world.

Changes in family size and structure have also had important consequences for the old. A reduction in family size has meant that there are fewer children to take care of their aged parents. The nuclear family, rather than the extended family, tends to exclude aged parents. When parents reach an advanced age, the children have already left the parental home to start homes and families of their own. Increased geographical mobility also means that young adults move to settle in another part of the country. These changes in family size and structure result in the social isolation and loneliness of the old.

A further decline in status and increasing loneliness can sometimes be brought on by retirement. In Britain, men retire at 65 and women at 60. These ages are fixed for social and economic reasons rather than for personal ones: they help to create vacancies for young and unemployed people and allow promotions within organisations. Peter Townsend in *The Family Life of Old People* writes:

The outstanding conclusion is that retirement is a tremendous blow to the man. It completely alters his life, lowers his prestige, thrusts him into poverty and near poverty, cuts him off from friendships and associations formed at work, and leaves him with few opportunities of occupying his time. He is thrown back on his wife and family. Here he finds his wife has the dominant place. He is thus often deprived of a useful function and finds his life difficult to justify. The sudden degeneration in his physical health may be, in part, a consequence of retirement itself.

We live in a society where a person's identity is often fused with his occupation. We would, for example, say that **Mr Jones is a teacher** rather than Mr Jones *works* as a teacher, and one of the first things we want to know about a person is what they do for a living. Not only does identity and status disappear with retirement, but also the friendships and the interests connected with the job.

Mr Wilkins is a retired welder:

I never thought retirement would be as lonely as it is. I still see my old workmates down the pub now and again but things aren't the same. I can't really join in with the conversations any more, and anyhow I think I make them feel a bit uncomfortable. There are a lot of things I miss about work – the outings, the do's at Christmas or when one of the youngsters gets wed. Funny really. I looked forward to the day when I could ignore the alarm clock. I'm just getting used to spending my days doing nothing and after 40-odd years hard graft it's taken some getting used to.

These comments highlight a further problem; the lack of preparation for old age and retirement. Work takes up a considerable chunk of our lives and to suddenly find ourselves with time on our hands can be quite startling. Few retired people have developed hobbies and interests during their long working lives to keep them occupied in retirement.

Many old working class people live on or below the border line of poverty. The old, along with single parent mothers, are the main receivers of supplementary benefits in Britain. Half the retired men and three-quarters of the retired women have no occupational pension, although of course nearly all retired people receive a State pension.

The main problems experienced by the elderly can be summarised as:

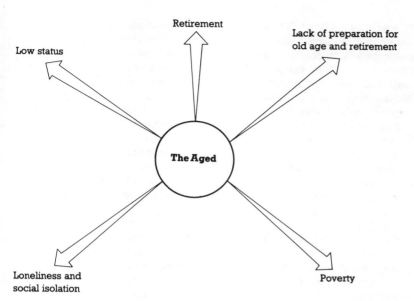

Retirement

Lack of preparation for old age and retirement

Low status

The Aged

Loneliness and social isolation

Poverty

Finally, the expanding number of elderly people has implications for society as a whole. The old, like the young (that is the under 16s), are economically inactive. A greater proportion of state spending must be allocated to both groups in future years in the form of state pensions, child benefit and extra provision of health and social services. Although not all elderly people are dependent on welfare and medical services they are more likely to need them, and after retirement less likely to be able to afford them.

EXERCISE

Discuss the following proposition: In order to create more jobs for young people, workers should be forced to retire once they have reached a certain age, say 60, even though they might wish to continue working and are capable of working.

QUESTIONS

1 *a* Which is the largest 10-year age group in the population? (2 marks)
   b Approximately what age shows the sharpest increase in numbers? (2 marks) Can you give an historical reason to explain why this number is so large? (3 marks)
   c Explain whether or not the secondary school population is likely to increase or decrease. (2 marks)

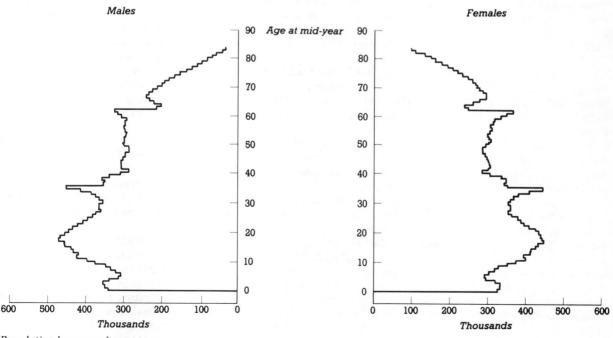

Great Britain

Males   Age at mid-year   *Females*

Thousands   *Thousands*

Population by sex and age 1982

d Which is the more numerous sex
   after the age of 80?   (1 mark)
e Explain why women tend to live
   longer than men?   (10 marks)

2 Changes in the size of a population
are affected by the birth rate, death
rate and migration. Explain the
relative importance of these factors in
Britain over the last 100 years.
(20 marks)

3 Explain the relationship between
social class and life expectancy.
(20 marks)

Working-class babies are more likely to die

**by ANNABEL FERRIMAN and
ARTHUR OSMAN**

Inequalties in health are becoming
increasingly class and race related,
according to an all-party
parliamentary report on baby deaths
published last week.

Stillbirths and deaths in the first
week of life, always considered one
of the most reliable indicators of a
nation's health, are more and more
linked to social groups, the report
shows.

Babies born into unskilled
working-class families are almost
twice as likely to die as those born
into professional families – and the
disparities are becoming more
clearly defined.

The report, drawn up by the
House of Commons Social Services
Committee, shows that the class gap
widened between 1978 and 1982,
despite repeated demands from
expert committees that increased
resources be put into reducing the
differences.

Mrs Renée Short, Labour MP for
Wolverhampton North East, and
chairman of the committee, said last
week she was 'deeply disappointed'
that the class differences had not
narrowed since the publication of
her committee's first influential
report on baby deaths in July, 1980.

She blamed the widening gap on
the economic recession, poor
nutrition among working class
mothers and inadequate health care
by inner city GPs, who fail to
encourage their patients to check
into ante-natal clinics early in their
pregnancy.

Overall, the perinatal mortality
rate (deaths at birth and in the first
week) has come down from 15.5 per
thousand in 1978 to 11.3 in 1982, and
to a provisional figure of 10.3 in 1983.

For babies born to parents in
social *Class 1* (professional), the rate
fell in 1978–82 by almost a third from
12 per thousand to 8.3 but in social
Class 5 (unskilled) it fell by less than
a quarter from 20.1 to 15.6.

It fell significantly among certain
ethnic minority groups, but still
remains high among women of West
Indian origin, and above all, among
women from Pakistan, where it is a
staggering 26.3 per thousand.

Studies have shown that Asian
women in certain areas attend
ante-natal clinics late in pregnancy,
and have bigger families than the
indigenous population, with the
mothers consequently being older in
later pregnancies, which increases
the risk of mishap.

One study carried out among
Pakistanis in Bradford in 1981 also
showed a high level of
intermarriages, with up to
three-quarters of pregnant women in
one clinic being married to their first
cousins.

Genetically transmitted
abnormalities may therefore have a
greater chance of occurring.
Congenital heart disease, for
example, is much higher among
Asian babies than white babies in
Bradford, and intermarriage is
thought to be a possible cause.

Professor John MacVicar,
Professor of Obstetrics and
Gynaecology at Leicester University,
said last week that the Asian women
attending his clinics, mostly Indian,
had a greater risk of having babies
with neural tube defects and babies
died inexplicably in the womb
before labour began.

He wants to see Asian women
making earlier visits to ante-natal
clinics to be screened by a simple
blood test for neural tube defects,
such as spina bifida, and also closely
monitored to ensure proper foetal
growth. If a baby showed signs of
ceasing to grow, it could be
delivered early.

The Government announced last
month that it is setting up a new
campaign with the Save the Children
Fund and the Health Education
Council to encourage Asian
mothers-to-be to make greater use
of maternity services.

Eighty workers, able to talk to the
mothers in their own language, are
being trained and employed for 2
years to spread the health care
message.

But last week's parliamentary
report on perinatal mortality, while
welcoming that initiative, criticised
the Government for taking so long to
set it up. 'The Committee had, after
all, drawn attention to these
difficulties in 1980,' it said.

The committee points out that
while most regions have seen a drop
in perinatal mortality, a few regions
have seen a disappointing increase.

The West Midlands Regional
Health Authority, for example, saw
an increase between 1981 and 1982
from 12.8 to 13.8 per thousand, and
its rate is now the worst in the
country.

So worried is that health authority
by its poor showing that it has set up
a £240 000 3 year study.

One reason is thought to be a high
concentration of mothers from ethnic
minorities in the area, but staff
shortages are also blamed and the
authority is planning to increase the

number of obstetricians by 4 to 5 a year for the next 10 years.

The West Birmingham Health Authority, which covers a population of about 300 000, has been researching perinatal deaths at Dudley Road Hospital since 1979. One fact that has emerged is that Indian women are more at risk than any other ethnic minority. Causes still remain elusive, though it is thought one might be a nutritional factor.

Mr Roy Condie, consultant obstetrician and gynaecologist at the hospital, said the coloured population using the maternity facilities tended to be mainly Bengali (Sikhs) and Pakistani Punjabis with a smaller number of Bangladesh origin.

The figures of perinatal deaths per 1000 was 13 for Europeans which was about normal, 16 for West Indians, 19 for Pakistanis and 27 for Indians. A continuing check in 1981 and 1982 showed that Indians were still by far the highest group. Their biggest babies – those of about 5 lb weight which would be expected to live – were most at risk. Research was continuing but Mr Condie said: 'We have not found the answers yet. There is much that is inexplicable.'

A more contentious issue, particularly with Asian community leaders, was the fact that there were larger numbers of congenital abnormalities among the Islamic population. They tended to intermarry and about 50% of the Pakistani population in the area were blood-related. Mr Condie said views on this had been submitted to the *British Medical Journal* but had been rejected as too contentious, too localised and too conjectural.

The language factor was an important barrier to many Asian women in terms of ante and post natal treatment. Islamics did not like male obstetricians, husbands objected, and this was particularly true of those from Bangladesh. Mr Condie said it was unlikely that

Mortality rate by mother's country of origin	Mortality rate by social group	Baby deaths per 1000 births in UK
Pakistan		27
West Indies		17
African Commonwealth	Class 5	15
India and Bangladesh		15
Irish Republic		14
United Kingdom	Class 4	13
	Class 3	11
	Class 2	10
	Class 1	9
Australia, Canada and New Zealand		8

smoking was a factor as it was not a habit among Asian women.

Source: Observer

QUESTIONS

1 In one sentence summarise the main message contained in the article.
2 Write short answers to these questions:
   a Define the terms: *i* stillbirth; *ii* indigenous population; *iii* antenatal; *iv* congenital heart disease.
   b What is the difference in meaning between the terms **infant mortality rate** and **perinatal mortality rate**?
   c Approximately what is the infant mortality rate experienced by West Indian mothers in the UK?
   d What reasons are given for the higher incidence of baby deaths among the working classes?
   e What is the infant mortality rate among women from Pakistan?
   f How does the government propose to encourage pregnant Asian women to make greater use of maternity services?
3 What have research studies revealed about the high incidence of perinatal mortality among Asian women? What can be done to reduce the risks of baby deaths among these women?
4 In which region in the UK has the perinatal rate increased? How is this increase explained?

Points for discussion

- We should do more to discourage poor working class families from having large families.
- Child benefit allowances should be increased substantially to help parents with large families.
- Extra medical and social care should be made available to reduce the infant mortality rate amongst certain ethnic minority groups.

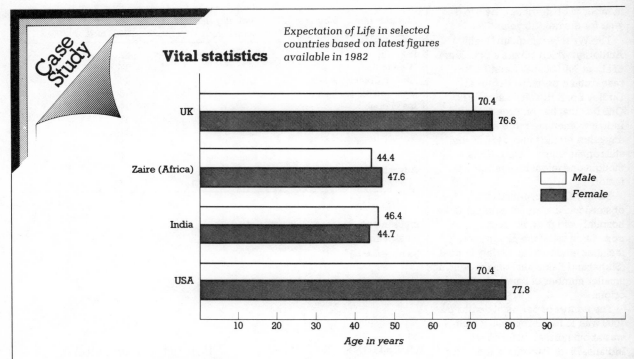

Vital statistics

Expectation of Life in selected countries based on latest figures available in 1982

Male
Female

UK — 70.4 / 76.6
Zaire (Africa) — 44.4 / 47.6
India — 46.4 / 44.7
USA — 70.4 / 77.8

Age in years

Source: United Nations

Perinatal and infant mortality rates by social class of father

England & Wales   Rates

| | Social class of father | | | | | | |
	Professional	Intermediate	Skilled non-manual	Skilled manual	Partly skilled	Unskilled	All classes
Perinatal mortality rates							
1970–1972	16.3	18.6	20.6	22.1	23.9	32.1	22.5
1976	12.7	14.3	15.6	17.1	19.2	24.9	17.0
1978	11.9	12.3	13.9	15.1	16.7	20.3	14.8
1979	10.3	11.8	12.7	14.3	16.5	18.7	14.0
1980	9.7	11.1	11.8	13.0	15.0	17.0	12.8
Infant mortality rates							
1970–1972	11.6	13.6	14.5	17.0	19.6	30.7	17.7
1976	9.4	10.5	11.2	12.9	15.3	22.3	13.3
1978	9.8	10.1	11.1	12.4	13.6	17.2	12.4
1979	9.8	9.7	9.8	11.4	14.3	18.7	11.8
1980	8.9	9.5	10.2	10.7	13.5	16.0	11.2

Source: Office of Population Censuses and Surveys

QUESTIONS

1 For how long can a newly born male child expect to live in Zaire?
2 For how long can a newly born female child expect to live in the USA?

3 Can you suggest 3 reasons why life expectancy is greater in the USA than in Zaire? Which one of your reasons do you regard as the most significant in extending life span?
4 Suggest at least 3 social reasons why

the life expectancy for men and women should be different in the UK.
5 What was the perinatal mortality rate for English children born to skilled manual families in 1976?
6 A child born in England or Wales in

Drinking habits of men by age and economic activity

Great Britain

	Type of drinker					
	Abstainer	Occasional	Infrequent light	Frequent light	Moderate	Heavy
Age 18–24 (percentages)						
Working	3	3	7	29	18	39
Unemployed	2	11	9	24	16	38
Economically inactive	9	3	8	39	23	18
All aged 18–24	4	4	7	30	19	37
Age 25–44 (percentages)						
Working	3	6	11	33	17	30
Unemployed	8	8	11	19	10	45
Economically inactive	9	10	18	27	7	30
All aged 25–44	3	6	11	33	16	31
Age 45–64 (percentages)						
Working	4	10	14	41	14	17
Unemployed	9	13	11	26	13	27
Economically inactive	11	12	12	39	11	14
All aged 45–64	5	11	13	40	14	17

Source: General Household Survey

Cigarette smoking by sex and socio-economic group

Great Britain

	Socio-economic group							
	Pro-fessional	Employers and managers	Inter-mediate and junior non-manual	Skilled manual and own account non-professional	Semi-skilled manual and personal service	Un-skilled manual	All persons	Average weekly cigarette con-sumption (numbers)
Percentage smoking cigarettes								
Males								
1972	33	44	45	57	57	64	52	120
1974	29	46	45	56	56	61	51	125
1976	25	38	40	51	53	58	46	129
1978	25	37	38	49	53	60	45	127
1980	21	35	35	48	49	57	42	124
Females								
1972	33	38	38	47	42	42	42	87
1974	25	38	38	46	43	43	41	94
1976	28	35	36	42	41	38	38	101
1978	23	33	33	42	41	41	37	101
1980	21	33	34	43	39	41	37	102

Source: General Household Survey

1970 would have had a better chance of survival in its first year than a child born in 1980. Is this true or false?

7 Explain why the social class of the father should be so important in determining the survival chances of his child.

8 In the table relating to the drinking habits of men, what kinds of people would be included in the category 'economically inactive'?

9 In the sample of working men aged 18–24, what percentage regarded themselves as heavy drinkers?

10 Generally speaking, which category of men, of all ages, did the heaviest drinking?

11 Of the unemployed in the 25–44 age group, 45% regarded themselves as heavy drinkers. As a sociologist, how do you explain this?

12 In 1980 what percentage of men and what percentage of women smoked cigarettes?

13 Is the social habit of cigarette smoking increasing or decreasing?

14 Which socio-economic groups smoke the most and which ones the least?

15 How is it possible for the average weekly cigarette consumption to increase as the percentage of people smoking decreased?

16 Give one social reason to explain why the rate at which women have given up smoking is less than the rate for men.

Points for discussion

- Women live longer than men because they lead easier lives.
- High infant mortality rates and early death should be encouraged in Third World countries to control population growth.
- All smoking should be made illegal.

Important points

- The increase in the size of the British population in the last 100 years has been mainly the result of a decline in infant mortality rates, with fewer children dying because of improvements in living conditions, nutrition and medical science.
- Birth rates have declined over the same period because of social and economic pressures on the family.
- Over the past 80 years more people have emigrated from Britain than have immigrated to Britain. Migration has not significantly affected Britain's population size.
- The distribution of a country's population will influence the availability of social facilities and economic opportunities for the individual.

- Babies born to mothers from social *Class 5* have a greater chance of dying than babies born to mothers from social *Class 1*.
- Life expectancy for the working classes is lower than for the middle and upper classes.
- Working class people tend to be generally less healthy than professional people and make less use of the National Health Service.
- Social factors are important in explaining why women live longer than men, although female life expectancy has decreased slightly because their lifestyles are becoming less different from men's.
- The proportion of aged people in Britain's population is increasing mainly because of the reduction in infant mortality rates.
- Changes in family organisation, loneliness, poverty, the pace of change, and sudden retirement from a working life, all contribute to a marked decrease in an old person's social status and prestige.
- Problems associated with the aged in future years will increase rather than decrease.

9 Social order

When you have worked through this chapter you should have a clearer understanding of

Social order · **The normative order** · **Deviance** · **Delinquency** · **Social control** · **Criminality** · **Law enforcement** · **Subcultural values** · **Youth culture** · **Anomie** · **Culturally defined goals and institutional means of achieving them** · **Illegitimate opportunity structures**

You are late for an appointment. You rush out of your house, run to the bus stop, and join a long queue. Ten minutes later a bus arrives and you can see it is almost full. You realise you are going to be very late for your appointment. The queue shortens as people board the bus but you know that you will not get on. You can, of course, push your way onto the bus, but you decide not to – you will wait your turn in the queue for the next one, just like everybody else.

The normative order

We have all been in such situations and by not pushing to the front of the queue we are conforming to what sociologists call the **normative order of society**. This lays the ground rules for behaviour in a variety of social situations. We know that if everyone pushed at bus stops, and if people didn't take their proper turn, chaos would reign and life would be difficult for everyone.

This social order is maintained both by individuals and by the behaviour of social groups. In fact,

all social behaviour is governed by complicated norms and laws. We use the term **norms** to describe the standard of behaviour expected of people by their social group. We learn these norms and laws – or at least we are made aware of them – first through our primary socialisation within the family and then through our experiences in the social world.

This overwhelming need for a normative order in society forces us to ask one of the crucial questions in sociology: how is society possible? How is order maintained in the numerous social situations in which we find ourselves? Think of your experiences in the classroom. Without you and the teacher having to draw up a signed contract you are both automatically aware of the norms which exist within the classroom setting. Without these norms it would be difficult to function and teaching and learning would be impossible. So strong is society's influence on us that we are usually unaware of the power of social order in controlling our behaviour until we experience the chaos that follows its breakdown.

Society is so persuasive in socialising us into this normative order that it can be said that we 'carry society around with us'. This means that social norms form part of our consciousness or our way of thinking about the world. Here is an example of how society can influence us even when we are alone:

Alison bought her magazine *Chart Toppers* from Roberts the newsagents. Mr Roberts was an old man who, years after he should have retired, ran his small shop just off the High Street. People liked going into Mr Roberts' shop because he was friendly and he made you feel welcome. When you went in he would often be at the back of his shop, in his living room, listening to the radio. Sometimes Alison waited for 5 minutes before he came to serve her. It was strange, given the number of stories in the newspapers about shoplifting, that Mr Roberts was still so trusting. Anyone could walk in and help themselves to whatever they fancied and then leave without paying. Although Alison realised that this would be a crime, there was more to it than that. Mr Roberts was a trusting soul and to steal from him would be a breach of that trust. In many ways it would be worse than the criminal act itself.

Can you think of similar situations in your own life where it would be easy for you to take advantage of someone?

Alison, alone in the shop, is being influenced by society even though there is no-one present to observe her behaviour. She knows that stealing is wrong, but she also feels that to steal from Mr Roberts would be an abuse of the bond he has developed with her and other customers. We all carry the norms of society around with us in this way, and how we behave is very much the result of socialisation and the social circumstances in which we find ourselves. In other words, we socially control ourselves.

EXERCISE

Here are a few common social situations. The norms that govern these everyday experiences reflect the culture of our society and guide our behaviour. Make a list of the kinds of behaviour you think are appropriate and inappropriate in each case:

- Attending a wedding at a church
- Going to a friend's 21st party
- Attending a funeral
- Sitting in a classroom during a lesson
- Shopping in a busy supermarket
- Watching TV in the company of your fiancé's parents
- Having an evening meal in a restaurant with friends.

Now compare your answers with a colleague's and you will find that their answers tally with yours in most respects. This is because you are both members of the same society and have, more or less, shared similar experiences and social influences.

Agents of social control

Society has to ensure that our behaviour can be controlled for us should we fail to control it ourselves. Serious breaches of social behaviour are dealt with by the legal system, especially by the police and the courts who are the key agents of social control. The legal system, and everything connected with it, exists to make society possible. Without a legal system social life would be difficult some of the time and occasionally impossible.

Thumbs down to Ellenstown!

When you want to travel to the Ellenstown suburb, don't shout for a taxi. No taxi driver will take you there. It's too risky. Only a week before I arrived in the city a taxi driver had been ambushed, dragged from his seat, badly beaten, robbed, and his cab burned in an orgy of destruction.

Strangers do not walk the streets at night in Ellenstown. In fact only fools with a death wish visit the decaying suburb. Gangs of youths roam the streets at night inviting the police in their patrol cars to come and get them. It's as if Ellenstown is spoiling for a fight with the rest of the law-abiding world. Murder, rape, burglary, robbery with violence are all commonplace in this part of the city where the normal rules of civilised behaviour have broken down.

In most places, you are likely to meet police officers who try to establish good relationships with the public. You can sometimes find churchmen who run community centres that provide much needed facilities, and armies of social workers grappling with social problems. But not in Ellenstown.

Any hope which once existed here has been mugged and left battered and broken on the streets. If you want to see civilisation falling apart – the show lasts 24 hours a day for 365 days a year – come to Ellenstown. But don't forget to come heavily insured – the whole area has been given a government health warning!

Despite the use of dramatic language, the article does alert us to a situation where the social norms and laws appear to have broken down. It also alerts us to the fact that although we accept the norms of society for the most part, there will be times when we will ignore or defy them for all kinds of complex social and economic reasons. A key task is not only to identify the normative order but to consider how particular social groups accept or reject it, and to offer an explanation for their behaviour. Sometimes a group will respond in an unexpected way. This is because we are all susceptible to different social influences which have powerful effects on how we behave. These influences are part of what sociologists call **social control influences** and we can identify these in the following way. It is important to remember that the degree to which each agent will influence us will vary from one person to the next.

The agents of social control

The central agent of social control is, of course, ourselves. Since we are not robots, programmed to behave in a given way, we each have some responsibility and control over the actions we take. However, as we do not live in social isolation our actions are bound to be influenced by general society. As we can see from the diagram, the individual is influenced by his family, the community he lives in, the friends he has, and the education he receives. All these social institutions exist to socialise us into the values of society. Should these controls fail and we become involved in law-breaking behaviour, the police, the final agents of social control, step in.

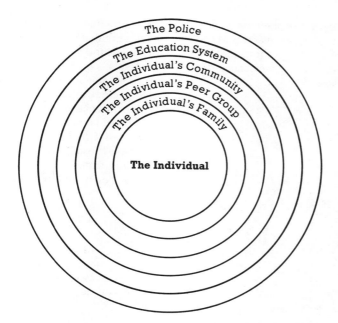

The Police
The Education System
The Individual's Community
The Individual's Peer Group
The Individual's Family

The Individual

laws will not only cause eyebrows to be raised but will provoke hostile reactions from those who are responsible for ensuring that laws are obeyed.

What are crimes?

We have pointed out that social behaviour is governed by unwritten rules which we call norms. If we break these unwritten rules we may incur the anger of those around us who will no doubt point out the error of our ways. However, if we dare break the prescribed or formal rules of society then we can expect the same punishment as the rule-breaker or the criminal.

We can define crime as any form of social behaviour that violates the laws of a given society. In Britain a crime is usually categorised as either:

- **An indictable offence** These are the most serious offences, including murder, theft, burglary and crime involving violence against the person. The accused is usually brought before a magistrates' or crown court by the police and, if found guilty, imprisoned or fined.
- **A non-indictable offence** These are the less serious but more common offences, including most motoring offences, damage to property and drunkenness. Guilty persons are usually asked to pay a fixed fine in a lower court.

Indictable and non-indictable offences are part of what is known as the criminal law, which normally implies some form of police involvement, although of all crimes reported to the police less than 30% are cleared up. Another category of offence can occur under civil law, where there is no police involvement. For

EXERCISE

Explain and illustrate with a few examples how the community might exert social control through the media. Can you think of any more agents of social control in the community?

Having established that we are subject to a host of social influences, we should appreciate that the norms and laws that govern social behaviour are not fixed and unchangeable. Although we take them very much for granted, they are nevertheless the products of decisions made by people. Another important point to note is how both the norms and the laws that govern behaviour can change over a period of time – change that can provoke comment from those who feel that change is never for the better, as this letter published in a local paper suggests:

Dear Sir,

I don't want you or your readers to think I'm an old codger but sometimes I have to stop and stare in amazement at some of the things I see these days as I go about my business. I'm a pensioner and while I'm not going to spout about the good old days I must confess that when I was young you could tell the difference between boys and girls.

The other day I was in a supermarket and I thought the people in front of me were young girls as they were wearing baggy trousers and earrings. Foolish old me! One was male and the other was female. Of course I should have known that these days both sexes wore earrings and – wait for it – MAKE-UP!!

Maybe I'm old fashioned but I really thought that this was too much!
A confused senior citizen

Although we associate the wearing of earrings and make-up with women, we know that there have been changes in the norms that govern this type of social behaviour. Fashions come and go and attitudes change. Of course we all accept that some norms are more important than others and while changes in the norms might provoke comment, changes in some laws can stimulate great controversy. Challenging existing

instance, if a neighbour of yours runs an all-night disco every Thursday night you might take him to a civil court to stop him causing you sleepless nights.

We have defined crime as social behaviour that violates the laws of a 'given' society. This means that each society will decide for itself what it regards as criminal behaviour. In one society smoking marijuana might be perfectly legal and in another country a criminal offence. In Britain, adultery and the public consumption of alcohol is lawful, but in Iran such activities are unlawful and are sometimes punishable by public flogging and imprisonment!

Nonetheless most societies would recognise the following behaviour as serious criminal offences:

increase in the percentage of violent offences over the past 30 years from 1% to about 5%. Similar trends have occurred in Scotland.

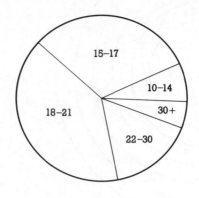

Source: Home Office

Proportions of males found guilty of serious crime by age

Source: Home Office

Indictable offences known to the police in England and Wales (excluding motoring offences)

Although these proportions relate to offences committed in the late 1970s, they do not change substantially from year to year. The amount of stealing has increased slightly in recent years as a proportion of all crime to over 90%, and there has been a gradual

The vast majority of crime is committed by young men. Although there has been a slight increase in the number of women committing serious crime, for every 35 men in prison in England and Wales there is only 1 woman.

What percentage of males committing serious crime would you estimate to be 21 years of age or under?

To ensure that laws are obeyed we have a number of organisations that are wholly concerned with the legal processes. The police represent the main body of law enforcement, and the courts exist to give the accused a fair hearing for alleged law-breaking behaviour. Officers of the court also have the authority to impose sanctions from fines to imprisonment on the guilty person.

EXERCISE

1 How many men and women in England and Wales were serving prison sentences in 1982?
2 Approximately what percentage of men and what percentage of women were sentenced for burglary?
3 Can you suggest any social reasons why a greater proportion of men than women commit burglary?
4 For what crime are women mostly imprisoned? Why is this particular type of crime committed by women?

How laws change

Laws exist in every society to serve and protect the interests of people in that society. Imagine what our roads would be like if we had no laws that tell motorists exactly what they can and cannot do? Not everyone, of course, agrees with all aspects of the law. This conversation illustrates what one individual thinks of the law relating to seat belts:

Dave I couldn't believe it when I was stopped last night.
Peter You always think it can't happen to you.
Dave I mean, I'm a law abiding citizen. You'd think I was a criminal or something.
Peter I don't think that – but the law is the law.
Dave Maybe, but it's a stupid law if you ask me. It's my life after all. If I want to

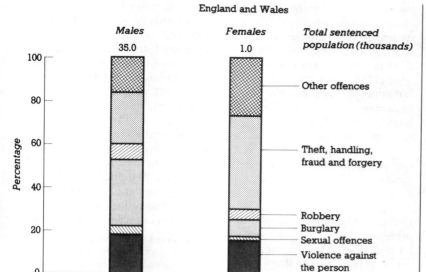

England and Wales

| Males | Females | Total sentenced population (thousands) |
| 35.0 | 1.0 | |

Percentage

- Other offences
- Theft, handling, fraud and forgery
- Robbery
- Burglary
- Sexual offences
- Violence against the person

Source: Prisons Statistics, Home Office

Prison population: sex and type of offence, 1982

drive without a seat belt, it's my business. The police should be chasing the real criminals.

Dave is angry at being caught not wearing a seat belt. If you were in conversation with him, what arguments would you put forward in favour of wearing seat belts?

Whatever our views, we have to accept that seat belt laws were introduced after years of careful research by experts who produced evidence to show that wearing seat belts reduced risks of injury and death for drivers and passengers. This research was noted by the government, and following debate in parliament our elected representatives voted to introduce this particular law relating to motoring behaviour. Some individuals, like Dave, may resent it, but when a law is passed it will be enforced by the police and any infringement will be dealt with in the courts. If a law proves to be unsatisfactory, members of parliament will consider changing it. Laws and norms are both man-made and are therefore responsive to change, as this story illustrates:

Backstreet blues

Some dates stick in the mind more than others. Thelma had never forgotten the 17th of April 1966. It was a Tuesday and she had got soaked on her way to work. She had thought of taking the day off but she couldn't afford to lose the money. What was going to happen at lunchtime was costing her enough anyway. It would take all her savings and some of her best friend's money too. There would be no holidays in Blackpool that year.

She thought of Alan's face when she had told him about the baby. He said he didn't want to know. It took him just 3 days to leave his job and digs to move to another town.

Ann had told her about this bloke who could help her out – at the right price. It was funny really. It wasn't the money that bothered Thelma as much as the prospect of losing her baby. But she had no choice because her widowed mother was an invalid and Thelma was resigned to the fact that she would have to spend the years ahead nursing her.

It took quite some time for Thelma to find the abortionist's house. It was the last one at the bottom of a narrow street, an ugly dark little terraced house. She remembered the dingy room and the damp bed and the smell of whiskey on his breath. There was the 'operation', his poking instruments, and the awful pain. She had been so ill afterwards.

'Don't tell anyone about this,' he had said after taking the money, 'we've both broken the law'. Thelma had become a criminal, and in her lunchtime too!

Whenever the 17th of April came around she would think of that day all those years ago. Her mother was dead now and she was living alone. She often thought of what would have happened had she not had the abortion. Her daughter would be grown up now.

Thelma had a dangerous and illegal abortion in 1966. Had she found herself in similar circumstances today her legal position would be different. She would now have the right in law to ask for a safe termination of her pregnancy by qualified medical staff in a NHS hospital. However, the law on abortion did not change overnight. It was changed, as all laws are changed, in response to the needs of a changing society.

EXERCISE

If you had an opportunity to change an existing law or to introduce a new law that would make a contribution towards a fairer society, what law would you choose? Explain in what way your law would change society.

Who influences changes in the law?

You might think that those of us who vote at elections have some indirect influence over the law-making process, but a number of writers question this. There are some lawyers and sociologists who argue that most laws represent and protect the interests of the most powerful groups within society. These groups are the social classes who control the means of production. From your reading of previous chapters you will know that this is a Marxist analysis of the legal system. These fragments are from a song describing an event in the USA during the 1930s:

Robbin' 'n' Stealin'

The men with the dollars closed the factory down
And ruined lives and killed-off the town
But the workers had their own ideas and plans
They took over the factory and put control in their hands.

The men with the dollars held an emergency meetin'
They wined and they dined, and after they'd eatn'
They called in the sheriff's men
To give the workers a good beatn'

Now the factory's closed and the assets bin stripped
And the workers' leaders have been savagely whipped.

Robbin' 'n' stealin' won't get you time
It's bein' poor and downtroddn'
That's really the crime.

These lyrics suggest that those with economic power have more influence on the law and the law enforcers than those without economic power. You might feel that the owners acted within their rights, and it was the workers who committed a crime by occupying property which was not theirs. A counter argument would be that the *real* crime was the closure of the factory and the effects of the closure on people's lives. Whether we accept this argument or not will depend on our views, but there is plenty of evidence to suggest that many laws in industrial societies exist to protect or at least favour the interests of the dominant economic groups.

Can you think of any law which serves the interests of powerful economic groups?

Hermann Mannheim, along with other sociologists, pointed to the large number of laws in capitalist societies that relate to the protection of property. He believes that this is an indication of how the law serves the interests of the ruling class. In a study *Amphetamine Politics on Capitol Hill* James Graham gives an interesting example of how powerful economic interest groups have a direct influence on legislation. In 1970 there were attempts made in the USA to control the manufacture of amphetamine. This drug, popular in drug subcultures, was manufactured legally but would often end up being sold on the illegal drug market. Graham shows how large manufacturing corporations put pressure on politicians to stop them from attempting to restrict the manufacture of the drug. While the government was declaring war on illegal drug use, the corporations made sure tnat this did not include drugs which made billions of dollars for them. The conclusion is that economic interests have priority when legislation is proposed, rather than the health of the people.

These arguments alert us to the complex process of law-making within society. Laws are not introduced and enforced only because they serve the well-being of the majority. Laws need not necessarily be neutral. They are the result of a variety of social, economic and political influences and pressures. We have seen that laws and norms can change over time and this reminds us of other important questions. Does social order exist for the benefit of all society or does the prevailing social order serve to protect the interests of the powerful? Are the police and the courts neutral in the way they apply the law? This is how one young black sees the situation in present-day Britain:

As soon as I see a police car I freeze. I know 'cos of past experience they will stop and search me and treat me different from the white kids in the area. I ain't sayin' all the police are bad – I'm not comin' out with that crap – but when you live in a racist society and you're stopped by the police all the time you start thinking that maybe the police are protecting all those racists. I mean, I can't see that the police are there to protect any of my interests.

This raises an interesting point. In a study called *Class and the Economics of Crime* David Gordon sees the practice of law enforcement as a means of protecting the interests of the ruling class. Gordon identifies the black population in the USA as the biggest threat to American capitalism. Although blacks form only about 12% of the population they appear more frequently than they should in the crime statistics. It is not that blacks necessarily commit more crime than whites; it is because the attention of the police is focused more on the black urban areas than on the white communities. In other words, it is too simplistic to argue that people who break the law will be dealt with equally by law enforcement agencies. The process of policing, arresting people, bringing them to court, and the overall maintenance of social order are activities that are influenced by other social forces.

EXERCISE

This point of view was expressed by a trade unionist on a TV news broadcast:

Anybody who believes that the police are on the side of the working man must be walking about with their eyes shut. I spent 2 months on picket duty outside a factory. Sometimes there were only half-a-dozen of us but about 25 police constables kept us company. In the whole 2 months there were always more police than pickets. At one time there must have been about 50 police officers showing off to the TV cameras. I can tell you this much, the criminals in this area must have had a marvellous 2 months.

1 What is the main point the trade unionist is making?
2 How would a sociologist, who believes that the laws main function is to protect the interests of the ruling class, explain the behaviour of the police?
3 What social reasons can you think of to justify the presence of the police in large numbers in an industrial dispute?

Problems with statistics

Statistics are gathered and presented to us by organisations to illustrate an aspect of social behaviour or a developing trend. Look closely at the table, and think about what it tells us about the crime rate in the Hilton area:

The table tells us that certain crimes are more common than others and that the number of people arrested for drunk and disorderly offences increased at the weekend. We have no reason to doubt these figures, nor should we. But how can we be certain that they tell the whole truth? One point that we must always keep in mind when we examine statistics is what they do *not* tell us. For instance:

- Who made the decision to select these particular crimes for presentation?
- Why were these crimes selected and not others? If car theft is included, why not embezzlement, computer fraud, currency and major income tax, customs and VAT offences?
- How do we explain the huge increase in assault on Wednesday? Was there a big social event in the Hilton area on that day? Was there a home football fixture or an industrial dispute perhaps?
- How is police manpower organised in the area? Are there more police on duty in the town centre on Saturday nights? Are the police willing and able to make more drunk and disorderly arrests on certain days or nights of the week? Are police officers on the lookout for certain kinds of crime?
- Do these statistics give us a fair indication of the amount of

crime in the area, or at least a reasonable idea of the proportions of selected crimes committed?

If we take the last point, and examine some statistics published by the government, we might get an idea of the scale of problems associated with crime statistics. You can see (page 154) that there is more crime in society than the official published figures normally suggest. There are more robberies, woundings and sexual offences, which cannot be described as minor offences. Yet even official statistics are not without criticism. We note that certain important types of criminal activity are not shown. As sociologists we must appreciate that statistics are not 'neutral' sets of facts that are chosen at random. They are selected for the specific purpose of drawing our attention to particular social problems. Unfortunately this usually means that certain types of crime get more publicity than others.

The first sociologist to look at what became known as 'white collar' crime was the American Edwin Sutherland. According to Sutherland, white collar crimes are committed by people of respectability and high social status in the course of their occupations. It includes taking bribes, fraud, embezzlement and financial misconduct by dentists,

Crimes committed in the Hilton area as reported to the police

Incident	Sun	Mon	Tues	Wed	Thurs	Fri	Sat	Total
Robbery from shops	13	9	11	16	3	7	28	87
Car theft	49	10	4	18	4	19	72	176
Drunk and disorderly	82	12	16	8	35	63	94	310
Assault	29	14	20	62	18	17	49	209
Robbery from person	12	17	16	9	41	57	44	196
Burglary	16	13	4	18	17	32	69	169
Major crime*	0	1(AR)	0	1(AR)	3(AR)	1(AR)	1(M)	7

*Murder/Manslaughter (M)
Armed Robbery (AR)

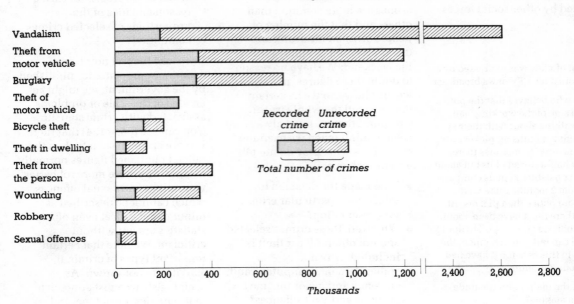

England and Wales

Vandalism
Theft from motor vehicle
Burglary
Theft of motor vehicle
Bicycle theft
Theft in dwelling
Theft from the person
Wounding
Robbery
Sexual offences

Recorded crime   Unrecorded crime

Total number of crimes

0   200   400   600   800   1,000   1,200   2,400   2,600   2,800

Thousands

Recorded and unrecorded crime in 1981: selected categories

lawyers and doctors. The most common white collar crime is of course tax evasion. In many countries tax evasion occurs on a vast scale and enormous amounts of money are unlawfully withheld from governments. Yet how often do we have a media outcry about tax evasion compared with, say, offences relating to social security fraud? Newspapers are always more eager to report and embellish statistics that expose 'scroungers', although the amount of money defrauded in this way is small compared with tax evasion.

We do know that certain types of criminal behaviour have increased in recent years. The increase in the abuse of drugs and of acts of violence against the person are examples. However, crime statistics are basically about people who have been caught committing crime. The reasons for capture (more police patrols in a

particular area) and the policy of the police force relating to particular crimes are factors we have to take into account. In short, we need to dig beneath the surface of statistical data. Even then, we cannot realistically consider deviant or criminal behaviour in isolation from social class and educational factors. To ignore these factors would be to underestimate the nature of social control in the organisation and maintenance of social order.

EXERCISE

Go back to the chart headed *Recorded and unrecorded crime in 1981: selected categories* and answer these questions:

1 Approximately how many recorded thefts were there from motor vehicles in 1981?
2 Approximately how many burglaries went unrecorded in the same year?
3 Can you think of the reason why virtually all motor vehicle thefts are reported to the police?
4 Suggest 3 reasons why so much crime is unreported.
5 Suggest 3 white collar crimes that are at least as serious as bicycle theft.

Conformity, deviance and crime

Peter sat in front of the mirror and carefully made up his face. He picked up the eye shadow and gently touched his eyelids with the brush. Then he applied the lipstick. It was a masterpiece. When he was satisfied he walked over to the wardrobe and took out a red dress on a hanger. The dressmaker had spent a lot of time stitching on the sequins. He quickly put the dress on and looked at himself in the long mirror. It was a perfect fit. He was more than pleased with himself . . .

In your view, would you say that Peter's behaviour is 'deviant' or 'normal'?

Most sociologists would argue that Peter's behaviour can be interpreted accurately only by taking into account the whole social situation. If Peter was an actor preparing for his role as the pantomime dame we would accept his behaviour as normal. If on the other hand he was going shopping in the High Street or going for a drink in the local pub we might have to think again, although we would have to be certain that Peter wasn't going to a fancy dress party. Indeed, most people would regard a man who often wears women's clothes in public places either as mad or deviant, which means that they think it is conduct which violates the norms of ordinary society.

When a sociologist discusses conformity and deviance he knows that he is dealing in relative concepts. An activity can be deviant in one situation and perfectly normal in another, which is what we mean by conformity. Look at this list of activities and note down which you think is deviant and which you think is normal. Explain your reasoning:

- Breaking into someone's house
- Walking naked on the street
- Talking to someone who is not there.

You will have worked out that it is the context in which people find themselves that determines whether or not their behaviour is deviant. If a friend has lost a door key you might have to 'break' into her home. Nudists, in their private colonies, are quite happy walking about naked. In fact, if you did wear clothing in a nudist colony you would be deviant! Kneeling and praying aloud in church or at home is also a common normal activity, yet it assumes an invisible God with whom one can have private conversations. Almost any type of behaviour that is deviant to you may be normal to someone else, and what is deviant to you in one situation might not be deviant in another. We also have to accept that an activity that is either deviant or normal in some circumstances may also be a crime in other circumstances. If our nudist went shopping in Woolworths he would probably be arrested on a charge of a breach of the peace.

Here is the view of a young person who regards himself as a 'punk'. He is describing to his friends some businessmen he saw drinking in a pub:

You should have seen them. You should have seen their clothes and their hairstyles. They were really weird. I just can't understand how people can behave like that. They were drinking wine out of funny little glasses and using knives and forks to eat meat pies and talking posh about classical music. I bet the wallies live in big houses. What a drag it must be to be like them. Weird, that's what I call them.

To this punk these conventional businessmen, with their dark suits and rolled umbrellas, are 'weird' or deviants. No doubt the businessmen would have similar views about him!

Another important point about deviance is that while people think of deviance as negative behaviour because it threatens the normative order, this is not always the case:

Breakthrough?

After 10 years of intensive research on fuel consumption, engineers at *Winfield Auto* have come up with what they see as a revolutionary way of reducing the amount of fuel needed to power motor vehicles. Everything is very hush-hush but a spokesperson for the company told us that what the engineers have discovered challenges all known engineering principles. A press conference has been called for next Tuesday when details of this thrilling breakthrough will be made known.

This article suggests that challenging the norm, within certain social settings, can have positive benefits, and such deviations from the conventional wisdom are usually welcomed and encouraged by society. When

sociologists talk of deviance, they usually mean social behaviour which is disapproved of in wider society.

Left-handed in a right-handed world

It began in school. A fuss was made when Susan started having problems with her handwriting. The teachers at first thought it was because she was stupid, but her writing did eventually improve. She struggled with games too but she did develop a taste for poetry. Her school friends laughed at her and her mother thought she was a dreamer. No need for that sort of thing for a girl who will work in a factory her mother had said. Susan was small and the children at school noticed her size. They said she would never have boyfriends and they laughed even more when she said it didn't matter.

Susan continued having problems at work. In the packing department the girls scoffed at her because she always had her head in a book. She didn't go out much, preferring to stay at home, locked away in her room scribbling and reading poetry. Her mother thought she was wasting her life and she would do better if she got herself a nice boyfriend.

Susan joined an evening class to improve her poetry, but everyone seemed cleverer than she was. The lecturer, a balding man with hair hanging down both sides of his head, used words she couldn't understand and made her feel ill at ease. She hadn't even heard of half the poets he talked about.

She felt awkward and began to believe she was awkward. People said she was different so she began to see herself differently. Her remaining few friends said they thought her a bit odd so she began to behave oddly. The odder they said she was, the odder she became. Susan gave the world what it wanted, and this made life easier for her. She lives alone now. We might say she is eccentric, but that's not the word her neighbours use – they aren't that polite. Sometimes she sits in her armchair for hours thinking about what went wrong.

What does this story tell us about deviant behaviour?

First it points out how a physical difference can be given a social meaning. Perhaps because Susan was left-handed she had difficulty learning to write at school. This was interpreted as a sign of low ability. She was also bad at sport and her peers thought her love of poetry amusing. Her mother saw her as a dreamer. All of this suggests that our family, our experiences in school and the reactions of our peers can not only define us as deviant but also lead us into thinking of ourselves as deviant. We also note that when Susan attended a poetry evening class she was made to feel out of place. She failed even here to fit into the expected role of 'artistic' student. The more society defined her as deviant, the more deviant she became.

The story helps us to understand that we are not born deviant, but that we become deviant because of society's reaction to our behaviour. The family, the school, our peer groups – all the elements of socialisation – help in the manufacture of the individual's deviant identity. Susan became labelled as an 'eccentric', or a 'nutcase'. This labelling, in its turn, became a self-fulfilling prophecy. The more hostile society was to her behaviour, the more her behaviour appeared to promote this hostility.

EXERCISE

Suggest 3 social groups or types of

social behaviour in general society that are regarded as deviant. Explain why they are regarded as deviant and mention some of the ways our society reacts to them.

When a person breaks the law the social response to the law-breaker is different. Here we see the social control agencies taking action. Historically sociologists have been greatly interested in the social factors which lead people to commit crime, and many believe that the influence of the social environment is the key explanation of criminal behaviour.

A term that is often used when discussing criminal behaviour is **subculture**. An example of this concept is contained in these comments made by a professional criminal:

It might seem strange to people outside my world but I grew up in a community where a lot of criminals lived. My own family were criminals. It wasn't unusual to have the police coming to our house at all hours of the night searchin' for something or other. My uncle was a well-known 'peterman'. He could blow open a safe dead easy and he was a bit of a legend when I was growing up. A lot of kids want to be professional footballers or pop singers. I didn't want any of that. I wanted to be a successful criminal.

This person grew up in an environment that had the norms and values of a criminal community, rather than the norms and values of a conventional community. This is what is meant by the concept of subculture. Many of the early social theories tried to explain criminal behaviour by placing great emphasis on the influence of subcultural values. Although these theories direct our attention to social influences, as opposed to theories that claim that criminals are 'born bad', they can be overstated to give the impression that an individual is somehow not in control of his own behaviour;

that is, if you programme in the required amount of social deprivation, with a dash of poor housing and education and a few 'bad' friends, then, hey presto! you have a criminal. As sociologists we know that life is more complicated than this. We will discuss the concept of subculture in more detail in the next section.

Most of the information on crime is provided by the courts, the police and the government and therefore is concerned with 'known' crimes or activities that have been defined as criminal by those in authority. As we have seen, there may be strong political reasons for the dominance of class-linked anti-authority type crimes within these statistics. Despite this, we should always seek to explain criminal behaviour by locating our enquiries within the social structure, and not simply to blame the individual as if he or she is isolated from the social world and its influences.

The sociologist David Matza makes an interesting point about social behaviour. Concentrating on delinquency, he points out in his famous study *Delinquency and Drift* that much delinquent behaviour can be seen as brief excursions from conventional behaviour. In other words, the delinquent is not that different from the non-delinquent. What makes the difference is whether we are caught or not. Most of us have committed a deviant or criminal act on occasion but this does not mean we are embarked upon a deviant or criminal career. The difference – between us and them – is that for a number of social and economic reasons we have tended to get away with it.

EXERCISE

What follows is a selection of social activities. Under the 3 set headings produce notes to show that you are aware of the complex relationship between conformity, deviancy and criminality. Try to resist the temptation to offer your own opinion, but do attempt to make an assessment based on attitudes and opinions in general society. Here is an example:

1 A man drives his car through a red traffic light on an empty road.

Degree of conformity	Degree of deviancy	Degree of criminality
Would not be considered as 'normal' behaviour in general society. In desperate circumstances, such as imminent childbirth or severe injury, driving carefully through a red light to get to a hospital would be desirable, even expected behaviour. Amongst certain groups of 'macho' young people 'taking a red light' might be fairly normal behaviour.	Most people would regard this as anti-social behaviour, especially pedestrians but probably would not report the offender to the police. Many drivers would be sympathetic towards someone who got caught since they themselves have often got away with it. A few drivers might feel guilty about doing it, but not too many.	Without doubt a criminal offence. The police would normally bring charges or at least give the driver a stern warning, unless the vehicle was an ambulance or a fire engine on emergency call. A police driver might feel justified in doing it if in pursuit of a dangerous criminal.

Now read through this selection and choose 3 examples to complete yourself. If you are working in pairs, select 6 different examples and compare your answers in the discussion that follows.

2 On a charity rag day a student throws a handful of flour at a passer-by.

3 A lone housewife kills a burglar with a hammer as he is climbing through her bedroom window.

4 A man who has a wife and 4 children frequently boozes away all his wages.

5 Because of low profits, an American multi-national closes a British factory throwing 250 employees out of work.

6 A soldier shoots dead a suspected terrorist escaping in a car.

7 A manufacturer announces massive profits following the launch of a new brand of cigarettes aimed at the teenage market.

8 A husband gives his wife a thrashing for sleeping with another man after a party.

9 A young mother allows her severely mentally handicapped baby to die of a chest infection without calling the doctor.

10 A lorry driver does window cleaning at the weekends to supplement his income but does not declare the income to the income tax office.

11 A man kisses and hugs another man in public.

12 In order to avoid personal financial loss, a company director flees to Spain to escape his creditors

13 A scantily-clad woman, with a string of carrots and onions round her neck, takes a walk down a road with a toy rabbit on a lead.

14 An anti-vivisectionist daubs paint over an animal researcher's car.

15 A private cleaning contractor employs under-age schoolchildren to clean a hospital.

16 A 17-year-old youth has consenting sexual intercourse with his 15-year-old girlfriend.

Social class and patterns of crime

Although sociologists feel obliged to try to explain why a person becomes involved in criminal activity, they have traditionally focused their attention on explaining patterns of working class crime and in particular crime committed by working class youth. As Mungham and Pearson write in their introduction to *Working Class Youth Culture*:

The adolescent boy has perhaps received more than his fair share of attention from sociologists, psychologists, criminologists, psychiatrists and welfare professionals.

Youth culture

A recurring feature of most industrial societies since the 1950s has been an obsession with the behaviour of youth. We know that young people, as far as the popular press is concerned, are often portrayed in headlines as 'juvenile delinquents' and 'mindless hooligans' and certain newspapers enjoy nothing better during the summer months than to report alleged gang warfare when ARMIES OF BIKERS INVADE SOUTH COAST BEACHES IN CLASH WITH MODS!! or YOUTHS RUN RIOT IN ROME CUP FINAL.

Why do you think youth gets such a bad press?

One of the factors we have to consider is that young people can now be identified as a distinct social group, and since the 1950s many industries have been set up to cater for their economic and social needs by providing records and tapes, clothes, magazines, special TV programmes, computer games and electronic devices. Popular discussion about young people usually includes references to the 'generation gap' and to the problems that society has in dealing with the 'teenager'. This notion of a generation gap suggests a clear distinction between young and old, and all other forms of social differentiation appear to be relatively unimportant. It is as if youth as a group is classless, that by buying the records of a particular band or by experiencing the threat of unemployment all young people are somehow united against a boring and oppressive adult world. As sociologists we should find these particular views unacceptable.

It is silly to say that because young people buy the same kinds of records or clothes they will share similar social experiences. The social experiences of a 16-year-old black working class male living in a high-rise area of a city will be different from the social experiences of a middle class female living in rural Surrey. It is also unwise to use the term 'teenager' when discussing young people's behaviour. If teenagers include everybody between 13 and 19 years of age then we know that society treats its 13-year-olds differently from its 19-year-olds and, equally important, it expects different behaviour and degrees of social commitment from a 13-year-old child than from a 19-year-old adult.

EXERCISE

To what extent do these social factors influence the cultural *differences* between young people
- Parents' income level
- The education they receive
- The kind of community in which they live?

We can say that much of the discussion about young people's behaviour is emotive and fails to take account of the complexities of social life in general. Some sociologists have also been found wanting in this respect. The neglect of female youth for example is apparent when we look at the research titles such as Willmott's *Adolescent Boys in East London*, Cohen's *Delinquent Boys* and Parker's *A View from the Boys* (although researchers are now facing up to this problem). However, with these thoughts in mind about young people, we can now turn to patterns of working class crime and to the question of why working class youth tends to come into conflict with the agents of social control. A useful concept in exploring this is the notion of a subculture, which we touched upon in the previous section.

Subcultures

When we talk of subcultures we are referring to social groups that have some norms and values that are different from the norms and values found in mainstream society. For instance, theft is not only a crime but also an anti-social or deviant activity in ordinary society. However, in certain subcultures, although theft is still regarded as a crime, it is not necessarily thought of as deviant. When sociologists try to explain criminal and deviant behaviour they take into account the origins of the behaviour in relation to the social structure. In other words, the nature of crime can only be assessed within the culture (or within the subculture) of an individual's community. Here is a description of such a subculture:

Pine Street people

Billy was late getting up because the law had called the night before. They came very late to question his brother Terry. This was nothing unusual; for as long as Billy could remember the police had been frequent and unwelcome visitors to the flat. A shop in the high street had been robbed and some grass had pointed the finger at Terry. But the police left empty-handed – they could pin nothing on Billy's brother.

'You'd better watch yourself,' his father had told Terry that morning, 'they've really got it in for you. It wouldn't surprise me if they don't try and fit you up one of these days.'

'The filth are pathetic,' Terry had said, 'they'd be better employed chasing the perverts and the tax dodgers.'

Billy had smiled at this. His brother had his own ideas about justice. He was always complaining that everyone was on the take – politicians, social workers, teachers, judges, and especially the filth – everyone was looking after number

one. The only difference was that no-one bothered them. The law only applied to the likes of Terry and the people of Pine Street, the people without contacts and money behind them.

When Billy left the flat the rain made him wish he had stayed at home by the electric fire. The electricity board had cut them off a few months back but it was a cinch to reconnect the supply. Now they used as much electricity as they wanted and no-one worried about bills.

Billy headed for the snooker hall. At least it would be dry and warm there, and he could have a chat with Seth, the manager.

'How's it goin' Billy?' Seth asked when he arrived. 'I hear the filth were round your place last night.'

'Yeah,' Billy joked, 'they came round for a night-cap. You know how it is.'

'Yeah, I know how it is with you lot in Pine Street.'

Although Billy was rarely involved in crime himself, being one of the Collins family had given him a reputation. All his family could look after themselves and his dad had done his fair share of time in prison. Billy thought the whole thing was funny, having a family with a reputation for being villains, but that's how it is in Pine Street.

'Hey! Billy!' George called over, 'I've got something here that might interest you.'

Billy went over to the table as George was pocketing his fourth red. George put up his cue, went to his bag, and got out a cassette to show Billy. 'What d'you think?' he asked.

'I like this band, but I'm not buying any old crap. Is this a fake copy?'

'No, this is the business. A mate of mine got them. He was up north and got them from a bloke who turned over a warehouse.'

Billy looked at the cassette. 'I'm a bit short at the moment,' he told George.

'Doesn't matter. See me when you've got a few quid.'

'Thanks,' Billy said, thinking George was a great mate.

Billy sat down and watched George finish the frame. George certainly knew snooker. Mind you, he'd had enough practice. Billy had been coming to Seth's for years, day in and day out. It wasn't as if work got in the way. Even if you had wanted a job you'd have been pushed to get one. Everything closed down years ago. Billy remembered the teachers saying how he and his mates should work that extra bit harder because jobs were in such short supply. What a joke! There was no work and if there were jobs they were an insult to your intelligence. At least the excitement from thievin' told you you were alive.

Billy looked about the hall. The people were OK, Billy thought. At least they were straight. They might be thieves but at least they admitted it. Terry was right. Everyone was at it, robbin' and thievin' in their own way and looking after number one. If the people who talked about law and order lived in Pine Street it would have been interesting to see what would have happened to them. They would have learnt that when there was nothin' going for you and you were skint, you might as well go robbin'. It was the only work not in short supply.

EXERCISE

1 How would you describe the culture of Pine Street?
2 What particular aspects of life in the Pine Street subculture would be regarded as deviant or criminal in conventional society?
3 How would you explain Billy's attitudes, and in what way do they differ from yours?

A sociologist looking at Pine Street would suggest that the social conditions were such that becoming involved in criminal activity was inevitable for some people. In fact, rather than seeing Billy's attitudes as irrational and irresponsible, some sociologists might argue that his attitudes and behaviour were rational and reasonable under those social circumstances.

Crime patterns and delinquency

One sociologist who has looked at the way we respond to our social conditions within the norms and values of ordinary society is Robert Merton in his book *Social Theory and Social Structure*. Merton's work deals with American society, which he argues places great emphasis on achieving 'success', particularly financial success associated with material possessions. In the USA people are encouraged to find success through what he describes as **legitimate means**, that is by gaining educational qualifications in the college system and through a well paid career. Since not everyone has the same opportunity to get to college and succeed in a career, what are they to do? According to Merton, failure to come up to par with this American ideal creates the condition of **anomie** in which we experience a sense of hopelessness that eventually leads to a moral collapse in society and an increasing unwillingness to obey laws. For Merton, the vast majority of us have to find other social strategies, other ways of satisfying the economic and social demands made by society to compensate for this sense of failure. He provides us with a model by which we can examine how people respond to these demands.

Merton's model describing responses to the accepted norms and values of society

	Values	Norms
Conformity	+	+
Innovation	+	−
Ritualism	−	+
Retreatism	−	−
Rebellion	−+	−+

+ *acceptance*
− *rejection*

- **The conformist** is a person who accepts the conventional values and norms of society and the means of achieving them. He or she will totally conform to the normative order and will therefore not fall foul of the law. The conformist is the ideal citizen whom Merton sees as a person striving desperately for social success through the conventional means of hard work and struggle. Most of us are conformists.

  The remaining 4 categories, for Merton, describe different types of deviant responses to the social system:
- **The innovator** will look for new ways of achieving success. He accepts the values of society, for instance the prestige enjoyed by the wealthy, but he will reject the conventional means of obtaining that wealth. He may be an inventor or a professional gambler (legal means) or rob banks or commit fraud (illegal means). He might desire respect and admiration in the community which spurs him on to collect money for charity or urges him to be tough or ruthless.
- **The ritualist** is someone who has lost all ambition for social success, status or prestige. He is content in the security of doing the same job day in and day out. He has accepted defeat by sacrificing the values of 'getting on' but willingly submits to the demands made of him by

accepting the approved means of ritual work.

- **The retreatist** abandons society both in terms of its values and its means of achieving what is considered socially desirable. The classic escape is through drink and drugs or by taking to the road and leading a nomadic life.
- **The rebel** rejects both the values of society and the means of achieving them, and wants to replace them with alternative values. Rebels are found in political groups that want a different kind of society but have abandoned traditional routes to power, like standing for parliament. The hippies in the 1960s who set up communes would be included in this category.

EXERCISE

Here are a few comments made by people in British society:

a I've been married now for 20 years and I like nothing better than doing the housework and getting Jim's meal ready for him when he gets back from work at 6.30. I've never felt the need to go out to work or to compete with anybody myself.
b I joined the IRA when my brother got killed by a Brit army lorry. I've done my fair share of action and I'm prepared to do anything to free my country from foreign occupation.
c After I left school I joined the staff of this publishing firm as a junior in the sales department. That was 5 years ago. Next week I hope to get the sales manager's job.
d Me and my mate Tony devised this brilliant scheme for burgling shoppers' houses. Tony's a great grafter (you know, good at pickin' pockets) and when we find out where the shopper lives from the purse we've nicked, I ring her up and pretend to be the manager of a shop. I tell her we've found her purse intact and would she like to come round to the shop to pick it up. Meanwhile Tony's watching her house to make sure she leaves the

house empty. Then we drive up in a van and clear the place out in about 3 minutes. Of course, we use her own front door key from her purse to get in – a nice touch is that. We feel really proud about our methods. You know, no violence, nothing like that, just brains and guts.
e I go to work regularly and keep myself to myself.
f I can't remember much about my late teens. I went to London when I was 18 and in 6 months I was a mainliner. I drifted from one hostel to another and now and then I'd go into hospital for a cure. I spent 2 years in a sort of dreamworld and I very nearly died more than once. I did shoplifting to pay for my habit. Then I met Wendy and we started to live together. She helped me back on the rails. That's a bit of a joke really because I worked as a porter for British Rail for the next 7 years. It was a dead end job but doing regular work without too much aggro was what I needed. I'm 33 now and I've started to do an Open University degree. Funny sort of life really. Some of our best friends died years ago.

Analyse these statements using Merton's categories as a guide. Explain whether or not you think any of these individuals are deviant in British society.

Many criminals fall into the category of innovators. Bank robbers rarely distribute money to the poor and some of them enjoy the same luxuriant lifestyles as the conventional rich. However, both groups accept the same values associated with wealth, but their methods of achieving wealth differ. At a lower level, many young people from working class communities who come into conflict with the police will gain a degree of status from their peers, as this 17-year-old explains:

I grabbed this handbag and I couldn't believe it when I found 350 quid tucked in at the bottom. For once I had real money and I went and bought some new clothes and treated my mates to drinks in the pub. I felt great

because I was thinking that I was somebody. I mean, they tell you in school that you've got to work hard to amount to something. So what happens? There's no work and you're a big nobody. My old man worked his guts out for over 30 years with the same firm, then they closed the place down and put him on the scrap heap. I bet he's never had 350 quid spending money.

For the sociologist Walter Miller, delinquency can be understood only by taking full account of the values of sections of working class cultural groups. According to Miller it is important to appear 'tough' in working class communities, to be able to 'look after yourself'. This emphasis on 'macho' behaviour encourages certain individuals to commit crimes of violence in order to gain respect and acceptance, which of course brings them into conflict with the police. Miller also suggests that there is, within working class communities, the search for excitement which sometimes leads young people into crime because there are few legitimate opportunities available. Many leisure activities, for example, are expensive and remain outside the range of unemployed youth. The streets are the only viable alternative:

There's nothin' around here to do ... so you look around and find a car ... you think about driving it ... not sell it or anything like that ... you'll only go for a short drive ... there's no car I can't get into and start ... the thing gives me a buzz ...

In their study *Delinquency and Opportunity* Cloward and Ohlin argue that the working class is under great pressure to deviate or to break the law because they have fewer opportunities to achieve anything of value within society by legitimate means. The study attempts to explain young people's involvement in criminal activity by looking at the structure of the communities in which they live. In some working class communities they identify the existence of **illegitimate opportunity structures**. This means that young people grow up in areas where there is an established pattern of crime and criminal activity and socialisation within this environment exposes them to anti-social values. Many autobiographies of ex-criminals seem to support this view. In *A Sense of Freedom* Jimmy Boyle, as a violent young criminal, describes growing up in a crime-ridden area of Glasgow during the 1960s. While most children have ambitions to be successful in sport or in a particular kind of work, some children in communities where there is a pattern of organised crime aspire to be professional criminals. Delinquency can almost be seen as an apprenticeship for this.

Finally, if we are to explain the high proportion of working class youths involved in delinquent and criminal acts we must consider social class. As we have seen in other chapters, sections of the working class experience social deprivations in education, housing and employment. If we live in a society that places emphasis on material success, yet denies many people the opportunity of achieving that success, it is not surprising that some individuals will come into conflict with the law. This is not the failure essentially of the individual but of a social structure which allows the persistence of glaring inequalities between different social groups.

EXERCISE

Can you identify any illegitimate opportunity structures in your town or city? They might be located in a particular pub or club or in a large residential area. Comment on the social problems that exist in this area and the kinds of temptations to which young people are subjected.

QUESTIONS

1 a Explain what is meant by deviant behaviour and why not all deviants are criminals. (6 marks)
  b Explain, with examples, how changes in the law and in social attitudes can lead to an increase or decrease in deviant behaviour. (14 marks)

AEB O Level 1983

2 What is the relationship between class and crime? (20 marks)

3 Drink-driving offences committed in the Haslow district in July – December 1985

July	Aug	Sept	Oct	Nov	Dec
20	16	12	14	15	38

  a What are statistics? (3 marks)
  b What further information do we require before we can draw sensible conclusions from these figures? (6 marks)
  c Supposing a device was introduced to make arrests for these offences easier and quicker:
    i What effect might this have on the statistics?
    ii Explain why a rising recorded rate of drink–driving offences might be misleading. (5 marks)
  d A drink–driving conviction is a serious criminal offence, yet some drivers regard getting caught as a form of bad luck. How do you explain this attitude? (6 marks)

Tristram's trouble

Sixteen-year-old Charlie Tristram has been sentenced to 3 months detention by the magistrates for stealing motor cars. It is his fourth conviction for theft in 2 years.

Researcher: Can you tell me something about your home life?

Charlie: Well, I live at home with my mum and dad and 2 brothers. My brothers are older than me. Actually it isn't my real dad. My real dad got killed in a road accident and my mum married again.

Researcher: What were you like as a youngster? Can you remember much about being at junior school? Did you get into trouble there?

Charlie: No. As far as I can remember, I was OK. I used to like going to school then. I was about average in lessons and I got on well with most of the teachers.

Researcher: What about your home life at that time?

Charlie: It was all right. But when my dad was killed I ran away from home. I was about 10 or 11 I think. I gave my mum a real bad time. When the policewoman brought me back home – actually I'd run away to Blackpool up north by stealing the train fare from my mum's purse – I couldn't really settle down at home. I think that's the time I started getting into trouble.

Researcher: What kind of trouble?

Charlie: You know, trouble in the street at first. I joined this gang of kids who were tearaways – always causing trouble and messing about. They were older than I was – about 13 or 14. We used to go round the shops nicking things. Woolworths was the best place. We'd go there and fill our pockets with chocolates and pens and things like that. Then we'd go down to the shopping centre to the clothes shops. The older kids would pretend to try on jackets while us smaller kids sneaked in behind the clothes racks to nick the jeans and pullovers. We never got caught.

Researcher: So when did you get caught?

Charlie: Tell a lie. We did get caught, but for doin' somethin' else. We broke into our school and messed things up a bit.

Researcher: Messed things up?

Charlie: Yeah. I was at the big school by this time, and we broke in on a Saturday night. We didn't break in for any particular reason. You know, just for summut to do, for a bit of excitement. Because I was small and thin they got me to climb through a small window so I could let the others in. When we got into the headmaster's office we smashed up his desk and poured ink on his chair and threw papers all over the place. Wilfie wrote a lot of obscene things about the teachers on the wall and spent about half-an-hour drawing nudes with coloured pens. Then we pulled out the drawers of this green cabinet thing and we found 2 bottles of wine hidden in a paper bag – I think it was sherry or somethin'. We reckon old Harris the head was a bit of an alco. That was when we did somethin' really stupid.

Researcher: Stupid?

Charlie: We got blotto. We drank the 2 bottles of sherry and there was only 3 of us. Drifter, he was the oldest, climbed on this bookcase and tried to do a handstand – he was good at that sort of thing. But he fell off and knocked himself out. We tried to lift him through the window but we kept falling down ourselves because we were so drunk. Then Wilfie was sick all over us. I'd just taken my jeans off to clean them when the law turned up. I suppose the caretaker or someone must have seen us.

Researcher: Then what?

Charlie: They took us down to the station. The coppers were all right with us – you know the coppers in uniforms – but the plain clothes coppers were nasty. Once they get you in their clutches and start questioning you, you haven't got a chance. They find out everything. They just don't stop until they

know everything. D'you want to know what they did to my mate Wilfie?

Researcher: No, not just now. What did your parents think about this?

Charlie: My mum was courting her new feller then. Naturally she wasn't very happy about it, but she wasn't all that bothered when they bound me over. She was more bothered about the stuff from the shops.

Researcher: What do you mean?

Charlie: She used to wear and sell a lot of the gear I nicked from the shops. She thought the police would find out about it so she went off on a fortnight's holiday to Spain with her boyfriend. I went to live with my grandad. I like my grandad.

Researcher: Did you go back to school?

Charlie: No, not to that school. I was kicked out of there. They sent me to Meadow Vale Comprehensive. I hated school by this time and I did a lot of skipping off. When I was 14 I got kicked out of there too.

Researcher: What for?

Charlie: Because I couldn't stand doin' school work and takin' orders from teachers, so I caused as much trouble as I could. I had a big bust up with the maths teacher, Mr Davies. I refused to do one of his stupid exercises so he sent me to the headmaster. He gave me a real good caning in his office. Then my mum came to the school and had a row with Mr Davies. Actually she gave him a thumping in the playground in front of all the kids. Then Davies reported my mum to the police, and then he started pickin' on me all the time in front of my mates. I got so mad that I found out where he lived and I went round there one evening and kicked in a few door panels on his car. He never found out who done it but he guessed it was me.

Researcher: What about your brothers?

Charlie: They're completely different from me. They both have good jobs. One of them is doing his A levels at college. I often wonder why things went the way they did. I was as clever as they were at school. I seemed to have gone downhill somehow. I suppose I must have had the same chances as they had?

QUESTIONS

1 What factors in Charlie's background do you think contributed most to his delinquent behaviour? Why do you think his brothers' behaviour was different?

2 Summarise Charlie's deviant activities towards his school and his teachers. Why do you think he held such hostile attitudes about his education?

3 Children from working class homes tend to commit more crime than children from middle class homes. What explanation can you give for this?

Points for discussion

- Once a person has turned 'bad' there's nothing much you can do about it.
- Criminals are people who want a fairer share of society's wealth.
- The cause of deviant behaviour is psychological and not social in origin.

Case Study

The Scarman Report

Following the 1981 riots in Brixton, a suburb of Lambeth in South London, the government asked Lord Scarman to 'inquire urgently into the serious disorder' and to produce a report. These are just a few extracts from the 137 page report:

Part I – Introduction

B – The two basic problems

1.2 During the week-end of 10–12 April (Friday, Saturday and Sunday) the British people watched with horror and incredulity an instant audio-visual presentation on their television sets of scenes of violence and disorder in their capital city, the like of which had not previously been seen in this century in Britain. In the centre of Brixton, a few hundred young people – most, but not all of them, black – attacked the police on the streets with stones, bricks, iron bars and petrol bombs, demonstrating to millions of their fellow citizens the fragile basis of the Queen's peace. The petrol bomb was now used for the first time on the streets of Britain (the idea, no doubt, copied from the disturbances in Northern Ireland). These young people, by their criminal behaviour – for such, whatever their grievances or frustrations, it was – brought about a temporary collapse of law and order in the centre of an inner suburb of London.

1.3 The disturbances were at their worst on the Saturday evening. For some hours the police could do no more than contain them. When the police, heavily reinforced, eventually restored order in the afflicted area, the toll of human injury and property damage was such that one observer described the scene as comparable with the aftermath of an air-raid. Fortunately no one was killed: but on that Saturday evening 279 policemen were injured, 45 members of the public are known to have been injured (the number is almost certainly greater), a large number of police and other vehicles were damaged or destroyed (some by

fire), and 28 buildings were damaged or destroyed by fire. Further, the commitment of all available police to the task of quelling the riot and dispersing the rioters provided the opportunity, which many seized, of widespread looting in the shopping centre of Brixton.

1.4 Two views have been forcefully expressed in the course of the Inquiry as to the causation of the disorders. The first is: – oppressive policing over a period of years, and in particular the harassment of young blacks on the streets of Brixton. On this view, it is said to be unnecessary to look more deeply for an explanation of the disorders. They were 'anti police'. The second is that the disorders, like so many riots in British history, were a protest against society by people, deeply frustrated and deprived, who saw in a violent attack upon the forces of law and order their one opportunity of compelling public attention to their grievances. I have no doubt that each view, even if correct, would be an over-simplification of a complex situation. If either view should be true, it would not be the whole truth.

Part II – Social conditions

A – Brixton

(1) LOCATION AND ENVIRONMENT

2.1 Brixton is an established commercial and residential centre within the inner area of South London. Administratively it forms part of the London Borough of Lambeth, one of the thirteen Inner London Boroughs.

(2) HOUSING

2.6 Nevertheless the general picture of housing provision both in the Borough as a whole and in Brixton in particular is one of considerable

stress. Despite a declining population, it was estimated at the time of the National Dwelling and Housing Survey (NDHS) in 1977–1978 that there was a shortage of about 20 000 dwellings in the Borough compared to the number of households requiring a separate dwelling. The local authority's waiting list alone currently numbers some 18 000 households. 37% of homeless households, compared to 20% of households overall in the Borough, are black. According to the HDH Survey, 10% of households in the Borough are overcrowded, ie one or more bedrooms below standard, compared to 9% for Inner London as a whole: but 13% of households in Brixton are one or more bedrooms below standard. Altogether Lambeth Borough Council has estimated that some 12 000 households in the Borough live in overcrowded conditions.

(3) LEISURE AND RECREATION FACILITIES

2.10 One other important aspect of the physical environment is the relative lack of leisure and recreation facilities in Lambeth, and in Brixton in particular. It is clear that the exuberance of youth requires in Brixton (and other similar inner city areas) imaginative and socially acceptable opportunities for release if it is not to become frustrated or be diverted to criminal ends. It is equally clear that such opportunities do not at present exist for young people in Brixton to the extent that they ought, particularly given the enforced idleness of many youths through unemployment. The amusement arcades, the unlawful drinking clubs and, I believe, the criminal classes, gain as a result. The street corners become the social centres of people, young and old, good and bad, with time on their hands and a continuing opportunity, which, doubtless, they use, to engage in endless discussion of their grievances.

B – The people of Brixton

(1) POPULATION

2.12 Like many other inner city areas the population of Brixton is falling. The population of the Borough of Lambeth as a whole dropped by 20% between the 1971 and 1981 census. It stands now at some 246 000. The major cause of this decline has not been natural change but the movement of people away from the inner city.

2.13 The population of Lambeth therefore tends to be relatively young, working-class and transient. The Borough has a higher proportion of children of school age than London as a whole, though lower than England overall, and a higher proportion of people in their twenties. Fewer Lambeth people are in professional or managerial occupations than in London as a whole, although the proportions of other non-manual, skilled or semi-skilled workers are similar. Other important features are a strikingly high figure of children in local authority care (2.3% of the population aged 18 or less) and an incidence of single-parent families which, at 1 in 6, is twice the national average. There is evidence of a higher rate of mental illness and of physical or mental handicap in the Borough than nationally.

2.15 There is also in Brixton a higher proportion of black people. Overall, some 25% of Lambeth's population were estimated in 1978 to belong to non-white ethnic groups. West Indians were the largest black group (12.5% of the Borough's population), followed by Africans (3.4%), Indians, Pakistanis, Bangladeshis (2.4%) and other non-white or mixed origin people (6.5%).

2.19 As the Select Committee in the same report wisely say, 'Disadvantage in education and employment are the two most crucial facets of racial disadvantage. They are closely connected. Without a decent education and the qualifications which such education alone can provide, a school-leaver is unlikely to find the sort of job to which he aspires, or indeed any job. Conversely, pupils who learn from older friends of the degree of difficulty encountered in finding employment may well be discouraged from striving to achieve at school. In other words, there is no point in getting ethnic minority education right if we do not at the same time sort out racial disadvantage in employment, and vice versa'.

2.20 When the young people of Brixton leave school, many of them, white and black, face unemployment. This reflects both the general economic recession from which the country is at present suffering and the contraction in the economic and industrial base of the inner city. In early 1981, unemployment in the area of Brixton Employment Office stood at 13%. For black people, the percentage is estimated to be higher. The level of ethnic minority unemployment as a proportion of total unemployment at Brixton Employment Office in May 1981 was 25.4%.

2.23 Many of the young people of Brixton are therefore born and raised in insecure social and economic conditions and in an impoverished physical environment. They share the desires and expectations which our materialist society encourages. At the same time, many of them fail to achieve educational success and on leaving school face the stark prospect of unemployment. Many of these difficulties face white as well as black youngsters, but it is clear that they bear particularly heavily on young blacks. In addition, young black people face the burden of discrimination, much of it hidden and some of it unconscious and unintended. Without close parental support, with no job to go to, and with few recreational facilities available, the young black person makes his life on the streets and in the seedy commercially run clubs of Brixton. There he meets criminals, who appear to have no difficulty in obtaining the benefits of a materialist society.

Part IX – Conclusion and acknowledgements

A – Conclusion

9.1 The evidence which I have received, the effect of which I have outlined in Part II, leaves no doubt in my mind that racial disadvantage is a fact of current British life. It was, I am equally sure, a significant factor in the causation of the Brixton disorders. Urgent action is needed if it is not to become an endemic, ineradicable disease threatening the very survival of our society. It would be unfair to criticise Government for lack of effort. 'Institutional racism' does not exist in Britain: but racial disadvantage and its nasty associate racial discrimination, have not yet been eliminated. They poison minds and attitudes: they are, and so long as they remain, will continue to be, a potent factor of unrest.

9.2 The role of the police has to be considered against this background. The police do not create social deprivation or racial disadvantage: they are not responsible for the disadvantages of the ethnic minorities. Yet their role is critical. If their policing is such that it can be seen to be the application to our new society of the traditional principles of British policing, the risk of unrest will diminish and the prospect of approval by all responsible elements in our ethnically diverse society will be the greater. If they neglect consultation and co-operation with the local community, unrest is certain and riot becomes probable.

9.4 On the social front, I find myself broadly in agreement with the House of Commons Select Committee. The attack on racial disadvantage must be more direct than it has been. It must be co-ordinated by central government, who with local authorities must ensure that the funds made available are directed to specific areas of racial disadvantage. I have in mind particularly education and employment. A policy of direct co-ordinated attack on racial disadvantage inevitably means that the ethnic minorities will enjoy for a time a positive discrimination in their favour. But it is a price worth paying if it accelerates the elimination of the unsettling factor of racial disadvantage from the social fabric of the United Kingdom.

QUESTIONS

1 Write short answers to these questions:

a When did the Brixton riots occur?

b What was the extent of the damage and injury?

c What views were expressed to the enquiry to explain the cause of the disorder?

d In the borough of Lambeth, what percentage of homeless households are black, and what number of households in the borough live in overcrowded conditions.

e What percentage of Lambeth's population is Afro-Caribbean?

f Of the total unemployed in Brixton, what percentage of the ethnic minority was unemployed?

g What particular problems does the ethnic minority school leaver have when searching for a job?

h Mention some of the factors that lead you into thinking that the population of Brixton is mainly working class.

i What illegitimate opportunity structures are identified in Brixton where young people are likely to come into contact with criminals?

j What did Lord Scarman mean by 'Institutional racism does not

exist in Britain'? Briefly argue whether or not you agree with this opinion.

2 What do you understand by the concept of the 'normative order'? Why do you think governments are concerned if social order and the agents of social control are threatened?

3 With reference to the extracts, discuss the relationship that might exist between social conditions and social unrest.

4 Briefly summarise, and comment on, Lord Scarman's conclusions.

5 Following the publication of the Scarman Report, urban riots have broken out in other major cities. Later in 1981, Liverpool (Toxteth) and Bristol (St Pauls) were hit, and Brixton was again the scene of serious disturbances in 1985. Birmingham (Handsworth) experienced the most serious riot in the summer of 1985, resulting in the deaths of 2 Asian shopkeepers, and many shops and factories were looted and burned to the ground.

a In what way is the Scarman Report helpful in throwing light on these subsequent riots?

b In what ways might a criminal element exploit an urban riot?

Points for discussion

- Police officers are always more eager to exercise control over young people's behaviour than they are to control older people's behaviour.
- Our society is now far more civilised than it used to be.
- Causing a riot is one of the best ways of getting noticed.

Prison rules, OK?

'We've got our own rules and regulations here,' Mitchell told Driscoll during his first morning on C wing, 'just like everywhere else.'

Driscoll welcomed his conversations with Mitchell. Mitchell was an old lag. He had done time in several prisons throughout the country. He was the kind of person to share a cell with. He made you feel at home.

'You see,' he told Driscoll, 'it's just like the outside world. You've got people at the top of the heap and you've got people at the bottom.'

'I thought we were all the same in here,' Driscoll said nervously.

'Life's never that simple. Even the screws know the score, and they know who to leave alone. You stick with me Driscoll. You've got to learn, so you might as well learn from me.'

That was just what Driscoll did during his first weeks on C wing. Mitchell was right. Prison was a complicated place. Some people fitted in and some didn't. Fortunately for him, Mitchell was well thought of by the other prisoners – nobody caused him any aggravation. It would pay Driscoll to keep on good terms.

Driscoll asked Mitchell about the three cons in the next cell. They were young and tough-looking. 'Just hooligans,' he said, 'they come ten a penny. You can hire kiddies with that kind of muscle any day of the week. One of them, Corrigan, has a big mouth. We think he might be running to the screws with stories. Sooner or later someone will stitch him up, mark my words. One of them in there got nicked thievin' from an invalid car. Pathetic, that's what I call them. Don't get mixed up with that lot. If you're looking for a caper when you leave prison, just let me know. I'll put you in touch with a firm who could use a smart boy like you.'

Even the prison officers were aware of the reputations the men had. The inmates who were respected by the other inmates got respect from the officers. It was the cons at the bottom of the pile who got pushed around, who got themselves into trouble and were given the dirty jobs.

'You know,' Mitchell said just before lights out, 'I reckon they should keep the sex offenders and junkies in different wings. I mean, you don't want to have to mix with that kind of rubbish. Why don't they put them in separate prisons?'

This was the first time Driscoll had heard him raise his voice. 'The thing is', he said, 'we've got to make sure that we get through our time here without any hassle. That's one of the reasons I don't smoke. Anyone who starts giving you problems can be bought off with snout. Then they'll leave you alone. It's crazy but that's the way it is.'

One night Mitchell was too quiet. As a matter of fact he had been too quiet all day. In the evening he told Driscoll he had received a letter from his wife. His son had been sent home from school for fighting. 'You know, Driscoll,' he said when the cell lights were out, 'it's not the fighting I mind so much – kids with fathers inside get a lot of stick – it's just that it's not necessary. The kid's got brains, so why doesn't he use them?'

As the weeks and months passed, Driscoll got to know Mitchell well, and many prisoners like him. They all had their own standards and their own sense of right and wrong. They hated sex offenders and young hooligans who knocked old people about.

'If you're gonna rob, rob from them that can afford it', Geordie said one morning when they were slopping out. Mitchell agreed. 'You give me a

professional thief or a forger anyday. There's a fella on E wing who got 25 grand from a bank and all he had was a computer. That's real class.' Everyone agreed.

Driscoll had a lot of learning to do about prison life. It wasn't just a place for prisoners and officers. It was a complicated world to understand. Like the world outside the high walls.

QUESTIONS

1 What is considered normal and deviant by the inmates in this prison?
2 How would you apply the concept of subculture to prison life?
3 In what way is life in prisons similar to life in the world outside?

Points for discussion

- Prison culture promotes criminal behaviour rather than discourages it.
- Prison regimes should be made tougher to deter offenders from committing serious crime.
- There are some people in prison who ought to be receiving treatment in hospital.

Important points

- The existence of a normative order makes society possible. It lays the ground rules for standard behaviour in all social situations.
- Norms and values are major components of the normative

order. They provide the standards and principles on which all societies are based.
- Social control describes the ways in which individuals and groups are influenced to conform with acceptable patterns of social behaviour.
- Crime is social behaviour that violates the laws of a given society.
- All laws and norms are man-made and are therefore subject to change.
- Some sociologists argue that laws exist to protect or favour the interests of the dominant economic groups.
- Law enforcement agencies, such as the police, may be influenced by social factors in the way they apply laws.
- Statistics are not neutral sets of facts; they are selected for the purpose of drawing our attention to a particular problem.
- Deviance is conduct that violates the norms of ordinary society.
- Conformity and deviance are relative concepts.
- Most recorded crime is committed by young working class males.
- Subcultures are communities that have some norms and values that are different from the norms and values found in everyday society.
- Most delinquent behaviour is associated with inequality, poverty, and deprivation in education, housing and employment.

10 Power

When you have worked through this chapter you should have a clearer understanding of

Democracy, totalitarianism and dictatorship · Power · Authority · Coercion · Charismatic, traditional and legal-rational authority · The structure of government and political parties in Britain · Political ideas · A pluralist society · The process of legitimation · Manifestos · Promotional and defensive pressure groups · Voting behaviour · Positive and negative abstainers

Power and politics

We are all members of a society in which numerous decisions are made that affect our lives. The type of education we receive, the availability of jobs and the services provided by the National Health Service are just 3 areas of social life which are influenced by people involved in political decision making. Of course the people who make political decisions are usually chosen by those of us who are entitled to vote in national and local elections, which includes virtually everybody over the age of 18 in the UK who are neither insane nor serving a prison sentence. The right to a free choice of political representative is part of what we understand as **democracy**.

We are often reminded that there are societies in which people cannot vote in the way that we vote. In some countries voting at elections is compulsory and it is sometimes possible to vote only for one party or for a single candidate, and there are other countries where the right to vote seems to have been withdrawn altogether. One question we might ask is: why bother to have a voting system at all if the people are only allowed to vote for one party or for one candidate? However, this is a complex question involving a discussion of the many factors which influence political decision making. It is the kind of question that is part and parcel of the function of sociology. In many ways the sociology of politics takes us behind the scenes of the formal political framework presented in the media and in textbooks on politics.

The **sociology of politics** is essentially a study of power in society, in particular the way power is distributed amongst different social groups. Sociologists are also interested in examining the reasons why certain social groups tend to have access to more political power than other groups both inside and outside of parliament. The following is a brief account of the experiences of a young Member of Parliament:

The Backbencher

Jim Cowley didn't feel like breakfast. He would catch the 8.45 train to London. His visit to the north had not been a happy one, but he had accomplished his mission. He had told the local party chairman, Frank Masters, that he would not be standing in the next election. He'd had enough of politics. Jim could see the chairman's horror-stricken face even now.

'What do you mean, you won't stand again?' Frank had exploded.

'I'm fed up with it. I'm getting nowhere. It's like I'm part of some stupid game.'

'What do you mean – *game*?'

'Well, that's all it bloody well is. Have you listened to the way they behave? Turn on your radio and you'll see what I mean. It's a bad joke.'

'Look, lad,' the chairman had said, 'a lot of people have worked damned hard to get you into parliament. A lot of silly buggers out there have faith in you – or should I say faith in the parliamentary system. You represent the ideals they have.'

Cowley thought about that. What Frank had said was true. That made it all the more tragic as far as he was concerned. All those people blindly believing in parliamentary democracy.

As he sat in his London-bound train, Frank's words began to eat into his brain. Soon he was travelling through the industrial wasteland of the once prosperous North of England. The derelict factory buildings and the rows of back-to-back houses reminded him of the way the voters are let down by the politicians. He thought of how he had first gone into politics, full of idealism. He had wanted to change the world – a world blighted by unemployment, poverty and injustice. But what had he achieved? He was just part of a cruel charade. He had sat in the Commons for endless hours working for policies which amounted to nothing more than half-baked compromises. Two years in politics had taught him that whoever wielded power in the country, it certainly wasn't the politicians. Everything Cowley had believed in, and everything his parents and his friends had believed in, suddenly seemed a lie.

Whatever we think of this account of the disillusionment of a Member of Parliament, it gives us an idea of how sociology can help us to understand the nature of political power. Despite the fact that, in theory at least, politicians of different political beliefs have the power to change existing laws, introduce new laws and substantially influence economic events, this does not always mean that great political or economic changes will occur. Indeed it might have struck you how Opposition parties suddenly become very much like their political opponents when they themselves form a government. This suggests that political power might not be quite as powerful as we might think. However, we will first look at a crude diagram of the structure of political power in Britain. (See below.)

This type of diagram is often used to illustrate the mechanics of government. But sociologists are more interested in putting politics into a wider social framework. When Jim Cowley saw the derelict factory buildings from the train window he associated them with his failure as a politician to influence events, particularly the rising levels of unemployment and poverty. Which is why we should not only be interested in the 'mechanics' of government but also in the general social forces that accompany political action. After all, the mechanics of government are exactly the same for all parties no matter which government is in power and no matter how extreme its policies. For instance, most politicians want to reduce unemployment in one way or another, but would nevertheless accept that at least part of the solution rests with powerful economic and social groups outside of parliament, such as multinational companies, influential newspaper owners and international financial speculators and investors. In other words, political power exists wherever individuals or groups are strong enough to influence social change.

EXERCISE

Iran bans kissing

Iran's legislators have ruled that

The government of Britain

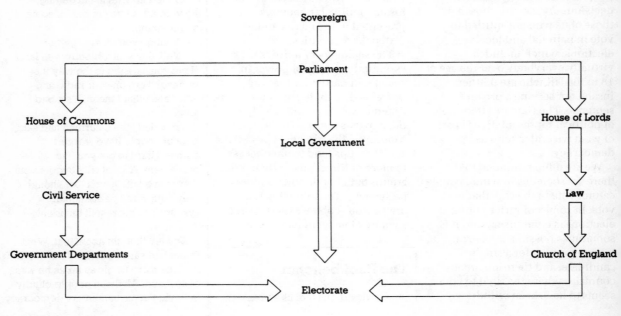

kissing for sexual pleasure has to stop.

Kissing for sexual pleasure, drinking alcohol and homosexuality are among a list of moral offences officially outlawed by legislation passed in Iran's parliament this week.

Teheran newspapers said today the law, which establishes punishment of 100 lashes for first-time offenders against the kissing ban, would run for an experimental period.

The law also establishes stricter punishment for recidivists–persistent homosexuality, for example, will lead to execution, the papers said.

Punishment for moral offences has been widespread since Islamic fundamentalists came to power in Iran more than 3 years ago. But the latest legislation is the first time such measures have been put into the statute book.

Under the new law sexual offences could only be proved if 4 men were brought as witnesses, the papers said. In the absence of a male witness, the court would accept 2 women substitutes, they added.

As a background to the new law, newspapers today published detailed accounts of punishments in force 14 centuries ago.

Up until now, the amputation of fingers and hands for theft and the stoning to death of adulterers have been relatively rare in post-revolutionary Iran. Newspapers said such penalties were likely to be more widespread under the latest legislation.

Source: *New Straits Times*, 26 September 1982, (Malaysia)

1 According to this newspaper article, what activities have the Iranian government defined as criminal?
2 In what major way do you think that the political decisions taken by Iran's government have been influenced by external social factors?
3 Can you think of any recent examples in British society where the introduction of legislation (new laws)

may have been influenced by powerful social or economic groups outside of parliament?

Power and authority

What do you think is meant by power?

Briefly discuss the nature and range of power exercised by:

- a trade union leader
- a magistrate
- a captain of a football team.

We know that in almost every sphere of human activity individuals and groups have power over others. Our parents have power over us as children in influencing and controlling our behaviour. They might insist, for example, that we should go to bed by a certain time or do the washing up. The police have special powers of arrest and teachers have power to control our behaviour at school. So we can see that the concept of power implies a degree of control or influence which an individual or group has over others. The German sociologist Max Weber defined power in *The Theory of Social and Economic Organisation* as:

The chance of a man or a number of men to realise their own will in a communal action even against the resistance of others.

Weber is telling us that power is nothing more than getting what we want in a social situation. He believed that all power is achieved either through **authority** or **coercion**, and he argued that authority is the more important source of power of the 2 in most societies. Weber identified 3 types of authority: **charismatic**, **traditional** and **legal-rational**:

- **Legal-rational authority** is by far the most common form of authority in a modern society. It is based on the relationships found in formal organisations, football teams, schools and colleges. It is an authority directly linked with people carrying out a particular role within a given context.
- **Charismatic authority** is based on the personal qualities of strikingly influential individuals who have made their mark in society, whether for good or evil. Christ and Hitler would be included in this category.
- **Traditional authority** is usually found in tribal societies where

Weber's three types of authority

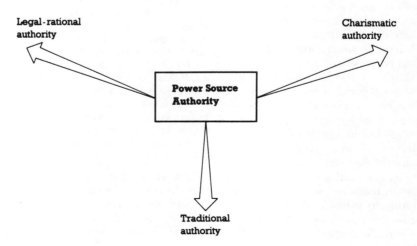

Legal-rational authority

Charismatic authority

Power Source Authority

Traditional authority

the chief or the witch-doctor is obeyed because they have always been obeyed. It can also be seen in some modern political parties where loyalty to the party or to the party leader is sometimes regarded as more important than the expression of true belief.

How do people achieve power?

Of Weber's 3 types of authority, the legal-rational type is by far the most significant in advanced industrial societies. In fact its existence is a key factor in the organisation of all modern societies. For example, it underpins the democratic process in allowing elected people to represent us in parliament. All those eligible to vote choose their own political representatives and the party with the largest number of MPs takes control of the decision-making processes of government. The minority parties and those of us who do not support the elected government nevertheless accept that the majority party is in charge and has the authority to run the country.

However, on a personal level, most legal-rational authority is vested in an individual's status. A person who happens to be a police officer has special powers as long as he remains a police officer, and he will lose this power when he leaves the police force. The power our parents have over us as children is likewise vested in their status of being parents. So, if a teacher at school tells us to shut up and get on with our work, we might feel obliged to take notice, but we would be put out and angry if the teacher were to talk to us in a similar way in our own living room. In a word, a person's authority is nearly always associated with their role in a particular context.

In what way do the following individuals exercise their authority:

- a carpark attendant
- a football referee
- a works foreman.

Describe one aspect of each individual's role that would be unacceptable outside the context described.

Weber's second dimension of power is the exercise of power through coercion or force. Usually a social group will reject the authority of those in power and make political decisions on their own behalf. Many observers would add that in some societies power is taken not through the ballot box but by powerful self-interest groups taking power by force. The armed dictatorships in Latin America are examples of this. However, even within societies which are described as democratic, certain social or political groups might claim that some forms of government exist against the interests of the majority of the people. An example of this could be the role successive British governments have played in the affairs of Northern Ireland. This is how one Irish woman sees the situation:

It's obvious to me that the Brits have no moral or political right to be in Northern Ireland. You can't divide a country up in the way Ireland has been divided and not expect trouble. The people who are dedicated to fighting the British army on the streets of Derry and Belfast do so, not because they are psychopaths or criminals – although it's easy for politicians in Westminster to see them like that – but because they believe that justice will only be done when Ireland is united. They believe that they have a just cause ...

Rightly or wrongly, this woman sees British rule in Northern Ireland as a form of coercion in that she rejects the authority of the British government to decide and control the political fate of some Irish people. She also believes that it is right in certain circumstances to use force – force which would be defined by the British government as unlawful – to bring about political change. We can see that the 2 major components of power, authority and coercion, are delicately intertwined.

On 29 July 1985 the BBC cancelled the television programme *Real Lives*, which featured an interview with the IRA's chief of staff Martin McGuinness, following government pressure. This is how it was reported in one newspaper:

BBC bans IRA film

Prime Minister Margaret Thatcher has rejected charges of censorship over the BBC's decision to cancel a documentary featuring the man alleged to be the IRA's chief of staff.

A storm of protest has erupted over the move, taken by the corporation's Board of Governors after a 7 hour meeting yesterday.

The board's chairman Mr Stuart Young denied there had been any retreat. But he said in an interview: 'When the Home Secretary says that any programme that deals with terrorist organisations should not be permitted to be broadcast that amounts to censorship.'

Mrs Thatcher said she was 'very pleased' by the move. 'I do not believe that any great body like the BBC should do anything which might be construed as furthering the objectives of terrorists.' But she added: 'I am never going to put censorship on – we are not that kind of party.'

Mr Robin Corbett, Labour spokesman, said: 'The BBC governors are acting as the Home Secretary's thought police.'

Journalists at the BBC yesterday

voted to strike over the governor's decision.

1 Describe how the government has exercised its power over the BBC.
2 What kinds of political or economic pressure can the government bring to bear on the BBC if it so chooses?
3 Why do you think the government did not want the programme to be shown?

Elements of political life

Politics is not simply a collection of individuals and institutions such as the Houses of Parliament, MPs, Law Lords and Cabinet Ministers. It is very much about making decisions based on political policies that embody a wide range of social ideas. Now we might think that some political ideas are difficult to understand, but this is not usually the case. After all, we carry our politics around with us all day. When we talk to our friends at school or at work we are almost bound to touch on one political topic or another. We might not think of them as political at the time, but on closer examination we will find that is exactly what they are.

EXERCISE

Here are a number of statements. Briefly record your views on each statement and compare them with a colleague's. Make a mental note of where you agree or disagree:

- Nuclear weapons should be abolished in Britain
- The government should reduce social security benefits to encourage people to find work
- Trade union powers should be increased
- People not born in Britain should be sent back to their country of origin
- Capital punishment should be reintroduced for some crimes
- The government should spend more money helping Third World countries

- The police should be given more powers to reduce the rising crime rate even if this results in a reduction of individual rights

Our views on these and other subjects will reflect our personal values and ideas. As we know, our ideas about the social world – and politics is an important part of the social world – will have been shaped and influenced by the vast range of experiences we have encountered during the whole of our lives.

The majority of us do not get involved in politics other than in voting for a local or national political party or by being an active member of a trade union. (Trade unions are a subject about which people have strong views.) Nevertheless we are political in the sense that we all have a few ideas of our own about how society should be organised. A political party, essentially, is nothing more than an organisation whose members share roughly similar ideas about how the country should be run. In order to put their ideas into effect, or to get political power, candidates have to persuade a majority of the electorate (more or less) to vote for them at elections. Commonly shared political ideas, then, lie at the centre of all political parties, and in Britain there are many parties who attempt, within their financial and organisational capability, to attract our attention.

According to the psychologist Hans Eysenck in *Sense and Nonsense in Psychology* a person's attitudes about a range of social issues may be linked with a tendency to support a particular political party. If you go back to your answers to the 7 statements, you may detect an emerging pattern of responses. For example, Conservatives, in general terms, tend to want to reduce trade union power, support the nuclear

deterrent, give more power to police, and reduce social security benefits in the belief that individuals are better off looking after themselves than by having to rely on state help and intervention. Of course, just because your responses to a whole range of social questions are similar to those of a Conservative, this does not mean that you are a Conservative, but it does point to the relationship between social ideas and political parties.

How many political parties can you name?

Most of you will have named the well known parties such as the Labour and Conservative Parties, the Liberal Party and perhaps the Social Democratic Party. Obviously there are many more political parties in Britain – far too many to mention – that represent the whole spectrum of political and social ideas from the Communist and Workers Revolutionary Parties on the 'left', the Ecology Party in the 'centre', and the National Front Party on the extreme 'right'. Although none of these lesser known parties are represented in parliament, they nevertheless form part of our political landscape. In its simplest form, the political spectrum can be shown as in the diagram on page 172.

Political parties and political ideas

Each of the following statements was made by either a Conservative, a Social Democrat/Liberal or a member of the Labour Party. Decide which statement was made by whom and explain how you arrived at your decision:

- *Statement 1*
  What we need is a movement

Communist Marxist Revolutionary	Labour	Liberal Social Democrat Ecology/Greens	Conservative	Fascist British Nazi National Front

Left-wing *Parties*		*Centre* *Parties*		*Right-wing* *Parties*

away from the old-style politics to the new-style politics. We need to work together to make this country great again. We don't want a society split by class divisions which are wholly out of date.

- **Statement 2**
  Wherever I look I see appalling injustice. We live in a society that is riddled with inequality and class difference. Look at the houses we live in, the education we receive, the bleak futures most people have. It is time to rid ourselves of governments that tolerate and perpetuate the haves and the have-nots.

- **Statement 3**
  When I think of this great country of ours, with its marvellous traditions, I realise that we became great, not because the government always steps in to help out at the slightest hint of trouble, but because people were allowed to thrive and prosper, they were left to their own devices, to use their initiative, and not treated like helpless children.

The first statement could well have been delivered by a Liberal or by a member of the newly-formed Social Democratic Party. The second statement comes from the left of the political spectrum, possible from a member of the Labour Party. The third statement expresses a Conservative viewpoint. Naturally, we know that political parties are complex organisations that like to present a clear-cut image of themselves to the voting public. Yet within each party there are factions who have political ideas, or at least wish to pursue political tactics, that are in

conflict with the views of their party's leader. For example, both the Conservative and the Labour Party have always been troubled or stimulated by groups of MPs who have attempted to offer different ideas from those of the mainstream party. The present leader of the Conservative Party, Margaret Thatcher, was herself a member of a radical group of MPs who were instrumental in ousting Edward Heath as the then leader of the party.

Can you name any groups or any individual MPs, within any party, who offer a different political perspective from their party's leader?

Despite the differences of opinion that exist within all parties, each political party relies on a set of fundamental beliefs to guide it in the conduct of its affairs. We can summarise the main political beliefs as:

Conservatism
Conservative Party
Preserve traditional institutions
Support for business and commerce
Less government interference
Reliance on market forces

Fascism
National Front Party
White supremacy
Single party rule
Inequality of the classes
Dictatorship

Socialism
Labour Party
A planned economy
Fairer share of wealth and income
Social and economic equality
Common ownership of the means of
  production

Communism
Communist Party
Political power through revolution
Creation of a classless society
Public ownership of property
State control

Liberalism
Liberal/Social Democratic Parties
Progressive social reform
More regional and less central
  power
Against state control and monopoly
More democracy and co-ownership
  in industry

Political parties are just one element of what we understand as a **democratic society**. As well as national and local political parties there is a permanent Civil Service whose main function is to administer the policy of central government, from advising Prime Ministers to paying out social security benefits. There are trade unions representing organised labour in industry and commerce. Industry is itself represented through the Confederation of British Industries. We also have thousands of organisations like the Campaign for Nuclear Disarmament and Animal Rights putting forward their ideas for us to consider. We have a legal system that attempts to ensure that something called 'justice' is available to all. These diverse elements of political life have led many observers to describe Britain as a **pluralist society**.

EXERCISE

Before every General Election, each political party publishes its own manifesto for distribution to the electorate. A manifesto is a document that outlines the party's policies and describes how the party intends to run the country if elected. What follows are extracts from 3 manifestos, published before the 1983 General Election, that deal specifically with the problem of unemployment. After reading the extracts carefully, state which political party you think is responsible for each extract and explain in detail how you came to your decision.

Extract 1

ENDING MASS UNEMPLOYMENT

Our approach is different. We will expand the economy, by providing a strong and measured increase in spending. Spending money creates jobs. Money spent on railway electrification means jobs, not only in construction, but also in the industries that supply the equipment – as well as faster and better trains. If we increase pensions and child benefits, it means more spending power for the elderly and for parents, more bought in shops, more orders for goods, and more jobs in the factories. More spending means that the economy will begin to expand: and growth will provide the new wealth for higher wages and better living standards, the right climate for industry to invest, and more resources for the public services.

Our central aim will be to reduce unemployment to below a million within 5 years of taking office. We recognise the enormous scale of this task. When we set this as our target, unemployment was 2.8 million, according to the official figures. On this basis it is now at least 3.2 million. Our target will thus be all the more difficult to achieve. It remains, however, the central objective of our economic policy.

To achieve it we will need 5 years of economic growth, with the government carrying through all of the industrial/financial and economic policies outlined here. But

we will also work with other governments to bring about a co-ordinated expansion of our economies.

Economic expansion will make it possible to end the waste of mass unemployment. But it will also reduce the *human* costs of unemployment – the poverty, the broken homes, the increase in illness and suicides. And it will provide the resources we need to increase social spending, as we *must*, at least in line with the growth of the economy.

Extract 2

UNEMPLOYMENT: COPING WITH CHANGE

During the last 4 years, unemployment in the industrialised countries has risen more sharply than at any time since the 1930s. Britain has been no exception. We have long been one of the least efficient and most over-manned of industrialised nations. We raised our own pay far more, and our output far less, than most of our competitors. Inevitably, this pushed prices up and drove countless customers to buy from other countries, forcing thousands of employers out of business and hundreds of thousands of workers out of jobs.

At the same time, there has been a rapid shift of jobs from the old industries to the new, concentrated on services and the new technologies. Tragically, trade unions have often obstructed these changes. All too often this has delayed and reduced the new and better-paid jobs which could replace those that have been lost.

REMOVING THE BARRIERS TO JOBS

We shall go on reducing the barriers which discourage employers from recruiting more staff, even when they want to. And we shall help to make the job market more flexible and

efficient so that more people can work part-time if they wish, and find work more easily.

That is why we have amended the Employment Protection Act and why we shall continue to:

- minimise the legal restrictions which discourage the creation of new jobs;
- encourage moves towards greater flexibility in working practices, such as Parti-Time Job Release, which makes it financially possible for people nearing retirement age to go part-time, and the Job-Splitting Scheme which helps employers to split a whole-time job into 2 part-time jobs;
- improve the efficiency of the employment services in identifying and filling job vacancies;
- ensure that Wages Councils do not reduce job opportunities by forcing workers to charge unrealistic pay rates, or employers to offer them.

Extract 3

2 Direct action to provide jobs

The immediate action we propose is targeted on those among the unemployed in greatest need, the long-term unemployed and the young. It does not throw money wildly about, but has been carefully drawn up to achieve the biggest early fall in unemployment we can manage at the lowest practicable cost. Out main proposals are:

- *to provide jobs for the long-term unemployed in a programme of housing and environmental improvement* – house renovation and insulation, land improvements; these jobs are real jobs crying out to be done. There will also be a major expansion of the Community Programme. We will back programmes of this kind with great determination to ensure that they generate at least 250 000 jobs over 2 years;

- *to extend the Youth Training Scheme so that it is available to all 16 and 17 year olds* and give real help to those who want to stay on at school after 16 or go to college or take a training course. Our long term aim is to see all 16–19 year olds either as students with access to work experience, or as employed people with access to education and training. But the extension of training proposed here would alone reduce youth unemployment by 100 000;

- *to create more jobs in labour-intensive social services.* There is a great need for extra support staff in the NHS and the personal social services. These services are highly labour-intensive and their greatest need for extra people is in regions of high unemployment. We propose the establishment of a special £500 million Fund for the health and social services in order to create an additional 100 000 jobs of this kind over two years;

- *to give a financial incentive to private firms to take on those longest out of work* – To boost jobs in the private sector, we propose to pay a grant to companies for every *extra* job they provide and fill with someone unemployed for over 6 months. The scheme will be for employment pay, not unemployment pay. The Government loses about £100 per week (in unemployment benefit and lost tax revenues) for every person unemployed, so it is not extravagant to pay £80 a week for each additional job. According to the best estimates this incentive could increase employment by around 175 000 jobs within 2 years of its introduction.

Britain as a pluralist society

When Britain is described as a pluralist society it is being suggested that within our democratic system there are so many political parties and interest groups openly competing against each other that a reasonable balance of power is achieved without any one party or group becoming excessively dominant. It also means that in such a society new people with fresh ideas are able to come forward to create different power groups to compete against or to share power with existing groups. For instance, in 1981 a group of rebel Labour MPs set up a new political party, The Social Democrats, to provide what they believed to be an alternative political viewpoint.

This concept of pluralism in British society is closely associated with what we call **democracy**. But do we know what is meant by this term? The popular definition of democracy as being 'government of the people, for the people, by the people' probably hides more than it reveals, and so we will turn for help to Seymour Lipset's definition in his book *Political Man*:

Democracy in a complex society may be defined as a political system which supplies regular constitutional opportunities for changing the governing officials and a social mechanism which permits the largest part of the population to influence major decisions by choosing among contenders for political office.

Since all political parties in Britain have to compete for our vote in a General Election within every 5 years, this means that we all have a real opportunity of influencing the way we are governed. The democratic system in Britain also provides safeguards against the possibility of a single political party taking absolute power to create a totalitarian society. These safeguards include:

- **Freedom of speech.** We can say or write more or less anything we choose to providing we don't make slanderous or libellous statements.
- **Pressure groups.** Literally thousands of non-party organisations exist in Britain which spend a great deal of time attempting to influence political decisions.
- **Local government.** Local people are able to elect their own councillors, who may or may not support central government, to represent them on local authorities. These bodies make important decisions about education, welfare, housing and transport that directly affect the voters.
- **A fundamental belief in individual freedom of action and choice.** A feature of all democracy is that everybody is entitled to seek political power regardless of class or origin and all voters are free to vote for the candidate of their choice.
- **Protection of minorities.** Britain has a tradition of safeguarding the rights of minorities who could always be outvoted by the majority, if put to the test. Minor religious and political groups, for example, are allowed to worship or promote their activities, and minority ethnic groups are offered legal protection under the Race Relations Act.

EXERCISE

Select one of the following self-interest groups and describe how it might seek to promote its interests in British society. Suggest at least one other group which will oppose these interests, and outline its opposing views and strategies.

- employers and employers' organisations

- supporters of the road haulage and road construction industries
- supporters of the nuclear power industry
- the tobacco industry.

Not all sociologists share this optimistic interpretation of Britain's democratic society. Some would challenge the view that voters or even the elected MPs are ultimately in control of the democratic processes or the government of the country. The exercise of political power, the argument runs, is much too important to be left entirely in the hands of the average voter. Sociologists might ask how much do we really know about the political parties who offer radically different ideas from the mainstream parties. For example, how much do you know about the Workers' Revolutionary Party or the Communist Party or the National Front Party? You may know something about the National Front because its alleged involvement in race riots and football hooliganism has been widely discussed in the media. But what of the other 2 parties?

The point being made here is that although we have a degree of choice about political representation, there are many political views and policies about which we know little or nothing. This is because, according to some sociologists, only certain acceptable or legitimate political views are made fully available to us. The reason for this, the argument continues, is that the control of information in our society and the discussion of political ideas, especially in the media, are carefully controlled by powerful social and economic groups. Sociologists point to the political stance taken by most British newspapers – evidence, it is claimed, that indicates that alternative political views are simply not heard or discussed

Top-selling British daily newspapers in 1983

Paper	Daily circulation (millions)	General political stance
Sun	4.1	Independent/Conservative
Daily Mirror	3.3	Labour
Daily Express	2.0	Conservative
Daily Mail	1.8	Conservative
Daily Star	1.4	Conservative
Daily Telegraph	1.3	Conservative

Source: National Readership Survey

seriously outside of narrow political circles.

In *Class in a Capitalist Society* Westergaad and Resler argue that it is the ruling class which control the major decision-making processes in British society. Through wealth and influence, this class manipulates the flow of information, and, put simply, the parliamentary system exists to protect the interests of this élite group. Of course, this does not mean that in our capitalist society laws and political decisions are never made which do not benefit the working class, but many sociologists argue that reforms which do take place fail fundamentally to change the structural inequalities in society.

Ralph Miliband in his study *The State in Capitalist Society* attempts to identify how the ruling class dominates society, and especially why the working class accepts the social organisation of a culture that is riddled with social inequality. Miliband calls this **the process of legitimation** which he regards as a form of indoctrination. In other words, we tend to take our political system for granted, we never seriously question it, and we are rarely offered any radical alternatives to the established political parties and policies.

In particular, this process of 'legitimation' enables members of the ruling class to present their political views unhindered to the

population because they effectively control the mass media and the education system. In the media, so much emphasis is attached to the importance of the democratic process in our culture that we tend to accept our parliamentary system without question. Although the Labour Party and the Conservative Party have different policies, these differences are not about issues that will radically change our society. Both parties believe in parliamentary democracy, and anyone who refuses to play the 'game' is seen as a revolutionary or a crackpot. This is what might happen when someone refuses to play the political game.

The radical

Wilson was surprised when he read about himself in the newspaper. There was a photo of him at the demonstration under the headline **Mindless Militant**. He was even more surprised when he heard a political correspondent on local radio describe him as a radical who had fed himself on the works of Karl Marx. Then a letter appeared in the evening paper which said that people like him were sick. Wilson wondered what he had done to deserve all this.

'I wish you'd pack the union in,' Marion said, 'People think I'm married to a lunatic.'

'Why?' he asked.

'Because you won't accept what's happened. The factory is closing down, and that's all there is to it.'

'Yes, but what about our jobs?'

'Well, you'll just have to go on the dole,' she told him.

'Are you saying that we just take it lying down?' He felt himself getting hot.

His wife looked at him softly. 'Look, it's not for people like us to ask the questions you are asking. Even the local MP says it's a waste of time. Anyway the kids are having a hard time at school because of it.'

Wilson didn't respond. He went out and began to walk down the darkening street. It started to rain. He could see his neighbours watching *Dallas*. He wondered how many more millions were getting caught up in the make-believe lives of television characters. How strange it was that people could talk for hours about *Dallas* and *Dynasty* and yet never talk about things that really mattered.

Wilson thought about his new-found fame. He was now a mindless militant! Of course that was all part of their strategy. It was an attempt to make him look foolish and by concentrating on him personally they could ignore the real issues of redundancy and unemployment. They could call him anything they wanted but he would not stop asking the questions they didn't want him to ask. He knew he wasn't alone in realising what a lie the democratic process was, and he wasn't going to play the political game by their rules.

This story attempts to show how a demonstrator was treated by the media because of his political actions and beliefs. It underlines Miliband's view that it is all right to be critical of the government's policies so long as open political action is not taken that directly challenges the acceptable face of democracy. More extreme examples are the actions of political groups who try to bring

about social change through terrorist activities. Usually such groups are labelled in the media as 'sick', 'psycho' or 'insane'. Rarely are the causes they believe in explained, let alone discussed, and the reason may well be that instant wholesale condemnation in the media serves the interests of a ruling class. It is more convenient to see these people as insane than admit they may have a cause to fight for.

EXERCISE

Go back to the story *The radical* and explain how a sociologist, who takes a critical view of our society, would explain the sequence of events.

Pressure groups and political power

Sociologists who argue that we live in a pluralist or democratic society not only point to a range of political parties offering alternative policies, but also to the existence of a large number of pressure groups (or interest groups). These groups, we are told, influence political parties in the democratic decision-making process. The importance of pressure groups is discussed in Jean Blondel's *Voters, Parties and Leaders*. In this book he argued that it is vital to have both political parties and pressure groups in a complex democratic society. Pressure groups help us to channel our ideas and demands in order to bring strong pressure on politicians to introduce new measures or to abandon existing ones. An example of how effective pressure groups can be is seen whenever the government attempts to site a third London airport. Faced with unremitting opposition from local pressure groups during the 1970s and

1980s, the government had to withdraw its proposals on no less than 3 occasions.

What are pressure groups?

We can say that a pressure group represents the views of a number of like-minded people on a particular issue. You might think that this is the same as a political party, but it is not the same. A political party has policies and ideas on a range of important issues, whereas a pressure group is only concerned with one issue or a set of related issues. So an organisation like the **Child Poverty Action Group** is interested in poverty in relation to children and families. As a pressure group it will produce reports on the needs of children in poverty, make public statements, bring the government's attention to the needs of children, and publicise the plight of needy children in Britain and elsewhere.

We can summarise the differences between political parties and pressure groups in the diagrams on page 177. Pressure groups also have many things in common with political parties. They both operate under hierarchial management structures and each has a membership that shares common aims and objectives. They also both try to court popular appeal and may well share similar political beliefs. The ideas of the CBI are not unlike those of the Conservative Party, for example, and the TUC has close links with the Labour Party to the extent of providing funds and sponsoring prospective candidates in a General Election.

EXERCISE

Here is a range of pressure groups that are fairly well known in Britain. Select 3 of them and describe briefly what

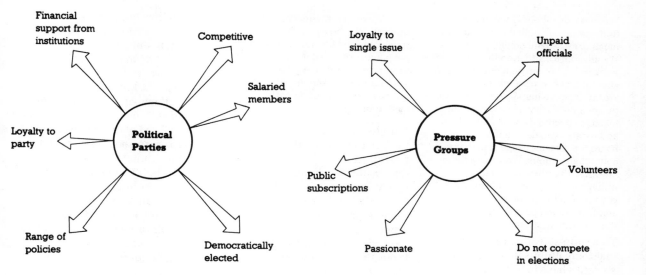

they stand for, and mention the tactics they might adopt to further their aims:

Royal Society for the Prevention of Cruelty to Children
Confederation of British Industries
Society of Motor Manufacturers and Traders
Royal Society for the Prevention of Cruelty to Animals
National Council for Civil Liberties
Age Concern
Alcoholics Anonymous
Automobile Association
Shelter
National Union of Mineworkers

A convenient way of identifying the different types of pressure groups is to arrange them under 2 headings: promotional groups and defensive groups:

- **Promotional pressure groups.**
  These groups try to draw as much attention to their causes as possible. In fact they go out of their way in deliberately creating a 'high profile' of themselves in the media in an attempt to stimulate our interest or to encourage us to make a financial or a personal contribution. The Child Poverty Action Group, for instance, is most anxious to promote its cause to all MPs to help it achieve its aims.

- **Defensive pressure groups.**
  These groups exist to protect the interest of their members. Common examples include trade unions and the British Medical Association. A trade union exists primarily to protect the pay and working conditions of its members against the interests of employers, and it will almost certainly belong to a larger body called the **Trades Union Congress (TUC)**. The TUC, in turn, will both defend and promote trade unions collectively in influencing government policy and to counteract the policies of the **Confederation of British Industries (CBI)** which is itself a pressure group representing the interests of employers. Although this is a useful way of looking at pressure groups, we must keep in mind that most groups are to some degree both defensive and promotional. The British Dental Association, for instance, not only defends the interests of its members but also has an interest in promoting healthy mouths. Now go back to the previous exercise and decide which of the 10 groups belong to

mainly promotional or defensive pressure groups.

When we think of the huge number and variety of pressure groups we can begin to build a mental picture of a society in which there is a diffusion of power throughout the population. However, if we look at what Marxist sociology has to say about the nature of power we may grasp at an inherent weakness in this pluralist argument. If power is based on the ownership of wealth, and from an earlier chapter we know that wealth is unevenly distributed, we might begin to see that the actions of pressure groups result in what is known as **institutionalised conflict**. This means that political conflict is only allowed to take place within limited, pre-determined lines. It is not allowed full reign to take its natural course and its supporters are punished if they attempt to challenge the political structures or the powerful social groups. Although we can think of trade unions as 'defensive' pressure groups, we know that their activities are strictly controlled by legislation. This is what a shop-steward had to say about workers crossing picket lines:

There is a deeply-held belief in the trade union movement that no union member crosses an official picket line. We now have a situation in which workers are not only encouraged by the government to cross picket lines but are given active help by the police. In this dispute we have workers being taken in coaches through picket lines and we are even denied the right to board the coaches to speak to them about their actions. Who made these laws? It certainly wasn't trade unionists. They were made by the government in the interests of employers and not in the interests of the majority on strike.

This shop-steward is suggesting that trade unions in democratic societies have to 'play the game' as defined by the government, and the rules of this game are often staked against the interests of unions and their members. Some sociologists argue that by containing conflict within democratic structures it will weaken the power of trade unions and therefore restrict workers' political actions. Ralph Miliband points out that trade union power is severely limited in industrial societies, and Richard Hyman, in *Strikes*, suggests that management is still very much in control, and trade union involvement in the democratic processes does not improve the low political status of workers. To a Marxist sociologist, the democratic process has effectively sidetracked workers from the possibility of revolutionary political change. Like the disillusioned MP at the beginning of this chapter, this full-time union official finds himself in a similar position:

It's when I go to meetings and hear the word compromise that I start to get worried. There you are, sitting opposite management. You know them on first name terms and you have a regular drink with them. They tell you that they respect what you are trying to do and they hope that you respect them. But when I think about it I know that we are not on the same side. We represent different class interests, and here I am, being reasonable and compromising, like a pet poodle, selling out my members for a few crumbs from the gaffer's table. That's how I'd describe trade unions in this country – part of a great compromise.

Pluralists counter this argument by drawing our attention to other pressure groups that have been responsible for dramatic changes in government policy, who have succeeded in influencing our ways of thinking about the world. Pressure groups are themselves important agents of social change. Protection from pollution and injury at work and on the roads, greater support for the aged, poor, sick and disabled, improved food hygiene and consumer rights, greater protection for women and ethnic minorities, all originate from the activities of pressure groups. The **Campaign for Nuclear Disarmament (CND)** has become as well known as most political parties in its staggeringly successful campaign to draw our attention to the dangers involved in the proliferation of nuclear weapons. The Labour Party has itself made a political commitment to abolish all nuclear weapons if it were to gain power. This commitment, a pluralist would argue, has largely come about because of the influence of the CND.

Nevertheless, even if the CND does achieve its aims, this does not mean that there has been a shift in the nature of political power in this country. After all, the CND, like most pressure groups, carries out its work legally within a conventional democratic framework. An example of what can happen to an organisation that is prepared to take a political initiative is the Anti-Nazi League. As an expression of their disgust of racism, a group with strongly-held opinions started a campaign which they hoped would make a contribution to the reduction of racism in our society. The movement got support from such people as the TV personality Michael Parkinson and the football manager Brian Clough. Members wore badges proclaiming their hatred of racism, and the group organised meetings and demonstrations which spoke out against political parties like the National Front. However when some Asian members started physically to defend themselves and their property against violent racist attacks in the Brick Lane area of London many celebrities resigned from the group.

This illustrates an inherent weakness of many pressure groups. They can survive and prosper, and get a large degree of support, as long as they act within the democratic structure and particularly within the law. If they step outside of these boundaries and deal with issues by taking direct action they will find themselves described in the media as the 'lunatic fringe' or 'the political bullyboys'. Pressure groups may well draw our attention to important issues, but they do so at the expense of being unable to deal with political problems head-on. We can say that their weapons for waging war have become institutionalised.

EXERCISE

This article appeared in a local newspaper:

Bullygirl tactics at nuclear base

Fifteen women were brought before magistrates at Newbury and charged with offences ranging from resisting arrest to damaging fencing and police uniforms. All the offences took place at the Greenham Common American nuclear missile base.

The women claimed to be members of the Greenham Women's Group, a pressure group dedicated to the elimination of nuclear weapons in Britain.

Sandra Collins, a defendant, claimed that she had the moral right to take whatever action was necessary, even unlawful action, to prevent the military might of the USA from destroying human life. The magistrate said that no one had any rights as far as he was concerned to take the law into their own hands in a democratic society.

The defendants were gaoled for 28 days after refusing to pay fines.

1 Explain in your own words what is meant by institutionalised conflict.
2 How would a sociologist explain the actions of the Greenham Women's Group and the magistrates?

Voting behaviour

The UK is divided into 650 constituencies, each returning one Member of Parliament to the House of Commons. Usually between 70% and 80% of those eligible cast their votes in General Elections, and between 30% and 50% vote in Local Elections. Of the 73% voting in the 1983 General Election, the results were:

government than voted for it.
3 A total of 843 700 people voted for the Labour Party in 1983.
4 Although 25% of the electorate voted for the Social Democratic/Liberal Alliance party, it gained fewer than 5% of parliamentary seats.

Questions that interest sociologists are: why do people vote or not vote in the way that they do? Is it possible to detect a pattern of voting behaviour in the various social classes? Do young people tend to choose a different party from their parents or does where you happen to live increase or decrease your chances of voting for one party or another? And what about you? Which party would you vote for if you had the chance?

You might say that since you voted for Tweedle Dum in the last election, this time you will vote for Tweedle Dee. You might say that you like a particular

you will choose not to vote at all! Now turn to the Registrar General's classification on page 25 and decide which of the 5 main classes are likely to vote for either the Conservative, Labour or the Alliance parties.

You may have decided that the Conservative Party will attract votes from the middle classes, the Labour Party votes from the working classes, and the Alliance Party votes from all classes. However, although you would be largely correct, politics is a little more complex than this. Since over 65% of the voting population are working class, all parties have to be attractive enough to draw votes from this large group. The Labour Party, too, will expect to attract votes from certain sections of the middle classes. It is obvious that voting behaviour is extremely complex and contains many shifting elements.

This unpredictability in voting

Voting by class in 1960s, by percentage

Class self image

| | 1963 | | 1970 | |
	middle class	working class	middle class	working class
Conservative	79	28	68	37
Labour	21	72	32	63

Source: Butler and Stokes

	Votes cast (thousands)	% share of vote	Seats won
Conservative	12 991	42	397
Labour	8 437	28	209
Social Democratic/Liberal Alliance	7 775	25	23
Others	1 420	5	21

Answer True or False to these statements:
1 In the UK, the party winning the most seats usually forms the government.
2 In 1983, more people voted against the party that formed the

candidate but not another, or that you prefer the policies of one party and detest those of another. It could be that you will vote for a party that represents what sociologists like to describe as your class interests, or perhaps

behaviour has come about mostly in the last 25 years. Until about 1960 the Labour Party presented an 'image' that was very attractive to working class voters, whilst the Conservative Party cultivated an alternative image that appealed more to the middle classes and to a smaller group of loyal working class Tories. Butler and Stokes in *Political Change in Britain* were the first to detect a change in the way working class and middle class people were voting during the 1960s (see table above).

You can see that in both 1963 and 1970 the middle class voted predominantly Conservative, and the working class voted predominantly Labour. Even so, within a short 7 year period a levelling process is detectable and class loyalties to parties are weakening.

During the 1970s and early 1980s the bond between class and preferred party continued to weaken:

Party is a matter of dispute. Despite all this, however, it is undoubtedly true that the Conservative and Labour Parties are still class parties, although it is less true that working class people can always be relied upon to vote Labour.

Why have working class voters become so unpredictable? What has happened in British society to create such a change in political loyalties?

labour, and this trend has accelerated recently as the manufacturing sector has gone into rapid decline. No-one is certain where the political loyalties of this new group of non-manual workers lie.

- **A more demanding electorate.** Loyalty to one party can no longer be guaranteed. Voters are more choosey and there is a weakening of party sympathies. The emergence of the Social Democratic Party is a further factor in this complicated process.

- **Current political appeal.** The previous Labour governments' economic policies and their failure to create a successful partnership with the trade unions did not impress all working class voters. The Conservatives offered 'strong' government under Mrs Thatcher, which made a big impression on the electorate during the Falklands war.

Movement of votes by social class, 1974–1983
Percentage of each class voting Conservative or Labour

		Middle class A+B	Lower middle class C1	Skilled working class C2	Unskilled and poor D+E
Conservative	1973	67	51	30	25
	1983	62	55	39	29
Labour	1973	10	21	47	54
	1983	12	21	35	44

Source: NOP and Gallup surveys

Answer True or False to these statements:
1 Between 1973 and 1983 the middle class Tory and Labour vote remained more or less unchanged.
2 Working class support for the Conservative Party decreased between 1973 and 1983.
3 Working class support for the Labour Party remained largely unchanged between 1973 and 1983.
4 On the basis of these tables it is possible to say that the electorate no longer vote along class lines.

If we look at the previous table with a fresh eye we can see that, roughly speaking, the middle classes have remained faithful to the Conservative Party, but working class loyalty to the Labour Party has markedly declined. Whether the Labour Party's lost support is moving across to the Tory or the Alliance

In his *Introduction to British Politics* P. J. Madgwick offers us three plausible explanations:
- **The emergence of a new working class.** Since 1945 there has been a big reduction in the number of workers engaged in manual

Of the factors that have been identified in influencing voting behaviour, the following are believed to be important:

Factors affecting voting behaviour

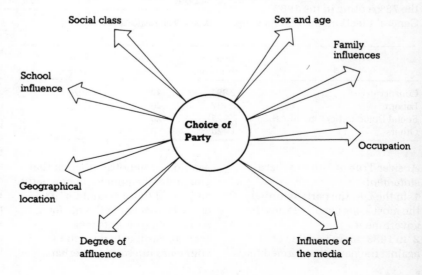

Social class

Sex and age

Family influences

School influence

Choice of Party

Occupation

Geographical location

Degree of affluence

Influence of the media

Most sociologists would accept that social class is by far the most important factor in predicting voting behaviour. Other factors such as age and sex are, of course, important. Generally speaking, older people and women have a tendency to vote Conservative, and voters who live in the north of the country and in Wales are attracted by the Labour Party. However, since family and school influences, occupation, degree of affluence, and where a person lives are clearly linked with social class, it is to a person's class we must finally turn in our quest to understand voting behaviour.

Some observers have suggested that since the material well-being of the working classes has improved, so there has been a corresponding shift in their political loyalties. Better-off people, the argument goes, are more likely to turn to the Conservative Party in a General Election. This is part of the debate on embourgeoisement which we looked at in the chapter *Social stratification and social class*. However recent research in this area has challenged the notion that the working class has become more middle class, and Frank Parkin in *Class Inequality and Political Order* suggests that many working class Tories have always accepted society's traditional values which the Conservative Party represents. Many working class families live in the suburbs of towns and cities, well removed from industrialised areas, and they like to think of themselves and their peers as a cut above the traditional Labour voter. Marx has described this attitude as **false consciousness**, which means that these workers think of themselves as middle class, although their actual social position does not support this. At the same time, workers living in traditional industrial areas solidly support

the Labour Party, particularly in mining, shipbuilding and heavy industries. Parkin also identifies numerous Labour voters amongst middle class groups such as social workers and teachers, professional workers who tend to have the same ideals and political philosophy as the Labour Party.

EXERCISE

Explain the likely relationship between social class and voting behaviour in the light of

- family and school influences
- family income
- occupation.

The abstainers

A group that we must consider seriously are the abstainers. These are people who are eligible to vote but fail or refuse to do so. Although they form only about one-fifth of the electorate, abstainers are important because they can tip the balance in favour of a candidate in a marginal seat, where the difference between the two leading candidates is only a few hundred votes. Since most of us vote loyally for the same party election after election, abstainers, or floating voters, are more susceptible to the silver tongues of politicians who try their best to persuade them either to vote for them or to abstain from voting for another party. As the difference in votes between the major parties in a General Election is often small (the 1983 General Election results were exceptional), it has been estimated that a less than 2% abstention rate of a party's supporters will usually allow the other party to gain power. Hence the great interest to understand why so many people do not vote in democratic societies.

Who are these abstainers and why do they abstain?

Since voting is voluntary in Britain (in Australia voting is compulsory) abstainers, like voters, can be found across the whole social strata. Of course they may have been voters themselves in previous elections, and may well return as voters in the future. However most abstainers, particularly those who have a negative attitude towards politics, are usually found amongst the youngest, oldest and poorest members of the community, and are rather more likely to be women than men. For example, a 25-year-old divorced woman living in a high-rise flat with her 2 children and ageing invalid father might be tempted to give the voting booth a miss during a howling gale. Her father might feel the same way.

Possibly of more interest to politicians are what we might call the **positive abstainers,** These are electors who deliberately choose not to vote, as opposed to the more numerous **negative abstainers** who either forget or just can't be bothered. Positive abstainers, who form over 10% of the electorate, are usually hostile to the idea of voting but who nevertheless are the target of politicians who try to woo them in their efforts to get them to vote. Positive abstainers may choose not to vote for one or more of the following reasons:

- After weighing up all the pros and cons, a voter might be unable to come to a definite decision, and so refrain from casting a vote for any party.
- The voter may not be able to bring himself to vote for his usual party because of his intense dislike of a particular candidate.
- The party of his choice may not

be fielding a candidate.

- Believing the result of the election to be a foregone conclusion, there seems to be no point in voting.
- He may wish to register his disapproval of the policies of the party he previously supported.
- He may be deeply cynical and hostile about all politics and politicians.

EXERCISE

'As far as I'm concerned, politicians are in it for the money. They couldn't care less about people like me. Once they get to parliament they forget all their election promises and start remembering their career prospects. I wouldn't vote for any of them – no way.'

This comment was made by a young woman abstainer who might be said to have a cynical and hostile attitude about politics. To complete this exercise, write 5 more typical comments, each of a similar length to the example, which could be said to represent the views of 5 different types of positive abstainers.

Although there has been a definite change in voting patterns during the first half of the 1980s, it is not possible to be certain why voters have chosen to elect two fairly right-wing Conservative governments. Nor is it possible to know whether we have witnessed the beginning of a long-term trend towards the right of the political spectrum or whether the process will go into reverse. Many commentators point to the popularity of the Centre Parties as a guide to future trends.

QUESTIONS

1 In the General Election of 1983 the Conservative Party had a landslide victory, winning many seats traditionally held by the Labour Party.

a What is meant by the term

Territorial distribution of seats in the General Election of 1983

	Conservative seats	Labour seats	Liberal/SDP seats	Nationalist seats
English counties (South & Midlands)	225	15	5	0
English counties (North)	38	25	2	0
Metropolitan England	99	108	6	0
Scotland	21	41	8	2
Wales	14	20	2	2

Source: Economist

'metropolitan England'? (2 marks)

b Describe briefly the geographical strengths and weaknesses of Conservative and Labour Party support. (6 marks)

c Can you suggest any reasons why Labour Party support is strong in metropolitan areas? (6 marks)

d Discuss the proposition that working class support for the Labour Party is in decline. (8 marks)

2 a What part do pressure groups play in influencing government decisions? (12 marks)

b What are the essential differences between pressure groups and political parties? (8 marks)

3 Using examples, explain the difference between power and authority. (20 marks)

Case Study

Against the odds

Stokes only drank when he was very depressed, so tonight he would work his way through a bottle of good port and maybe just a drop more. The campaign he had been involved in for the past 18 months had come to an end. In fact it had failed miserably. Along with other residents on the Compton housing estate, he had formed a pressure group to try and stop the Langhill Waste Disposal Company from building a waste disposal plant nearby and filling dozens of deep mineshafts with industrial toxic waste. Stokes and his group *Save All Future Environments (SAFE)* had fought a hard battle, but, on reflection, the odds had been stacked against them. Even though they had done everything they could think of, they had failed to win against the might of a company which was part of a multinational organisation.

'I think you've got a good case,' the editor of the local newspaper had told him when they had met months before, 'but I think you're standing in the way of progress.'

'Progress?' Stokes had queried, 'I thought we were being responsible in protecting the environment. We're not just thinking of ourselves, you know, but of future generations'.

Stokes imagined he had detected a knowing smile creep across the editor's deadpan face. 'Look here,' the editor said, 'and this if off the record, the Langhill Company are part of a huge organisation which places many advertisements with us. Do you really think in these difficult times we would put our advertising revenue at risk by attacking them? Please stop being an idealist, Mr Stokes, and join us in the real world. After all, that site is just as safe as it can be in the circumstances'.

So much for the freedom of the press, Stokes had thought when he left the editor's office. But he was determined to carry on. Who needed the support of the local paper anyway? Do they think for one minute that someone as stubborn as a mule would back off at the first obstacle? All his life he had believed in the democratic system, a system that allowed all voices and opinions to be heard. The fight was on, and *Save All Future Environments* was born.

A petition was drawn up and more than 2000 people registered their opposition to the waste disposal plant. Letters damning the scheme were written to local and national newspapers. Stokes himself appeared on a local radio phone-in programme. A public meeting was called, chaired by the local vicar, and there were guest speakers from Friends of the Earth and the Campaign for Clear Air. The town was literally buzzing with excitement and protest. Stokes was delighted with the response to his campaign. Surely nothing could stop them now.

'Look, I don't want to see you getting upset,' his wife had said to him, 'but since this campaign has started you really have changed. The kids hardly see you any more and I can't remember the last time we spent any time together'.

'But I'm doing it for you and the kids,' he had protested.

'Well, there are times when I wish you wouldn't'.

'What do mean by that?'

'It's just that people think that you're a bit of a fanatic. I don't want people to laugh at you.'

'I don't care what people think,' he had said.

'You might not,' his wife had protested, 'but then you don't see the smirks on people's faces when I bump into them in the supermarket.'

With that she went to retrieve a brochure which had sailed through the letterbox. It was a glossy, well-printed information leaflet produced by the Langhill Waste Disposal Company that explained the safeguards the company were taking when dealing with industrial waste. It certainly looked impressive and

made interesting reading. There were statements from three of the country's leading scientists who described the company's excellent safety record. IF YOU CAN'T TRUST LANGHILL, WHO CAN YOU TRUST? the bold lettering had asked, and DO YOU WANT TO THROW AWAY AN EMPLOYMENT OPPORTUNITY? Stokes had to admit that it had made their cheaply-printed handout look pathetic.

He thought about that day the leaflet had been delivered. It had been an important day because it marked the beginning of his failure. As he sipped his port he realised how the odds had always been stacked against *SAFE* from the start. He had believed that he was living in a society that allowed all the arguments to be heard, but what had happened in the last months made him doubt all this. The plant was going to be built, so that was that.

QUESTIONS

1 What does this case study tell us about democracy?
2 How does the concept of 'power' help us to understand the relationship between SAFE and the Langhill Disposal Company?
3 a Describe the actions taken by *SAFE* to achieve their aims.
  b What other forms of political action were available to them?

Points for discussion

● The existence of pressure groups proves that political parties have failed
● Most pressure groups are self-serving organisations who are interested in perpetuating traditional ways of life against the march of progress
● A pressure group that I would like to start up is . . .

Class & Politics

These extracts are taken from 'Britons observed', an article written by Katherine Whitehorn and published in the *Observer* magazine on 28 November 1984. The statistics are based on a survey conducted by the Harris Research Centre who interviewed 1084 respondents.

'There's much more intermingling goes on these days. People from the upper class are staunch socialists and people from the working class are staunch Conservatives.' It might be easier to locate a staunch Conservative in Bradford than a staunch socialist at Blenheim Palace, but the engineer who said this realised that things are very different from the way they were 20 years ago.

There was a famous poll done then by Butler and Stokes, and by comparing the results of that one with our own, some differences between then and now stand out sharply. More of us today feel badly off – in spite of having, in real terms, more cars, carpets, telephones, holidays. More of us expect to become worse off – in the early Sixties everyone thought they were on the up and up, that all men were equal and also doing fairly well.

There's been a 10% drop in those who call themselves Labour, though not much change in those who'd say they were working-class. But the working classes always vote Labour, don't they? Since the war it's certainly looked as if they did. Yet the identification of the labouring masses with Labour was never complete: it couldn't have been, or

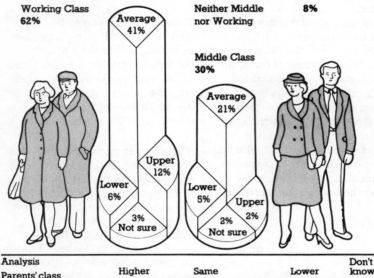

QUESTION: a Most people say they belong to either the middle class or the working class. Do you ever think of yourself as being in one of these classes? If 'yes', which class is that?

b Would you say that you are about average, or that you were in the upper or lower part of that class?

c (to those specifying a class): Would you say that this is the same as your parents when they were your age? If not, were they higher or lower?

Working Class 62%

Average 41%

Neither Middle nor Working 8%

Middle Class 30%

Average 21%

Upper 12%

Lower 6%

Lower 5%

Upper 2%

3% Not sure

2% Not sure

Analysis Parents' class	Higher	Same	Lower	Don't know
All	8%	52%	33%	7%
Of those saying they are Middle Class	7%	48%	39%	6%
Of those saying they are Working Class	9%	54%	30%	7%

the Conservatives would never have got in again.

Twenty years ago, 4 people out of 5 had always voted for the same party, but now the old attachments are cracking up. Conservatives still do look like the Haves, I admit. In our survey they were more likely to be well off and think they were getting better off, to trust the police and get the best out of the Health Service. Just under half of Conservative voters are middle-class, but that still leaves 43% of them workers. Less than half the working-class votes Labour – or did last time around, at any rate.

At the same time, class itself has

changed. Many reckon your job determines your class – which of course makes it all the more awful if you lose it. True, a lot of working-class people see the middle classes as mainly professional – doctors, lawyers; so they go on calling themselves working-class, even when they've quite a bit of money. It doesn't stop them behaving in middle-class ways.

To say that the classes are mixed and intermingled doesn't mean, though, that there's a vast equal pool – quite the opposite. It was the Sixties that used to talk as if class no longer existed – the upper classes were never even mentioned. There

were stories of duke's daughters getting their posh accents fixed, and even if it never happened, the point was we thought it did. Diamond galas were out, and the élite university students dressed in jeans to a unisex. But when the cold winds of the Seventies blew a little more job-conscious reality into the middle-class young, the upper classes rose back into view. Of course the money had always been there; but now the notion that you can't tell princess from shopgirl has finally gone.

It's my belief that British society has polarised again – but in two very different ways. The real one is the upper/lower split, which is financial: the rich get richer and the poor get much poorer (the Civil and Public Services Association recently reckoned that the pay of the bottom tenth in the wages league was down 1% while that of the top tenth was up 16.6% in real terms). Inflation has actually benefited the landed and the house-owning; and when it come to prices, the gap between the highest and lowest is far wider than it was in the Sixties. The dole may be better than before the war, but it's still nowhere near a good wage; there's no way the long-term jobless can be anything but poor.

The other polarisation is entirely artificial. It's created by the 2 main parties to make themselves visibly more different. Hence the grabbing of any new idea by one party, so that it is automatically denounced by the other.

We are surely into an era, not of automatic loyalty to the party of your class, but of issue politics, pressure groups, local causes; with a crucial middle area up for grabs.

QUESTIONS

According to the Harris survey:

1 a What percentage of people thought they were members of the middle class?

b What percentage of the working class thought that their parents

QUESTION: *a* Do you remember when you were young whether your father had any particular preference for one of the parties? If yes, which party was that?

b And when you were young did your mother have any particular preference for one of the parties? If yes, which party was that?

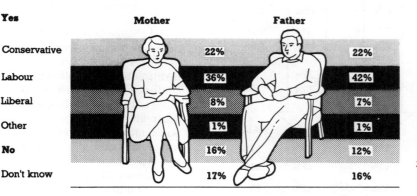

Yes	Mother	Father
Conservative	22%	22%
Labour	36%	42%
Liberal	8%	7%
Other	1%	1%
No	16%	12%
Don't know	17%	16%

QUESTION: Generally speaking, do you normally think of yourself as Conservative, Labour, Liberal, SDP, or what?

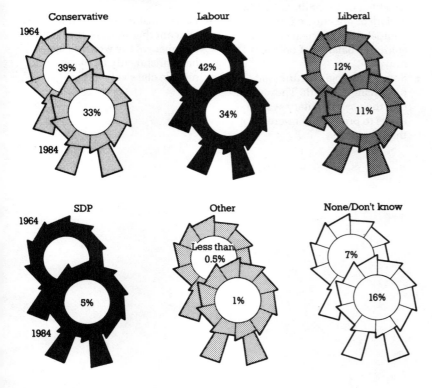

Conservative	Labour	Liberal
1964: 39%	1964: 42%	1964: 12%
1984: 33%	1984: 34%	1984: 11%

SDP	Other	None/Don't know
1964: (—)	1964: Less than 0.5%	1964: 7%
1984: 5%	1984: 1%	1984: 16%

were in a lower class than themselves?

c Which political party was most preferred by the respondents' parents?

d Of the three major political parties in 1964, which party had lost the most ground by 1984?

e Why was the SDP so unsuccessful in 1964? What do the initials SDP stand for?

f Which political party do the most well-off tend to support?

g Which party do the least well-off tend to support?

h What percentage of respondents thought they were fairly/very badly off?

i What percentage thought that their parents were fairly/very badly off?

2 According to the author:

a What is the name of the poll that was conducted in 1964?

b How does the writer characterise Conservative voters?

c At what period in recent history did class appear not to exist?

d What evidence is provided by the writer to suggest that society is becoming polarised?

e What does the writer mean by the final phrase 'with a crucial middle area up for grabs'?

3 What is meant by the term **embourgeoisement**? According to the article, what evidence exists to support or refute this theory?

4 What is false consciousness? Why do you think that some people in the 1960s believed that class difference was diminishing?

5 Explain why in the 1983 General Election about two-thirds of manual workers voted for the Labour Party and about three-quarters of white-collar workers supported the Conservative Party.

Important points

- The sociology of politics is essentially a study of the way power is distributed in society.
- Political power exists both inside and outside of parliament and local government.

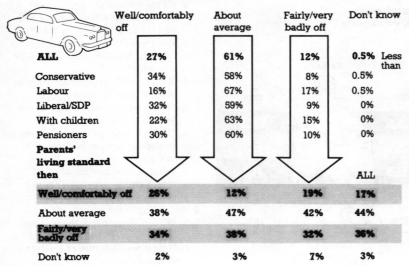

Own standard of living now

	Well/comfortably off	About average	Fairly/very badly off	Don't know
ALL	27%	61%	12%	0.5% Less than
Conservative	34%	58%	8%	0.5%
Labour	16%	67%	17%	0.5%
Liberal/SDP	32%	59%	9%	0%
With children	22%	63%	15%	0%
Pensioners	30%	60%	10%	0%

Parents' living standard then				ALL
Well/comfortably off	26%	12%	19%	17%
About average	38%	47%	42%	44%
Fairly/very badly off	34%	38%	32%	36%
Don't know	2%	3%	7%	3%

- The exercise of power implies an ability to control or change events, even against the resistance of others.
- Power is gained through the exercise of authority and coercion.
- Authority is the legitimate exercise of power that has been accepted by most or all of the population. Weber identified three types of authority: charismatic, traditional and legal-rational.

- Our social attitudes are linked with a tendency to support a particular political party.
- A pluralist society is a society in which many political parties and ideas are allowed to compete against each other to achieve a balance of political power.
- Some sociologists think that pluralism is a myth. They argue that the parliamentary system exists to protect the interests of the ruling class.

- A political party is an organisation, which has a range of policies on offer, whose goal is to gain or keep political power.
- A pressure group is an organisation that represents the like-minded views of its members on a single issue. It attempts to control or effect social change by employing methods that are either defensive or promotional.
- Institutionalised conflict is conflict that is allowed to take place only within politically acceptable limits.
- Social class is the most important factor in influencing how a person will vote.
- The Labour and Conservative Parties are still basically class parties, but fewer working class people are voting for the Labour Party.
- The attitudes of positive abstainers are extremely important in determining the outcome of General and Local Elections.
- False consciousness is a Marxist concept that implies that some members of the working class have mistakenly taken on middle class values.

11 Mass media and youth culture

When you have worked through this chapter you should have a clearer understanding of

The functions of the media · Media–person interactions · The hypodermic theory · Over-reporting · Stereotypes · The teenager · Youth and social class · Youth subcultures and counter cultures

The mass media

There are 2 features in our present-day society which have made the mass media possible: a large literate population and mechanisation. During the 19th century a growing urban population not only provided a ready market for mass media products, it also permitted a simpler method of delivery to the family doorstep. You can imagine how difficult it was to distribute newspapers to an isolated rural population. The second feature, mechanisation, allowed newspapers and books to be printed quickly and cheaply on steam-driven printing presses, and the newly-invented steam engines ensured rapid distribution throughout Britain. This process of mechanisation has, of course, led in turn to electronic and computer-based techniques in the manufacture of mass media products and to communication satellites which provide a long-range method of delivery to an even bigger audience.

What are the mass media? Why should they be of interest to sociologists?

We can define the mass media as those systems of communication which transmit ideas, values and information to a large, socially mixed and geographically dispersed audience. The main media are television, radio, newspapers, advertising, films and recordings of one sort or another. These media are an important part of any modern industrial society, and sociologist are interested to know;

- What effects, if any, does a medium have on its audience?
- What purpose do the media serve in general society?
- What use is made of the media by audiences?
- In whose interests are the media acting?

Perhaps the most important thing to keep in mind is that we are not just passive receivers of media outpourings. We have the luxury of choice, although factors such as social class, sex and age are important modifiers of that choice. Nor do we all receive either equal quantities or equal qualities of media output. For example:

- There are significant sex, age and social class variations regarding both what and how much is watched on TV or listened to on the radio. This table should give you an idea of variations in TV viewing. You might like to ask yourself why the over 55s and adult women tend to watch more TV than other groups:

Television viewing, by age and sex, Jan–Mar 1984

Age group	Weekly hours
4–15	17.5
16–24	14.0
25–54	23.0
55+	30.0

	Weekly hours
Adult males	22.0
Adult females	25.5

Source: BBC

- Newspaper readership has remained a class-based activity.
- Cinema attendance depends to some degree on specific age

groups and where people happen to live.

- The ownership, reading and buying of books are all related to age, social class and education.

EXERCISE

	Percentage of adults in each social class reading each paper in 1982					
	A	B	C1	C2	D	E
Daily newspapers						
The Sun	7	11	23	37	41	28
Daily Mirror	6	10	19	32	33	19
Daily Express	15	16	17	13	11	8
Daily Mail	17	18	18	10	8	7
Daily Star	1	3	6	15	16	10
The Daily Telegraph	34	22	11	3	2	1
The Guardian	9	10	4	1	1	–
The Times	14	6	2	1	1	–
Financial Times	10	4	2	1	–	–
Any daily newspaper	77	71	72	76	76	62

Source: National Readership Survey

To answer these questions you will need to refer to the Registrar General's social classification on page 25. You can also find some newspaper circulation statistics on page 175.

1 Which is the most popular newspaper read by the working class?
2 Which is the most popular newspaper read by the middle class?
3 What percentage of social *Class A* and *E* read newspapers?
4 What is meant by the term **tabloid**? Which of the 9 newspapers are tabloid?
5 Can you think of a reason why the tabloid shape appeals more to the working class newspaper reader?
6 Which newspaper would you say appealed to the widest *range* of classes?

Before we discuss audience interest in the media, let us look at a newspaper article that was published in the Spring of 1985.

Similar reports were broadcast on TV and radio news:

Costa del Dole kids to get evicted

The government has introduced new regulations cutting unemployment benefit to youngsters who stay too long at boarding houses. The regulations will affect thousands of young people in bed-and-breakfast accommodation throughout Britain.

The limitations on board and lodging allowances are being introduced after relevations about the 'Costa del Dole' scandal in which youngsters spend months at seaside boarding houses while supposedly looking for work.

They are aimed at reducing the rising costs of board and lodging allowances, which rose from £200 million in 1983 to £570 million in 1984.

Under the new rules, youngsters can stay in big cities like Cardiff and Leeds for up to 8 weeks, in most other areas for up to a month, but at the seaside for only 2 weeks.

The government is determined to put a stop to the practice of thousands of young people taking what amounts to free sea-side holidays on the state.

A reasonable question to ask is: what is the purpose of this and similar articles that are read by over 15 million British newspaper buyers every day? A simple answer might be that we want to know what's going on in the world, we like to be informed. Sociologists, however, are able to dig a little deeper than this.

Researchers at Leeds University have studied the different uses people make of the media. They have identified 4 categories of what they term **media–person interactions**, which simply means how each of us makes use of the media. These are:

- **Diversion.** The media offer escape and emotional release from the stresses of everyday life.
- **Personal relationships.** We come to know certain characters or situations on the TV or radio. For example, well known soap operas can provide us with both 'characters' and 'situations' that we have come to love or hate.
- **Personal identity.** Items in the mass media come to be valued for reflecting one's own personal experiences and prejudices. We might turn to an article or a documentary that we anticipate will fulfill our needs.
- **Surveillance.** Information and opinions are looked for. For example, TV and radio news broadcasts, weather reports, regular articles by our favourite writers, cartoon strips and TV guides in newspapers.

If we go back to the article *Costa del Dole kids to get evicted* we can see how a reader might regard it as a useful source of up-to-date information, and its general tone about young people, in particular the hostile heading, might appeal to certain prejudices in the adult population.

In *Sociology of the Mass Media* David Glover supports much of the research done at Leeds University, but offers a broader interpretation of the functions of the media. He suggests that the media act as:

- **Rituals.** Buying and reading a newspaper or watching breakfast TV may mark the beginning of the day, just as switching on the TV in the evening may mark the end of an active working day.
- **Information.** The media provide up to the minute information.
- **Social prestige.** Reading a certain newspaper may communicate a person's social class to others as well as reinforce the reader's own class consciousness.
- **Relaxation.** The radio, for example, can provide background music which aids relaxation, even in active periods like driving and doing housework.

So each mass medium may have different functions depending on who is using it and what that individual's motives are. However, there may not always be a motive for using a mass medium. Those researchers who have investigated the uses people make of the media have ignored the extent to which some activities are unplanned and casual.

EXERCISE

Using 3 of the 4 Leeds University's media-person interactions, investigate how a person might use a mass media product. You can conduct your research on any daily or Sunday newspaper or you can review any evening's TV transmission (all channels), an example of which can be found on pages 34–5.

Pick out what you believe to be examples that can be said to reflect the needs of an average reader or viewer, and set them out under the following headings. The exercise will be completed when you have recorded 7 examples of each.

Mass Media Product		Date
Personal relationships	Personal identity	Surveillance
1	1	1
2	2	2
3	3	3
4	4	4
5	5	5
6	6	6
7	7	7

The effects of mass media

The first studies into the effects of the media were based on the view that the media affects us in simple and direct ways. This became known as the **hypodermic theory**. The media are the hypodermic syringe, and the audiences are the veins into which ideas and attitudes are injected. The injection is usually harmful but occasionally beneficial.

According to the 'hypodermic' view, the portrayal of, for example, violent crime on TV will tend to stimulate criminal behaviour, especially if the viewer is a person who is easily led. That the media are capable of provoking certain types of behaviour is an idea deeply ingrained in the thinking of modern societies, as these examples illustrate:

In 1938 the H. G. Wells' story *The War of the Worlds* was dramatised on radio in the USA. It is a story about an invasion of the Earth by belligerent aliens who proceed to destroy our civilisation with death rays from their flying saucers. The broadcast was so convincing that many people fled for their lives, and over one million people were frightened or affected in some way. This incident led to a change in the rules governing broadcasting in the USA.

Eysenck and Nias in *Sex, Violence and the Media* quote the example of the famous 'Moors Murderers', Ian Brady and Myra Hindley, who were convicted of torturing and murdering a 10-year-old girl. They were found to possess sadistic literature at home. Also quoted is the 16-year-old boy who broke into a neighbour's house and attacked a sleeping woman with a knife. An identical incident had occurred in *Starsky and Hutch* just 2 hours before.

The question arises as to whether these acts would have occurred without exposure to the media which supposedly created them. A fundamental weakness of the hypodermic view is that audiences are assumed to be impressionable and passive receivers of media messages, rather than people who are capable of making up their own minds about what they choose to accept or reject. However this is not to say that the media do not affect our lives in significant ways. The media play a vital role in shaping our view of the social world.

Effects of the media on children

The most powerful and influential medium is arguably television, and sociologists are interested in assessing its effects, particularly on children. We can accept the potential power of this medium if we realise that over 93% of households in Britain have TVs and that the average child spends as much time in a year watching TV as attending school. If TV is a potent social tool, then its power is likely to be even greater in influencing children whose values and attitudes are not yet fully developed.

As we have discussed in the chapter *Family*, the nuclear family is a close-knit unit that tends to enjoy its pleasures at home. As the supreme entertainer, the TV set has become the centre-piece in most living-rooms, and for many families watching TV provides the main, if not the sole, evenings activity. Television has become an agent of socialisation in itself. It offers standards to which children can aspire and models on which they can base their behaviour; it is a spreader of what we know as culture. Families themselves also use TV as a device for promoting desirable social behaviour, as this fragment from a 10-year-old's story shows:

My dad tells me to get to bed about 9 o'clock. Sometimes my mum and dad argue about what time I should go to bed. They let me stay up late if there is a good film on but I have to keep quiet and not argue with my older sister. Sometimes my dad lets me stay up late on Saturdays to see the horror film but I have to be a really good boy all week for that.

One subject that has attracted discussion are the effects of violence on TV. Does violence on TV encourage violent behaviour in children? Are violent acts portrayed on the screen copied by children or do they help children to cope better with violence both in the family and in wider society? If we are influenced by TV advertisements, plays and documentaries, then why not by programmes with a high content of violence? Unfortunately watching TV is not as simple as this. It is difficult to know what programmes are less or more violent than others. Should we prevent children from watching news broadcasts because they frequently show acts of appalling real-life cruelty? Is *Tom and Jerry* violent? Are children likely to be influenced more by fictional or factual violence? The truth is that we do not really know the answers to any of these questions.

Some research suggests that there is a link between violence on TV and behaviour problems in children. In *TV Violence and the Adolescent* William Belson argued that TV violence, especially violence that had been glamorised, can lead to real-life aggression in unstable young people. However, Grant Noble in *Children in Front of the Small Screen* suggested that some forms of TV violence are cathartic, which means that children get released from their own aggressive feelings by watching simulated violence on TV. What we can be sure of is that the media cannot be the single cause of deviant behaviour in children, and perhaps not even an important contributor.

What is far more likely is that television, and all the media for that matter, form just a part of a child's social experience that may or may not lead to the development of deviant behaviour. As sociologists we know that it is silly to make hasty judgments about any group until we have investigated the social setting in which the group develops. Children are no different. Children, like adults, differ from each other in terms of social class, sex, intelligence and age. Before we can even approach the question of the effects of TV violence we need much more information about children's social backgrounds. Knowing what disturbed children watch on TV is not nearly enough, and may be only a minor component in a generally deprived social condition.

EXERCISE

This reader's letter was published in a local newspaper:

Sir,
I am convinced that the increase in street violence perpetrated by young hooligans has its roots in the corrosive influence of certain TV programmes.

These thugs have as children been brought up on a diet of violence, rape, robbery and murder that can be seen every night on our TV screens.

We could help ourselves a great deal by cleaning up the violence on TV. Then we might begin to rid ourselves of a social problem that obviously starts in childhood.

Mr Warrilow.

Using your own words, explain the weaknesses in Mr Warrilow's arguments, and suggest a more satisfactory approach towards an understanding of the causes of deviant behaviour in children. Include in your answer references to the kinds of social problems that are more likely to be found in the lives of deviant children.

Are the media biased?

In the chapter *Power* we have given the daily circulation figures for the 6 top-selling newspapers in 1983. Together, the *Sun* and the *Daily Mirror* sold over 7 million copies per day, which gives a readership of over 20 million, since at least 3 people read each newspaper. A question worth asking is: what is so special about these papers? How did a paper like the *Sun*, for example, manage to gain a million extra readers between 1981 and 1982?

Although there are many different answers to this question, there can be no doubt that for many people reading the *Sun* is to read a newspaper that provides both interest and excitement. It provides so much interest and excitement that we have a right to ask how much news and how many articles published in it and in other tabloids are actually true or at least fairly reported. The following extracts are from an article published in the *Sun* on 21 May 1985:

The most dangerous streets in Britain

by PETER CLIFF

 Britain's cities used to rank among the safest in the world, night and day.

But a rocketing crime wave has turned many urban jungles into virtual no-go areas.

 Many ordinary folk are afraid to set foot outside their own front doors for fear of being attacked by hoodlums.

Often they don't even feel safe barricaded inside their own homes.

 These are the shocking findings of a nationwide Sun survey of five of the hardest-hit areas in which we talked to YOU – the people living on the front line – as well as police, doctors and social workers battling to protect us.

People are most terrified of mugging – especially by gangs of young thugs – and house-breaking, which has reached epidemic proportions.

 We blame soft sentencing, unemployment and the scourge of drug abuse for making our lives a misery.

Vital

The conclusions are echoed by top police officers and backed by hard statistics in an age of violence where the biggest offender is a 15-year-old boy or a 14-year-old girl.

 In 1984, the total number of offences recorded in England and Wales was 3.5 million – 8% up on 1983.

This shocking figure included:

- **BURGLARY** 897 500 – 10% up.
- **ROBBERY** 24 900 – 13% up.
- **VIOLENCE** 114 000 – 3% up.

Home Office Minister David Mellor says: 'Burglary and the number of kids involved in crime are major causes for concern.

 'It is vital that parents, schools and neighbours, as well as the police, play their part in helping to turn the tide.'

LONDON, Peckham (pop. 90 000)

The street-wise kids and Flash Harrys have often found a bolt hole in this rabbit warren of tower blocks and council estates south of the Thames.

But the chief worry now is the sickening violence which accompanies so many petty crimes. King's College, the area's biggest hospital, treats at least one major stabbing victim a day.

Dr Robert Ware, the head of intensive care, says: 'The current macho thing is to carry a knife with a blade at least eight inches long.

'It's almost impossible to shove that into sombody without hitting vital organs.'

Break-ins	174
Muggings	46
Assaults	29
Sex attacks	0
Murder	0

LIVERPOOL, Copperas Hill (pop. 7000)

Life on the streets of a major port is always hard, even away from the waterfront.

'The Hill' is no exception, and its police station is reckoned to be the second busiest in Britain.

Every day, more than a million people pass through the area, which includes the business centre, top stores and a thriving clubland.

Superintendent George Mothers, head of Copperas Hill police, says: 'This is a violent city and always has been.

'Once you get a reputation it tends to stick. Innocent people do fall victim to thugs, but I believe people can walk around the centre without fear.'

Local Labour MP Bob Parry says: 'Many people are avoiding the city because they are afraid.'

Break-ins	143
Assaults	31
Muggings	12
Sex attacks	2
Murder	1

GLASGOW, East End (pop. 106 500)

Lawlessness is rife in this tough-talking district of a city legendary for its violence.

A crime is committed in Glasgow every two minutes and housebreaking has reached epidemic proportions.

Pensioners live in constant fear of attack or robbery and often leave a few pounds on the kitchen table when they go out, in the hope that it will satisfy callous thieves.

One old man says: 'Only the unemployed, the elderly and those in dead-end jobs are left here. It's a breeding ground for crime.'

Hardened detectives in a police force which is 700 officers under strength confess they are in danger of losing the battle against housebreaking.

Vicar John Lang has had his church broken into 40 times in recent months. Hoodlums have stolen organ pipes, brass vases and stripped lead from the roof.

Break-ins	188
Assaults	61
Muggings	33
Sex attacks	3
Murder	1

It would be easy to be critical of this article. For the moment, we can capture its tone by re-reading the second paragraph which describes Britain's cities in terms of 'a rocketing crime wave has turned many urban jungles into virtual no-go areas'. However, we can say that this kind of over-the-top reportage seems to sell newspapers. What we should be asking is just how far will a newspaper go in the creation of exciting material. Will it go as far as actually 'manufacturing' news or conflict in order to feed on the whipped-up fears of an anxious or excited readership? In short, do newspapers tell lies.

Stan Cohen's *Folk Devils and Moral Panics* is a classic study of how the media contributes to the creation of deviant behaviour. Cohen was interested to see how certain events are highlighted in the media and how this influences the likelihood of them recurring. He chose to analyse the media treatment of a conflict that took place between two rival youth cultures of the 1960s, the Mods and the Rockers.

The Mods and Rockers phenomenon began in Clacton-on-Sea in 1964 during the Easter holidays. Over the weekend, groups of young people were involved in scuffles, windows were broken and there was a lot of noisy riding about on bikes. The police were surprised at the number of young people on the streets.

Cohen argued that the language used by the media grossly exaggerated the incident and inflated the fears of many readers who were shocked by misleading articles and alarmist headlines. *The Daily Telegraph's* headline read: DAY OF TERROR BY SCOOTER GROUPS, whilst the *Daily Express* told its readers that YOUNGSTERS BEAT UP TOWNS — 97 LEATHER JACKET ARRESTS. Cohen also drew an interesting comparison between the reporting of these events in local and national newspapers. He found that the local papers' accounts contained more detail and were less sensational. He suggested the reason was because local people would easily recognise any false or misleading statements or descriptions of events.

These incidents were, in Cohen's view, 'over-reported'. He described 3 main ways in which the media over-report:

1 Exaggeration. In this case there was an over-estimation of the numbers of people involved and the scale of the damage caused. Also the emotive language used to describe events, such as 'riot', 'orgy of destruction' and 'siege', distorted the facts. The reports highlighted the motor-bikes and scooters, although young people with their own transport were in a minority. Most people came by train or hitched. Furthermore, only 24 out of the 97 arrested were charged.

2 Prediction. Where reports imply a future performance of events (ie: IT COULD BE YOUR TOWN NEXT!!).

3 Symbolisation. This occurs where the media build associations around words, styles or individuals. In this case the Mods' anoraks and the Rockers' leathers became symbols of delinquency.

Cohen shows how a 'moral panic' can be created by the media from fairly trivial incidents. By 'moral panic' he implies that society's major values and institutions appear to be under attack. This leads to two distinct responses. First, deviant behaviour is portrayed as far more serious than it is, and this produces the very behaviour the media are condemning by confirming the deviant's self-image. In other words, if the Mods and Rockers weren't quite sure that they were locked in mortal combat, they would soon find out by reading the newspapers. Second, the police, the courts and local communities — elements of what Cohen referred to as the **control culture** – become more responsive, over-reactive and less tolerant of deviant groups. This leads to an increase in the numbers of individuals being harassed or arrested (think of football crowds), which in turn provides more 'news' for the media.

But what of serious crime? Since we derive much of our knowledge about crime from reading newspapers, is crime fairly and accurately reported?

In 1983 Jason Ditton and James Duffy investigated the reporting of crime in 6 Scottish newspapers for March 1981. Their investigations focused on the Strathclyde region (Glasgow area) which had the most reported crime in Scotland and also a very high newspaper readership.

They found that crime reports made up 6.5% of all news, but there was bias in favour of the reporting of sexual and violent crimes. The authors argued that this press scaremongering heightened people's fear of crime, particularly vulnerable groups such as the elderly. They also pointed out that the way in which crime is reported misinforms the public with its emphasis on crimes that are relatively untypical. (Actual crime statistics can be found on page 150.)

In *Policing the Crisis* the Marxist writer Stuart Hall examined the role of the media as 'an arm of the state'. He argued that during the 1970s the media helped to create a moral panic by over-reporting the incidence of muggings, which eventually enabled the state to exert more power. The police, the power of the courts and the law were all strengthened, 'law and order' became central themes of debate and people were encouraged to believe that a stronger state was needed.

Hall suggested that the

reporting of mugging helped to create and sustain social anxieties about social order. He pointed out that 'mugging' as a legal term does not exist. It is an American import which first appeared in the British press in the late 1960s in stories about urban crime. Criminal offences that the media call 'muggings' are in fact 'robberies' or 'assaults with intent to rob'. Hall noted that the rate of increase in these offences had actually fallen by over two-thirds between 1955—1965 and 1965—1975. Even so, there was an increase in police activity and the setting up of special squads to deal with urban crime during this period.

EXERCISE

Go back to the article *The most dangerous streets in Britain* on page 191 and answer these questions:

1 In what sense would Cohen regard the article as being over-reported?
2 a In what way would Ditton and Duffy regard the statistical data as misleading?
  b What kind of useful data are missing?
3 How would Stuart Hall interpret the use of the term 'muggings'?
4 What overall impression are readers likely to get of crime in Britain?
5 Whom or what does the writer blame for the increase in crime? What evidence does he produce?

Media techniques

If the media do exercise bias in the reporting of events, what then are the techniques involved? Perhaps the most common technique is the creation of what are called **stereotypes**. Stereotypes are distorted, over-simple and misleading images, created by the media to get across quickly to an audience fixed ideas about people and situations.

The reporting of industrial disputes will provide an example of how the media use stereotypes. We are often presented with newspaper headlines like **Militants in Strike Action** and **Pickets Force Factory Closure**. In the text of articles trade unions are described as making wage 'demands' or 'forcing' a claim on employers. Rarely do we read of workers who are, say, 'exercising their legal rights to strike in a bid for a fair increase in wages'. On TV workers are usually interviewed in the noisy outdoors, sometimes in the vicinity of picket lines or a mass meeting, with reporters pressing around with microphones, asking more questions about the problems the strike is causing than about the problems that led to the strike in the first place. The presentation of the management's position is usually in stark contrast. Here we see a well-dressed, quietly spoken representative being interviewed in an office, by one reporter, against a backdrop of books or curtains. The employer is usually presented as a sensible and reasonable chap, whereas the workers are shown as difficult and uncompromising. Both are stereotypes.

Another media stereotype is sometimes disguised under the general term of 'immigrant'. If we read an article with the headline **Police Van Stoned in Immigrant Area** and are then informed that 'up to 20 black youths are helping the police with their enquiries', we might be getting a false impression of a social event. A moment's thought will tell us that the association of the words 'immigrant' and 'black youths' is completely misleading. Black youths, who are almost certainly British-born and probably speak with regional accents, are not immigrants at all. We can only suppose that the stereotype of the 'immigrant' has been created to frighten us (or deflect us) into believing that the cause of riots has more to do with a black alien culture than with British urban deprivation.

Research into the media's treatment of race over the years suggests that the reporting of race has been limited, stereotyped, and hostile. A study which analysed the national press between 1963 and 1964 was carried out by Hartmann and his associates in 1974. It showed that coverage of race relations tended to focus on the visible signs of racial conflict, with little attention being paid to factors such as access to housing, education and employment which most social observers regard as the underlying causes of tension.

Race became associated with trouble. The clichés 'race riot' and 'immigrant no-go areas' emerged from the press and stories often gave a misleading view of black people as a social problem in themselves. In many ways these stereotyped images reinforce prejudices as well as perpetuate the social disadvantages experienced by ethnic groups.

EXERCISE

What makes the perfect woman?

One vision of the perfect woman emerged yesterday – mother-of-four Mrs Annie Wilton-Jones.

Annie is proud that she is obedient and submissive to her husband Ian, a computer scientist. And she is glad that they are not equal.

Add to that her willingness to let her husband have the last word and it's easy to see why Annie has been voted Feminine Woman of the Year by an anti-women's lib group.

Annie, who lives in Llanelly, Gwent, said: 'My husband makes the most important decisions in our lives and he always has the overall veto on what I do. I obey him and if we ever disagree, I feel it is my duty as a wife to give way.'

She was given her award by Campaign for Feminine Women, an organisation set up to promote the 'value and validity' of the different sex roles.

Source: Daily Mirror

1 In what way does this article contribute to the creation of a stereotype?
2 Can you suggest other ways in which television and newspapers promote the stereotype woman?
3 Can you name any other groups that are stereotyped to their disadvantage by the media?

We can summarise other media techniques as:

- **Selectivity.** This lies at the centre of the media's influence. As more news pours into the newsrooms than can be published, so a group of people must decide which items are newsworthy and which are not. News, therefore, is an individual's or a group's opinion about what is newsworthy.
- **Omission.** The inclusion of some news items involves the exclusion of others. What does not appear in the news can be very important. For instance, the editor of *The Times* during the war used his power to omit references to Nazi atrocities.
- **Facts and opinion.** These may be cleverly combined and disguised so that the reader is uncertain about what is fact and what is opinion. The previous article *The most dangerous streets in Britain* is a typical example.
- **Character assassination.** This occurs when the audience is persuaded to adopt a low opinion of a public figure. Tony Benn became the target of a character assassination in the 1970s as was in more recent times, Arthur Scargill, the miners' leader.
- **Special campaigns.** These focus our attention on a particular current social problem such as drug abuse. There is danger in exaggerating the extent of a problem one minute and ignoring it the next.
- **Headlines.** The language, size and position of headlines all contribute to our views of 'important' news.
- **Technical factors.** Galtung and Ruge in *Structuring and Selecting News* point to the practical contraints such as time, money and location which influence what does or does not become news. Only some events have a suitable time span for news reporting. Events that happen quickly are easily reported (strike action) whilst long-term processes are not (background to the strike). Also unpredictable events tend not to get covered due to the absence of journalists and cameras (natural disasters in remote regions of the world).
- **All-bad news.** Negative news gets transmitted more often than positive news. A possible reason is that agreement on bad news is likelier than agreement on good news amongst the public and broadcasters.

Since the media are important interpreters of events occurring in the social world, it is essential for us to be aware of the dangers of misrepresentation. There is enough evidence to suggest that not only are deviance and crime sometimes seriously misreported, but articles on race, women, and industrial relations have also been the subject of intense criticism. Whether we accept the Marxist view that the media are controlled by the ruling class to serve its interests, or that they are channels of free speech in a democratic society, will depend on our political point of view. These two views are explored in the chapter *Power*.

The importance of the mass media in shaping and manipulating social attitudes cannot be ignored. Although we can rightly argue that as individuals we are much too intelligent to be influenced, say, by an hysterical article in a tabloid or by a frivolous TV advertisement, we are not nearly intelligent enough to resist the relentless and overwhelming pressures that are exerted by the countless channels of communication in a modern society. The fact that over £1 billion is spent on advertising each year in Britain testifies to the belief that we are capable of being influenced.

EXERCISE

Here are some average daily circulation figures for 3 newspapers in 1984, and the cost to advertisers to insert a full-page advertisement for one day only:

The Sun	4 150 191	£21 896
The Guardian	466 376	£13 200
Financial Times	164 163	£15 904

1 What advertisements are more likely to appear in *The Guardian* than in *The Sun*?
2 The cost of advertising in *The Sun* is only about £6 000 more than advertising in the *Financial Times*, yet *The Sun's* circulation is 25 times greater. Can you suggest any explanations for this?

We conclude this section by drawing your attention to a few extracts from a newspaper article which could be said to represent what is best in British journalism:

(These extracts are taken from an article published in *The Observer* on 2 June 1985. It describes the events surrounding the European Cup Final in Belgium between

Liverpool and Juventus in which 39 fans were killed, following a charge of Liverpool supporters.)

Taming the beast

Once Belgium had been chosen, Heysel was the only option – the only large capacity ground available in the country. But it is very far from ideal. An old athletics stadium, it has flimsy crash barriers, crumbling concrete flooring and dangerous walls.

Interior Minister, Charles Northomb, subsequently admitted that 'our safety measures were never good enough.'

Arguably, this would not have mattered if the game had been policed and ticket arrangements fixed in the manner that is now standard practice for any major soccer fixture in Britain.

In the wake of it, more opaque views have emerged. One, from John Smith himself, can be largely discounted. The Liverpool chairman laid much of the blame on members of the National Front who, he said, had fomented the trouble.

But Liverpool fans have no need of the NF to teach them anything. John Williams, co-author of 'Hooligans Abroad,' a study of British soccer thugs on the Continent, said: 'Most Liverpool fans take a very anti-Fascist stance and if there had been any NF members passing themselves off as supporters, they would probably have been attacked themselves.'

More convincing is the suggestion that among the fans is a solid core of hardened youths, many from deprived inner cities where they live without jobs, hope or stable moral values.

'They are the product of our class structure,' says Eric Dunning, a Leicester university sociologist. 'They are best described as a raw lower working class.' Many of them come from what the Bishop of

Liverpool, David Sheppard, has called 'the left-behind communities.'

'We were harassed by policemen all the time' said one Liverpool fan, 26-year-old Peter Keatley. 'They kept forcing us to move on every time we stopped to sit at verges or at cafés. Then they made us go to the stadium a couple of hours before the match was due to start.'

On top of this there was a fatal lapse in control over the sale of tickets, resulting in the close proximity of Liverpool and Juventus fans – thus breaking one of the basic rules governing first class football matches.

For the Liverpool crowd, many of whom had been drinking steadily in the hot sun, the proximity of their rivals was a fatal provocation.

The panic increased. Above the terrace, a giant electric sign blinked out its message 'Welcome.' Below, fans struggled towards the front, south west end of section Z. A wall there collapsed under the pressure of bodies. The result was carnage.

Most victims died of suffocation, others were killed by chest compression and shock. A few may have died because they choked on their own vomit while others succumbed to internal ruptures, of livers and spleens.

'People died standing up, crushed to death,' said one survivor, Mr Alan Hibbert, a plasterer from Wallasey. 'They were pushed against a wall chest-high. Their faces were purple and black. It was horrible.'

All this provides Mrs Thatcher with more than enough lessons on controlling crowds. But it was the savagery of the Liverpool attacks that shocked the Prime Minister. No one has seriously denied that the responsibility for the violence which erupted lay with them.

At one stage she suggested holding all games behind closed doors, without fans at all. At another she told them: 'There are three

sources of violence in our society; Ulster, football hooliganism and picket-line violence,' then lectured them for two minutes about the lessons of the miners' strike. Although she listened to their views attentively, she countered them with a specific checklist of reforms: a ban on alcohol; ticket-only matches; registered supporters with identity cards.

Although this article attempts to correct some of the myths surrounding the stereotype of the soccer hooligan, we must keep in mind that it deals only with a small section of young people who regularly attend football matches. There are numerous images presented by the media on youth, ranging from the self-conscious dancers posing for the cameras on *Top of the Pops* to TV documentaries and newspaper articles on drug addiction and 'dole queue kids'. The mass media depend a great deal on youth, both in terms of providing the raw material for our consumption and in the creation of a lucrative buying market for their products. The way youth is presented in the mass media reflects some of society's concerns and misconceptions about young people in society generally.

EXERCISE

There are many magazines that are published for the female teenage market. They include *My Guy, Loving, 19, Mizz, Honey, Girl, Just Seventeen, Blue Jeans* and *Romance*.

1 What kind of articles are commonly featured in these magazines?
2 Get hold of one of these magazines and calculate roughly the percentage of advertising that is directed at young women readers in particular.
3 Can you think of any reasons why magazines for teenage girls (but not comics), which were unheard of 30 years ago, are now so popular?

Youth culture

In the UK in 1985 there were about 6.7 million people aged between 13 and 21. It is therefore not surprising that sociologists have shown a great interest in the culture of a social group that comprises nearly 12% of the population. In fact, the term **youth culture** has been invented to describe the way in which young people are socialised into a common, all-embracing but different set of values, beliefs and general lifestyle from that of the adult population. Youth culture implies that there is a fundamental difference, even a conflict, between the older generation and the younger generation. The sociologists Berger and Berger in *Sociology* have gone as far as suggesting that youth might be a social class in its own right, a class that recruits its young members from different social backgrounds, giving them a special status in the process.

In *Youth in a Changing Society* Fred Milson provides a helpful guide in showing us the forms that youth cultures are likely to take:

- The **assenters** are the most common groups whose members prefer to conform to the values of ordinary society. They are mainly regarded as well-adjusted youths who ritually strive for economic and social success, who willingly search for conventional pleasures and enjoyments. The vast majority of young people can be found in this category.
- The **experimenters** are activists and revolutionaries who wish to change society either through direct political action or by personal involvement. Student protesters and hippies are common examples.
- The **socially rejected** includes delinquent youth, the escapists and the plain disgruntled. In an economic slump these groups tend to increase in size as unemployment, poverty, homelessness and drug addiction rise.

How did this concept of youth culture originate? Has there always been a thing called youth culture?

During the mid-1950s many young people in Western Europe and the USA were subjected to a range of cultural experiences that seemed at the time to have a special meaning. The Rock 'n' Roll music of Bill Haley and the Comets, Elvis Presley, the later lyrics of Bob Dylan and the moody anti-authority acting of James Dean, symbolised for many young people the rejection of both the restrictions of childhood and the authority imposed by the adult world. Where previously a person was described either as a child or an adult, a new word or concept came into being – the teenager. A teenager, throughout the 1960s and 1970s, was a young person who characteristically attempted to challenge authority through direct action, music, clothes and lifestyle, in order to establish a personal independence. From the disturbances caused by the film *Rock Around The Clock* and the Teddy Boys of the 1950s, to the Hippies and Skinheads and the anti-Vietnam war demonstrations of the 1960s and 1970s, we have a continuing saga of young people, moulded into a separate and coherent body, that we can identify as a youth culture.

But can we be certain that there is a separate and unique social phenomenon called youth culture? Is it really a culture, a way of life, or is it something that has been created by the mass media to further their commercial ends? In a word, is youth culture a rip-off? Do we seriously believe that Elvis Presley, James Dean, Bob Dylan, Mary Quant, The Beatles, The Rolling Stones, The Who, Duran Duran, Tamla Motown, the reggae stars and Bruce Springsteen provide a focus for a youth culture, or are they just the talented sharp end of a money-grabbing Hollywood and the music business? When Presley's manager asked Elvis to stick a rubber pipe down his jeans to enhance his sexual profile, was this done to promote social rebelliousness among the young or was it a brilliant strategem to boost record sales by creating a monster for parents and a hero for youth? Sociologists are uncertain about these and other questions about the relationship between the media and youth culture.

In *Folk Devils and Moral Panics* Cohen suggested that the mass media may have helped to create the youth cultures on which they later depend for their stories. Youth cultures, Cohen noted, tend to fit neatly into the values of the tabloids and adult myths about 'how young people behave these days'. Can you think of any other commercial advantages to the mass media of a thriving youth culture?

The use of the terms **youth culture** and **teenager** as all-embracing concepts can be seen to be lacking in real meaning if we think about the unlikely possibility of 6.7 million people sharing similar, let alone identical, values and attitudes just because they fall into the same age group. This would smack not of rebelliousness but of slavish conformity. In the chapter *Social order* we have shown this to be an unattractive idea, as unattractive as the notion that you can have an all-embracing geriatric culture for all old-age pensioners. Young people, like old people, individually have different ideas about the world. In fact it might be more true to say that groups of young and old people from similar backgrounds are more likely to have common or shared values than groups of 18-year-olds from different backgrounds.

Society treats its youth in a variety of ways. As in the family home, young people in wider society are given more and more responsibility as they grow older. The law itself recognises growing up as a gradual process. The age of criminal responsibility, for example, does not begin until a child has reached the age of 10; so a 9-year-old cannot technically commit a crime. But with increasing age comes increasing responsibilities. At what minimum age can we:

- go into a public house
- pay adult fares on British trains
- consent to heterosexual acts
- consent to homosexual acts in private
- take out a credit agreement
- be asked to fight for our country
- leave home
- buy alcohol
- get married
- drive a car
- start work full-time or part-time
- place a bet in a betting shop?

The different ages at which we are allowed legally to carry out these activities demonstrates the difficulty society has in dealing with young people. Young people are encouraged to 'enjoy their youth' and 'sow their wild oats' (especially boys) before settling down to the routine of work and married life. At the same time they are expected to be 'responsible' and 'mature' in the way they conduct themselves. It is this inherent conflict which leads to rebelliousness and sometimes aggressiveness within sections of youth groups.

Much of the popular discussion on youth is based on sensationalised stories sometimes literally manufactured by the media. **Young People in Sex and Drugs Horror! Homeless Teenagers Enjoy Hotel Bonanza on the State** scream the headlines in the tabloids. The study of youth in sociology also leaves a little to be desired. This is especially true of the study of working class youth which invariably seems attractive to some middle class sociologists who seem to enjoy exploiting alleged anti-authority attitudes in young people, usually from the security of the university common room. Nevertheless, this area of study has progressed apace in the last 10 years and in the remainder of this chapter we will consider some of these advances. We will conclude this section with an article which portrayed the lifestyle of a teenage girl in the 1960s.

Suzy Goodtimes
by JANET ELLIS

Something exciting is happening in the land. Young people are behaving as they have never behaved before, and I for one wish I was sweet 17 all over again. Suzy works in her father's office in central London, and while she will *settle down* (her own words) in her 20s, from now until then it's *gonna be fun, fun, fun.*

She talked me through a week's gruelling social schedule. Monday night saw her dancing to the latest Tamla Motown records at *Upstairs*. Tuesday she went out for a drink with Phil (met him the night before) and Wednesday she had drinks with her friends Ann and Judy. Thursday was Gino's coffee bar in Oxford Street, a meal, then home and early to bed as the weekend approached. Friday, a late night at the *Stax* club. Saturday morning a lie-in and Saturday night the *Carlton Blues* club. Sunday night a drink with the DJ from the *Carlton*, Delroy D. *He was fun.* Goodbye Phil!

I bet you're exhausted just reading this, but for Suzy Goodtimes it was just another week in a life devoted to having fun in the endless search for pleasure. And this isn't something that only happens in the capital. No, it's something that's happening all over the country in these swinging times. Oh! to be 17 again!!!

EXERCISE

In what way do you think this description of the lifestyle of a young woman office worker in 1960s London is misleading?

This type of article promoted the myth of the swinging sixties. The idea that life was the same for all young people throughout the UK was a creation of the media, and though certain cultural changes were indeed taking place, the social structure hardly changed at all. The reason why such stories of young people were so wide of the mark was that they failed to take account of social differences between young people.

The most important social difference is social class. Think of Suzy Goodtimes for a moment. To enjoy her type of lifestyle a great deal of money is required, plus a car or the use of taxis and access to all the social facilities mentioned. In spite of what was implied, what happened in swinging London in the 1960s was unlikely to be happening in Cleethorpes or Wigan. In fact this is how one person remembers her youth in a northern industrial town:

I got a job in the local factory – I suppose that's something when you think about what's happening to school-leavers today – but all this talk of the swinging sixties seemed to pass me by. Sure I had a good time. I wore what every one else wore, but a lot of what went on only seemed to go on in the papers or on the telly. It wasn't for people like us. There was what they said was happening and what I knew was happening down the Locarno.

Youth and social class

As we have said, much of the sociology of youth cultures has failed to consider young people within a social context. The argument that *all* young people, by virtue of their age, are united and stand apart from adult society has 2 serious flaws:

- it oversimplifies and exaggerates the differences between 'adults' and 'youth'; and
- it fails to take into account the differences between young people from different social backgrounds.

The sociologists Murdock and McCron in *Youth and Class* explained it in this way:

Restoring class to the centre of the sociology of youth does not mean evacuating age. Clearly age is an important factor in structuring the social situation of young people. Some experiences, notably compulsory schooling, are youth specific. Similarly young people entering the labour market are particularly vulnerable to shifts and uncertainties in the structure of employment. Age also plays a key role in determining the range of options and choices available within the leisure environment. It is not therefore a question of simply substituting class for age at the centre of analysis but of examining the relations between class and age and more particularly the way age acts as a mediation of class.

This simply means that although age is important in locating young people within a legal and economic framework, the overriding feature of the sociology of youth is social class. As we have seen throughout this book, social class influences most aspects of

our life and experiences, from the type of houses we live in to the state of our health and the kind of education we receive. It would be sociologically unwise to ignore or underestimate social class when considering youth in our society.

In what way does class influence the social behaviour of young people?

We know from earlier chapters that the class to which we belong provides us with a particular set of life chances. Put simply, the expectations and opportunities for the sons and daughters of unemployed dockworkers are likely to be different from those of the sons and daughters of merchant bankers. The following story illustrates the social divisions which exist between young people:

Backpacking to nowhere

It was a wet August day as Winston stood distributing leaflets at Victoria Station. The leaflet informed anyone who bothered to read it about the wonders of FASTFOOD CITY which was located 100 metres from the station. Winston got paid in cash at the end of the day, not very much, but it boosted his dole money.

A young couple came towards him. 'We don't want one,' the girl said, as he tried to thrust a leaflet into her hand. 'We're heading for Greece'.

'Yeah,' her boyfried chipped in, 'we'll be gone for about 6 weeks.' They walked on, leaving Winston with one more leaflet to get rid of. He looked at them as they headed for the Dover train. It was all right for some, he thought.

Working at the station really depressed him, especially seeing all those kids who were heading for the sun on their holidays. They seemed

different from Winston in more ways than one. They were so bloody confident about everything they did. Nothing seemed to bother them like it bothered Winston. He heard them talking loudly and cheerfully to each other about how they would be 'doin' Europe' with their travel passes – sleeping rough, eating cheaply, thumbing lifts, visiting hostels, and maybe coming home at the end of September. That was the thing that got up Winston's nose, them coming home after 6 weeks' holiday and then going back to college. They would be the ones who would be getting the good jobs and turning out kids just like themselves when they got married.

He thought about how far he'd come since his father had arrived in Britain with Winston's grandmother. His father had got a job with the council, at least till he was made redundant. But somehow Winston hadn't quite made it. He knew that he was a bright kid, and not because the teachers at school had said so, but being bright wasn't enough. In fact it was a handicap – it let you know that you were being screwed into the ground.

The leaflets felt heavy in his hand. He looked about him and saw another young couple approaching, holding hands and listening to music on their Walkmans. Probably some song about social deprivation and injustice. Winston decided he had had enough. He tossed the leaflets into the air and walked through the tumbling cascade to the exit. When he was outside he realised that he had nowhere to go.

This story illustrates the differences in lifestyles between an unemployed working class youth who is drawn into low paid and illegal work to supplement his dole, and some carefree middle class youths who are 'doin' Europe' before returning to higher education. This suggests that any serious discussion of youth cultures must take into account the social and economic positions in which young people find themselves. The lifestyle of most youngsters on a Youth Training Scheme, for example, will differ markedly from the lifestyle of sociology students at university. Although members of both groups might enjoy similar types of music and clothes and cultivate their own forms of behaviour, some of which will incur the disapproval of the adult world (eg: smoking pot, buying motorbikes, sleeping rough, heavy drinking, fast driving, tattooing, striking fashions, football hooliganism), there remain none-the-less greater *differences* between the 2 groups. These differences are based on social class, which suggests that it is a mistake for sociologists to speak of an all-embracing youth culture in British society.

EXERCISE

Suggest in what way the lifestyles of these 18-year-olds are likely to be similar or dissimilar with regard to

a recreational pursuits   c type of friends

b personal finances   d prospects

- the daughter of a British managing director who is attending a Swiss finishing school for ladies
- the pregnant daughter of an unemployed one-parent West Indian family who is receiving training in shopwork on a Youth Training Scheme
- the son of a British Member of Parliament who has failed his A levels at public school.

Changing youth in a changing world

Since we have rejected the likelihood of a single, all-embracing youth culture, we will now consider the proposition that middle class and working class

youth have developed their own separate and special subcultures. In other words, how likely is it that youth subcultures originate and grow within the class system itself, with each youth group reflecting the wider problems and aspirations of its own class base? After all, as sociologists we know the importance of the family, peer group and education in shaping our life chances, so we must not be surprised to learn that young people are likely to be drawn to those subcultures that most closely fit their class needs.

Many sociologists regard youth subcultures as mutually antagonistic. The formation of Skinhead youth groups, for example, is thought to represent a hostile working class response to the 1960s middle class Hippies. Paul Willis in *Profane Culture* suggested that the hippy counter-culture, which was largely made up of college students and ex-students rejecting middle class values, was mostly ignored by working class youth, and positively unloved by the 'bike boys' who detested what were to them their weak and effeminate ways.

But how did these class-based youth subcultures develop? If they didn't exist 50 years ago, what made them suddenly appear and become a focus of interest to social scientists?

Until the late 1950s one unavoidable prospect facing all 18-year-old men in the UK was being called up for National Service in the armed forces. On average 160 000 men a year were recruited for a minimum two-year period. This removed young people from their communities, and especially from their peer groups, and placed them within a restrictive military discipline. The abolition of National Service in 1960 allowed

these young people to remain in their home towns to exploit new-found leisure time and the extra money they could earn in employment. Of course, as we have already mentioned, this trend began before 1960, and a key factor in the establishment of youth groups was Rock 'n' Roll music. An ex-Teddy Boy put it this way:

I remember hearing Little Richard's records for the first time. It was like listening to someone from another planet ... before then there had been just some old crooner singing about the girl next door, falling in love and getting married ... there was no excitement in that for an 18-year-old ... then came Elvis singing *Blue Suede Shoes* and Lonnie Donnegan's *Rock Island Line* ... and when I heard Elvis' *Jailhouse Rock* for the first time my head nearly exploded ...

The arrival of the Teddy Boys in the 1950s (so-called because their clothes were similar to those worn by dandies in the reign of Edward VII) represented the first identifiable group of young people who established a 'style' of their own. Their drainpipe trousers, 'beatle-crusher' suede shoes and striking hair styles made them stand out both from adults and other young people in the community. The Teds were essentially working class youth, who, with leisure time on their hands and some money in their pockets, were intent on doing their own thing, much to the disgust of their elders and the delight of the media. They formed their own subculture which made them distinct in what they perceived as a dull, boring world of adult rules and regulations.

The 1960s saw the rise of a number of different youth subcultures. Although the Rockers of this period, with their leather and bikes, were seen as extensions of the Teds, the Mods were different in that they were clean cut, smartly dressed and newly attached to the ultra-respectable scooter, which they managed to convert into a symbol of aggression and group solidarity. What made the Mods so different was their obsession with clothes and music which previously had only been 2 of many ingredients in popular youth culture. Artistes like Otis Redding, Sam and Dave and Wilson Picket, whose music had never been played on radio, performed in Mod clubs throughout the country. Whereas the Teds and Rockers emphasised their working class backgrounds, the Mods sidestepped theirs, distorting to some extent their lower middle class origins and values. Of course, any social movement involving large numbers of young people with an interest in clothes and music is bound to attract the attention of commercial interests, and the decline of the Mods was signalled when shops and chain stores began cashing in on Mod styles. One recurrent feature of youth subcultures is that once commerce, TV and radio take an interest, and the quality Sunday papers devote space to them, they soon tend to die.

Since the Mods and Rockers we have seen the emergence of Hippies, Skinheads, Punks and New Romantics. Of all youth subcultures, the Skinheads of the late 1960s and early 1970s are interesting to researchers because they reinforced and shared many working class adult values, rather than developed their own distinctive alternatives. They presented a masculine image, had short hair, were clean shaven, wore industrial safety boots, supported their turned-up jeans with old-fashioned buttoned-up braces, and preferred beer and pubs to wine and night clubs. They were antagonistic towards students and Hippies, and they gained a reputation for deviant behaviour towards certain minority groups that was eagerly reported in the press under the headings of 'queer bashing' and 'Paki-bashing'. In its way, the Skinhead subculture provided an example and a reminder of the relationship between youth culture and social class.

Another important youth subculture in Britain is based on the Caribbean religious cult of Rastafarianism. This movement draws its members mainly from young blacks living in inner city areas who look towards Ethiopia as their spiritual and racial home because it was an African country that was never colonised by white races. The importance of the Rastafarian movement to black youth should not be underestimated because it gives many alienated young British blacks a sense of identity in a society in which racist acts against black people are commonplace.

But the adoption of dreadlocks and an unusual style of dress has not only alienated young blacks from the wider white society, it has also brought them into conflict with their elders. However, since a Rastafarian is a member of the same society that has produced Skinhead and Bike Boy subcultures, he can expect to suffer the same kinds of disadvantages in education and job opportunities as poor white working class youth. In fact, as a member of a large black minority group, he has the added burden of having to cope with a white society that has given a hostile meaning to blackness.

The situation that many young people face today is one of long term unemployment, or at best a series of training opportunities which, for many, will not lead to a real job. What effect this will have on youth is something we will have to wait for, but there is no doubt that any new youth subcultures will be greatly affected by the social and economic position in which young people find themselves.

EXERCISE

Slam-dancing craze 'cover for violence'

STAFF REPORTER

Teenage thugs are using a dangerous dance craze as a cover for violence at pop concerts in the Midlands, it was claimed today.

Gangs of 16 and 17-year-olds are travelling to live pop shows in and around Birmingham to drink and fight – under the guise of the violent 'slam dancing' craze.

Trouble is breaking out as the teenagers leap around in a frenzy, barging into each other with fists and legs flailing in the dance craze which is alarming local doctors.

One Birmingham band, Balaam and The Angels, has had repeatedly to appeal to fans to stop. It believes trouble has been caused deliberately.

Mrs Kerry Jennings, 22, from Solihull, who helps manage the band, said: 'Teenagers are doing it purely to cause trouble and aggro. They aren't there to dance to the music.'

Doctors fear that there could be a tragedy.

The dance is associated with 'psychobilly' bands and recent shows by The Cult, The Meteors, and Primal Trash have been frenzied scenes. There was a brawl at The Meteors show at Burntwood Recreation Centre in Staffordshire.

Nationally known band The Cult said in a statement today: 'We do not want anyone to get hurt at any of our shows. We do not discourage genuine fans from dancing – but we are totally against violence.'

Source: Birmingham Evening Mail

Write short answers to these questions:

1 What evidence is given in this article to support the claim that there is increasing violence at pop concerts?

2 Why does the media take such an interest in reporting the deviant activities of youth?

3 As a student of sociology, make comments about the likely social backgrounds and cultural influences of these 'teenage thugs'.

QUESTIONS

1 'The reader's taste in political news is affected by his own political opinions, especially if they are strong ... most readers probably prefer news which confirms their own opinions to news which does not.'

Source: *Public Opinion: Changing Attitudes on Contemporary Political and Social Issues,* ed R Chandler, Bowker 1972

a What does this suggest about the possible effect of the media on the political attitudes of audiences?   (5 marks)

b If the statement above is true of media generally why then should people worry about the effects of TV on children?   (15 marks)

Source: AEB, 1981

2 a To what extent do you believe that audiences are susceptible to the control of the mass media?   (10 marks)

b Why is the research into the effects of television on deviant behaviour so inconclusive?   (10 marks)

3 'Youth is a class of its own'. Discuss   (20 marks)

Inquest on a rural riot

A pitched battle between police and hippies near Stonehenge last weekend has raised disturbing

questions about police methods of crowd control. **NICK DAVIES describes a police operation that went far beyond the 'doctrine of minimum force.'**

This weekend, the twisting country lanes of Wiltshire are witness to a bizarre and very un-English scene. Along the grassy verges underneath the beech trees, riot police sit waiting in their vans, windows darkened and reinforced.

On the A303 towards Amesbury there are road-blocks. And around the ancient monument of Stonehenge are rings of a peculiarly unpleasant type of barbed wire known as razor wire.

Just up the road, in Savernake Forest, is the object of this formidable concentration of police power – a group of some 300 hippies, members of the so-called Peace Convoy, whose battered buses and cars are drawn up between the trees, and who play rock music around camp fires late into the night.

Between the police and the Convoy stands the unlikely figure of David Michael James Brudenell-Bruce, the 32-year-old Earl of Cardigan, secretary of the Marlborough Conservative Association, Old Etonian and now, surprisingly, a passionate defender of the Convoy.

As the owner of Savernake Forest, Lord Cardigan has been drawn into a long and bitter feud between police and hippies which culminated last Saturday in scenes of extraordinary violence. Precisely what happened when 700 police officers in riot gear poured into a bean field at Park House near Cholderton, to take on 500 men, women and children, was witnessed at first-hand by relatively few outsiders.

All of us were shocked by what we saw: police tactics which seemed to break new bounds in the scale and intensity of its violence. We saw police throw hammers, stones and other missiles through the windscreens of advancing vehicles; a woman dragged away by her hair; young men beaten over the head with truncheons as they tried to surrender; police using sledgehammers to smash up the interiors of the hippies' coaches.

Lord Cardigan, who was in the field throughout, said: 'One image will probably stay with me for the rest of my life. I saw a policeman hit a woman on the head with his truncheon. Then I looked down and saw she was pregnant, and I thought: "My God, I'm watching police who are running amok."'

The events of last weekend raise a series of disturbing questions. Not just because this was a police operation that apparently slipped out of control, but because the officers involved seemed to be applying a new approach to policing.

The Wiltshire officers in charge, like those from the five other rural forces who helped them, have all been on duty at Greenham Common and throughout the miners' dispute. Their tough and aggressive attitude to the hippies owed more to the picket line than to normal standards of crowd control.

It was hard to discern in the events of last Saturday, the doctrine of minimum force that is enshrined in section three of the 1967 Criminal Law Act: 'A person may use such force as is reasonable in the circumstances in the prevention of crime, or in the effecting of, or assisting in, the lawful arrest of offenders ...'

That is not to say that the Peace Convoy and its advance towards Stonehenge was in any way a run-of-the-mill affair. The Convoy has been an annual irritant in Wiltshire since the first festival in 1974, when a small group of people who still clung obstinately to the ideals of the 1960s joined together to escape city life by living on the road.

Over the years, the Convoy has

expanded, picking up young unemployed, punks and Hells Angels, the inadequate and outcast.

They have cultivated an archaic faith in the power of the moon and the trees, and, more than anything else, in Stonehenge, where the Convoy was born, and where they go each year for their pilgrimage. At the summer solstice, on 21 June, they cross the road from their site to the stones and baptise their babies.

Their public face has been quite different. Absurdly exaggerated Press stories have pictured them overdosing on drugs, laying waste to the country, terrorising whole towns and beating the police into submission. 'Sex-mad junkie outlaws make Hells Angels look like Little Noddy,' as the *News of the World* put it. (In fact, the Convoy has one strict rule: no hard drugs.)

The Conservative MP for Salisbury, Robert Key, raised the matter in the Commons, where he spoke of hand-grenades, shotguns and armed law-breakers. He called for the army to be brought in. Later, he conceded that he had no direct evidence to support his allegations.

Source: *The Observer* (extracts) 9 June 1985

QUESTIONS

1 What is the media stereotype of the Hippy?
2 What advantages does the hippy lifestyle have compared with the lifestyle of a conventional nuclear family?
3 Why do you think the police acted with such violence against the Hippies? Do you think there is much support for this type of police action in general society?
4 In what way does a hippy counter culture depend on the support of mainstream society?
5 Suggest why social class is an important factor in the study of youth culture.

Points for discussion

● Social groups who create their own cultures ought to be supported by general society.
● Hippies are deviants who should be pressured into changing their lifestyles.
● Children brought up in a hippy culture are more likely to develop into wholesome citizens.

Case Study

To what depths can people sink? Just how much degradation and shame can people stand? This article, by our reporter Joss O'Riordan, makes horrific reading. It describes life as it really is some of our towns and cities. It could be happening on a housing estate near you right now! These are not isolated scenes but a sickening feature of life in Britain today.

Amongst the living dead

Janice is a bright, 19-year-old hardened drug addict. I met her in the Lord Nelson bar on the Ashton housing estate – SMACKLAND as it is known locally – and during my time with her I had insights into what life is like with the **Living Dead**. Janice sees herself as a cut above the rest of the **Smackheads**. She talked to me over pints of lager in the crowded pub.

'Sure, I'm into heroin, but I'm not totally without control. I've got a habit but I can manage it. I don't have to rob old ladies to get money for smack. I know some people do, but I don't.'

I asked Janice how she supported her habit.

'Whoring,' she glibly told me, 'I do a couple of tricks a night'.

I must have looked shocked because she went on to explain her 'street philosophy'.

'Most women give it away for nothing to their boyfriends – I just charge.'

I brought up the subject of boyfriends, loving relationships and marriage, but these were not on her agenda.

'C'mon,' she continued, 'you get married, get a crappy little house, a couple of kids, and the old man, Mr Wonderful, falls asleep every night on the settee in front of the telly with a gut full of beer – that's love and marriage? You can keep it. Anyway half the blokes I pick up are so-called happily married men. I'd rather be dead than live like that.'

I told Janice that if she persisted with her present way of life her death might be sooner than later.

'Sure,' she said with a frightening casualness, 'it could happen, but at least I'm dying the way I wanna die.'

Listening to Janice in the Lord Nelson, I wondered if all the anti-drug publicity and campaigns were a waste of effort. It seemed to me that people like Janice are hell bent on destroying themselves, and we are wasting our time and money trying to save people like her.

Later in the evening she took me to a derelict building on the north side of the estate, here I met more **Smackheads**. Heroin had just been shared out and bodies littered the floor and people mumbled incoherently to one another. A large bundle of what looked like old rags lay in the corner of the room. Janice told me it was Dave and Patsy with their arms wrapped around each other. She told me that they were in love. They were in love all right, they were in a **Death Embrace**!

The room stank of stale urine and wherever you walked you stepped on used syringes and bits of crinkled silver paper funnels.

'It's OK in here,' Janice told me,

'one of the best squats I've been in.'

This I could hardly believe! I had a feeling welling up inside me that I was having a glimpse of hell. **And these people were the Devil's disciples**!!!

I sat on the floor and tried to make out what was being said, but it was impossible. The heroin was speaking and conversations were unintelligible, a collection of meaningless words and desperate moans. I stayed in this hell-hole for an hour before Janice told me it was time for her to go to work. The pubs would be turning out soon and she would be ready to entice some drunk up a back alley to get money for her habit.

'I'm off now,' she said, 'I hope you got what you wanted.'

I said nothing as we walked towards the Lord Nelson. As I turned away I couldn't help wondering whether she would be around in a year's time. The one thing I was certain of was that there are thousands more like her. The youth of Britain in the 1980s are, it seems, hell bent on destroying themselves, and I had the terrible feeling that there was very little society could do to help. **Something told me that on the Ashton estate I witnessed the beginning of the end of our society with its long traditions and once-cherished values.**

QUESTIONS

1 a What stereotypical picture does the writer paint of the heroin addict?
  b Are there likely to be other types of heroin addicts? Explain.

2 a What types of deviant behaviour has the journalist observed in this drug subculture?
  b What other forms of deviant behaviour are likely to be present?
3 a What techniques does the writer adopt to bring drama to the story?
  b What kinds of information has the writer chosen to omit that might have thrown more light on the causes of drug addiction?
4 How can articles like this lead to a moral panic?
5 The stereotype is a useful if distorting device used frequently on TV. Explain how British TV writers tend to stereotype:
  a Nazi army officers
  b Mothers-in-law
  c Irishmen
  d KGB agents
  e Male homosexuals
  f Barmaids.

Points for discussion

- Newspapers have very little effect in changing people's minds.
- News doesn't happen – it is made.
- We can thank the media for protecting us against vested interests.

Important points

- Mass media are systems of communication which transmit ideas, values and information to a large dispersed audience.
- There are significant social class, age and sex variations regarding the quality and quantity of media products consumed by the general public.
- The media's function is to fulfil important personal and social needs, such as the need for information, diversion, ritualisation, and to communicate social class.
- The media play a vital role in shaping our view of the social world. They are agents of **secondary socialisation**, providing models on which children can base their social behaviour. The media are a major disseminator of culture.
- Sociologists are unsure about the relationship between violence portrayed in the media and behaviour problems in children and young people.
- There is evidence to suggest that the media contribute to the creation of deviant behaviour amongst young people, and to the exaggerated fear of deviance in the general population.
- The media simplify messages through the creation of stereotypes. Stereotypes are false, short-hand images of people and situations that may promote prejudice in the general population.
- Youth cultures, which originated in the 1950s, are usually associated with music, clothes, behaviour and the general lifestyle of groups of young people.
- The concept of a common youth culture ignores the important fact that young people are themselves brought up in different social class backgrounds.

12 Social change

When you have worked through this chapter you should have a clearer understanding of

Industrialisation · **Urbanisation** · **Conurbations** · **Community** · **Simple and diverse economies** · **Social mapping** · **Concentric zones** · **Macro and micro effects of social change** · **Belief systems** · **Functions of religion** · **Secularisation**

Industrialisation and urbanisation

In a world that is constantly undergoing social change, part of the task of the sociologist is to identify and explore these changes and to try to explain why they are taking place. From other chapters in this book you will know that throughout this century the family, the education system and the structure of the population have all undergone change and you should now be aware of the social and economic factors which brought about these changes.

To bring your thinking back into focus, describe briefly the way in which family structures have changed during the last 100 years.

You will have noted that we have changed from a society of extended families to a society of nuclear families and that most families in 20th century industrial societies live in towns and cities and not in the countryside. This movement of people from rural to urban areas to create a population that lives mainly in large towns and cities is called **urbanisation**. We also use the same term to describe the spread of urban

values and culture throughout the whole of our society, even to those families who continue to live in the countryside. This means that urbanisation is both a movement of population *and* a movement of culture and ideas.

As sociologists we know that social change *does not happen by chance*. It occurs as a result of a combination of social and economic influences. We also know that social change *does not stop* but continues as part of an endless social and historical process. The world as we understand it is different from the world of our parents when they were young, and will no doubt differ from the world we will experience in 30 years' time.

However, the most dramatic social change in European society came with the introduction of industrialisation, mainly during the 19th century. In fact sociology itself developed as a response to the social and political changes resulting from the industrial revolution in Britain and the political revolution in France. Both revolutions changed the social fabric of society, and the sociologist Durkheim wrote his

study *The Division of Labour in Society* in an attempt to understand the changes resulting from the transition of simple traditional rural communities to modern complex societies. Durkheim saw that life in rural societies was close-knit, with country people depending on each other for most of their material and social needs within communities that gave great support to the individual. Life in urban areas was vastly different in that it was impersonal and people were, to a great extent, strangers to each other. For Durkheim, the central question was how could society survive this change.

His answer lies buried in the title of his study *The Division of Labour in Society*. He argued that in village life, in a traditional society, people often share the same values and religious beliefs. However, as urban dwellers come together from different social and economic cultures (perhaps from other countries) something else is needed to bind people and groups together to prevent social chaos. This something else is the **division of labour**, which refers to the way work is broken down into specialised tasks to be carried out by different workers. Think for a moment of a shipyard. No one worker or even a single group of specialist workers builds an entire ship. Individuals with different skills combine to build a ship, each group of workers making a contribution by producing a different part. This specialisation binds urban workers together. Put simply, in an industrial society workers depend on each other for their own social and economic survival.

EXERCISE

According to Durkheim, urban society is possible because the division of labour gives work an enhanced social meaning. In your school or college, explain in what way these specialist workers might find social satisfaction in their jobs:

- the school caretaker
- the cleaners
- the dinner ladies
- the lollipop man.

How would Durkheim explain the connection between urbanisation, the division of labour and the growth of trade unions?

Town and country life

Although we can appreciate that the growth of industrial society brought about great changes to the social organisation of Britain, we should not see this development as anything other than a complex and lengthy process. In the 1801 *Census* 9.73% of the population of England and Wales lived in the London area and only a further 7.21% lived in towns of 20 000 people or more. It wasn't until the middle of the 19th century that the urban population was greater than the rural population, and since 1911 about 80% of the population of Britain have lived in urban areas:

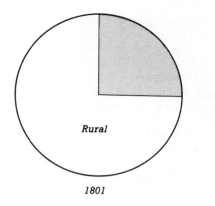

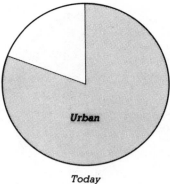

Today, of the people who live and work in large towns and cities, over 50% of them live in the 7 **conurbations**, which are large geographical areas so dense with towns and cities that they each form one huge urban sprawl:

The urban and rural population balance in 1801 and today

The seven conurbations

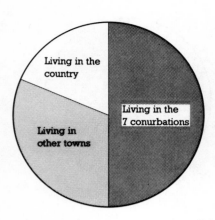

Where people now live in Britain

The 7 conurbations are: Greater London, Clydeside, West Yorkshire, Merseyside, West Midlands, Tyneside and South East Lancashire. You might like to identify the conurbations for yourself by matching them with the black areas on the illustration of Britain.

However, we should note that the pattern of industrialisation and urbanisation during the last 200 years differed from region to region and was dependent on the growth of the population and the availability of work in the developing industries. Far too often a picture of 'instant' industrialisation is painted when we are led to believe that suddenly armies of people left the fields and farms to seek work in the towns. This is an over-simplification of a social process that took many decades.

Some sociologists like to draw a distinction between social life in the country and in towns and cities. Robert Redfield in *The Little Community* thought that rural or village life tends to produce fewer social problems because communities are small and the inhabitants tend to share the same social and economic experiences within a common culture. In fact,

to all sociologists a community is not just a collection of individuals living together in one great jumble. It implies a society of people that have many things in common to form a coherent social group who generally get on well together. This does not mean that a community is a simple form of society. Although it might appear simple, small and economically unimportant, it will be bursting with complicated social relationships, as this woman can testify:

I was glad to leave the village and come and live in town. I feel much freer here. In the village it was impossible to be alone. Everybody knew what you were up to and people were always poking their noses into your business. Everybody knew everybody else. They were all very friendly, like, but I prefer to be more independent. But it's hard to get used to the idea that there are people living on this estate I have never even met.

Redfield would argue that although these folksy close-knit communities can no longer survive in a modern world they are nonetheless the basic units of society. He would point out that large towns and cities should not automatically be thought of as communities just because of their size and importance. Indeed, forcing people to live in urban areas can lead to:

- **Loneliness and alienation** People may find difficulty in making friends and creating a neighbourhood atmosphere in a big impersonal city. Close relatives living miles away may well increase the sense of isolation and loneliness, and the more hurried way of life only adds to the tension.
- **Social problems** Congestion of population in towns and cities, and overcrowding in particular areas, give rise to acute social problems involving ill-health, poverty, pollution and growing

crime rates. Whether crime actually increases in urban areas is arguable, but it *seems* to be more prevalent because there are more opportunities to commit crime and a greater chance of getting caught because there are more police officers on duty. Suicide and mental breakdown are also more common in urban areas.

As you might expect, not all sociologists share this opinion of urban life. In *The Urban Villagers* Herbert Gans chose to study a slum area called the 'West End' in Boston, USA. He described a population of several ethnic groups, including Italians, Jews, Poles, Albanians and Greeks, many of whom lived in run-down poorly maintained tenement flats separated by rubbish-strewn, vermin-infested alleys. It was a poverty-stricken modern American city suburb of a classic variety.

Gans was surprised to find not loneliness and alienation but a basically friendly neighbourhood in which people were eager to say hello to each other and share each other's problems. Although drunkenness, bad debts, mental illness and street violence were common enough, most people were quick to offer a helping hand if their neighbours were in trouble, especially if they were of the same ethnic group. Unlike middle class families in the outer suburbs, the inhabitants of the West End found group comfort in knowing a lot about each other's business as it was difficult to be completely hidden from view in this overcrowded, bustling slum community. Gans concluded that social relationships prospered in this 'urban village' just as effectively as they would in a rural setting because of ethnic loyalties *and* because survival in such a difficult urban environment depended on close human ties. In a word, the West Enders needed each other.

These conflicting views of rural and urban communities were brought together by Ronald Frankenberg in his *Communities in Britain*. He argued that urban life has a slight edge over rural life in the advantages it offers, although he accepted that the initial shock of moving into a city from the countryside can cause loneliness and alienation. Frankenberg maintained that there are important differences between living in 'truly rural' and 'less rural' areas of Britain. You will have gathered from these studies that we should not be too hasty in drawing conclusions about rural and urban life. We must not fall into the trap of thinking that there is a simple country life on one hand, and a complex urban life on the other. One of the consequences of industrialisation and urbanisation is that they produce in many of us, perhaps in some researchers too, an idealised view of what it means to live in rural Britain.

Examples from Frankenberg's model of rural and urban life

Rural Life	Urban Life
Community In a rural society people meet frequently, and they often have many interests in common to create a community atmosphere. The village postman might simultaneously be your best friend, your landlord, the publican, and captain the village darts team. There will be fully attended meetings in the village hall to discuss vital issues, and regular village fêtes.	**Association** In cities, people might have a large number of relationships based on personal needs, but they do not often overlap. You will tend to have different personal friends from the people you work with, and it is unlikely you will know the name of your postman or be friends with the person who delivers your newspapers.
Simple economy Most inhabitants will be engaged in agriculture or rural crafts, and the whole social and economic life of the village will revolve mainly around this single activity.	**Diverse economy** The population will be engaged in whole range of different productive activities, and there may be a greater readiness for individuals to switch from one type of occupation to another.
Little division of labour Country people expect to turn their hands to anything. A farmworker might drive the tractor, herd cattle, fell trees, pick fruit and mend the roof of the barn.	**Specialisation** In urban societies few jobs overlap. Industrialisation has traditionally led to specialised jobs requiring long periods of training.
Ascribed status In rural societies social position is often determined by family origin. Status is strongly associated with *who* the person is, which will usually determine how he is treated.	**Achieved status** This is determined more by *what* the individual has become, rather than by his family background. A person's occupation, and not his birth, will be more important in determining status.
Integration To the worker in a rural society there is often an obvious link between him and his family and the produce of his labour. Most of the family might be working in agriculture and occasionally consume produce from the farm.	**Alienation** To the urban worker, factory and office work has little personal meaning. The products of work are mere commodities. Thus a typist can see no direct link between what she produces and her personal life experiences.

What does living in the countryside mean to you?

Most urban dwellers see the 'nice' side of rural life. The pace of life is gentler and there is something satisfying about the idea of 'working the soil' and 'growing your own food'. Everything is neat and tidy, rather like the scenes printed on postcards and chocolate boxes. Of course rural life is, and always has been, nothing like this. There is social and economic inequality in the countryside (who owns those large farms?), poverty (farm workers are amongst the lowest paid in the country) and danger (the number of accidents with machinery is substantial) just as there are in urban society. We should also be aware that social and economic changes are still rapidly taking place in rural communities, with the farmer working just a few acres a thing of the past. Land is very valuable now, and most farms are highly mechanised. A new word has entered our language: **agribusiness**, to describe how large farms are often owned by international corporations and run as very efficient businesses.

Many villages are now attracting wealthy young couples from the cities either to buy second homes in the countryside or to live in the villages and travel to work on the recently-built motorway system. Some villages are filling up with retired couples who have been drawn by the chocolate box image, but who nevertheless help to push up house prices, often to the point where farm workers are forced to leave their low paid jobs to find work in the towns. Whatever may be happening in any particular village, the image of the pipe-smoking gentleman farmer, leaning against a 5-bar gate watching his cows go by, is based on a rural myth and certainly has no place in the competitive and harsh world of rural life in the late 20th century.

EXERCISE

Taking a small Welsh mining village of 250 inhabitants as an example, what would be the likely consequences of major coalmine closure on:

- family life
- local commerce
- social problems in the community
- the size and composition of the village population and the population of a nearby city?

The growth of cities

We have seen that the process of social change known as urbanisation is the movement of people from rural communities to towns and cities. For the American sociologist Louis Wirth a city has 3 essential features: population size, population density and heterogeneity, which means it contains several groups of people of different cultures living closely together. Although a city dweller might experience many more social contacts than his rural counterpart, he might equally experience a feeling of isolation and alienation. In Wirth's opinion, an individual's social experiences in the city are likely to be of an impersonal and threatening nature. Wirth was one of the many sociologists who established themselves and their work in the 1920s and 1930s to become known as the 'Chicago school'. They were basically a group of social researchers who were interested in the way cities develop.

A leading thinker of the Chicago school, Ernest Burgess, in his *The Growth of the City*, provided us with a useful concept of 'social mapping' to help us to understand social change within heavily populated urban areas. His idea, based on a study of the growth of Chicago, was that pressure of population led to an expansion of a city in patterns of concentric circles, rather like the waves caused by a pebble thrown into a pond. This encouraged Burgess to consider cities in terms of what he called 5 **concentric zones**.

If you imagine for a moment that you are accompanying Burgess through the various zones he identified within city areas, your journey might take you through the following scenes. Starting in **Zone 1** you find yourself in the central business district where the cost of land is extremely high. Here you find the Town Hall, banks, various commercial and government offices and insurance companies. Travelling from Zone 1 into **Zone 2** you enter an area of run-down, deteriorating, multi-occupied houses, flats and bedsitters, badly in need of repair, housing various groups including newly arrived immigrants, students and poor single parent families. In **Zone 3** you observe a more established and settled area where well-constructed houses, laid out in neat housing estates, are occupied mainly by working class people. Travelling to **Zone 4** takes you into a well-established middle class residential area of more expensive and desirable properties, before you finally enter **Zone 5**. This zone is many miles from the city centre and most of the families are multi-car-owning and affluent. They are living in high-status very expensive detached houses and bungalows near to parkland and the greenbelt.

Burgess argued that each zone was in itself a 'natural area', attracting and retaining particular social groups who tend to share a common lifestyle and culture. For example, a young single person with artistic ambitions might feel more comfortable living in Zone 2 than in Zone 5, at least to begin with. Although we cannot always identify city life exactly in the way Burgess did, there are certain valid and interesting points to be drawn from his observations.

In fact it was Zone 2 that

Concentric zone development of cities

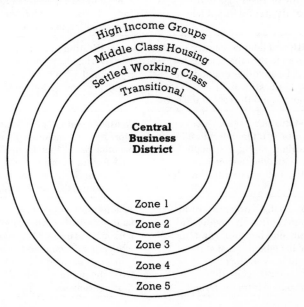

Zone 1
Zone 2
Zone 3
Zone 4
Zone 5

became the focus of interest for many sociologists because they identified it as a setting without a well-defined community atmosphere, and a source of social and economic deprivation. The famous study by Coates and Silburn, *Poverty: The Forgotten Englishman*, with its description of the St Ann's area of Nottingham, is an interesting example that can be found in the chapter *Education*.

However, not all cities are laid out like this. In some British cities many people live in or near the city centre in 'high rise' developments, usually council owned, or in small private housing estates built in sheltered enclaves and convenient for shopping. A famous piece of research, conducted by the *Centre of Urban Studies* in the 1960s on some high rise council flats in London called Churchill Gardens, found an active Tenants' Association which helped to foster a vigorous community atmosphere. Even so, many cities present a drab, soulless image and it is unrealistic to think that all or even most of the occupants of high rise flats, which often house a large proportion of unemployed and poor families, enjoy anything but an unsatisfactory lifestyle. Robert Roberts' *The Classic Slum*, based on Salford and describing much poverty and hardship, is probably more representative. Perhaps the most important point about all the studies of city life is that they tell us that a city is a very complex social place indeed and we must be on our guard against over-simple explanations.

EXERCISE

Select any city that you know fairly well and discuss how it compares with Burgess' zonal model. Taking each zone of your city in turn, try to assess differences and similarities with regard to

- ethnic groups
- social class grouping
- living accommodation.

Social change and consciousness

As we have already discussed consciousness in the context of social class, we can now broaden our understanding of this concept in more general terms. Put simply, consciousness relates to our attitudes, values and thoughts about a number of different social matters. It derives from our experience of the world, our background, and from our primary and secondary socialisation. We can best understand this difficult concept by examining how people from different social groups, with differing kinds of consciousness, see an identical event:

Women win support

The new town of Keating today experienced its first taste of old-fashioned trade union solidarity. Fifteen sewing machinists went on official strike at Blanchard Garments and found instant support from other trade unionists in the area. In sympathy, workers from a nearby engineering plant and white-collar trade unionists from the Town Hall marched behind the women strikers as they paraded through the town. One full-time union official expressed his surprise this way: 'What this shows is that solidarity between different workers is alive and well. This is a great day for Keating.'

Indeed, Keating had never seen anything like it. The peaceful march, led by trade union leaders carrying their bright banners, was reminiscent more of union activity in mining communities than a market

town. Whatever the outcome of the strike, and the women are convinced that they will resist the introduction of short-time working, life in sleepy Keating will never be the same again.

How does this account help us to understand consciousness?

Look at these occupations and indicate how each person might describe what is taking place in Keating. You should explain why you think each person might see events from a different angle:

- a stockbroker
- a miner
- a female clerical worker
- an employer.

The differences in opinions and attitudes will to some extent be related to the social class to which the person belongs and to the individual's personal experiences. In other words our experiences in the social world are likely to shape our awareness of the world and strongly influence how we see particular events, which is what we mean by 'consciousness'. But how does this help us to understand the nature of social change? Look carefully at the 2 photographs on page 210. Having examined the illustrations, write down what each one means to you and the kind of life you associate with it. Compare your answer with a fellow student's to see where you agree and disagree.

Your own response will be influenced by your past experiences and your social background. Those who have lived in a large town or city with little experience of rural life will see the countryside illustration differently from those with mainly rural backgrounds. Similar interpretations can be made about the urban scene. In short, our understanding of the illustrations

an expensive car.

How do your attitudes, values, hopes and fears compare with a poor person's attitudes who happens to live in famine-torn Africa? How do people in that desperate setting understand the future? What views do they have about violence on TV, inflation and nuclear war? The answer is none at all. Such matters have no meaning in a society of starving people. Their consciousness is determined by their horrific social and economic conditions, and the thrust of their thinking is directed at when (or if) they are to get their next mouthful of food.

In discussing consciousness we are suggesting that we all carry society around with us, inside our heads, and the values and attitudes of our society impinge on us constantly, even when we are alone. So when we think of social change we not only have to consider factors such as the breakup of traditional communities and the growth of urban societies, but also how our awareness of the world and our consciousness changes. Consciousness is an important aspect of social change and one we should not ignore.

EXERCISE

April 1911
Bronwen had been walking out with Hugh for nearly 3 years. They had known each other since childhood and everyone said they were made for each other. So it was no surprise when they announced they would marry in early summer. Hugh had a steady job as a machine fitter and Bronwen's parents thought he would be a good provider. Bronwen was level-headed and she could turn her hand to anything. She would make a good wife and home for them both.

April 1986
Carole met Spencer at a disco at the end of a great evening. He said he'd phone her at the office the next day. She didn't think he would, but he did.

(and of the real world) differ not because we see them differently but because we *interpret* them differently, depending on our individual social experiences.

Taking this idea a little further, let us think about our hopes for the future as an example. You may know only too well that because of high unemployment jobs will be scarce, and this will force you into a position where you will soon have to make some crucial decisions about your lifestyle and social behaviour, such as whether to stay on at school or college or attempt to find work as soon as

possible. Although you don't really know how life and circumstances will change for you in the next 20 years, your present consciousness or awareness will alert you to certain possibilities that are within the range of your cultural expectations. Your consciousness will in effect be instrumental in determining how you will change or modify your social behaviour. For instance, it is unlikely that you seriously entertain the possibility of starving to death, but you know that you will have to secure a well-paying job before you can buy

They had a whirlwind romance and after a holiday in Spain together they announced that they would get married in the autumn. Carole had a good job at the bank which she enjoyed, and Spencer made a lot of money in the building trade.

These accounts describe similar social events in 1911 and 1986. When you have answered the following questions you will be able to see that not only have the couples' circumstances changed materially, but also culturally. These cultural changes in social expectations are an indication of the shifting nature of consciousness. (You might find it helpful to re-read the chapter on *The family*.)

What would be considered the expected social behaviour and attitudes of both couples towards:

- Finding somewhere to live
- Relationships with relatives
- Divorce
- The role of men and women at home and at work
- The size of family
- The education of children.

Macro and micro effects of change

One way of understanding the nature of social change is to think of it as operating at 2 distinct levels. The first is the **macro** level, which refers to change affecting institutions that make important contributions to the organisation of society, such as families, schools and businesses. The second is the **micro** level, which describes the effects of social change on an individual, on a person's behaviour and consciousness.

The following account was written by a sociology student researching into aspects of social change in a small town. She provides an excellent description of both the macro and micro effects of this social process:

Life in Millbank

Thirty years ago Millbank was a thriving town of 10 000 people. Industry was centred on two factories which provided employment for the majority of the townspeople. One factory, Millbank Electronics, produced radios and hi-fi equipment, and won numerous international awards for its products. The second factory, Millbank Garments, produced high quality men's shirts which again were internationally known. The local shops, pubs, small businesses and housing market thrived as these two industries prospered. Millbank was a good place to live. It was situated near to the coast and surrounded by magnificent countryside, and boasted of a close-knit community atmosphere. People worked hard for their money, but they enjoyed spending it, and each summer the townspeople, almost to a person, made a contribution to the Millbank Community Festival. Then the decline set in.

The electronics industry was the first to experience competition from Hong Kong and it soon became clear that Millbank Electronics could no longer survive. Cheap imports flooded the home market and it wasn't long before the factory closed down. If cheap imports had destroyed the electronics industry, the other factory, Millbank Garments, was soon to suffer the same fate.

'It was the beginning of the end,' Bill Sykes, a local councillor, told me 'It wasn't long before the full economic effects were felt in Millbank. Takings were down in the shops and the folks couldn't pay their rents or keep up with their mortgages. Suddenly we were a community in crisis.'

One of the immediate effects of this was that the young people started to move away. There was no work in the area so they had to find work in the larger towns and cities. This started to shift the balance in the structure of the population of the town.

'Now we're faced with an ageing population,' Bill continued, 'which is a drain on the social services. Because sons and daughters live miles away they are not available to deal with any problems facing their parents – so more social workers and home helps are needed. It is a vicious circle.'

As you walk through the town it is hard to imagine that once this was a thriving community. There is a general air of hopelessness and despair. Many shops are boarded up and, as someone told me in the deserted White Swan, anyone who starts a business in Millbank wants their head examined. The landlord told me that the spirit of Millbank had been destroyed. 'People don't get on as well as they used to,' he said, 'everyone keeps themselves to themselves. We used to organise lots of events from this pub. Now no-one wants to know.'

The people who don't want to know are the young people. It's a short step from school to the dole for the youngsters and one thing they hate hearing about is the good old days. Gary Clarke told me outside the Jobcentre (renamed in grafitti the Jokecentre): 'My old man always goes on about how good it was to live in Millbank. Well, as far as I've known, this place has always been a dump. I grew up with my dad out of work, and now I've joined him. It's the same everywhere. The place is dead. Everywhere's dead.'

Talking to Gary about the 'good old days' is like talking about life on another planet. It's so remote from his experience that it has no real meaning. Both young and old in Millbank agree that their future is bleak.

EXERCISE

1 What were the economic effects

of factory closures in Millbank?

2 How did the people respond to this change?

3 How can we explain the attitudes and behaviour of the young people?

4 Suggest the macro and micro effects of social change in your own town or city if a major company were to close. What effect would the closure have on you or your family?

Belief systems and social change

One aspect of human activity affected by social change during the industrialisation of Britain was religion. Until this time Christian religious worship had been an activity conducted mainly in small, dispersed churches throughout rural Britain. Of course, religious rituals and ceremonies, often taking magical or superstitious forms, have always been associated with rural societies, and many of our Christian festivals have their origins in ancient pagan cults. Late December, for example, which was the high point of pagan religious life that heralded the new year, was chosen as a suitable time to celebrate Christ's unknown birthday about 300 years after his death.

During the 19th century the urbanisation of Britain involved the widespread building of churches and chapels on a scale similar to that of factories and houses. Religious worship, along with almost everything else, became urbanised on a grand scale. This didn't mean that the urban population was becoming more religious. Urban church building is not an accurate indicator of religious feeling, any more than the crudely-built rural churches of earlier centuries had more

religious significance than the forest temples and stone monuments of pre-Christian Britain.

But why should sociologists be interested in religion anyway?

Wherever we are in the world it will not be long before we come across a building, of one sort or another, which is set aside for the purpose of religious worship. There are vast numbers of religions in human society and what they have in common is that their followers believe in the existence of a supernatural Being or a divine force that is alleged to exist outside the normal world. This Being or divine force might be called God, Buddha or Mohammed. Whether or not supernatural Beings exist does not really concern sociologists. What does concern them is the social significance of religion and its relationship to other aspects of society.

Sociologists acknowledge that everybody is committed to a range of beliefs or attitudes of one form or another. When sufficient numbers of like-minded people begin to hold similar deeply-held beliefs and join together to form a coherent body of believers, religious or otherwise, they are said to be engaged in a 'belief system'. This means that group members hold a wide range of similar ideas about how to live and behave in society. In other words, belief systems eventually become ingredients in the overall culture of society. A description of a religious belief system, Hinduism, which is deeply embedded in Indian culture, can be found in the chapter *Social stratification and social class*.

Just because a group of people share a belief system that they hold to be right and true does not of course mean that it is right and

true. After all, most religious beliefs, taken literally, exclude the possibility of other belief systems being true. Membership of the club is exclusive. Neither does it mean that members can necessarily 'prove it' or completely understand their beliefs to the point at which they can argue a powerful case. Nor does it mean that a person cannot hold say 2 sets of contradictory ideas at the same time, or be aware that not all religious creeds can possibly be true simultaneously. A belief system is essentially a *belief*, and it does not depend on rational or scientific argument for its existence. Here is the view of a leading space scientist:

The more mankind discovers about the universe, the more I am convinced in my belief in the existence of God. It is inconceivable to me that the vastness of the cosmos, governed as it is by precise laws of science, can possibly be the result of random godless events.

However, we must not think that all belief can be expressed in this cosy armchair way. Strongly-held belief systems have drawn people to bitter controversy, banishment, torture, death and bloody war. In the late middle ages the Crusaders (Christians) were prepared to fight and die not only for war booty but to 'punish the infidel Turks' (Muslims) for their capture of Jerusalem and cruelty to Christians, and an estimated 10 000 'witches' were burnt on the stake by Christians in 17th century Europe. Today, rigidly-held beliefs in one political or religious creed or another are important components in conflicts in the Middle East, India, and nearer home in Northern Ireland.

Although a religious belief system, Christianity, dominates religious thought in our present-day society, we know that there are many other religious groups outside the Christian faith. We also know that within Christianity there are several different 'Churches', such as the Church of England, the Catholic Church and the Methodist Church.

EXERCISE

Strange objects found in wood

Mysterious occult objects, including a broken cross on which symbols were engraved, and fragments of charred animal flesh, were discovered in Pipers Wood near the A34 early on Thursday morning.

Farm labourer Ray Birch, aged 25, stumbled upon these strange objects as he took a short cut through the wood on his way to work. He immediately alerted the police.

Police constable George Millar was called to the scene, and he discovered further items scattered around a small clearing deep in the wood. These were a bloody knife, fragments from the headstone of a grave, oddments of clothing and a great number of shoeless footprints.

A police spokesman later said that although he didn't believe that criminal offences had been committed, the police were anxious to interview anyone who had seen or heard anything suspicious around Pipers Wood late on Wednesday night.

How might a sociologist interpret these strange events in Pipers Wood? In your answer, comment on

- belief systems
- the reasons for secrecy
- the significance of the objects found in the wood.

Religion in society

Before we discuss religious life in society

- draw up a list of as many religious groups as you can think of which practise their faith in Britain, and
- choose one group and explain in what way its faith influences its members' everyday behaviour.

Sociologists have always been fascinated by the number and variety of religious beliefs in the world because religion has a great influence not only on how people think (their religious consciousness) but also on how they behave. The French sociologist Emile Durkheim was very interested in religion and he defined it as:

A unified system of beliefs and practices relative to sacred things, uniting into a single moral community all those who adhere to those beliefs and practices.

What does Durkheim mean by this? In your own words, explain the meaning of the phrases 'a unified system of beliefs and practices' and 'a single moral community'.

To Durkheim, religion gives meaning to people's lives. In his *The Elementary Forms of Religious Life* he argues that simple rural societies rely on religion to ensure survival by appealing to the gods for short term benefits such as rain during drought and protection in battle. Durkheim himself did not believe in the supernatural, but he did believe that human beings need religion to provide a symbolic and awe-inspiring divine force to help them cope with the apparent meaninglessness of their lives. He argued that religion binds us together, within a common moral order, not in the worship of a supernatural god, but in worship of ourselves. Durkheim is saying that since gods do not exist, then the only thing left to worship is society itself.

What, in ordinary human terms, does all this mean? Can it be possible that millions of religious worshippers are deluded, that since the beginning of human society they have been praying to non-existent gods? How would Durkheim understand and interpret this man's beliefs, for example?

The Believer

Mr Harris took his usual place in the church. He always sat just about halfway from the main aisle. He had taken this same place for many years now. In fact most of his memories were centred on Saint Gregory's. He was married there more than 30 years before. His children had been baptised there and his eldest daughter had been married there only a few weeks back.

Since he had been made redundant, Mr Harris not only attended church on Sundays but on other days too. He found it a peaceful place where he could sit and think. He would stay for an hour or so, then visit his wife's grave in the churchyard. He took great pride in keeping the grave nice and tidy and he would often be seen kneeling there in quiet prayer.

When Mr Harris looked around him in church he would see people he had known for years. In this small community most people knew one another. The church was where everyone was brought together – men and women, young and old and the rich and not-so-rich. It was a great comfort for Mr Harris to share his troubles. News of his redundancy had come as a bitter blow. His pride and self-esteem had been shattered and he had spent hours questioning the justice of it all. In his brooding despair he felt there was something totally unfair about life. The rich could always survive a recession – it was those at the bottom of the ladder who seemed to suffer most.

But he had to rid himself of such

thoughts. He told himself that his plight, and the plight of millions like him, was ordained by God. God had created the world and each person had his or her cross to bear. If God had wanted the world to be different it would have been different.

Now he was in church, none of his problems seemed important any more. The gentle arms of the church offered him security, a way of understanding all that had happened, and much more too. Without his beliefs life would indeed be difficult. Nothing would make sense and he would be lost in the world.

EXERCISE

1 What does religion mean to Mr Harris?
2 What contribution does religion make to his community?

According to Durkheim, Mr Harris is mistaken in his belief about a divine god. Whatever happens in the world, whether it happens to Mr Harris or not, is not ordained by God or by any other supernatural force. There is simply no need to explain man-made actions (his redundancy) or chance events (his wife's death) by inventing a god. But there is a need for religious worship in human society because it gives 'sacred authority to society's rules and values'. If we didn't have religion we would have to invent it. For Mr Harris, religion brings him into contact with the people who care for him and who are prepared to help him with his problems. It also encourages him to communicate with his fellow men and women in common worship and provide instructions and guidance about his duties and responsibilities in society.

Durkheim is only one of many sociologists who have written about religion and its functions in society. Marx and Weber are 2 other important contributors.

The functions of religion

We can summarise the functions of religion in this way:

- **The integrative function** The members of a community can be united in their shared belief in a particular religion. Belief can cut across social class and age barriers, and private conflicts can be put aside or settled as people come together in joint worship.
- **The personal support function** Religion can help us with the BIG questions we all like to ask, such as: Why did such a terrible thing have to happen to me? What is the purpose of life? Why does God allow innocent children to die? Religion also provides us with caring support in times of personal crises, such as bereavement and unexplainable catastrophe. It also helps us to release personal guilt and anxiety through confession and prayer and it may contribute to a believer's emotional needs and sense of worth. A common function of religion is of course the provision of rituals and ceremonies as we progress through life: baptism, confirmation, marriage and burial.
- **The social control function** Religion as an agent of social control is of great interest to sociologists. It is convenient to divide this into:

External control Religion can be an important ingredient in the promotion of social order and stability. Traditionally the church tends to support the existing political structure. It will bless the state's soldiers going to war and crown the monarch during the Coronation. Anti-social conduct is branded as 'sin' and followers are urged to obey the law of the land. Karl

Marx argued that the sole purpose of religion is to help the rich and powerful hold on to power by keeping the exploited and the gullible in their place.

Internal control Religion provides its adherents with a set of moral codes on which they can base their social conduct. Religious codes may reinforce society's existing norms about what is permissible and what is not and thus contribute to the development of the individual's awareness of right and wrong.

EXERCISE

Here is a modified version of the *Ten Commandments*:
1 I am the Lord thy God: thou shalt have none other gods but me.
2 Thou shalt not make to thyself any graven image (false gods) or bow down to them or worship them.
3 Thou shalt not take the name of the Lord thy God in vain (blaspheme).
4 Keep holy the Sabbath day.
5 Honour thy father and thy mother.
6 Thou shalt do no murder.
7 Thou shalt not commit adultery.
8 Thou shalt not steal.
9 Thou shalt not bear false witness (tell lies).
10 Thou shalt not covet (wish for wrongfully).

QUESTIONS

1 Explain how a Christian might find comfort and security in these Commandments.
2 Explain why a sociologist might understand them as important agents of social control – both for the individual and for society as a whole.
3 How might a religious non-Christian interpret these Commandments? To what extent do they conflict and correspond with the moral codes of any other religious faith you may be familiar with?

Secularisation

Raindeath

The elders of the tribe had gathered to discuss the failure of the crop.

'We have not worked hard,' one elder said.

There were few who disagreed with this.

The elders decided that the Gods were angry, for it had rained continuously for four weeks and the fields were flooded. There would be no crop to harvest and the people would go hungry.

Raindeath.

That was the punishment. The skies had always opened and the Gods had poured water onto the land when there had been wrongdoing amongst the people. The people were to be punished and their crop destroyed.

In the 1980s, in a modern industrial society, heavy rainfall would not be explained in terms of the 'anger of the Gods' but by careful calculation based on a scientific assessment of weather patterns. The rise of science and the increase in the need for scientific explanation is part of the process known as **secularisation**. Secularisation is simply the process whereby religious and supernatural ideas and practices lose their social significance.

Many sociologists think that this rational and scientific way of understanding the world began with the industrial revolution. In simple societies religion tends to dominate people's lives, but as they begin to move away from small rural communities to live in industrial towns and cities their traditional ways of explaining the unknown become less convincing. In *Raindeath* it is much easier for people to accept a supernatural explanation of rainfall (coming as it does from the sky-God), since rainfall, crop-growing and food are directly linked with their survival. It is less easy for the new industrial workers, working in factories and coalmines, to see the supernatural significance of steam hammers and spinning jennies which are obviously man-made but equally important to their survival. Supernatural explanations were becoming more and more irrelevant.

Religion in urban societies also became separated from many of its traditional social functions. Sermons from the pulpit and congregational gossip had always been focal points of communication in village life and church schools and bible classes made substantial contributions to the spread of literacy in rural societies, as well as acting as crude channels of social welfare. Most of these functions were to be taken over by the state and the media.

One sociologist who believes that religion is in decline in Britain is Bryan Wilson. In his book *Religion in a Secular Society*, and in other published articles, he provides us with a mass of statistical evidence that shows a massive decline in church attendance. Wilson believes that the only satisfactory way of measuring secularisation is by trying to assess how the Christian Church is 'losing direct influence over the ideas and activities of men'. Here are a few points from his statistics:

- In 1851, 40% of the population attended church each week. Today, only between 10% and 15% attend regularly. (By 1986 church attendance had fallen to 6%.)
- Between 1964 and 1974 the number of confirmations in the Church of England fell by 30%. A similar fall was recorded in the Catholic Church. The Methodist Church lost 34 000 members in the same period.
- By 1979 more couples were being married at registry offices (civil marriage) than in Church (religious marriage).

Wilson argued that religion is in irreversible decline. The Christian message is no longer valid or relevant to most people and they are voting with their feet. He believes that there will always be some form of religious worship, but it will be the preserve only of minority groups.

Other sociologists, including David Martin in *A Sociology of English Religion*, suggest that Wilson's interpretation of his statistics might be misguided. Church attendance cannot in itself be the only or even the main measure of religious feeling. A person might be religious and *not* go to church, or attend church only occasionally. In fact, Martin found that 45% of the population attended church at least once a year. He also suggested that although many people may reject the established Churches, there has been a growing interest in alternative religious thinking, particularly by young people in less conventional religions such as Rastafarianism and Hari Krishna:

I just didn't like the idea of organised religion. The religion I was brought up with has no meaning for me. I find peace and happiness in this movement of ours. It's not boring like the established church.

A *Harris* survey published in the *Observer* in 1984 indicated a sustaining interest in religion in Britain, or at least a desire to support the moral codes of Christian life. The respondents were asked: How important do you think it is that this should be a Christian country?:

34% thought it very important
32% thought it fairly important
19% thought it not very important
12% thought it not at all important
 3% didn't know.

Although we can be certain that there has been great change in the way we understand and practise religion since the growth of industrial society, we must not be too eager to assume that this amounts to a rejection of religious feeling. After all, the anthropologist Anthony Wallace has estimated that humankind has produced in the order of 100 000 religions in the last 60 000 years. It hardly seems likely that we would want to stop now. Some sociologists think that religious practices have merely become **privatised**, which means that people are getting their religion at home via radio and TV in a more private, personal way. Whatever view we take, religion still has real meaning for millions of people.

EXERCISE

Find out as much as you can about the work of the 19th century naturalist Charles Darwin. Explain why his ideas upset so many of his religious contemporaries.

QUESTIONS

Faith, hope and cavities
by **Brian Deer**

Government hopes of bringing more enterprise into health care got a new boost this weekend with the arrival in Britain of Willard Fuller, the American dental psychic, who yesterday dropped in from Geneva for a week of public meetings.

In more than 25 years of dentistry, Fuller has attracted a crescendo of carping. The root of the trouble is not merely the matter that he has no licence to practice, no equipment and no fixed address. What has really excited the establishment is Fuller's bold claim – which he has hawked around the world – that a drill can make you ill and that faith can fill your cavities.

As he addressed 500 frenzied fans at the Conway Hall in London, it was obvious to an onlooker how Fuller has found his following. 'Do you believe God can fill teeth?' he asks quietly of the throng. 'Yes', they call back as one. 'Do you believe God will fill teeth?' 'Yes' is the reply. 'Do you believe,' in a tremulous crescendo, 'that God will fill teeth for you?' The answer is inescapable.

'In the name of Jesus, be thou whole,' he intones, with a slap on the patients' cheeks. And lo the teeth were filled and enjoyed all manner of oral improvements. Or at least many of the multitude were more than ready to believe it. And looking carefully with mirror and flashlight. I'll be damned if I'll say it wasn't true.

Attempts to place advertisements for his meetings in the British Dental Journal were curtly rebuffed.

Before the meeting, Fuller said: 'After 40 000 successes all over the world, I'm not interested in proving that it works. And that's just dental healings. I have four times as many successes with other parts of the body. But we have found laboratory conditions are not conducive to healing.'

'I am convinced that God gives you what you want, if you really want to believe it,' says Fuller, with resonant reassurance. 'I am convinced that if people lived their whole lives by the laws of God they would never get sick at all.'

According to Fuller's philosophy, doctors and dentists should make themselves redundant – and certainly, if he had his way, they wouldn't be getting much work.

Source: *The Sunday Times*

1 a Briefly describe the nature of the belief-system contained in this article. (3 marks)
  b Define a belief-system. (2 marks)
  c In what way do belief-systems, and religions in particular, contribute to social control in a modern industrial society? (15 marks)

2 a What is meant by urbanisation? (3 marks)
  b What kinds of social problems are likely to be found in towns and cities? (8 marks)
  c Suggest at least 3 distinguishing features of life in an urban society that are unlikely to be found in traditional rural communities. (9 marks)

3 Discuss the proposition that Britain is becoming a secular society. (20 marks)

Case Study

Village schools to close

The closure of two more South Warwickshire village schools was brought a stage closer this week – but there was new hope for a third school which has been under threat of being shut down for the past seven years.

County education officer Michael Ridger announced on Monday that the working party on the rationalisation of primary education in the county had recommended the closure of Stourton and Cherington Church of England School and Whichford junior and infants' school at the end of the 1986 summer term.

In each case places would be available for pupils at Brailes Church of England School and Long Compton junior and infant school.

Mixed
The closure proposals have had a mixed reception in Cherington and Whichford. Mr George Jackson, headmaster of Stourton and Cherington school, said that at meetings with members of the county working party last June and in February this year parents had made it clear to chairman Fred

Parrott that they would prefer to see the school remain open.

Mr Jackson said that he supported the parents' view, even though, as a result of pupils leaving for secondary education or going to other schools, numbers had fallen in the last year from 16 to 6.

The sharp drop in numbers at Stourton and Cherington has been partly caused by the transfer of children to Brailes school by parents who did not want their children to go to Long Compton because of the traffic problems in that village.

Mrs Susan Parker, who has a daughter, aged eight, at Cherington, said that if the school closed her daughter would have a change of school at the final stage of her primary education, which would probably set her back 12 months.

She said, 'Education standards here are terrific, and at least you can get to your children if anything goes wrong and there is no transport problem. I do not see how the county are going to save money because they will have to pay for the buses to take the children to the other schools.

'At present children have the advantage of attending part-time school in the mornings but that will not be possible if the school is closed as the children will not be able to get home at lunch time as they do at present'.

Sorry

Mrs Mary Thompson, headmistress of Whichford school, said parents were naturally exceedingly sorry at the possibility of losing the school. Whichford was a very rural village with no prospects of new houses being built so there was little possibility of school numbers increasing. When she arrived 5 years ago there were 25 children at the school, and this was now reduced to 15.

Mrs Thompson said the main concern was that the children should have the best possible provision that

could be made for them, and it was a changing world. Small village schools could not provide much that larger schools had: they had no computers and team games were out of the question.

Mr Martin Harvey, chairman of Whichford school governors, said the governors were considering calling a meeting of the whole community later next month to discover its feelings and decide whether or not to oppose the closure plan. 'Obviously it is a loss to the community when a small school closes', he said.

Source: Stratford upon Avon Herald

Background information from the 1981 Census:

	Population
Brailes (Upper and Lower)	925
Cherington	252
Long Compton	621
Stourton	135
Whichford	298

QUESTIONS

1 Produce short answers to these questions:

a What are the main proposals contained in the article?

b What reasons are given to explain the school closures?

c According to the article, what problems will result from school closures?

2 Write an interesting letter for publication in the *Stratford upon Avon Herald* explaining to less knowledgeable readers why these school closures may be unavoidable. (You might find it helpful to read the chapter on *Population*.) Your letter should cover the following points:

- Population trends and family size
- The continuing process of urbanisation
- The general social and economic prospects of small villages.

3 What are the social and economic effects of school closure on village life?

Points for discussion

- Village life offers a more satisfying way of living.
- Most poverty occurs in towns and cities.
- Life is much better now than it used to be.

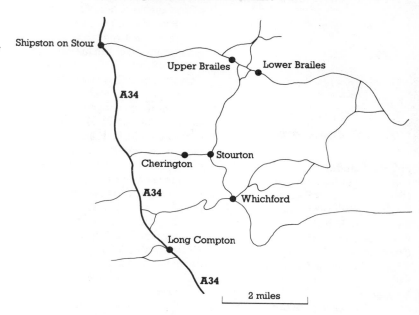

Sketch of part of South Warwickshire

Astral Voyagers

Bob Fletcher didn't know what to do with the letter from his daughter, Claire. Should he tell his wife, Margaret, about it? It had been 4 years since Claire had walked out of the house without a word, and it was 3 months later when they heard from a friend that she had joined a religious cult called the Astral Voyagers.

'How could she have done this to us?' Margaret had asked a thousand times, until the pain and the bitterness prevented her from mentioning Claire's name again.

'I don't know,' he had said, 'I just don't know'.

But perhaps he did know more than he let on, although he could never share his suspicions with his wife. Maybe they had been too hard on her as parents. Maybe his wife had told Claire too many times how grateful she should be for the wonderful home she had and how lucky she was to have had such caring parents. Perhaps if they had listened to her more, and had tried to answer all those probing questions she had asked, instead of fobbing her off with a 'because we say so'. Fletcher couldn't be certain whether he was right or not, but he had come to believe that things had been going wrong in his family for a long time.

Claire had won her battle to get to university (wouldn't you be happier working in a bank, my dear, then you could find a nice boyfriend and settle down with a family of your own? her mother had asked) and she had become increasingly unwilling to come home in the vacations, and on no account were her parents allowed to visit her there. The more Fletcher thought about it, the more he realised how life with his daughter had been a series of events that had driven them further and further apart.

The problems began with their work for the Church. He played the organ every Sunday, and whenever the vicar asked for volunteers to help to clean the church and arrange the flowers his wife was the first person to put her name on the list. 'Religion is such a comfort,' Margaret would say, 'it helps one through life'.

But whatever religion did for Mrs Fletcher it did nothing for her daughter. 'You and your religion make me sick,' she had shouted during one of many rows with her mother. 'You're just a hypocrite. You go to church on Sunday for the same reason that you wash your net curtains and put out rinsed milk bottles on the front doorstep, you want to impress the neighbours with your *goodness*.'

Perhaps there was just a fragment of something in what Claire had said, Fletcher conceded, some grain of truth within all the hatred that had been welling up inside her.

'Maybe we're too concerned with the technicalities of religion,' he had suggested to his wife, 'and not concerned enough to put religion into practice.' But Margaret ignored him and spent even more time with her bible and her flower arranging, and talking more frequently of the evils of the flesh and of the pain and misery of hell.

Fletcher read the letter again. Claire said she was safe and well and that for the first time she was happier than she had ever been – she had *found herself*, her true self, and with the Astral Voyagers she had *become a complete person*. He read and reread every word and wondered what it all meant. One thing was clear, conventional religion had failed her, her family had failed her, and whatever he thought about this obscure sect he had to admit that it gave his daughter something he and his wife could not give – meaning to her life. Claire had rejected their ways and their church and had gone on her own unconventional way. But isn't there only one God who serves all men and women? Does it really matter which God we pray to or which religion we serve? Fletcher didn't know any more. He had heard of other families who had lost their children to religious groups whose beliefs he found utterly incomprehensible.

Claire's flight into the arms of the white robed Astral Voyagers could be explained by her unhappiness and their offer of sanctuary and peace of mind. It was all escapism, Fletcher concluded, a delusion, but she did say in her letter that she was happy. The Astral Voyagers, with all their sinister ceremonies, had given Claire something he had failed to give her. What right had he to deny her that?

Fletcher carefully folded the letter and put it into his pocket. Better not to let Margaret know about this, he thought.

QUESTIONS

1 Explain why you think Claire rejected conventional religion.
2 What attracts young people to sects like the Astral Voyagers?
3 In what way does religion provide comfort for Claire?
4 What are the social functions of religion?

Points for discussion

- God has been created by society for its own purposes.
- There are some belief systems that are socially superior than others.
- Religion plays an important part in influencing people's lives.

Important points

- Social change does not happen by chance. It is caused by social and economic factors.
- About 80% of the British population live in urban areas and 50% of the urban population live in the 7 conurbations.
- Social problems, loneliness and alienation tend to increase as people move from rural to urban areas.
- Many sociologists have discovered thriving communities in the midst of cities and in city suburbs.
- A city has 3 features: population size, population density and heterogeneity. Many cities in industrial societies tend to expand along certain predictable lines.
- The way we think about the world, our consciousness, will determine how we interpret our social expectations.
- Both micro and macro factors are likely to exist before the social process of change occurs.
- A belief system exists when sufficient numbers of people hold similar deeply-held beliefs and join together to form a coherent body of believers. It does not depend on rational or scientific proof for its existence.
- Sociology is concerned with the social significance of religion and its relationship to other aspects of society.
- Religion is important as an agent of social control.
- Secularisation is associated with the growth of science and industry in an urban society.
- Whether or not religion has declined in Britain is a matter of dispute amongst sociologists.

Glossary

absoute poverty   A condition in which the basic needs essential for survival are absent or in short supply.

affluent society   A society which contains a large proportion of people who can afford many goods once regarded as luxuries.

alienation   The feeling of non-involvement, usually in the workplace.

anomie   A social condition in which the norms which govern social behaviour are absent or unclear.

anthropology   The study of the structure and the processes of social interaction of the societies of simpler peoples.

argot   The slang or jargon used by the members of specific social groups.

authority   Power which is accepted as right and just by those subject to it and therefore obeyed.

automation   The process of advanced mechanisation in which complex machines perform tasks formerly completed by humans and often replacing people who operated simpler machines.

blue collar workers   A class of worker who is engaged in manual labour, such as a factory production worker.

civil law   That part of the law concerned with the rights and duties of individuals towards each other. Unlike criminal law, legal action is taken by the private citizen against another citizen.

classless society   A concept used to describe a society in which the divisions between the proletariat and the bourgeoisie and the exploitation and domination of one group over another no longer exist.

closed shop   A worker must join a union before he or she can be employed.

coercion   The exercise of power without the acceptance of those subjected to it. Commands are obeyed because there is some compulsion to do so, rather than because they are considered to be fair.

communism   A social and economic system that is based on the belief that no individual should possess significantly more property than any other individual, and that all wealth and property should be held in common ownership by the state.

community   A collection of people who share similar social and economic experiences. They may live close together, as in a mining community, or they may live apart, geographically, as in the black community.

concepts   Words or phrases which sociologists can apply to social behaviour expressing ideas or notions.

conjugal roles   The relationship between the marital roles of husband and wife. Sociological studies have distinguished two different types of conjugal roles:

   segregated conjugal roles   Characterised by separate husband and wife roles. Each has specific duties and responsibilities within the family.

   joint conjugal roles   Those marital relationships where the roles of husband and wife are not so clear cut. Responsibilities for decisions which affect the family tend to be shared between the wife and husband.

conservatism   A political outlook which seeks to conserve the existing order of things that are thought to be safe, valuable and familiar. It is naturally opposed to radical changes in society that are based on liberal and idealistic doctrines.

counter culture   A culture that is in opposition to the values of the dominant social culture.

criminal law   That part of the law which defines certain kinds of behaviour as offences against the state. Police are public servants whose duty is the prevention and detection of crime and the prosecution of offenders before the courts.

culture A concept used to describe the beliefs, values, customs and ways of life of social groups.

de-skilling The process of reducing the level of skill required to complete a job. This is usually achieved either by the reorganisation of the workforce into smaller productive units to reduce the range of skills required (car production lines) or by the introduction of machinery (welding robots or word processors).

delinquency Usually associated with juveniles. It covers a range of criminal offences from theft to joy-riding. Unlike deviant behaviour which can take place within the law, delinquent behaviour is usually illegal and considered by many to be morally reprehensible.

democracy A form of government in which the population (excluding non-voting groups) are able to influence political decisions by electing people to represent their interests in government.

demography The scientific study of human population.

deviant behaviour Non-conformist behaviour. The individual does not conform to the norms of society or to specific social situations. Whether or not an act is deviant depends on the particular social circumstance.

dictatorship Power vested in one person or a small group of people. This form of government is usually but not necessarily restrictive of individual freedoms.

distribution of wealth and income The way in which all available money and assets are apportioned to individuals in society.

diverse economy The population is involved in a wide range of productive activities and services.

division of labour The division of a work process into a number of parts, each part undertaken by an individual worker or group of workers.

divorce The legal termination of a marriage, so allowing either partner to remarry if they so wish.

egalitarian marriages Marriages in which there is equality between the marriage partners. Husbands and wives share domestic responsibilities and have an equal say in running the home.

embourgeoisement A theory that proposes that the working classes are becoming middle class.

empirical support Supporting evidence that derives from sociological study.

empty-shell marriages A condition where the marriage has broken down even though the spouses live together and remain legally married.

extreme occupations Jobs that involve a high degree of physical exertion, danger or skill, in which various aspects of a worker's life are affected because of the nature and demands of the work.

extrinsic job satisfaction The job gives the worker little or no satisfaction: the wage packet provides the main satisfaction that can be obtained from work.

fascism A nationalistic attitude that is hostile to democracy, egalitarianism and communism. It attempts to perpetuate the cult of the 'leader', and members hold symbols, uniforms, hatreds, marches and rigid discipline in high regard.

family as a unit of production A family in a pre-industrial society produces its own goods and services with other families in the community.

feminist sociology This concentrates specifically on the role of women in society.

forces of production A Marxist concept which refers to the materials, tools and techniques used in production in capitalist economies. The bourgeoisie are said to own and control the forces of production.

fringe benefits Benefits that workers receive in addition to their regular pay.

gender messages The many and varied ways in which boys and girls are taught behaviour considered appropriate to their sex. Examples of gender messages are to be found in toys, books and television programmes.

gender roles The culturally determined roles which we attach to masculine and feminine aspects of behaviour in the family and other social settings.

gender socialisation The process whereby boys learn masculine behaviour and girls learn feminine behaviour.

hidden curriculum The subtle ways in which certain values and attitudes are conveyed and emphasised in educational institutions.

high and low status subjects Not all school subjects are considered to be of equal importance. Success in high status subjects is thought to require more effort and intelligence than for low status subjects though this is not necessarily the case.

higher education Education of a more advanced nature than that provided in schools or further education institutions. Universities, polytechnics and teacher training colleges are examples.

historical perspective Using the past to understand more about the present.

industrialisation The transition of an economy based on agriculture to a factory-based economy.

intrinsic job satisfaction The pleasure and satisfaction gained from doing the job.

labelling process In education, it describes how a pupil's behaviour, through being interpreted in a positive or negative way by teachers or others in authority, leads to a negative or positive label being applied to that pupil. Subsequent behaviour is interpreted by both the teacher and the pupil in the light of whichever label has been applied.

leisure   A non-contractual activity enjoyed during our free time.

liberalism   Recognition of the supreme value of the individual and his rights, which should as far as possible be both independent of government interference and protected by the laws of society.

life chances   The opportunities an individual has of obtaining the material and cultural rewards that society has to offer, such as a well-paid job or a 'good' education. People from the same social class are thought to experience the same life-chances.

marriage   A socially and legally approved union between a man and a woman.

mechanisation   A process of performing or completing tasks with the help of machines that are operated by humans.

methodology   The whole range of techniques and research available to the sociologist in his study of society or social groups.

myth   A commonly-held belief that is probably untrue, or without foundation.

normative order   The system of norms present in society which ensures social order. The more important norms are called *mores*.

observer bias   A term used to describe how an observer's own prejudices or attitudes may influence his judgment of the group under study.

opportunity structures Opportunities present in a community which can be either legitimate or illegitimate. *Illegitimate opportunity structures* describe the opportunity to gain

access to a criminal subculture. An example might be a particular locality, an amenity or someone you know within a well-established criminal subculture.

peer group   A group of interacting persons of similar status, usually of similar age, who share many common norms and values.

pilot study   A preliminary investigation of the subject under study. Its aim is to identify possible weaknesses in the method of research that has been chosen and to correct any errors before the full-scale investigation is carried out.

power   The ability of an individual or group to exercise its will over other people. It is the extent to which an individual or group can get its own way.

prejudice and discrimination   Prejudice denotes certain negative ideas, attitudes and assumptions held by an individual often about members of a social group. Discrimination occurs when prejudiced ideas are put into action.

pressure group   A voluntary association where members join together to try to influence outside agencies. Some groups attempt to influence MPs and civil servants and others direct their attention more towards the general public.

primary education   The compulsory education which takes place in Infant and Junior schools between the ages of 5 and 11.

primary and secondary breadwinners   Within a marriage or a family the primary breadwinner is the main income provider. The secondary breadwinner provides the income which is regarded as supplementary to the main income.

process of legitimation   A

concept that describes the ways in which the ruling class exerts power in society through the control of important influences on our lives such as the mass media and the educational system.

psychology   The study of the mind and of individual behaviour.

pupil identities   The image pupils hold of themselves.

pupil strategies   This concept refers to the many ways in which pupils can exert an influence over what goes on in the classroom.

qualitative data   Sociological research often requires qualitative analysis of findings because it is the aim of research not simply to collect facts but to understand social life.

quantitative data   Information that can be presented in statistical form to allow comparisons to be made between groups in a relatively straightforward manner.

relative poverty   The deprivation we experience when our standard of living falls below the normal standards of our society.

Registrar General   The Government's chief keeper of official records.

role conflict   In the study of social behaviour the concept of role conflict refers to the conflicting demands made upon the individual.

role in the family   The part each person plays in the family group. It is the result of the interaction with other members of the family which determines how we are expected to behave.

secondary education   The education a child is legally required to receive in secondary schools between the ages of 11 and 16.

secularisation   The process whereby the influence of religion in various areas of social life diminishes.

self-fulfilling prophecy   In education, the process whereby a pupil's self-image is shaped by the definitions imposed by the teachers. The pupil will tend to accept the teachers' definition and will behave accordingly, to confirm the evaluation.

sexual stereotypes A set of assumptions concerning male or female social behaviour.

shop stewards Ordinary employees who have been elected by union members where they work to represent their views to the employer.

simple economy Most common in non-industrial societies. The population is involved mostly in agriculture and rural crafts and few goods and services beyond those that are required are produced.

social construction of self The way an individual develops as a result of his or her social experiences.

social hierarchy A concept used to describe how people are organised into a system of higher and lower social ranks according to the degree of power they exercise over others.

socialisation The process whereby people learn the norms and values of the society in which they live. The process can be divided into 3 stages: *primary*, *secondary* and *adult* socialisation.

social control The concept that describes the way we exert pressure on each other in many different ways to ensure conformity to the norms and values of society.

social interaction The communication that takes place amongst individuals.

socialism The notion of human

equality, and of equal rights and opportunities for all citizens. The government is seen as the main agent that guarantees and distributes benefits among the people, following the abolition or reduction of class privilege, class control and excessive personal wealth.

society Everybody within a particular culture experiencing an organised system of social life.

sociological theory An explanation of a social phenomenon such as crime, derived from observation and testing.

status A person's social position as defined by other members of the community.

status quo A continuing state of affairs in society.

subcultural values Values are learned beliefs about what is right, good or worthwhile. They exert a strong influence on a person's actions by setting standards for correct or appropriate behaviour. A distinguishing feature of a subculture is that its own values differ from those of mainstream society.

subcultures Cultures which exist *within* mainstream cultures. The group identified as a subculture enjoys a distinctive way of life, and exercises its own beliefs, values, codes, knowledge and prejudices.

subjective experience The way we personally respond or feel about something that happens to us.

sunrise industries Industries employing the latest computer-based technologies, especially

those engaged in producing computers and computer software.

supplementary benefit Cash given by the state to a person in need to bring them up to a basic standard of living acceptable in our society.

Totalitarianism An extreme form of anti-democratic government in which an individual or group is solely responsible for political decisions. Individual freedoms are usually severely restricted.

trade unions Organisations which defend and promote the interests of their members in the workplace and at national government level.

urbanisation A growth in the proportion of a country's population living in large towns and cities.

values The guiding principles and fundamental beliefs that influence our social conduct.

voting behaviour A general term used to describe the voting intentions and tendencies of different groups in the electorate.

wages or income differentials The difference between levels of income received.

white collar workers A class of workers who are *not* engaged in manual labour, such as office workers and teachers.

work deprivation The inequalities found at the workplace; for example, in earnings, welfare schemes and opportunities for promotion.

youth culture The distinctive but diversified lifestyles, norms and values of young people.

Bibliography

Chapter 1

Booth, Charles. *Life and Labour of the People of London* New York, Kelley, 1970

Cohen, Stanley. *Folk Devils and Moral Panics* Oxford, Martin Robertson, 1980

Patrick, James. *A Glasgow Gang Observed* Eyre Methuen, 1973

Whyte, W. F. *Street Corner Society: Social Structure of an Italian Slum* University of Chicago Press, 1955

Willmott, P. & Young, M. *Family and Kinship in East London* Penguin, 1969

Chapter 2

Engels, Friedrich. *The Condition of the Working Class in England* Panther, 1969

Goldthorpe, J. H. *Social Mobility and Class Structure in Modern Britain* Oxford, Clarendon Press, 1980

Goldthorpe, J. & Lockwood, D. *The Affluent Worker in the Class Structure* Cambridge University Press, 1969

Martin, F. M. *Social Mobility in Britain* Routledge & Kegan Paul, 1954

Turner, R. *Education, Economy and Society* Free Press, 1962

Weber, Max. *Class, Status and Party* Ed by H. Gerth & C. Mills, Routledge & Kegan Paul, 1970

Chapter 3

Burgess, Ernest, & Locke. *The Family* Reinhold, 1971

Cooper, David. *Death of a Family* Penguin, 1972

Dickens, Charles. *Hard Times* Penguin, 1970

Fletcher, R. *The Family and Marriage in Britain* Penguin, 1969

Hart, Nicky. *When Marriage Ends: Study in Status Passage* Tavistock Publications, 1976

Laing, R. D. *Divided Self* Penguin, 1970

Mead, Margaret. *Male and Female: A Study of the Sexes in a Changing World* Penguin, 1970

Parsons, T. & Bales, R. *Family, Socialisation and Interaction Process* Routledge, 1956

Schapera, I. *Married Life in an African Tribe* Royal Anthropological Institute, 1963

Willmott, P. & Young, M. *Family and Kinship in East London* Penguin, 1969

Willmott, P. & Young, M. *The Symmetrical Family* Penguin, 1975

Chapter 4

Bernstein, Basil. *Class, Codes and Control* Routledge & Kegan Paul, 1971

Bourdieu, P. & Passeron, J. *Reproduction in Education, Society and Culture* Sage Publications, 1977

Coates, K. & Silburn, R. *Poverty: The Forgotten Englishman* Penguin, 1973

Dale, R. & Griffiths, S. *Downstream: A Study in Failure* International Library of Sociology, 1965

Floud, Halsey & Martin. *Social Class and Educational Opportunity* Heinemann, 1956

Hargreaves, David. *Social Relations in a Secondary School* Routledge, 1970

Johnson, Linton Kwesi. *Inglan is a Bitch* Race Relations Publications, 1980

Karabel, J. & Halsey, A. *Power and Ideology in Education* Oxford University Press, 1977

Little, Alan. *Schools and Race: Five Views of Multi-Racial Britain* Leicester, National Children's Bureau, 1978

Pryce, Ken. *Endless Pressure: A Study of West Indian Lifestyles in Bristol* Penguin, 1979

Sharpe, Sue. *Just Like a Girl: How Girls Learn to be Women* Penguin, 1981

Veness, Thelma. *School Leavers* Penguin, 1962

Wright, J. & Norris, R. *Schools Council Project at the University of Birmingham* 'Teaching English to West Indian Children', Methuen, 1970

Chapter 5

Blauner, Robert. *Alienation and Freedom* University of Chicago, 1967

Dennis, N., Henriques & Slaughter. *Coal is Our Life* Tavistock Publications, 1969

Halsey A. *Origins and Destinations: Family, Class and Education in Modern Britain* Oxford University Press, 1980

Miliband, Ralph. *The State in a Capitalist Society* Quartet Books, 1973

Parker, Stanley. *The Future of Work and Leisure* Paladin, 1972

Sampson, Anthony. *The New Anatomy of Britain* Hodder & Stoughton, 1983

Townsend, Peter. *Poverty in the United Kingdom* Penguin, 1979

Tunstall, Jeremy. *The Fishermen* MacGibbon, 1969

Chapter 6

Benet, Mary. *Secretary: An Enquiry into the Female Ghetto* Sidgwick & Jackson, 1972

Caplow, Theodore. *The Sociology of Work* Greenwood Press, 1978

Coyle, Angela. *Redundant Women* Women's Publications, 1984

Delamont, Sara. *The Sociology of Women* Allen & Unwin, 1980

Klein, Viola. *Britain's Married Women Workers* Routledge & Kegan Paul, 1965

Mackie, L. & Patullo, P. *Women at Work* Tavistock Publications, 1977

Mead, Margaret. *A Study of Sexes in a Changing World* Penguin, 1970

Millet, Kate. *Sexual Politics* Virago, 1977

Oakley, Ann. *Housewife* Penguin, 1976

Oakley, Ann. *Sociology of Housework* Martin Robertson, 1974

Oakley, Ann. *Subject: Women* Fontana, 1982

Sharpe, Sue. *Just Like a Girl* Penguin, 1981

Stanworth, Michelle. *Gender and Schooling: A Study in Sexual Division in the Classroom* Hutchinson Educational, 1983

Chapter 7

Abel-Smith, B. & Townsend, P. *The Poor and the Poorest* Bell & Sons, 1965
Atkinson, Anthony. *Unequal Shares: Wealth in Britain* Penguin, 1974
Booth, Charles. *Life and Labour of the People of London* New York, Kelley, 1970
Coates, K. & Silburn, R. *Poverty: The Forgotten Englishman* Penguin, 1973
Gans, Herbert. *More Equality* New York, Pantheon, 1973
Kelly, George. *Psychology of Personal Constructs* W. W. Norton, 1980
Lewis, Oscar. *La Vida* Panther Books, 1968
Piachaud, David. *The Causes of Poverty* HMSO, 1975
Rowntree, S. & Lavers, B. *Poverty and the Welfare State* Longman, 1950

Chapter 8

Blythe, Ronald. *A View in Winter: Reflections on Old Age* New York, Allen Lane, 1979
Campbell, Beatrix. *Wigan Pier Revisited* Virago, 1984
Howe, George. *Man, Environment and Diseases in Britain* David & Charles, 1972
Hurd, Geoffrey. *Human Societies: A Sociological Introduction* Routledge, 1973
Oakley, Ann. *Sex, Gender and Society* Maurice Temple Smith, 1972
Oakley, Ann. *Subject: Women* Fontana, 1982
Titmuss, Richard. *Essays on the Welfare State* Allen & Unwin, 1976
Townsend, Peter. *The Family Life of Old People* Penguin, 1970

Chapter 9

Boyle, Jimmy. *A Sense of Freedom* Pan, 1977
Cloward, R. & Ohlin, L. *Delinquency and Opportunity* Free Press, 1968
Cohen, Albert. *Delinquent Boys: The Culture of the Gang* Free Press, 1971
Gordon, David. *Class and Economics of Crime* New York, John Wiley & Sons, 1976
Graham, James. *Amphetamine Politics on Capitol Hill* New York, John Wiley & Sons, 1976
Lord Scarman. *The Brixton Disorders* (Report), HMSO, 1981
Matza, David. *Delinquency and Drift* New York, John Wiley & Sons, 1970
Merton, Robert. *Social Theory and Social Structure* Free Press, 1968
Miller, Walter. *Lower Class Culture* New York, John Wiley & Sons, 1962
Mungham, G. & Pearson, G. *Working Class Youth Culture* Routledge, 1976
Parker, H. *A View from the Boys: Sociology of Downtown Adolescents* David & Charles, 1975
Willmott, Peter. *Adolescent Boys of East London* Penguin, 1979

Chapter 10

Blondel, J. *Voters, Parties and Leaders: Social Fabric of British Politics* Penguin, 1969
Butler, D. & Stokes, D. *Political Change in Britain* Macmillan, 1975
Eysenck, Hans. *Sense and Nonsense in Psychology* Penguin, 1970
Hyman, Richard. *Strikes* Fontana, 1977
Lipset, Seymour. *Political Man* Heinemann, 1963
Madgwick, P. *Introduction to British Politics* Hutchinson, 1984
Miliband, Ralph. *The State in a Capitalist Society* Quartet Books, 1973
Parkin, Frank. *Class Inequality and Political Order* Paladin, 1971
Weber, Max. *Theory of Social and Economic Organisation* Free Press, 1964
Westergaad, J. & Resler, H. *Class in a Capitalist Society* Penguin, 1976

Chapter 11

Belson, W. *TV Violence and the Adolescent Boy* Saxon House, 1978
Berger, B. & Berger, P. *Sociology: A Biographical Approach* Basic Books, 1975
Cohen, S. *Folk Devils and Moral Panics* Martin Robertson, 1980
Ditton, J. & Duffy, J. *Bias in Newspaper Crime Reports* Pressgang, 1983
Eysenck, H. & Nias, D. *Sex, Violence and the Media* Paladin, 1980
Glover, David. *Sociology of the Mass Media* New York, Causeway Books, 1984
Hall, Stuart. *Policing the Crisis* Macmillan, 1978
Hartmann, P. & Husband, C. *Racism and Mass Media* Davis-Poynter, 1974
Milson, Fred. *Youth in a Changing Society* Routledge, 1972
Murdock, G. & McCron, G. *Youth and Class: The Career of a Confusion* Routledge, 1976
Noble, G. *Children in Front of the Small Screen* Constable, 1975
Wells, H. G. *The War of the Worlds* Pan, 1975
Willis, Paul. *Profane Culture* Routledge, 1978

Chapter 12

Burgess, Ernest. *The Growth of the City* American Sociological Society, 1923
Coates, K. & Silburn, R. *Poverty: The Forgotten Englishman* Penguin, 1973
Durkheim, Emile. *The Division of Labour in Society* Free Press, 1947
Durkheim, Emile. *The Elementary Forms of Religious Life* Allen & Unwin, 1976
Frankenberg, Ronald. *Communities in Britain* Penguin, 1970
Gans, Herbert. *The Urban Villagers* Free Press, 1962
Martin, David. *A Sociology of English Religion* Heinemann, 1967
Redfield, Robert. *The Little Community* University of Chicago Press, 1960
Roberts, Robert. *The Classic Slum* Penguin, 1973
Wilson, Bryan. *Religion in a Secular Society* Watts & Co, 1966

Index